AUSTR

good food

GUIDE 2019

EDITED BY

MYFFY RIGBY

SIMON &
SCHUSTER

London · New York · Sydney · Toronto · New Delhi

A CBS COMPANY

Our Thanks

Our thanks to Vittoria Coffee and Citi whose generous support ensures the Good Food Guide continues to be trusted and independent.

National Editor Myffy Rigby

Melbourne Editor Roslyn Grundy

Reviewers Steven Amsterdam, Arizona Atkinson, Lee Atkinson, Rachel Bartholomeusz, Joel Beerden, Ardyn Bernoth, Callan Boys, Max Brearley, Lucy Carter, Paul Chai, Gemima Cody, Sasha Cody, Kate Cox, Pete Cruttenden, Claire Davie, Mariam Digges, Larissa Dubecki, Jill Dupleix, Terry Durack, Rita Erlich, Marc Fennell, Daniel Findlay, Daniela Frangos, Jess Gardner, Cathy Gowdie, Kye Greenacre, Roslyn Grundy, Michael Harden, Neil Hargreaves, Michael Harry, Jil Hogan, Dugald Jellie, Megan Johnston, Jordan Kretchmer, Andrew Levins, Les Luxford, Caitlin Mahar, Andrea McGuinness, Lyndey Milan, Pilar Mitchell, Peter Munro, Kenneth Nguyen, Sarah Norris, Jane Ormond, Michelle Potts, Phillip Putnam, Myffy Rigby, Besha Rodell, Nina Rousseau, Lucinda Schmidt, Melissa Singer, Annabel Smith, Belinda So, Daniela Sunde-Brown, Andrew Taylor, Dani Valent, Anna Webster, John Weldon, Patrick Witton, Helen Yee

Reviewing Panel Ardyn Bernoth, Callan Boys, Lara Caraturo (wine awards), Gemima Cody, Jill Dupleix, Terry Durack, Roslyn Grundy, Myffy Rigby

Josephine Pignolet Award Panel Margie Agostini, Damien Pignolet, Myffy Rigby, Ben Russell, Alla Wolf-Tasker

Life Editor Monique Farmer

Publishing Director Trudi Jenkins

Publisher for Simon & Schuster Julie Gibbs

Designer Daniel New

Managing Editor Pru Engel

Typesetting Post Pre-press Group

Maps Hannah Schubert

Hat logo design David Band. Hat logo is the registered trademark of Fairfax Media Publications Pty Ltd

Photographs Courtesy of restaurants and the Fairfax Media photo library. Cover and section opener patterns: Shutterstock.com

Second edition of the national guide published by Simon & Schuster Australia, 2018. First edition published by Fairfax Media, 2017

37 editions of *The Age Good Food Guide*, 32 editions of *The Sydney Morning Herald Good Food Guide* and five editions of *The Brisbane Times Good Food Guide*.

Fully revised and reset for this edition

A catalogue record for this book is available from the National Library of Australia

Visit thestore.com.au to buy this book online. For more reviews, visit goodfood.com.au

Your feedback is welcome at goodfoodguide@fairfaxmedia.com.au

MIX
Paper from responsible sources
FSC® C001695

Printed and bound in Australia by McPherson's Printing Group

ISBN 9781925791457

Contents

Introduction

It's said to have been the toughest year in hospitality since 2008's Global Financial Crisis. But then, they say through periods of challenge come great art. Restaurants are no exception. This year, the watchwords are focus and connection. For diners, that means full-circle cooking where ingredients are grown, cured and cultured on premises. Even the ceramics are often thrown by the chefs themselves – sometimes from the very clay the restaurant is built on. Yes, the future is live and local with plenty of heart.

The second annual national *Good Food Guide* is a reflection of the thousands of voices that make Australia one of the most diverse and delicious places to eat in the world. Every one of the 500-plus restaurants featured within the pages of this book is a summation of all those moving parts, from kitchen hands to executive chefs, glassies to sommeliers, restaurant managers to directors of vibe.

Our aim is to create a restaurant guide that showcases what it means to dine out in Australia today. We review more than 700 venues before selecting the best 500 for the Guide. To receive a hat, a pinnacle moment in a chef's career and a restaurant's history, that restaurant must score a minimum of 15 out of a possible 20. Reviewers visit unannounced. They book under an assumed name and pay for their own meals. Every score in the book is finalised by a senior review panel – if a final score can't be settled on by the group, we revisit the restaurant.

The national *Good Food Guide* builds on a proud 39-year tradition across *The Sydney Morning Herald* and *The Age*. We remain independent, always.

Myffy Rigby, editor

BRAE

ABOUT THIS GUIDE

The *Good Food Guide* is a compilation of independent, anonymous reviews written by a panel of professional restaurant critics. Restaurants in NSW and Victoria must score at least 14 out of 20 to be included in the guide. All other states must score a minimum of 15 (a chef's hat). Restaurants are chosen at our discretion.

SCORE BREAKDOWN

14 Good

♟ **15** Very good

♟♟ **16** Great

♟♟ **17** Excellent

♟♟♟ **18** Outstanding

♟♟♟ **19** Incredible

♟♟♟ **20** Perfection

SYMBOLS

🍷 Good wine list

AE American Express

DC Diners Club

MC MasterCard

V Visa

$ mains under $20

$$ mains $20–$40

$$$ mains over $40

Please note, **BYO** means a restaurant has BYO on at least one day – please check details and corkage fees with venue.

THE HATS

Three hats

NEW SOUTH WALES
Momofuku Seiobo
Quay
Sixpenny

SOUTH AUSTRALIA
Restaurant Orana

VICTORIA
Attica
Brae
Minamishima

Two hats

AUSTRALIAN CAPITAL TERRITORY
Aubergine

NEW SOUTH WALES, SYDNEY
Aria, Automata, Bennelong, Bentley
Restaurant and Bar, Bert's Bar and
Brasserie, The Bridge Room, Cirrus,
Est., Ester Restaurant, Firedoor, Fred's,
Icebergs Dining Room and Bar, Lucio's,
LuMi Dining, Monopole, Mr Wong,
Ormeggio at The Spit, Oscillate Wildly,
Pilu at Freshwater, Porteno,
Restaurant Hubert, Rockpool Bar
and Grill, Saint Peter, Tetsuya's, Yellow

NEW SOUTH WALES, REGIONAL
Biota Dining, Fleet, Muse Restaurant,
Paper Daisy

QUEENSLAND, BRISBANE
Aria, Otto, Stokehouse Q,

QUEENSLAND, REGIONAL
Wasabi Restaurant and Bar

SOUTH AUSTRALIA
Hentley Farm, Magill Estate

TASMANIA
The Agrarian Kitchen Eatery, Franklin

VICTORIA, MELBOURNE
Amaru, Cutler and Co., Dinner by Heston
Blumenthal, Flower Drum, Grossi Florentino
Upstairs, Ides, Iki Jime, Ishizuka,
Lume, Matilda 159 Domain, O.My,
Rosetta Ristorante, Vue de Monde,
Woodland House

VICTORIA, REGIONAL
Igni, Lake House, Laura, Provenance,
Wickens at Royal Mail Hotel

WESTERN AUSTRALIA
Cullen Wines, Vasse Felix,
Wills Domain, Yarri

♕
One hat

AUSTRALIAN CAPITAL TERRITORY
Bar Rochford, Courgette, Eightysix, Italian and Sons, Morks, Ottoman Cuisine, Temporada

NEW SOUTH WALES, SYDNEY
10 William St, A1 Canteen, Acme, The Apollo, Bacco Osteria, The Bathers' Pavilion, Billy Kwong, Bistro Guillaume, Ble Restaurant, The Boathouse on Blackwattle Bay, Bodega, Buon Ricordo, Catalina, Chin Chin, China Doll, Cho Cho San, Continental Deli Bar Bistro, Cottage Point Inn, The Dolphin Hotel, Felix, Fratelli Paradiso, The Gantry, Glass Brasserie, Hartsyard, Hotel Centennial, Izakaya Fujiyama, Jonah's, Kepos and Co, Kepos Street Kitchen, Lankan Filling Station, LP's Quality Meats, Nomad, Otto Ristorante, Paper Bird, Poly, Queen Chow, The Restaurant Pendolino, Rising Sun Workshop, Rosetta Ristorante, Sagra, Sake Restaurant and Bar (Double Bay), Sean's Panorama, Sokyo, Sotto Sopra, Spice Temple, Stanbuli, Sushi e, Three Blue Ducks (Bronte), Uccello, Yan

NEW SOUTH WALES, REGIONAL
The Argyle Inn, Bistro Molines, Bistro Officina, The Byron at Byron Resort, Caveau, Clementine, Fumo, Harvest, Lolli Redini, Margan Restaurant, Muse Kitchen, Pearls on the Beach, Restaurant Mason, Shelter, St. Isidore, The Stunned Mullet, Subo, The Zin House

NORTHERN TERRITORY
Hanuman

QUEENSLAND, BRISBANE
1889 Enoteca, Blackbird Bar and Grill, E'cco Bistro, Gauge, Gerard's Bistro, GOMA Restaurant, Montrachet, Tartufo, The Wolfe

QUEENSLAND, REGIONAL
The Fish House, Hellenika, Homage, Kiyomi, The Long Apron, Nu Nu, Rick Shores, Rickys, Spirit House

SOUTH AUSTRALIA
Africola, Appellation, Bistro Blackwood, Botanic Gardens Restaurant, The Currant Shed, d'Arenberg Cube Restaurant, FermentAsian, Osteria Oggi, The Pot by Emma McCaskill, Press Food and Wine, Shobosho, Stone's Throw, The Summertown Aristologist

TASMANIA
Dier Makr, Fico, The Source, Stillwater, Templo

VICTORIA, MELBOURNE
Anchovy, Atlas Dining, Bacash, Bar Carolina, Bar Liberty, Bar Lourinha, Cafe Di Stasio, Carlton Wine Room, Caterina's Cucina e Bar, Cecconi's Flinders Lane, Centonove, Coda, Cumulus Inc., Da Noi, Donovans, Elyros, Embla, Ezard, French Saloon, Greasy Zoe's, Highline at the Railway Hotel, Il Bacaro, Kakizaki, Kenzan, Lee Ho Fook, Lesa, Maha, Marion, Miznon, MoVida, Noir, Osteria Ilaria, Pascale Bar and Grill, The Press Club, Ramblr, The Recreation, Rockpool Bar and Grill, Ryne, Saint Crispin, San Telmo, Saxe, Scopri, Spice Temple, Stokehouse, Sunda, Supernormal, Tempura Hajime, Tipo 00, Tonka, Trattoria Emilia, Tulum

VICTORIA, REGIONAL
Captain Moonlite, Doot Doot Doot, Ezard at Levantine Hill, Ipsos, Masons of Bendigo, Midnight Starling, Montalto, Oakridge, Paringa Estate, Pt. Leo Restaurant, The Public Inn, Sardine Eatery and Bar, Source Dining, Stefano's Cantina, TarraWarra Estate, Terrace Restaurant, Tulip, Underbar

WESTERN AUSTRALIA
Amelia Park Restaurant, Balthazar, Billie H, Bread in Common, Garum, The Heritage Wine Bar, Il Lido, Lalla Rookh, Liberte, Long Chim, Lulu La Delizia, Millbrook Winery, Petition Kitchen, Rockpool Bar and Grill, Wildflower

The
Awards

Vittoria Coffee Restaurant of the Year

Ticks every box. The winning restaurant does not need to receive three hats, but must capture the mood of the nation right now and exemplify what it means to be a world-class restaurant.

RESTAURANT ORANA
Adelaide, South Australia

There's plenty of sincerity and zero earnest hand-wringing here at this gutsy little Adelaide restaurant. Yes, much of the food is based on head chef Jock Zonfrillo's personal history and that of the Australian landscape. But it's the collective team narrative that makes this such a captivating place to be. That, and a menu that's as fun as it is delicious, spanning 20 or so small courses, starting with damper skewered on young eucalyptus branches brought to each table on smouldering coals, perfuming the spare, mid-century dining room with the comforting smell of the bush. Each dish is served with a story and a sense of place, navigating deep sea, low-lying scrub, unforgiving desert plains and outback marshlands. Sit still, breathe in. This one's a game changer.

New Restaurant of the Year

*The most exciting opening in the past 12 months, this restaurant sets
the eating agenda and starts conversations. It represents everything
that's fresh, hot and interesting about dining.*

LAURA
Merricks, Victoria

It was a bold pitch to build a $40-million sculpture park, winery and double-restaurant phenomenon overlooking Victoria's Western Port Bay, then to lure chef Phil Wood, the most wanted man on the market after Neil Perry's Eleven Bridge closed last year, to head the kitchen. But the Gandel family does not bluff, and Point Leo Estate has emerged every bit as beautiful as dreamed. Surrender to restaurant manager Ainslie Lubbock's soothing service and a wine list as impressive as your surrounds. Stepping from the raucous main dining room into the taupe terrarium that is Laura, you'll see views of Jaume Plensa's eight-metre statue of a girl's head (the restaurant's namesake). Listen to the sound of whisks gently striking pans as Wood transforms the Mornington Peninsula's vines, land beasts and fish into modern classics. It's a trip. Take it.

Santa Vittoria Regional Restaurant of the Year

The best beyond metro limits. The winning establishment must provide a restaurant experience comparable to anything in the city but remain uniquely regional.

BRAE
Birregurra, Victoria

It's a restaurant that lives and breathes the seasons, fed directly by what's growing out the front of the restaurant, found in the foothills of the Otway Ranges. Chef Dan Hunter's cooking, though bound by the garden, is almost otherworldly. There's a single mouthful of cooling scallop, rich urchin and musky truffle. Or the earthiness of baked beetroot, the sweetness of local honey and brine of trout roe. Bonito cured overnight with kelp and mountain pepper is soft and warm with just the right balance of sweetness and savour. Dining in this sprawling, converted weatherboard house is all about deep, unhurried comfort from immaculate service, a roaring fire in the lounge, onsite accommodation complete with vinyl record collection and a pre-dessert stroll through the gardens, backlit by the setting sun.

———— ✳ ————

Citi Chef of the Year

*This chef is at the forefront of dining, setting new standards,
creating new flavour combinations, doing something original, and
adding something extra to the Australian dining scene.*

PETER GILMORE
Quay, Sydney, New South Wales

Cue sound of a record breaking. This is the 17th consecutive year that
Peter Gilmore has steered Quay to its coveted three-chef-hat status. In that
time, he has introduced us to red speckled peas, tennouji turnips, hatsuka
radishes, red orach, pea flowers, okra shoots and native violets. He's the crackling
king, creating crisp deliciousness from maltose, sea cucumbers, and even the frill
of an oyster. He has produced the most acclaimed dessert this country has ever
seen, with the extraordinary Snow Egg. This year, he threw his entire menu out
the window and started again, creating future classics for a new generation
– Oyster Intervention, Hand-Harvested Seafood and the airy, fragile White
Coral. His cooking is luxurious, but still connects us back to earth and ocean,
creating texture, harmony and surprise.

THERE'S A BRAND NEW *WORLD OF FLAVOUR*

Find your new favourite restaurant
with the Citibank Dining Program.

citibankdining.com.au

Firedoor, NSW

Vittoria Coffee Legend Award

For an outstanding long-term contribution to the industry,
chosen from a short list by Les Schirato of Vittoria Coffee.

STEFANO DE PIERI

Stefano's Cantina, Mildura, Victoria

Long before 'local and seasonal' became a restaurant mantra, Stefano de Pieri was serving Mildura's story on a plate at Stefano's Cantina. This from a man with no formal training as a chef who was born almost 16,000 kilometres away in Treviso, Italy. Since 1991, de Pieri has turned a hotel cellar in a remote Victorian town into a destination restaurant, accidentally becoming a celebrity chef along the way with his 1990s television series and cookbook *A Gondola on the Murray*. De Pieri has used the restaurant as a springboard, starting a cafe-bakery, a brewery, a wine label and the annual Mildura Writers Festival, all intended to help the desert city bloom. This while being a fierce champion of the Sunraysia region's food producers, its arts scene and the environment.

Josephine Pignolet Young Chef of the Year

*This award is chosen by a panel of food professionals led by Damien Pignolet.
It celebrates the memory of a great young chef and is the ultimate accolade
for a committed and talented young cook.*

JODIE ODROWAZ
Iki Jime, Melbourne, Victoria

Don't worry, citizens of planet Earth. The future is safe in the hands of chefs like Jodie Odrowaz. Before she stepped from front of house into the kitchens of Vue de Monde, she worked overseas in restaurants focused on reducing waste. Now she's landed back in Shannon Bennett's fish house Iki Jime, where sustainably sourced, humanely killed seafood rules. In her current role, she's been learning to trace fish from its source and dry-age it for fullest use. She even saves the restaurant's kelp, fire ash and coffee to make body scrub. In time she plans to be the change she wants to see in the world, operating as an all-preserving, carrot-championing connector between producers and the people. As someone who lists a Sharpie and knife as kitchen weapons, you know she's got the detailed determination to do it.

Citi Service Excellence

*The winner of this award executes the highest standard of restaurant
service, from attitude and skill to knowledge and personality.*

KYLIE JAVIER ASHTON
Momofuku Seiobo, Sydney, New South Wales

She has been one of Momofuku Seiobo's few constants since its early days of pork
buns and pet-nat at The Star. Those famous steamed baos have long gone, but the
general manager's professionalism has maintained Momo's vitality through the
Noma-via-New-York cooking of chef Ben Greeno to the flavour-driven haute
Barbadian cuisine of current chef Paul Carmichael. With a resume listing
fine-dining temple Tetsuya's and wine church Bentley Restaurant and Bar,
Javier Ashton greets guests with warmth, extols Bordeaux and jumps behind the
pass when needed to keep the open kitchen humming. Don't you dare think about
stealing the bespoke cutlery, either. When Javier Ashton isn't ensuring that every
diner is having the most delicious fun possible, the industry ambassador takes
names in the amateur boxing ring. Can talk Left Bank. Will throw right hooks.

Food For Good Award

*The winner of this award, which celebrates innovation, social enterprise and
sustainability, goes above and beyond to contribute to the broader community.*

SYDNEY DOESN'T SUCK
New South Wales

Australians use 10 million plastic straws a day, which end up in our waterways as
a threat to marine life, and ultimately break down into microplastics that enter
the food chain. It's this staggering number that prompted City of Sydney Deputy
Lord Mayor Jess Miller to create the #sydneydoesntsuck campaign, working with
small bars across the city to reduce single-use plastic. As ever, little things grow,
and major venues soon signed up to go straw-free (always keeping some to hand
for those with disabilities), including Solotel venues across the Sydney Opera
House and Opera Bar, the International Convention Centre, and the Museum
of Contemporary Art. Combined with online resource, laststraw.com.au, which
provides know-how and lists straw-free venues, #sydneydoesntsuck aims to
put 2.3 million plastic straws out of business. Cheers to that.

Bar of the Year

The best all-round bar that nails service, drinks, vibe and decor.
The winning bar adds something new or different to the drinking scene.

THE DOLPHIN WINE ROOM
Sydney, New South Wales

If you want a bourbon and Coke, move on. If you're keen on local whisky with small-batch cola, come on down to Maurice Terzini's Pub For The 21st Century where post-mix soda is out and Harvey Wallbangers are in. A middle finger to Coca-Cola is only the tip of the Icebergs legend's initiatives with chef Monty Koludrovic and wine director James Hird that have seen The Dolphin become a bellwether boozer for the local community. Australia's best chefs guest star at the Delfino Aperitivo afternoons (hey, it's up-and-coming talent Ben Shewry!) and a wine list bursts with new-wave producers and sustainable Italian deliciousness. Also: tins of Boags. At its core, The Dolphin is still an Aussie pub. A place to shoot the breeze and yell at the footy. All the better with a first-rate cotoletta and a few schooners, too.

———— ✳ ————

Sommelier of the Year

The successful wine professional is able to demonstrate an in-depth knowledge of their subject, while helping to influence and educate diners. They must be personable, inclusive, curious and driven to constantly deliver the highest level of service.

TRAVIS HOWE

Carlton Wine Room, Melbourne, Victoria

When it comes to his gift of the pour, this isn't the first time in lights for the ex-Coda and Tonka sommelier. But it's the first time with skin in the game. A refit of the Carlton Wine Room and installation of chef John Paul Twomey has given the Melbourne institution its mojo back, but it's the ever-approachable steerage by Howe through a 100-bottle list that's given the name over the door its weight again. Throw any brief at Howe and watch him nail it with *Rainman*-like accuracy and a puzzle-lover's delight from a list that runs an all-embracing spectrum including flinty chablis, juicy Burgundy and grower Champagne. He's even coded his list with user-friendly graphics for those who prefer to self-navigate. Amen to having this professionalism freed from fine diners, on tap with your spaghetti on a Monday night.

Wine List of the Year

A diverse and high-quality by-the-glass selection alongside an accessible bottle list that displays a good range of vintages and complements the restaurant's food and style.

OTTO
Brisbane, Queensland

Everything about this tightly run Sydney offshoot nudges you to exhale and relax. Riverside views, sparkling glassware and convivial vibes make cracking open a magnum of Champagne here all but irresistible, especially with a list as tight as this one. The wine list is a celebration of Italian and Italianish wines that can be taken as seriously as the purse-strings will allow, in just about any format you'd care to throw at sommelier Alan Hunter. There's a strong selection of Coravin wines – a perfect way to try a glass of something from the deep and far-reaching wine list without breaking out a full bottle and a second mortgage – hello Radikon, Passopisciaro and Serragghia, old friends.

Regional Wine List of the Year

Honouring a wine list outside the city limits that displays a diverse selection that complements the restaurant's food and style while reflecting the unique qualities of the region.

WICKENS AT THE ROYAL MAIL
Dunkeld, Victoria

All hail the Royal Mail's showstopping new dining room, giving uninterrupted hi-def views of Mounts Sturgeon and Abrupt. But as exciting – if not more so for oenophiles – is the new, tourable cellar housing the 28,000-bottle-strong collection. Owner Allan Myers has long held the Southern Hemisphere's largest privately owned collection of Burgundies and Bordeaux, which is backed by a just-as-heavy-hitting stable of heroes from the old world and old school to progressive punks from Austria to the US. Going head to head with chef Robin Wickens' revamped degustation, driven by that impressive kitchen garden, you'll find 800 of those bottles displayed in three temperature-controlled cellars.

Australia's Best New Restaurants

A1 CANTEEN
Chippendale, New South Wales

Is Clayton Wells' muffaletta-style pressed sandwich Sydney's most Instagrammed dish of 2018? It's in the running. But the good times go well beyond lavish sandwich action at the buzzy, high-ceilinged space, rolling from LP sausages for breakfast to pre-batched negronis and whole flounders at night.

BERT'S BAR AND BRASSERIE
Newport, New South Wales

In a year where the apocalypse has felt especially nigh, Bert's has emerged as the lavish last-days-of-Rome hero we need to face the end with reckless grace. It's Pittwater's bold new beauty where Siberian caviar meets fat lists of grower Champagnes, $125 mud crabs and plates of pasta just casually rolling deep with an entire lobster. No big deal.

BISTRO BLACKWOOD
Adelaide, South Australia

It's third time lucky for Jock Zonfrillo's understudy to his fine diner, Orana. After a second renovation, a firepit now drives an agenda that's in its own way as captivating as the offering upstairs. Veg, squid and beasts are expertly charred and matched with a brilliantly fun bracket of small producer wines and a floor team led by the brilliant Greta Wohlstadt.

IKI JIME
Melbourne, Victoria

It's the fish, the whole fish and almost nothing but the fish at Shannon Bennett's replacement for Bistro Vue in the city. Here, against a room of squid ink darkness, line-caught, humanely killed fish emerge as buttery tarts filled with finger lime and just-set bug meat, and miso-enhanced, crisp-fried barramundi head for finger-picking fun. It's all backed with the impressive cellar and service you expect of the Vue group.

LAURA
Merricks, Victoria

Combine $40 million worth of landmark Australian sculpture, a slick winery restaurant with panoramic ocean views and some of the country's hottest talent, and you have a destination to be reckoned with. That's Pt. Leo Estate, which at its heart has lovely Laura, a gentle taupe terrarium where ex-Rockpool chef Phil Wood is applying classic techniques to the Peninsula's best produce while service gun Ainslie Lubbock calmly steers the ship.

LESA
Melbourne, Victoria

Embla's upstairs restaurant has finally opened its doors with plenty of fans, and delicious fare. The decor is all moody light and dark timbers - central casting for renaissance nudes - while the menu is a celebration of chef Dave Verheul's more technique-driven days at the Town Mouse with lessons from Embla's wood-fire. Large format wines meet big groups and fun times. Embrace it.

MATILDA 159 DOMAIN
South Yarra, Victoria

Chef-restaurateur Scott Pickett hit the jackpot formula with his new fire-fuelled South Yarra restaurant. A powerful room in the dusty, rusty tones of Australia plays backdrop to a gently smoked and charred dinner suited to big groups with its whole crabs, burnished ducks and wines of both the interesting and lifetime investment variety.

POLY
Surry Hills, New South Wales

Is it a natural wine bar, a casual restaurant – or a bar-staurant? Er, yes, probably. Chef Mat Lindsay's punk kitchen glows with grills (all coals, no gas) and the bold flavours are carried by buttery sauces, ferments and duck fat. Garlic bread is warm, puffy and stuffed with a green mulch of young garlic. Blood pie, heir apparent to Ester's renowned blood sausage sanga, is a tennis ball of earthy black pudding wrapped in dark, malty pastry – ridiculously good. Poly is whatever you like, really, as often as you like.

MATILDA 159 DOMAIN

QUAY
Sydney, New South Wales

Quay is back, and it's definitely a brand-new invention. The cool $4 million renovation has turned Peter Gilmore's flagship into what looks like first class on an actual ship. And that's just the beginning of a super-luxe dining experience starring rockpools of sealife benefiting from Gilmore's magic touch, truffle-buttered crumpets from custom-made toasters and an adventurous drinks match that genuinely deserves to be called a journey.

SHELTER
Lennox Head, New South Wales

Embrace the breeze and almost excessive beauty of this stunning dual-purpose cafe/restaurant in Lennox Head. Its polished woods, native flowers and sharp, clean dishes are well suited to the beachy surrounds. Be as one with the beautiful people, drinking natural wines, eating raw fish and cultured cream or beautifully bolstered brussels sprouts.

SUNDA
Melbourne, Victoria

Captained by young gun chef Khanh Nguyen, Sunda is winning hearts and minds with smart, sharp plays on Indonesian, Malaysian and Vietnamese flavours. It's a brutalist industrial space using scaffolding to strangely beautiful effect, where service is sleek and dishes are elegant, but moreover fun, from rendang buns to XO noodles tossed with chicken crackling.

YARRI
Dunsborough, Western Australia

Margaret River's loss is Dunsborough's gain. Chef Aaron Carr has ditched the tweezers of Vasse Felix in favour of simpler but no less compelling dishes at this Dunsborough resto-bar, which takes cues from the six seasons recognised in Nyungar country but also fire cooking and the international flavours Carr loves. Hence, cured emu with muntries meets wood-grilled prawns in miso butter and beachside good times.

Cirrus Dining, NSW

CELEBRATE
A BRAND NEW
WORLD OF FLAVOUR

Congratulations to our Citibank Dining Program partner restaurants.

Quay, NSW
Sixpenny, NSW

Bennelong, NSW
Bentley Restaurant & Bar, NSW
Biota Dining, NSW
The Bridge Room, NSW
Cirrus Dining, NSW
Firedoor, NSW
Muse Restaurant, NSW
Ormeggio at the Spit, NSW
Otto Ristorante Brisbane, QLD
Pilu at Freshwater, NSW
Yellow, NSW

The Bathers' Pavilion, NSW
Caveau, NSW
The Gantry, NSW
Glass Brasserie, NSW
Highline at the Railway Hotel, VIC
Homage, QLD
Kepos & Co, NSW
Kepos Street Kitchen, NSW
Kiyomi, QLD
The Long Apron, QLD
Long Chim Perth, WA
Muse Kitchen, NSW
Otto Ristorante Sydney, NSW
Paper Bird, NSW
The Restaurant Pendolino, NSW
Sokyo, NSW
Sotto Sopra, NSW

citi®

BAR ROCHFORD

♛♛

Aubergine

Australian
Capital
Territory

♛

Bar Rochford
Courgette
Eightysix
Italian and Sons
Morks
Ottoman Cuisine
Temporada

Agostinis

KINGSTON
East Hotel, 69 Canberra Avenue
02 6178 0048

ITALIAN   **14.5/20**

Casual Italian with a little bit of glamour

You can't beat this lively spot if you're dining with kids but still want food worthy of a grown-up's night out. From the glamorous fit-out with plenty of pink, leopard print and touches of gold, to dyed rope hanging from the ceiling to resemble spaghetti drying in the sun, and the lush outdoor dining area filled with plants, it's the sort of space you'll want to stick around in. The giant pizza oven is on full display in the open kitchen. It's cooking not only traditional-style pizza but also Queensland scallops, served in their shells, fragrant with lime and herb butter. Agostinis is focused on fresh produce and meals are definitely share-friendly, like the Milanese-style golden-crumbed veal cutlet, or the calamari, lightly fried and beautifully crisp as the Italians do so well, and served on a zesty lemon and mint aioli. Service isn't always forthcoming, but who's in a hurry anyway? All the more time for dolce and/or vita.

Try the Italian wines on tap – there's pinot grigio, rosé or sangiovese

Open	L D Daily
Price	$$
Cards	AE MC V eftpos
Chef	Francesco Balestrieri
Features	Bar, licensed, outdoor seating, private dining, wheelchair access
Website	easthotel.com.au/eat-and-drink/agostinis

Aubergine

GRIFFITH
18 Barker Street
02 6260 8666

CONTEMPORARY   **16.5/20**

Destination dining spotlighting the region's best produce

Dramatic sheer black curtains, Scandi-style furniture and wine service that never misses a beat make this much-loved fine diner the sleekest spot for a big night out in the capital. Wildflowers bring warmth to the room and owner/chef Ben Willis brings comfort to the table with a refined four-course menu that's high on flavour and low on gimmicks. Spanner crab is handsomely plated with crunchy apple, almond cream and kohlrabi to create a many textured thing laced with basil seeds and a bass note of avruga. Pork loin is gently barbecued to create a trembling layer of fat that's terrific with buttery soubise and the pop of pickled riberries, and saltgrass lamb rump is a heavy-hitting main plated with grilled sweetbreads, cabbage and tangy green persillade. Cracking fodder for a local cool-climate shiraz (check out that vertical selection of Clonakilla) while calvados rounds out the evening with yuzu brulee lifted by mandarin sherbert.

It's no problem to swap dessert for the optional cheese course

Open	D Mon–Sat
Price	$$
Cards	AE MC V eftpos
Chef	Ben Willis
Features	Licensed, outdoor seating, wheelchair access
Website	aubergine.com.au

AUBERGINE

Bar Rochford

CANBERRA
Level 1, 65 London Circuit
02 6230 6222

CONTEMPORARY   **15/20**

A smart, handsome bar for dinner and dancing

'Zibibbo upstairs' touts a blackboard outside this bar walking a line between elegance and grunge. It's a direction worth following for the wine, of course, but also to find Bob Dylan vinyl, bottle-green booths and a fireplace made for drinking vermouth near. Assured cooking makes this a dining destination, too – at least until 10pm, when the soul music starts thumping. Grilled cos is spangled with shiny crisp chicken skin that shatters into a mess of stracciatella, cured egg yolk and dehydrated kale – the younger, cooler cousin of caesar salad. Eggplant is slow-roasted in mushroom dashi for savoury, earthy excellence, bolstered by tahini and a soft smoked egg. Winter carrots love their woody bed of spiced almond puree and a squeeze of grilled blood orange zips the plate mates together. Later, a rosy strap of lamb is dressed with local barberries and quince. Phone ahead and book a table by the beautiful arched window. It's a fine time listening to Tom Waits in the late Canberra sun.

An in-house bottle shop facilitates natural wine and negronis for home use

Open	D Tue–Sat
Price	$$
Cards	AE MC V eftpos
Chef	Louis Couttoupes
Features	Bar, licensed
Website	barrochford.com

Chairman and Yip

BARTON
Burbury Hotel, 1 Burbury Close
02 6162 1220

CHINESE   **14.5/20**

An old favourite for Northern Chinese with modern flair

This institution has been providing pollies with duck pancakes and pinot for more than 20 years, first in Civic and now at Hotel Realm in the serviced apartment-lined suburb of Barton. With the spire of Parliament House looming super close by, it's a quick jaunt for cabinet members to power lunch on dumplings and write off a few bottles. Staff flit around a room of lacquered black and lipstick red, keeping glasses full and carting scallop toast, hotpots and fragrant stews. Fall-apart Shantung lamb belly is a menu mainstay with crackling invigorated by soy and tamarind, and there's new joy to be found in deep-fried zucchini blossoms crammed with crab and prawn. Sichuan-style chicken is crisp-fried and juicy with a chilli punch tempered by caramelised onion and barley. Desserts lean west (macadamia brownie, sticky ginger toffee pudding) and there's a cheeseboard, too. Hey – where's the Act of Parliament saying you can't enjoy post-Chinese comte?

Sister restaurant Lilotang is next door for a sushi snack or sake before dinner

Open	L Tue–Fri; D Tue–Sat
Price	$$
Cards	AE MC V eftpos
Chef	William Suen, Andy Ho
Features	Bar, licensed, outdoor seating, private dining, wheelchair access, BYO
Website	chairmangroup.com.au/ chairmanyip

Courgette

CANBERRA
54 Marcus Clarke Street
02 6247 4042

MODERN EUROPEAN   **15/20**

Modern European fine dining with a sense of occasion

Chef James Mussillon has sold his second venue to put all his focus and energy into this city fine diner, where it's all about relaxed comfort. Charming young waitstaff know their way around the menu and are eager to please with a wine match. Biodynamic riesling from Canberra region's Lark Hill winery works its zesty magic with rare yellowfin tuna that's buzzing with cumin and coriander, and gets an added fruity kick from compressed watermelon, and lime and yuzu mayonnaise. A full-bodied Bordeaux blend packs a punch against the rich combination of juicy Hunter Valley beef fillet and a tender braised wagyu cheek, with potato salad, sweet and sour cabbage, and celeriac puree. Save the pleasingly crunchy caramelised onion cigar for last. Sink into a plush chair for venison checkered with luscious corn croquettes, mirrored by beetroot carpaccio topped with a fragrant truffle mayonnaise. Death by chocolate for dessert won't kill you, but will end the evening on a suitably sweet note.

Extra special occasion? Dine surrounded by hundreds of bottles of wine in the cellar room

Open	L D Mon–Sat
Price	$$
Cards	AE MC V eftpos
Chef	James Mussillon
Features	Licensed, private dining, wheelchair access, BYO
Website	courgette.com.au

Eightysix

BRADDON
Corner Elouera and Lonsdale streets
02 6161 8686

CONTEMPORARY   **15/20**

Smart, social, casual, confident: a go-to eatery for those in the know

Five years on and Eightysix's number still comes up. Address? In on-the-rise Braddon. Architecture? Timelessly modern (timber chair legs on polished concrete, tan leather banquette, louvred glass, undressed black tables). Ambience? Think designer handbags under the bar, swinging among an inner-city crowd who get the clever, snappy menu (salt and vinegar potato scallops, say) that still pops and sizzles. Food arrives fast, from spot-on fried chicken bombs with Kewpie mayo and chilli-hot sriracha sauce, to a slow-roasted lamb shoulder as upright as the Brindabellas, on a creamy mash as rich as you like. The living is good (and easy) with perfectly soft duck buns, or crisp-skinned salmon fillet, baked in a paper bag and served with a playful flourish of colours (pink pickled ginger, red onion, orange wedges, red radish, green shiso mint). You can bet that sticky caramel popcorn sundae is going nowhere fast, either. Hands clap and flames hiss in the open kitchen. Casually on-trend? You betcha.

Peckish? There's a gourmand's all-you-can-eat menu for $100

Open	D Daily
Price	$$
Cards	AE MC V eftpos
Chef	Jiwoo Kim
Features	Bar, licensed, outdoor seating, wheelchair access
Website	eightysix.com.au

Italian and Sons

BRADDON
7 Lonsdale Street
02 6162 4888

ITALIAN   **15.5/20**

A buzzy, well-oiled trattoria in the heart of Braddon

Braddon was a sleepy part of the city before this chic tratt opened a decade ago and jolted Lonsdale Street to life. Date-nighters, birthday revellers and Canberra's social elite still can't get enough of the joint, meaning you'll absolutely need a reservation to experience its classic Italian cooking at the weekend. At the end of an elongated dining room warmed by a wood-fired oven, you can find the marble counter of Bacaro wine bar, a slick spot to swipe semolina scarpetta ('little shoes') through deep-flavoured suckling lamb ragu, before hitting the restaurant proper for house-made pasta – a slippery black tangle of squid ink linguine, say, rich with tomato, spanner crab and chilli. Grilled cotechino is the perfect picture of comfort on its bed of veal stock-braised lentils while wood-roasted Bangalow pork with bitter greens, pan juices and stone fruit mostarda has the type of crackling that sticks to your teeth and needs loosening with lambrusco. Here's to another 10 years of la vera cucina.

Groups can 'eat like an Italian' with the $75-a-head tasting menu

Open	L Tue–Fri; D Mon–Sat
Price	$$
Cards	AE MC V eftpos
Chef	Pasquale Trimboli
Features	Bar, licensed, wheelchair access
Website	italianandsons.com.au

Lilotang

BARTON
Burbury Hotel, 1 Burbury Close
02 6273 1424

JAPANESE   **14/20**

A fun-time eatery for sushi, beer and sake

Bento boxes are big business at this mix of izakaya, kiosk and restaurant in Barton's parliamentary precinct, where cabinet types huddle over lunch specials of chicken katsu, agedashi tofu and Japanese curry. There's a fast casual vibe thanks to quick service and the biff-bam-pow of manga comic murals, but the kitchen provides surprises and skills that invite a longer stay. The sushi carte is healthy with scampi, sea urchin and saltwater eel while a composed sashimi course of koji-cured kingfish is elevated with the savoury kick of nameko mushrooms. There's more fungi magic in a sweet and salty bowl of vegetable sukiyaki teeming with enoki, shiitake and an onsen egg, and binchotan-grilled chicken thigh is wonderfully tender and aromatic after 48 hours marinating in sake lees – white sesame chilli sauce sends the smoky flavours into overdrive. Sakura cheesecake is dense and creamy and the right way to cap an evening with refreshing umeshu riding shotgun.

An $85 tasting menu is where chef Ota really showcases his sushi talents

Open	L Tue–Fri; D Tue–Sat
Price	$$
Cards	AE MC V eftpos
Chef	Shunsuke Ota
Features	Bar, licensed, outdoor seating, wheelchair access, BYO
Website	chairmangroup.com.au/lilotang

Monster Kitchen and Bar

NEW ACTON
Ovolo Nishi Hotel, 25 Edinburgh Avenue
02 6287 6287

CONTEMPORARY   **14.5/20**

Creative hotel dining without a club sandwich in sight

It's farewell Hotel Hotel and greetings to Ovolo, the new Hong Kong-based owners of Canberra's top spot for crumpets in bed. The change of hotel management hasn't affected the bold-flavoured cooking, and the dining room is still a wonderful mismatch of terrazzo table tops and white wrought iron, but certainly the young service team needs organisation – especially when it comes to suggesting and pouring wine from Monster's cracking cellar. Spiced lamb ribs with curry leaves love a local cabernet, with braised meat that slides off the bone and demands a squeeze of lime. The earthy tang of rare Flinders Island wallaby is enhanced by smoked beetroot and pan-fried snapper is a rich and juicy treat with burnt butter and leek. The shattering of chocolate tuile against ganache with Fernet Branca and fresh mint is a delicious time in any situation, but if you're staying at the hotel, consider having it in the room and pouring your own booze. There's nothing like eating dessert while dressed in a waffle robe.

The new 'chop-chop' pick-up menu is ideal for New Acton workers keen for banh mi or katsu to go

Open	B L D Daily
Price	$$
Cards	AE MC V eftpos
Chef	Daniel Flatt
Features	Bar, licensed, outdoor seating, private dining, wheelchair access
Website	monsterkitchen.com.au

Morks

KINGSTON
18 Eastlake Parade
02 6295 0112

THAI   **15/20**

Modern Thai that doesn't take itself too seriously

There's a wall of wine at the entrance, a mural up the back and not much else when it comes to interiors at this mod-Thai restaurant. Instead, the food does all the talking at the lively Foreshore eatery. Brothers Mork and Benn Ratanakosol have put their second-generation restaurateur spin on a menu that's to-the-point and doesn't take itself too seriously. Scallop, squid and pork salad is fresh and light, driven by fish sauce and lime. Poached chicken is served like a Buddha bowl but tastes like a laksa. Stir together the chicken, witlof, mustard leaf, noodles and curry, for a dish that delivers all of the beautiful Thai flavours and leaves quite a lingering heat in your mouth. Dessert's where the fun is at, from the cheekily named 'Pikachu I choose you', to the 'monkey magic' (which translates as deep-fried ice-cream). Want to try an unusual wine by the glass? This is the place to do it, with plenty of options and staff who are more than happy to offer suggestions.

Bag a seat in the leafy outdoor area in the warmer months

Open	L Wed–Fri, Sun; D Tue–Sun
Price	$$
Cards	AE MC V eftpos
Chef	Mork Ratanakosol
Features	Licensed, outdoor seating, wheelchair access
Website	morks.com.au

Otis Dining Hall

KINGSTON
29 Jardine Street
02 6260 6066

CONTEMPORARY   **14.5/20**

Modern bistro cooking in old English setting

You won't find any tapestries or candelabras in this dining 'hall' which is really more of a spacious wood-panelled dining room punctuated by brass, brown leather and banker's lamps. The kind of place Winston Churchill might drink 10 martinis for lunch. Salted wallaby tartare is a healthier midday option, wrapped in pickled vine leaves and mellowed by macadamia floss. A young service team stumbles and the dining room can feel hollow if it's not at capacity, but certainly there's talent on the pans and local wine to fill your glass. Burnt butter and sage roll with sweet pumpkin tortellini is fine-tuned with aged balsamic to create a pasta perfect for cool-climate chardonnay. Lip-sticking shiraz jus enhances just-pink lamb rump served on a bed of nutty braised farro, and duck neck sausage with plump golden raisins comes from the same world of European comfort. Creme caramel is a fantastic finish with Japanese whisky and sea salt taking baked custard to new heights.

Cocktails are best ordered in the evening when there are senior staff on deck who know how to stir them

Open   L D Tue–Sat
Price $$
Cards   MC V eftpos
Chef   Damian Brabender, Adam Wilson
Features   Bar, licensed, wheelchair access
Website   thisisotis.com.au

Ottoman Cuisine

BARTON
9 Broughton Street
02 6273 6111

TURKISH   **15/20**

Expect old-fashioned hospitality and new-fashioned Turkish food

The banquet trade is strong at this powerbroker favourite in the Parliamentary Triangle, where private rooms might facilitate a leadership challenge by day and birthday celebration in the evening. A sprawling dining room with views to an ornate courtyard and water lilies makes Ottoman a popular choice for date-nighters too, and knowledgeable staff are ready to rise to any occasion and tailor menus on request. Rolls of crisp yufka pastry are essential, packed with shredded duck, currants and pine nuts, lifted with fresh mint and yoghurt. Juicy char-grilled chicken skewers keep it simple with a subtle saffron marinade and barberry pilaf, while a Turkish-spiced pot pie is rich with the greatest hits of Sunday lunch, featuring slow-cooked Cowra lamb, carrots and onion with big whacks of garlic. Semolina cake is the right size to share, served with honey yoghurt sorbet to cut through the orange syrup-soaked sponge. Don't forget to pinch a complimentary Turkish delight on the way out.

The most simple deliciousness can be found among the daily specials

Open   L Tue–Fri; D Tue–Sat
Price $$
Cards   MC V eftpos
Chef   Serif Kaya
Features   Licensed, private dining, wheelchair access, BYO
Website   ottomancuisine.com.au

OTIS DINING HALL

Temporada

CANBERRA
15 Moore Street
02 6249 6683

CONTEMPORARY   **15/20**

TEMPORADA

Refined everyday eating in a chic, relaxed setting

From the team behind fine diner Aubergine, this come-as-you-are bar and restaurant provides dishes than never trade substance for style. A plaid-clad waiter hangs jackets and suggests cocktails, and the central bar is a perfect perch for margaritas and crumbed oysters on a bun with kohlrabi remoulade. Share a bowl of roast chestnuts with softly cooked barley boosted by black garlic and mushrooms. In a dining space where rough wood walls meet a pressed metal ceiling, Civic workers roll up their sleeves for skewers of wagyu intercostal braised in masterstock and grilled for a sticky crust barely containing fall-apart rib goodness - brilliant with fresh lime and salsa negra featuring five types of chilli fried in duck fat. Flinders Island lamb rump is a dish less intense, served with buttery soubise and gently grilled to let the meat's grassy-sweet flavour come forward. Kudos for the American graham cracker crumb in a creamy mascarpone cheesecake with strawberry sorbet.

Share wood-grilled T-bone with chimichurri to seal a business deal

Open	B L Mon–Fri; D Mon–Sat
Price	$$
Cards	AE MC V eftpos
Chef	Ben Willis, Dave Young
Features	Bar, licensed, outdoor seating, wheelchair access
Website	temporada.com.au

citi®

THERE'S A
BRAND NEW
*WORLD OF
FLAVOUR*

Proud Presenting Partner of the
Good Food Guide 2019.

citibankdining.com.au

Otto, QLD

QUAY

New

South

Wales

♔♔♔

Momofuku Seiobo
Quay
Sixpenny

♔♔

Aria
Automata
Bennelong
Bentley Restaurant and Bar
Bert's Bar and Brasserie
The Bridge Room
Cirrus
Est.
Ester Restaurant
Firedoor
Fred's
Icebergs Dining Room and Bar
Lucio's
LuMi Dining
Monopole
Mr Wong
Ormeggio at The Spit
Oscillate Wildly
Pilu at Freshwater
Porteno
Restaurant Hubert
Rockpool Bar and Grill
Saint Peter
Tetsuya's
Yellow

♔

10 William St
A1 Canteen
Acme
The Apollo
Bacco Osteria
The Bathers' Pavilion
Billy Kwong
Bistro Guillaume
Ble Restaurant
The Boathouse on Blackwattle Bay
Bodega

Buon Ricordo
Catalina
Chin Chin
China Doll
Cho Cho San
Continental Deli Bar Bistro
Cottage Point Inn
The Dolphin Hotel
Felix
Fratelli Paradiso
The Gantry
Glass Brasserie
Hartsyard
Hotel Centennial
Izakaya Fujiyama
Jonah's
Kepos and Co
Kepos Street Kitchen
Lankan Filling Station
LP's Quality Meats
Nomad
Otto Ristorante
Paper Bird
Poly
Queen Chow
The Restaurant Pendolino
Rising Sun Workshop
Rosetta Ristorante
Sagra
Sake Restaurant and Bar (Double Bay)
Sean's Panaroma
Sokyo
Sotto Sopra
Spice Temple
Stanbuli
Sushi e
Three Blue Ducks (Bronte)
Uccello
Yan

Sydney

10 William Street

PADDINGTON
10 William Street
02 9360 3310

ITALIAN   **15/20**

A bar that's a restaurant that's a bar that's a . . .

You'll want to be happy to wait, or happy to eat extremely early if you have intentions around trying chef Enrico Tomelleri's esoteric Italianese menu. And don't be surprised if you're turned away at the door point blank if you show up mid-evening on a Friday night. But if you've made it this far and have a table in the dark, dinky room where the bar dominates, you'll be rewarded with the likes of a juicy, sweet black tomato and bread salad balanced with just the right amount of acid. Crisp, golden wedges of chickpea cake are draped in silken ribbons of prosciutto and the smoky whipped bottarga served with a big, sweet malty pretzel is perfect to linger with over wine. On that, the list is Italian-leaning, but not Italian-only. And there are plenty of treasures to dig up – especially if your tastes lean to naturalists and small producers. Pasta, like a cacio e pepe crowned with a raw duck egg yolk, is always a winner but it's the sideshows that bring it tonight, like a bowl of mussels that arrive stinking of garlic and rosemary and wonderful for it. Just like everything here, it's beautifully unapologetic.

Come early in the week and take a seat at the bar for relaxed snacks

Open	L Fri–Sat; D Mon–Sat
Price	$$
Cards	AE MC V eftpos
Chef	Enrico Tomelleri
Features	Bar, licensed, private dining
Website	10williamst.com.au

12-Micron

BARANGAROO
Level 2, 100 Barangaroo Avenue
(enter via Shipwright Walk)
02 8322 2075

CONTEMPORARY   **14/20**

Native Australian ingredients with water views

Can you get any more So Australian Right Now than Sydney rock oysters with Davidson plum or roast lamb with warrigal greens? We reckon not. Contemporary Australian cuisine can mean pretty much anything these days but 12-Micron (a restaurant *and* a premium wool fibre measurement) is noticeably earnest about trumpeting native produce using refined techniques. Sweet, plump yabby tails are seasoned with lemon myrtle and garnished with ice plant – a crunchy edible succulent that looks like it's covered in frost. Crisp-skinned barramundi is almost outshone by a support cast of carrots and leeks that have been variously roasted, charred, sauteed and pureed. Foams are still in vogue here, but worked with a deft hand, contrasted against charred corn kernels and chicken with skin so crisp it snaps like crackling. Finish with the 'coconut rough' for dessert, an elaborate plating of chocolate mousse, coconut and rainforest lime, while you soak up the twinkling Barangaroo water views through the floor-to-ceiling glass windows.

Sweet tooths can go hell for leather with the dessert degustations

Open	L Tue–Sun; D Daily
Price	$$
Cards	AE MC V eftpos
Chef	Justin Wise
Features	Bar, licensed, private dining, wheelchair access
Website	12micron.com.au

1821

SYDNEY
122 Pitt Street
02 8080 7070

GREEK   **14/20**

Classic meets contemporary Greek in this bright oasis

Amid the skyscraper scale and shambolic traffic of Pitt Street, it's possible for the eye to skate over the grandeur of 1821. Pass over the threshold, though, and you've entered an establishment that knows what it's about – a small slice of Greece in the CBD. The bright room radiates pride in the fatherland with stylised muskets from the war of independence adorning the wall to a massive Greek flag mural. So it is with the kitchen. Slow-cooked lamb shoulder is a flawlessly executed classic but even more delight is to be found in the marriage between old school comfort and modern flair. Mushroom and truffle moussaka takes the original eggplant and potato dish to earthy, smoky new heights. The prawn saganaki is less assured in the sweet cinnamon-heavy sauce but a passionfruit bougatsa spins the custardy treat into fresh and fruity territory. Order a glass of the lush, spicy Alpha Axia syrah-xinomavro and revel in the union.

Grab a booth if you can – it's the safest place to wield the tall menu

Open	L D Daily
Price	$$
Cards	AE DC MC V eftpos
Chef	David Tsirekas
Features	Bar, licensed, outdoor seating, private dining, wheelchair access
Website	1821.com.au

A Tavola

BONDI
Shop 2, 75-79 Hall Street
02 9130 1246

🍷

ITALIAN   **14.5/20**

The best of Abruzzo cuisine two blocks from Bondi Beach

Complimentary soft and fluffy house-made focaccia with extra virgin olive oil is a small touch but reflective of the warm Italian hospitality that underlies this local favourite, specialising in Abruzzo dishes from Italy's central east. The airy dining room is all copper light pendants, Bentwood chairs and crisp tablecloths, dominated by a massive marble slab that could comfortably seat 30. Blackboard specials will test your high-school Italian but don't fret, staff will automatically present an English version. Choices abound, from a silky lemony polenta strewn with spanner crab and sorrel, to a single curl of masterfully cooked octopus on a saffron potato puree. The house-made pasta is what really shines, though, like the linguine alla vastese hearty with seafood and the dramatic squid ink ravioli in deepest ebony, wrapped around pockets of mulloway. Their signature dessert, cremino al cioccolato, is deservedly so – an espresso cup layered with chocolate hazelnut ganache, salted caramel gelato, amaretti biscuits and blow-torched meringue.

Arrive early for an al fresco pre-sunset drink and watch the world go by

Open	L Wed–Sun; D Daily
Price	$$
Cards	AE MC V eftpos
Chef	Marco Masotti
Features	Licensed, outdoor seating, wheelchair access
Website	atavola.com.au/bondi

60TH

ANNIVERSARY

1958 - 2018

Vittoria®

Coffee

A1 Canteen

CHIPPENDALE
Ground floor, 2-10 Kensington Street
02 9280 3285

CONTEMPORARY   **15/20**

Workers rejoice! Automata gives birth to a snack-happy, all-day diner

OK, so it's not really a canteen. There are no trays, and no queues lining up to be served. Automata's Clayton Wells has walked across Kensington Street to open this buzzy, high-ceilinged, light-filled all-day diner, with its coffee window up front, cafe seating, curved booths and long, padded banquettes. The food and mood change from dawn to dusk – from cheerful breakfasts of curried scrambled eggs with LP's sausages and lunchtime muffuletta-style pressed sandwiches to a more intimate vibe at night, complete with pre-batched negronis and haute bistro food. There's drama in a daring pairing of deeply rich, sweetly savoury, house-made blood cake with swathes of pickled beetroot, and whole flounder awash in peppery espelette butter under a shower of crisp curry leaves. Dinner winner is the kibbeh-like, hand-chopped lamb tartare entwined with eggplant and embellished with pickled green almonds. For dessert, slow-poached quince teamed with a rich pistachio sorbet nails the season. It might not be a canteen, but at least it's A1.

The lunchtime muffuletta looks set to become a Sydney icon

Open	B L Daily; D Tue–Sat
Price	$$
Cards	AE MC V eftpos
Chef	Clayton Wells, Scott Eddington
Features	Licensed, wheelchair access
Website	a1canteen.com.au

Abhi's Indian Restaurant

NORTH STRATHFIELD
163 Concord Road
02 9743 3061

INDIAN   **14/20**

A reliable local favourite that's well worth travelling for

The table next to us are locals. So are the table next to them – and they urge us to order the 'amazingly hot' vindaloo. They've been coming here for 20 years, so we take the tip. "It's not Indian-hot," the waiter tells me with a wink and smile as he sets it down. "It's Aussie-hot." He's right – the beef ambotik, described as a 'Vindaloo variation' is more tang than tingle – a sharp balance of tomato, ginger and cumin-y hunks of tender meat. There's more serious heat to be found in street-food style entrees – crisp potato alu tikki patties with piquant tamarind chutney, and smoky tandoor-roasted pieces of marinated chicken with punchy lime pickle. Flavours in the seafood moily get a little overpowered by the coconut base but the scallops, prawns and chunks of barramundi are plentiful. A sticky spoonful of the rose and pistachio kulfi and it's abundantly clear why this place has been packed out by Strathfield locals for nearly three decades.

Almost everything is gluten-free, and they will happily adapt their banquet menus to suit vegetarians

Open	L Sun–Fri; D Daily
Price	$$
Cards	AE MC V eftpos
Chef	Kumar Mahadevan, Ranjan Choudhury
Features	Licensed, wheelchair access, BYO
Website	abhisindian.com.au

Acme

RUSHCUTTERS BAY
60 Bayswater Road
0435 940 884

CONTEMPORARY   **15/20**

The spiritual home of rap, Jatz and pig's head pasta

"You've got to try the dehydrated chocolate mousse," says Acme co-owner and world's friendliest floorman, Cam Fairbairn. "It legit tastes like Ovaltine." He's right, too, and the dried cocoa is straight-up delicious shattered through Jerusalem artichoke ice-cream. Hat tips to high-school snacks and Aussie kitsch are threaded through Mitch Orr's cooking, where Jatz have found their way off the regular menu and into alphabet soup, toasted and reduced into a broth with hispi cabbage for a salty savoury hit like no other. That baloney sandwich and glossy pig's head macaroni still bookend a menu also featuring 'steak and eggs' (wagyu tartare popping with avruga, tobiko and salmon roe) and malloreddus – rich and green with stinging nettles, potato and a pinch of chicken salt. Pasta is still number one at this buzzing little restaurant and spaghetti with smoked eel bordelaise is every bit as boisterous as the rap soundtrack and cocktails. Bring a crew and kick off with Korean tinnies for a super swell time.

The $65 'crush me' menu is one of the best bangs for your buck in town

Open	D Tue–Sat
Price	$$
Cards	AE MC V eftpos
Chef	Mitchell Orr
Features	Licensed, private dining, wheelchair access
Website	weareacme.com.au

Aki's

WOOLLOOMOOLOO
Shop 1, 6 Cowper Wharf Road
02 9332 4600

INDIAN   **14.5/20**

Modern Indian plus your go-to favourites in a ritzy wharfside location

As the first stop on a long wharf of upscale restaurants, the sunny outdoor tables are perfectly positioned for watching the who's who of Sydney arrive to dinner – by car, foot or yacht. And yet despite the stately surrounds, there's a relaxed charm that makes you feel comfortable enough to gnaw at your tandoori lamb bone, or double dip the noodle-like string hoppers into a fragrant crab sauce. Smiling staff add to the allure, as does a well-loved red carpet leading into a double-storey space decked out in decadent splashes of pink, black and silver. It's a colourful mix of classic and contemporary, just like the food. Grilled quail comes with an alluring spice mix of dried chillies and browned coconut, generously coating crunchy charred onions. Then there are your regulars, like silky chicken korma and wafer-thin naan. They're a cut above your local Indian joint, as is the bill. But then that sunset view of the city skyline is priceless.

Be sure to order a flaky paratha lacchadar flatbread to soak up the curry

Open	L D Daily
Price	$$
Cards	AE MC V eftpos
Chef	Kumar Mahadevan, R.J. Dahnasekaren
Features	Bar, licensed, outdoor seating, private dining, wheelchair access
Website	akisindian.com.au

Alibi Woolloomooloo

WOOLLOOMOOLOO
Ovolo Hotel, 6 Cowper Wharf Road
02 9331 9000

CONTEMPORARY, VEGETARIAN   **14/20**

Designer plant-based dining

Alibi is an unusual but timely
choice for the entrepreneurial Ovolo
Woolloomooloo. The vast interior is
broken into playful, urban-backyards
of sofa and communal table seating,
with luminous trees that are more
like art installations. Controversial
California-based consultant chef,
Matthew Kenney, has created a menu
of plant-based, nut-enriched dishes
such as cacio e pepe with kelp noodles
entwined with slivered sugar snap peas,
pea sprouts, and a light black pepper
cashew cream. Kimchi dumplings
made from compressed coconut flesh
and coriander and filled with pureed
kimchi, cashew and tahini are light and
fresh, and a straightforward smoked
hummus with crisp-fried chickpeas is
a winner-winner-no-chicken dinner.
Udon noodles in a rich pool of cashew
hoisin sauce with shiitake and chickpea
tempeh might be a step too close to
peanut butter, but let's face it, vegan's
here to stay, so we may as well
have some fun.

**The #hashtag cocktail of pisco,
yuzu and mandarin coloured with
activated charcoal comes with an
edible fruit gel lipstick**

Open	L Sat–Sun; D Tue–Sat
Price	$$
Cards	AE DC MC V eftpos
Chef	Matthew Kenney, Michael Nicolaou
Features	Bar, licensed, private dining, wheelchair access
Website	alibibar.com.au

Alpha

SYDNEY
238 Castlereagh Street
02 9098 1111

GREEK   **14.5/20**

Greek classics served in a stylish taverna

The Greeks have long claimed
democracy as their greatest invention
but the golden, flaky pastry of chef
Peter Conistis' spinach and feta pie
deserves its place in the Mediterranean
sun. So too his creamy taramasalata
and tzatziki dished up with stacks
of puffy, grill-scorched pita. But
bread and dips do not begin to hint
at the delights of Alpha's menu,
which serves the classics – moussaka,
souvlaki – alongside inventive
new flavours such as the pineapple
ouzo sorbet that accompanies the
tongue-twisting galaktoboureko, a
passionfruit custard encased in Conistis'
signature golden pastry. The baked
barrel-aged feta, joined by a cast of
flavours – lemon, capers, garlic and
pickled peppers – delivers freshness and
the gentlest of kicks. That light touch
is evident in the spiced lamb shoulder,
a hearty dish ideal for sharing. The
relaxed air and pale interior, with its
high ceiling, fishing net hanging lights
and wall inscribed with the Greek
alphabet, evokes the atmosphere of
an island taverna.

Find out Yia Yia's secret ingredients in Alpha's foodstore

Open	B Mon–Fri; L D Daily
Price	$$
Cards	AE MC V eftpos
Chef	Peter Conistis
Features	Bar, licensed, private dining, wheelchair access
Website	alpharestaurant.com.au

Annata

CROWS NEST
69 Willoughby Road
02 9437 3700

CONTEMPORARY   **14.5/20**

Crows Nest finally gets a spot for natural wines and technically focused plates

This quiet and dimly lit restaurant on Willoughby Road has one of the best wine lists this side of the bridge. You'll spot Annata's owner Christian Blair working the floor on any given night of the week – he's the dude with the grapes tattooed on him. He may offer up a glass of crisp, just-amber white blend by Swinging Bridge (this may, in fact, be the first spot on the North Shore to offer up some great skin contact wine options). Food-wise, you should opt for the more surreptitious vegetarian options on the menu, like the crisp onion puffs. You'll dip the golden fried petals into a quenelle of buttery parmesan custard, which feels like eating a high-end Le Snak. Or try the aromatic mushroom broth, which has a pho-like intensity of flavour, with hunks of king brown and shiitake mushrooms, sitting pretty with brown quinoa. It may read healthy on the menu, but it's a warming, complex bowl of deliciousness.

Order on your own here – while the five-course degustation is tempting, it doesn't showcase the true stars of the menu

Open	L Fri; D Mon–Sat
Price	$$
Cards	AE MC V eftpos
Chef	Dan Webb
Features	Licensed, outdoor seating, BYO

The Apollo

POTTS POINT
44 Macleay Street
02 8354 0888

GREEK   **15/20**

There's comfort in things that remain constant here at this swish Greek diner

That wild weed pie is still deliciously filled with tender bitter greens, the pastry light and flaky. The fried cheese, which comes sizzling in the pan doused in oregano-flecked honey and olive oil is still just as fragrant, stretchy, and deliciously moreish as the day chef/restaurateur Jonathan Barthelmess first fired up those individual cast iron pans back in 2012. The little glass jars of taramasalata remains a must-have thinking-snack – lightly sour and creamy with the pop of trout roe on top. The warm, fluffy pita bread on the side could be eaten by the pound alone. That slick, dimly lit concrete room designed by starchitect George Livissianis is just as busy as it's always been, too. It's walk-in only for small groups and near impossible to get a table unless you rock up very early or very late. Floor staff are as friendly as they can be under the pressure of all those diners, and happy to find you place to have a glass of assyrtiko while you wait. Same as it ever was.

Take a crew and book a table, then slide in like you own the place

Open	L Fri–Sun; D Daily
Price	$$
Cards	AE MC V eftpos
Chef	Jonathan Barthelmess, Stefano Marano
Features	Bar, licensed, outdoor seating, private dining, wheelchair access
Website	theapollo.com.au

Let us serve
you Australia's
best dining
experience

goodfoodgiftcard.com.au

goodfood
RESTAURANT GIFT CARD

Quay

Aubergine | Grossi Florentino Upstairs | Otto, Brisbane | Rosetta Ristorante, Melbourne
Bennelong | Icebergs Dining Room & Bar | Pilu at Freshwater | The Agrarian Kitchen Eatery
Firedoor | Ormeggio at The Spit | Rockpool Bar & Grill, Sydney | The Bridge Room
Flower Drum | | |

ACME | Eightysix | Rosetta Ristorante, Sydney | TarraWarra Estate
Bacash | Elyros | Sagra | Temporada
Bacco Osteria | Ezard | Sake Restaurant & Bar, Double Bay | The Boathouse on Blackwattle Bay
Bistro Guillaume, Sydney | Gerard's Bistro | Sotto Sopra | The Zin House
Catalina | Homage | Source Dining | The Gantry
Caterina's | Jonah's | Spice Temple, Sydney | The Heritage Wine Bar
Caveau | Otto, Sydney | Spice Temple, Melbourne | The Long Apron
Coda | Rockpool Bar & Grill, Melbourne | |
Courgette | Rockpool Bar & Grill, Perth | |

goodfood
RESTAURANT GIFT CARD

Aqua Dining

MILSONS POINT
Corner Paul and Northcliff streets
02 9964 9998

ITALIAN   **14.5/20**

A picture-perfect way to enjoy Sydney Harbour, without getting your feet wet

There's a whiff of chlorine in the air and the sound of swimmers slapping the water in the fading sun. From up here, their laps look like voluntary water-torture. The restaurant balcony boasts some of the city's best waterside seats, with unspoilt views of North Sydney Olympic Pool, the Harbour Bridge, Opera House and Luna Park. While soaking up the sights, dip into some fine Italian fare that's more than a little fun, from a honeycomb negroni to veal sweetbreads marinated with Peruvian chilli paste and served with smoked cauliflower and pickled enoki mushrooms. Globetrotting chef and co-owner Davide Rebeccato worked across Italy, England, the Caribbean and India, before settling in Sydney. Sweet and simple tagliolini with pureed artichokes and prawns is a trip back to his hometown near Venice, while crisp-skinned Murray cod with braised brussel sprouts in a clear cabbage consomme adds an Australian flavour to the evening. Leave the laps to the swimmers. You're better off being happy, high and dry.

There's a discount set menu on Saturday lunch and Sundays

Open	L D Daily
Price	$$
Cards	AE MC V eftpos
Chef	Davide Rebeccato
Features	Licensed, outdoor seating, private dining, wheelchair access, BYO
Website	aquadining.com.au

Aria

SYDNEY
1 Macquarie Street
02 9240 2255

CONTEMPORARY   **17/20**

Fine dining complete with fine views, wine and service

Succession planning is all the go at the moment. With an eye to the future, Matt Moran has appointed Joel Bickford, former head chef of The Gantry as executive chef of his Circular Quay flagship, and a new grace and precision is applied to some of the state's finest produce. The snacks are serious, from tricornes of compressed beetroot enfolding Kristen Allan goat's cheese to cigarillos of sweet potato around chicken liver parfait. Dining flows through slow-cooked pork belly with shavings of abalone, and the luxury of poached WA marron grounded by pan-fried sweetbreads to a celestial, lightly steamed Murray cod from Griffith paired with a chilled angasi oyster on warm celeriac with miso cream – a thrilling combination of texture and taste. It feels as if all the many aspects of Aria are coming together in one delicious whole. Bickford's food is exciting, with a clarity and seasonal synchronicity that lifts the dining experience to a new high.

Dip your toe in the water with an early pre-theatre menu for $90 for two courses

Open	L D Daily
Price	$$$
Cards	AE DC MC V eftpos
Chef	Joel Bickford
Features	Bar, licensed, private dining, wheelchair access
Website	aria.com.au

Automata

CHIPPENDALE
5 Kensington Street
02 8277 8555

CONTEMPORARY   **16.5/20**

**Intelligent, striking cooking served
in an industrial-chic setting**

While other restaurants at the
Kensington Street 'lifestyle' precinct
are in a state of flux or closure, this
beautifully brutal restaurant, with its
motorcycle cylinder lights, concrete
and timber, keeps getting better. This
is confident, unflashy cooking and
chef Clayton Wells excels at plating
hyper-seasonal produce with house-
cured deliciousness. Fermented and
pickled celery is cross-hatched with
cuttlefish on a thick pool of squid ink
enhanced with shallot oil for depth
of flavour. Snapper is cured in koji to
bring out its delicate sweetness and go
one-for-two with desert lime cream
and batons of apple-like jujube. All
the better with a vibrant sake from
sommelier Tim Watkins' left-field
drinks list, like a juicy red with black
Angus tri-tip powered-up by white
miso. The seven-course option (instead
of the standard five) is a nifty idea,
especially when it includes fresh
shiitake pasta flecked generously
with mudcrab. Automata's new
A1 Canteen is open for breakfast or
drinks just a few doors down, too.

**Tim Watkins can deliver a powerful
version of *Happy Birthday* in Italian
for special occasions**

Open	L Wed–Sat; D Tue–Sat
Price	$$
Cards	AE MC V eftpos
Chef	Clayton Wells, Sarah Knight
Features	Bar, licensed, wheelchair access
Website	automata.com.au

Azuma

SYDNEY
Level 1, Chifley Plaza, 2 Chifley Square
02 9222 9960

JAPANESE   **14/20**

**The delicate arts of Japanese cuisine
continue to thrive in the CBD**

Outside the towering home to wheelers
and dealers, ironically named after the
Labor leader who tried to nationalise
the banks, ties are loosened as the
alcohol begins to flow. But inside
Chifley Plaza, hand-thrown dishes of
agedashi tofu, bathed in dashi broth
and topped with daikon, and plump
slices of sashimi are served with hushed
reverence by the quietly efficient
waitstaff. Slivers of grilled wagyu, richly
marbled and bathed in sweet sauce and
served with rocket and eschalot crisps
are a work of art. The delicate tempura,
served with flavoured salts, maintains
a high standard. A couple at a nearby
table excitedly tend to their shabu
shabu cauldron of vegetables, tofu and
udon noodles, but the atmosphere is
serene in Kimitaka Azuma's restaurant.
It is hard to disguise Azuma's location
in a food court (albeit upmarket)
but the wall hangings and screens
elevate the dining experience, especially
as the shadows fall on commuters
heading home after a day of work.
Sake and shochu supplement the wine
list and staff are on hand to offer their
expertise in Japanese alcohol.

**Don't forget to admire the art displayed
throughout the restaurant**

Open	L Mon–Fri; D Mon–Sat
Price	$$
Cards	AE MC V eftpos
Chef	Kimitaka Azuma
Features	Licensed, private dining, wheelchair access
Website	azuma.com.au

Bacco Osteria

SYDNEY
Shop 1, 2–12 Angel Place
02 9235 3383

ITALIAN   **15/20**

The city osteria that's blessed Angel Place

Missed Vini? Pining for 121BC? Mourning Berta? That's fair. The three enoteca/osteria/wine bars really set the tone for mod-Sydney Italian for the better part of a decade. Owner-chef Andrew Cibej sold them last year and now runs this slick CBD espresso bar-tavern with chef Scott Williams (ex-Sagra). The layout has the same simple, unaffected style and vibe as Cibej's other venues, where office workers are made as comfortable as first daters and everyone is getting down with the Italian wine list. Start with firm strands of bucatini tossed with pork jowl and tomato, made creamy with fresh borlotti beans and finished with a few leaves of basil. Or the almost dessert-like sweetcorn-and-ricotta-stuffed ravioli dressed with artichoke honey. Move on to grilled spatchcock scattered with raisins and toasted pine nuts and order a side of cucumber and air-dried ricotta for a perfect feast of leisure. Dessert? Maybe. Another run at the wine list? Definitely.

Try for a window seat to watch the human circus of the Ivy unfold in the evenings

Open	L D Mon–Fri
Price	$$
Cards	AE MC V eftpos
Chef	Scott Williams, Andrew Cibej
Features	Bar, licensed, outdoor seating, wheelchair access
Website	bacco.com.au

Bad Hombres

SURRY HILLS
40 Reservoir Street
0410 191 441

MEXICAN, VEGAN   **14/20**

Meat-free with a Mexican spirit

Forget any crunchy notions of meat-free fare – this hot little spot offers good vegan eating from a Mex-leaning menu so tight you could (and should) order the lot. Housed in the old Sugarcane digs, the space retains the same spunky casual-canteen spirit, with an extra lick of bold red paint. Snack your way through sweet/salty cobs of corn, charred then dusted with Japanese seasoning, and oh-so-smoky black-bean tacos dressed with pickled shiitake and cucumber slivers. Or split a pretty patch of pureed peas and translucent radish flecked with olives on crunchy tostada. Main courses get hands-on: a toasty cauliflower number comes with raw onion, coriander, salsa and cashew cream, all prepped for a session of fold-your-own pancakes while the single sweets option, a rosy tequila-watermelon popsicle, is summer incarnate. A fun-sized drinks menu of naturals and locals keeps the compact theme and good times rolling.

Take your omnivore mates. And don't miss the margaritas

Open	D Tue–Sat
Price	$$
Cards	AE MC V eftpos
Chef	Toby Wilson
Features	Bar, licensed, wheelchair access
Website	badhombres.com.au

Bambini Trust

SYDNEY
185 Elizabeth Street
02 9283 7098

EUROPEAN   **14/20**

A culinary tour of Europe with multiple stops in Italy

Eating at Bambini Trust is like being in the dining car of a luxury train meandering around Europe. It's comfortable, the waiters are polite and efficient, the food is immediately recognisable. Your fellow travellers are business people, young lovers, well-heeled retirees and the occasional discerning tourist. The train starts in France, touches Spain but spends most of its time in Italy. The Roman is impressed by the creamy interior of a mini suppli served as an amuse bouche. The Milanese couple love the mushroom risotto with a restrained truffle flavour, and a perfectly crafted cotoletta Milanese is bigger than they expected. A lady from Torino enjoys the vitello tonnato even if she doesn't recall the veal being pink in the middle, but the Neapolitan thinks his spaghetti vongole has a touch too much garlic. And the Aussies? They love the familiar sweetness of pavlova. Bambini may not be modern, but the cooking is classically European, highly satisfying and the welcome is pure Italian warmth.

Try a European wine you've never heard of – they have plenty

Open	B L Mon–Fri; D Mon–Sat
Price	$$
Cards	AE DC MC V eftpos
Chef	Kevin Coux
Features	Bar, licensed, outdoor seating, private dining, wheelchair access
Website	www.bambinitrust.com.au

Banksii Vermouth Bar and Bistro

BARANGAROO
Shop 11, 33 Barangaroo Avenue
02 8072 7037

citi

CONTEMPORARY   **14/20**

A waterside botanical oasis in the stealy heart of Sydney

Everything's bold at Barangaroo, where the combined wealth of the corporate denizens is higher than some second-tier nations. Where else might you buy a cappuccino and a company before breakfast? Those bullish towers and smart-casual suits almost put Sydney Harbour in the shade. So it's nice to take a break at Banksii, where the focus is on botanicals rather than big business. Husband-and-wife team Hamish Ingham and Rebecca Lines love plants so dearly that they named their restaurant after botanist Sir Joseph Banks. The drinks menu is a lively toast to vermouth (wine infused with botanicals), from the crisp blanc spritz to the prettiest darn dry martini this side of the CBD. A plate of prosciutto, fennel salumi and fresh figs is equally cheery. Grilled prawns in glistening curry leaf butter with pickled turmeric are sweet, smoky and suitably rich. While the vibrant Banksii trifle with dollops of custard and hibiscus jelly is the business, no matter your bank balance.

Save some room for a sweet treat at RivaReno Gelato around the corner

Open	L D Daily
Price	$$
Cards	AE MC V eftpos
Chef	Hamish Ingham
Features	Bar, licensed, outdoor seating, wheelchair access
Website	banksii.sydney

Bar Patron by Rockpool

CIRCULAR QUAY
2 Phillip Street (entrance off Albert Street)
02 9259 5624

MEXICAN   **14.5/20**

Mexican dining gets Perry'd

What was the very French cafe, Ananas, has been given a breezy, high-end hacienda treatment by Neil Perry's Rockpool Dining Group and Patron Tequila. Think faded floor tiles, embossed tables, a glorious long marble bar stocked with top-level tequila, and real freshness and joy in head chef Pamela Valdes' upmarket handling of classic Mexican street food. A soft taco enveloping a fried finger of flathead with sour cream and a tangy pico di gallo is fun and streety, and the bright green guacamole is hand-pounded to order. Cochinita pibil – red rice, cabbage salad, pickled red onion and shredded, slow-cooked pork shoulder and steamy tortilla – is a feast in its own right, and pozole, a silky, rich porky soup studded with hominy (soft, puffy maize kernels) with lettuce, radish, chilli, oregano and corn chips for crumbling, is downright heartwarming. It's a mix of big-city glitz and back-country basics that fits neatly into today's high/low dining ethos.

To make the most of the views (of the harbour, and the tequila), grab a seat at the bar

Open	L D Daily
Price	$$
Cards	AE DC MC V eftpos
Chef	Neil Perry, Pamela Valdes
Features	Bar, licensed, wheelchair access
Website	barpatron.com.au

Bart Jr

REDFERN
92 Pitt Street
0402 567 134

CONTEMPORARY   **14.5/20**

Generous bar with neighbourhood spirit

This bar-restaurant is named for Redfern's most famous ginger tomcat, Bart, and his many, many local offspring – arguably the greatest ode to deadbeat dads since Darth Vader. The only thing that matches the inventive ever-changing menu of share plates and cocktails is the people-watching on a Saturday night. Through the huge windows, Bart Jr creates a sort of open dialogue with the area – you want to invite people in to join you for dinner and you also feel like you're part of everyone's Saturday night plans. The focaccia is a charred and fluffy brick redolent with the scent of warm fermented chilli butter. The almond hollandaise that accompanies the grilled broccolini should be sold in bulk so diners can take it home and mainline it in private. The absolute highlight is haloumi that is drowning – or at the very least gasping for air – under a lake of nutty burnt honey, rosemary, verjuice and currants. And the best bit is it can very easily double as dessert.

Get a window seat and let the bartenders do the rest

Open	L Fri–Sun; D Wed–Sun
Price	$$
Cards	AE MC V eftpos
Chef	Wesley Jones, Georgia Woodyard
Features	Bar, licensed, wheelchair access
Website	bartjr.com.au

ACQUA PANNA
THE FINE DINING WATERS
S.PELLEGRINO

Tastefully Italian
@sanpellegrino_au

For trade enquiries, please contact 03 9560 4011

Barzaari

MARRICKVILLE
65 Addison Road
02 9569 3161

citi

MIDDLE EASTERN   **14/20**

Marrickville mezze done with imagination and flair

Dedicated labne lovers know the hung yoghurt should be spread thick enough to leave clearly defined teeth marks when you take your first bite. Thankfully, the crew at Barzaari know this too. And when it's served in abundance with soft pita bread straight out of the wood-fire, there's no need to hold back. The generosity extends to the buttery pickled octopus reclining in fragrant oil, modesty preserved by a layer of cracking house-made kipfler chips. It's louche, tender to the point of fall-apart and hints at the richness in store further down the menu. Haloumi decked with peach and molasses adds a spark to a classic and deboned spatchcock wrapped in vine leaves takes wing again with a slash of creamy, garlicky toum. Against the bare brick and polished concrete, the wine takes a pleasing trip straight outta Marrickville via Serbian pinot gris and Austrian rosé by the glass and the only thing to do in the face of such hospitality is to ask, "What's for dessert?"

Ask about dishes from the wood-fired oven – it's the star of the show

The Bathers' Pavilion

BALMORAL
4 The Esplanade
02 9969 5050

citi 🍷   👑

EUROPEAN   **15.5/20**

Modern French plates at the beachhouse of your dreams

There's no shortage of views here. Bifold doors open right onto the beach, with the expanse of harbour and heads front and centre. The high continues to the food, where technical plates are as faultless as they are fulfilling. Fork-tender pork cheek is well served by smoked yoghurt and an almost drinkable chicken jus. Likewise, the dashi saucing on the superb Murray cod and squid linguine deserves a straw. Flavours come together with finesse in the Moreton Bay bug tail – the chorus of sweet corn polenta, finger lime, squid ink crisps and seaweed butter could, in less-confident hands, have played out a jumble. A chocolate cremeux log is a delight but the accompanying coriander croquant lacks polish (as does the haphazard service). Date night out? Ask for a leather banquette and let those views do the talking. Reunion over a long lunch? It's made for lingering and ordering another bottle of wine from the excellent list.

There's an excellent vegetarian menu to hand here

Open	L Fri–Sun; D Tue–Sat
Price	$$
Cards	AE DC MC V eftpos
Chef	Darryl Martin
Features	Bar, licensed, outdoor seating, private dining, wheelchair access
Website	barzaari.com.au

Open	L D Daily
Price	$$$
Cards	AE DC MC V eftpos
Chef	Serge Dansereau, Alexis Bessau
Features	Bar, licensed, private dining, wheelchair access
Website	batherspavilion.com.au

Bea

SYDNEY
Level 1, 35 Barangaroo Avenue
02 8587 5400

CONTEMPORARY   **14.5/20**

It's been a long time since anyone's opened anything so Sydney in, well, Sydney

Here's Barangaroo House, a triple-threat venue resembling three artful salad plates resting on top of each other. At ground level, House Bar offers jugs of Pimm's and chicken schnitzels. On the roof, Smoke Bar features everything from $100 Cadillac margaritas to bowls of house-made salt and vinegar crisps. The middle section, however, is the jewel in the crown. This is chef Cory Campbell's arena, where creamy burrata relaxes on the plate overlaid with slices of winter zucchini, their flowers gently shredded over the top. Tuna tartare is scooped up with house-made potato crisps and a tart quandong sauce. Juicy spatchcock, sticky and sweet, does its best work when paired with a simple butter lettuce salad. And while at first glance there's a lot more going on with a composition of beetroot (roasted, pickled, raw, pureed), elevated with chewy little nibs of beef tongue, there's an elegance in its simplicity when it comes to flavour.

All hail the rocky road dessert – a miniature Barangaroo House extravaganza of chocolate, cherry, marshmallow and coconut

Open	L D Daily
Price	$$$
Cards	AE MC V eftpos
Chef	Cory Campbell
Features	Bar, licensed, outdoor seating
Website	barangaroohouse.com.au/bea-restaurant

The Bellevue Hotel

PADDINGTON
159 Hargrave Street
02 9363 2293

citi   CONTEMPORARY   **14/20**

Pub food served with a lack of fuss and plenty of polish

Queen Victoria was still on the throne when The Bellevue opened its doors in 1880, but the Paddington pub is not hidebound by tradition. The ponies might be tearing around the racetrack on wall-mounted tellies but pass through the public bar to the smart restaurant out the back for a menu that promises far more than standard pub fare. Sweet figs are expertly balanced with house-smoked ricotta, pedro ximenez and dandelions. Whipped feta and nectarine accompanies ribbons of serrano ham. A crunchy coating gives way to the juicy interior of crumbed lamb cutlets served with potatoes and spring onions, while an impressive scotch steak from the grill, served with smoked herb and garlic butter, is tender and rich. The waitstaff are friendly and solicitous if occasionally distracted by the roar of gamblers celebrating or commiserating their wager. The allure of coffee brulee and an extravagant cheeseboard are regretfully rebuffed for a lighter dessert offering of poached peach with raspberries and meringue.

Treat yourself to a glass of something from the Bellevue's Coravin collection

Open	L Wed–Sun; D Tue–Sun
Price	$$
Cards	AE MC V eftpos
Chef	Robert Te Whaiti
Features	Bar, licensed, private dining, wheelchair access
Website	bellevuehotel.com.au

Bennelong

SYDNEY

Bennelong Point, Sydney Opera House
02 9240 8000

citi ♟

CONTEMPORARY   **16/20**

Be a one-percenter, if only for an evening, at this glittering piece of Sydney history

Is there anyone this restaurant doesn't tick a box for? It's parent-friendly. First-date bait. Anniversary and proposal heaven. A business lunch deal-sealer. You could even eat here if you're (gasp) just out with friends for a fun time. Peter Gilmore and head chef Rob Cockerill have created a menu that, while on the safe side, is entirely pleasurable and delicious. Nothing more so than eggplant caught in a pale, airy tempura batter set alongside chubby scallops, seared until golden. Warmth and depth comes from bacon pieces, fried and bound in house-made XO sauce. Grass-fed lamb from Margaret River, rare and tender while still maintaining flavour and chew, is brightened with sweet and pretty little broad beans and crunched up by papery deep-fried Jerusalem artichoke skins. Desserts? Sure. There's that famous pavlova and the cherry jam lamington, but there's nothing like the simplicity of fresh persimmons and wild thyme honey ice-cream to remind you that seasons can be fleeting.

Eat a sausage roll with one of the best views in Australia at the Bennelong bar

Open	L Fri–Sun; D Daily
Price	$$$
Cards	AE DC MC V eftpos
Chef	Peter Gilmore, Rob Cockerill
Features	Bar, licensed
Website	bennelong.com.au

Bentley Restaurant and Bar

SYDNEY

27 O'Connell Street
02 8214 0505

citi ♟

CONTEMPORARY   **17/20**

Glittery CBD dining that still pushes all the right buttons

How many diners here have actually driven a Bentley? A few, you'd guess. But if Brent Savage's glittery flagship restaurant in the old Fairfax building exudes 'moneyed business lunch', the fresh and bold menu never pulls its punches. The degustation jumps from easy snacking in cheesy bush tomato-dusted tartlets that taste like fancy Barbecue Shapes, and the world's most luxurious potato skins filled with creme fraiche and chives. But then, plush cured kingfish pings with cape gooseberries and warmed oysters pop with luminous scampi roe and finger lime. Pairing smoky pork neck with a bitter, fermented sauce of green peppers is a risk for some chefs, but not Savage's crew. They speak vegetable as fluently as they do grill, dispatching perfect nine-score wagyu alongside so-fresh watermelon radish curls with camel's milk curd. Pinion it all with a wine party. Nick Hildebrandt's list will always challenge you to take the road more textural, but can fulfil any fantasy you can pay for.

Snacks at the bar are just as much fun as the full dinner experience

Open	L Mon–Fri; D Mon–Sat
Price	$$$
Cards	AE MC V eftpos
Chef	Brent Savage, Aiden Stevens
Features	Bar, licensed, private dining, wheelchair access
Website	thebentley.com.au

MELBOURNE

ALL-DAY BREAKFAST
ALL-NIGHT NOODLES

MELBOURNE
A TWIST AT
EVERY TURN

🔍 melbourne twist

Berowra Waters Inn

BEROWRA WATERS
Via East and West Public Wharves
02 9456 1027

citi

CONTEMPORARY   **14.5/20**

A waterside gem that should be on any food lover's hit list

'Arrive by seaplane', 'free upgrade' and 'clothing optional' are among the most sublime phrases in the English language. Diners here might come by air or sea, opting for their own pleasure craft or a private ferry puttering up the Hawkesbury River. The journey to the stunning Glenn Murcutt-designed building is part of its charm, cleansing the mind of clutter. Kick things off with a fragrant botanical cocktail before settling into the cryptic set menu. 'Crab, coconut and cucumber' is an alliterative joy of refreshing confit crab and coconut mayonnaise with compressed cucumbers. 'Hapuka, mussels and herbs' is a sweet and smoky square of hibachi-grilled fish with a rich mussel sauce and flourish of fresh herbs. And 'pork, apple and bacon' is gloriously gooey slow-cooked Tenterfield pork with fermented apple, bacon puree and candied barley. This is Sydney at its best: vibrant food and spot-on service in a sun-drenched setting. It's well worth the trip, no matter your mode of transport.

Search for a nearby river stay so you needn't worry about driving home

Open	L Fri–Sun; D Fri–Sat
Price	$$$
Cards	AE DC MC V eftpos
Chef	Brian Geraghty
Features	Licensed, private dining
Website	berowrawatersinn.com

Bert's Bar and Brasserie

NEWPORT
2 Kalinya Street
02 9114 7350

CONTEMPORARY   **16/20**

Evoking the golden age of dining on the Northern Beaches

It's excess all areas at this next-level Newport offering from the indefatigable Merivale group. Vulgar to mention money, we know, but you're going to need it, for the vast Champagne list, live sea urchins, $125 mud crab and $295 Siberian caviar. The room is splendid in its scope, with a lovely sweep of window offering glimpses of Pittwater and the pub grounds below. Three golden, toasted brioche fingers topped with buttery roasted chicken fat and tongues of sweet sea urchin are a luxurious kick-off, and fleshy, hand-filleted Cantabrian anchovies come with their own crisped bones as a crunchy garnish. Tables for two share house-made tagliolini of lobster in a gentle tomatoey, herby, winey sauce. It's rich right through to the finish line, with a wow-factor mango and toasted pav hit with the pop and ping of native finger lime. At Bert's, you will eat too much, drink too much, spend too much money, and end up wanting to do it all over again.

Allow time for parking – it can be tricky at weekends, for you and the locals

Open	L D Wed–Sun
Price	$$$
Cards	AE MC V eftpos
Chef	Jordan Toft, Sam Kane
Features	Bar, licensed
Website	merivale.com/venues/berts

Bibo

DOUBLE BAY
7 Bay Street
02 9362 4680

🍷

MEDITERRANEAN **14.5/20**

Great things can happen when fine dining chefs head up neighbourhood wine bars

This is the sort of place where you arrive for a 6pm booking only to wander out minutes before midnight. The wine list at Bibo is serious, courtesy of young gun sommelier Louella Mathews, but it's by no means intimidating, with by-the-glass numbers accompanied by helpful haiku-like tasting notes ('dried cherries, red apple skin, bright'.) They take a similarly accessible-yet-awesome approach to snacks, too – flambeed chorizo, shareable meat and cheese platters and a knock-your-socks off peri peri. The chilli- and garlic-laden sauce is everything it should be – fiery, glossy and aromatic – and comes slathered on tender chicken thigh or across silky slow-cooked eggplant. Don't bother sharing dessert – here it's all about an individual Portuguese custard tart. It's the same recipe as chef Jose Silva bakes at his Petersham bakery, Sweet Belem, and rounds out a trifecta of Portuguese perfection (peri peri, tarts and wine) that give you three good reasons to slink down to Bibo, stat.

Request a seat at the bar or at the window to watch staff in action

Open	L Fri–Sat; D Tue–Sat
Price	$$
Cards	AE MC V eftpos
Chef	Jose Silva
Features	Bar, licensed, private dining, wheelchair access, outdoor seating
Website	bibowinebar.com.au

Big Poppa's

DARLINGHURST
96 Oxford Street
0499 052 201

🍷

ITALIAN **14.5/20**

Pitch-perfect Italian in the company of some special wines

If Biggie and Al Capone pooled ideas and decided to open a slick speakeasy, this would be it. Hip hop enough to impress the heads and Italian enough to please la famiglia, though they definitely wouldn't approve of the volume in the dining room. Dark and raucous, with some serious heat by the glass, this is a restaurant going undercover as a bar – or maybe it's the other way around. Either way, be sure to visit both floors for the full experience. Up top, food is king and the snapper crudo is so fresh and so clean, arriving with a generous cacio e pepe heavy with pecorino and parmigiano – just the way it should be. Citrusy Jerusalem artichokes kick the background as a lowkey but could also star as a not-to-be-missed vego hit if that's your jam. Follow the recommendation of the chatty crew and pair any one of the (mostly) organic red bangers with the lamb shoulder ragu over pappardelle and you won't die wondering what it's like to live the life of a baller.

Don't get lost in it all and forget the time – last kitchen orders are at 2.30am

Open	D Daily
Price	$$
Cards	AE MC V eftpos
Chef	Jason Barron, Liam Driscoll
Features	Bar, licensed, wheelchair access
Website	bigpoppa.com.au

Bills Bondi

BONDI BEACH
79 Hall Street
02 8412 0700

CONTEMPORARY **14/20**

Granger's cookbooks spring to life at this bright beachside diner

Bondi suits Bill Granger's food and aesthetic – light, clean and bright – and while he's off opening restaurants in Tokyo and Hawaii, you can still find his Mod-Oz staples all here (including those corn fritters). The menu plays a ping pong match between sweetness, smoke and a little spice. Take the burnt peaches with honey, which veers towards being a dessert, only to be put back on course with the earthiness of thyme, fennel and smoky goat's curd. Or a fillet of nicely cooked salmon, which sits in a light soy and mirin broth. And the steak 'okonomiyaki', which sees sweet teriyaki and creamy mayo zig-zagging across slices of juicy charred steak. You're not visiting here for an essay on wine (it's a succinct list with drops like the orchard fresh Sons of Eden riesling) but the Bloody Mary is renowned for good reason. You may know Granger's recipes off by heart but to truly see his cooking ethos in action, book in here.

This may be a brunching destination but book in for a lunch so you can try the all-day breakfast and a selection of dinner winners, too

Billy Kwong

POTTS POINT
Shop 1, 28 Macleay Street
02 9332 3300

CHINESE **15.5/20**

The Sydney stalwart that never fails to delight

There are some things you can be sure of when dining at chef Kylie Kwong's restaurant. The signature XO fried eggs will be on the menu. Their whites will bloom like lotus blossoms, with crisp frills around the edges, all hidden under a ground covering of thinly sliced green onion, fresh chilli and blobs of fiery XO sauce. Order steamed rice to dull the heat. There'll be a natural-leaning drinks list with a focus on local producers. Shanghai-style shallot cakes are given an Aussie twist and filled with saltbush. Douse them in chilli sauce to up the tempo or enjoy the short pastry as is. Mussels, tender, plump and stir-fried with surf herbs, are given a little bit of extra help thanks to crisp-fried batons of pork hock. Big Boss Kwong still fires the pans here regularly, but whether she's here or not, the cooking remains balanced, assured and three dimensional when it comes to fat, smoke and spice.

Want to experience BK in private surrounds? Book 'Kylie's Table' and be personally welcomed by the chef herself

Open	B L D Daily
Price	$$
Cards	AE MC V eftpos
Chef	Jordan Wijeadasa
Features	Bar, licensed, outdoor seating, wheelchair access
Website	bills.com.au

Open	L Sun; D Daily
Price	$$
Cards	AE MC V eftpos
Chef	Kylie Kwong
Features	Licensed, private dining, wheelchair access
Website	billykwong.com.au

Bishop Sessa

SURRY HILLS
527 Crown Street
02 8065 7223

🍷

CONTEMPORARY   **14.5/20**

Surry Hills is a fast-paced suburb, but Sessa plays the slow game

Things come down in tempo when you enter this Crown Street restaurant. It's a small operation (one waitress, one chef) with soft dusty blue velvet seats, heavy leather-bound menus and wine bottles stacked high. The soundtrack is relaxed – Boy & Bear, Father John Misty and Fleet Foxes all get a spin – and matches what's happening on your plate. It's all about comfort: a hearty ragu lets slow-cooked lamb shine without being weighed down with excessive tomato or herbs and comes served with great little dense shells of pan-fried gnocchetti. A hunk of pork belly is like a sample slice of the perfect Sunday roast (crisp crackling included), while Cone Bay barramundi comes with soft roasted fennel and sour segments of grapefruit that punch through the buttery fish. Bishop Sessa takes cues from the music it plays – warm, comforting and familiar. And that will keep locals coming through the doors for years to come.

As we went to press, Bishop Sessa refashioned itself as a wine bar called The Bishop Wine Bar

Open	L D Tue–Sat
Price	$$
Cards	AE MC V eftpos
Chef	Craig Gray
Features	Licensed, wheelchair access, private dining
Website	bishopsessa.com.au

Bistecca

SYDNEY
3 Dalley Street
02 8067 0450

🍷

STEAKHOUSE   **14.5/20**

Sydney basement bar and steakhouse with Tuscany in its bones

There will be steak. In fact, as far as main courses go, there will only be steak, and only one steak at that. Owners James Bradey and Warren Burns have dedicated their hustly-bustly laneway CBD basement bar and steakhouse to the glories of bistecca, the titanic Tuscan T-bone traditionally sourced from Chianina beef. In the charming, vaulted ceilinged dining room, the grain-fed black Angus (marble score 2+) from the Riverine region is cut to order, grilled over the coals until scorchy, smoky and the recommended medium-rare within. Snacks run from house-made focaccia with beef dripping 'candlewax' to shavings of pecorino with truffled honey, and sides include crisp cos leaves under a smoked mussel emulsion, and a bowl of herb-flecked, properly cooked white beans. The choices are as wide with dessert as they are with the main course – it's either tiramisu or tiramisu. There are aperitivi and digestivi for days – and nights, given the bar opens from 4pm to 2am.

There are so many negronis on offer, they're practically on tap. Oh wait, there's one on tap as well

Open	L Wed–Fri; D Mon–Sat
Price	$$$
Cards	AE MC V eftpos
Chef	Pip Pratt
Features	Bar, licensed
Website	bistecca.com.au

BISTECCA

Bistro Guillaume

SYDNEY
259 George Street
02 8622 9555

FRENCH **15/20**

Greatest-hits French bistro, from parfait to profiteroles

Butter, salt, cheese – the three pillars of classical French cooking – are delivered in luxe style at Bistro Guillaume. Plush and padded, it's a favourite of the business set chasing a quality, easy-pleaser meal and a posh bottle (ka-ching goes the expenses on a $450 Chateauneuf-du-Pape). Don't be surprised if a table of seven all order steak frites, grass-fed sirloin with textbook bearnaise and crunchy shoestring fries. Trad-classics keep on coming with onion soup that's almost knife-and-fork hearty with crunchy gruyere croutons bobbing in the rich broth. Or try the country-style terrine, a porky puck licked with Dijon, with toast and cornichons on the side. Cheese hounds unite over the twice-baked souffle with roquefort sauce (oh, yeah). Order a solo serve or upgrade to jumbo and feed five. Executive chef Guillaume Brahimi's famed Paris mash is there, as is duck a l'orange. Dessert? It's got to be those profiteroles with warm chocolate sauce poured at the table.

Grab pastries and coffee to go from the attached Bistro Guillaume Bakery

Open	L Mon–Fri; D Mon–Sat
Price	$$$
Cards	AE MC V eftpos
Chef	Guillaume Brahimi
Features	Bar, licensed, private dining, wheelchair access
Website	bistroguillaumesydney.com.au

Bistro Moncur

WOOLLAHRA
116A Queen Street
02 9327 9713

FRENCH **14/20**

Classic French bistro that's still going strong

Everything sounds better in a French accent, whether you're riffing about liberty, equality or programmatic specificity. So when your Gallic waitress says the salmon entree is "not too fishy", she's practically speaking in sonnets. Evenings at Bistro Moncur are similarly easy on the senses. This perennial Woollahra bistro, celebrating its 25th year, is that reliable and relaxed fine diner that every suburb deserves. Locals keep coming back for classics that have been on the menu since day one, such as a slab of smooth chicken liver pâté with lively confit onions and house-made brioche, or the salt-cured salmon – fresh, clean and marinated in more sauvignon blanc than an eastern suburbs hen's night. Pan-fried WA barramundi with old-school mushy peas, folded with creme fraiche and confit spring onions, tastes even better than it sounds – and is not too fishy by half. The airplane hangar ceiling adds to the feeling that you have arrived somewhere that never goes out of style.

Pop into Moncur Cellars next door for a bottle of Bordeaux

Open	L Mon–Fri; D Daily
Price	$$$
Cards	AE MC V eftpos
Chef	Mark Williamson, Damien Pignolet
Features	Bar, licensed, outdoor seating, private dining, wheelchair access
Website	bistromoncur.com.au

Bistro Rex

POTTS POINT
Shop 1, 50–58 Macleay Street
02 9332 2100

FRENCH **14/20**

All hail this neighbourhood bistro serving a perfect Gibson

Potts Point was crying out for a place where locals could drop in for steak frites and Burgundy and disappear just as quickly. And Rex, for the most part, delivers. If you can grab the attention of a waiter. Though what they're missing in terms of attentive staff, they make up for with a pissaladiere so flaky it all but floats off the table, weighted only by slivers of anchovy and sweetly caramelised onion. Chef Jo Ward's flair for all things vegetarian shines when it comes to cauliflower 'rice' – tiny tender florets crunched up with toasted pine nuts and a little dill. Crisp-skin chicken verges on entering far-too-salty territory, but is tempered by a black garlic puree and a green salad. And yes, there's the steak, scarlet and perfectly rested, Cafe de Paris butter dripping over crisp fries. Is it a perfect bistro experience? Not quite. But there's plenty of heart in the kitchen that keeps Potts Pointers coming back.

Take a group of three or more people and go for the fantastic-value Le Grand banquet – the best of the menu for just $88 a head

Open	L D Daily
Price	$$
Cards	AE MC V eftpos
Chef	Jo Ward
Features	Bar, licensed, wheelchair access
Website	bistrorex.com.au

Blanca

BONDI BEACH
Shop UG4, The Hub, 75–79 Hall Street
02 9365 2998

CONTEMPORARY **14.5/20**

Leave your preconceptions at the beach – this is clever modern Asian

Even if Bondi is not your scene – even if a Japanese-Mediterranean restaurant with a white-on-white interior and a Scandinavian influence doesn't sound like you – you might just love Blanca. The welcoming staff get it so right you'll be convinced even before you've had a mouthful. That mouthful, by the by, should be a black bun, steamed and filled with fried soft-shell crab, spicy cabbage and XO mayo. Order heavily from the snack selection, such as dumplings filled with braised oxtail meat, and aged raw beef wrapped in sesame leaf. The big umami flavour of miso drives the menu, cut through with fresh, raw and pickled things, and the occasional dab of mayo from Finnish hands in the kitchen. The signature pork ribs in miso caramel fall off the bone, but vegetarians will also leave happy – this is Bondi after all. Bondi Sands, a dessert of mascarpone-vanilla creme and chocolate ganache, is rich – excellent cocktails offer a happy alternative.

Snack at their next-door bar for a casual vibe, but beach hair is fine at both

Open	L Fri–Sun; D Daily
Price	$$
Cards	AE DC MC V eftpos
Chef	Tomi Bjorck, Samuel Cole
Features	Bar, licensed, outdoor seating, wheelchair access
Website	blanca.com.au

Ble Restaurant

RAMSGATE BEACH
Shop 2, 203-207 Ramsgate Road
02 9529 4335

GREEK   **15/20**

A beachside Greek hotspot in the making

It's not every day Ramsgate hits Sydney's radar, but former Alpha and Beta chef Natalia Gaspari is making quite an impact at her new Greek restaurant – a lean, clean, modern space where cliche is thin on the ground. Armed with a kitchen full of cast-iron skillets and a mighty charcoal grill, Gaspari draws heavily on the influences of her island home of Kefalonia. Don't miss taramasalata peppered with avruga, ready to slather on smoky, warm, char-grilled pita bread. Some dishes get a restaurant upgrade – kakavia is more than a stew of fleshy mussels, vongole and diamond clams here, with the addition of silky lobster and haloumi ravioli. There's lamb, of course, the shoulder braised for 12 hours with lemon, garlic and sumac, but it's hard to go past a whole snapper straight from that magical grill. Greece and Australia link arms in a pagoto that sandwiches lemon ice-cream and chocolate kataifi pastry and tastes disarmingly like chocolate ripple cake.

Get a group together and pre-order the whole lamb souvlaki cooked over the charcoal grill

Open	B Fri–Sun; L D Tue–Sun
Price	$$
Cards	MC V eftpos
Chef	Natalia Gaspari
Features	Licensed, outdoor seating, wheelchair access
Website	blerestaurant.com.au

The Boathouse on Blackwattle Bay

GLEBE
123 Ferry Road
02 9518 9011

CONTEMPORARY   **15.5/20**

Sets the standard for impeccably sourced seafood

Just try and not order the snapper pie. Nearly every table requests the puff-pastry crowned, truffle-infused dish (it's been on the menu for almost two decades). Think of it as the Christy Turlington of the pie world: bombshell with substance. It's silver-served tableside but the theatrics are not overdone – a key theme underpinning the Boathouse's entire offer. After all, you wouldn't want to compete with the floor-to-ceiling, 180-degree Blackwattle Bay vistas. The seafood here is a geography lesson in the country's most pristine estuaries, inlets and bays, with lesser-seen, more sustainably caught species getting top billing. Shucked-to-order rock oysters are served simply with a classic mignonette. Coffs Harbour red mullet is fork-flaky, while the Swansea bonito makes for a fine sashimi brightened with ponzu, pickled young ginger and shiso. Smart, professional waitstaff dart between tables, offering encouragement on another bottle of Sancerre or the chocolate custard-filled cannoli with poached cherries. A real-deal dining institution.

The corner table with the Anzac Bridge front-and-centre is the money

Open	L Fri–Sun; D Tue–Sun
Price	$$$
Cards	AE MC V eftpos
Chef	Colin Barker
Features	Bar, licensed, wheelchair access
Website	boathouse.net.au

Bodega

SURRY HILLS
216 Commonwealth Street
02 9212 7766

TAPAS   **15.5/20**

Where hillbilly beats, Latin heat and Asian treats somehow meet

Bodega delivers one of the highest surprise-per-mouthful ratios in Sydney. There's the heavily spiced hot cross buns that open to reveal salty corned beef, sharp kimchi and a smoky oyster mayo. Or you can go sailing with the crisp duck and apple upon a mini lake of chocolate mole. The slow-cooked lamb with harissa, yoghurt, hummus and eggplant is rich and warm but can seem a little cloying. It could do with something light and acidic to cut through all that creamy sweetness. Best of all is the savoury inversion of the traditionally sweet Portuguese tart, here stuffed with king crab, while the pastry shell has been given a miso makeover. There's a certain school of thought that 'good' food is the stuff you want to shovel in your mouth at warp speed while truly 'great' food is so complex and unexpected that it actually forces you to slow down to fully appreciate each little bit. Bodega displays all of the rewards of the latter eaten with the enthusiasm of the former.

Order more than you think you'll need. Yes, you will be fat in the morning. But so very happy

Bodega 1904

FOREST LODGE
The Tramsheds, 1 Dalgal Way
02 8624 3133

TAPAS   **14/20**

Elevated tapas in fun and accessible surrounds

At 6pm, the shift change starts at the Tramsheds. Shopping bags are exchanged for handbags, sneakers swapped for leather, and the centre transitions from a family-friendly food court to something a little more grown-up. Teenagers still circle the place eyeing each other, and there's a dwindling trickle of grocery buyers but plant yourself at the bar with your back to the thoroughfare and focus on what's important. The smart, sexy tapas, that is, and the warm and talented team running Bodega 1904. For a bold start, the blood cake with a mojo verde made from pickled jalapeno can't be beat, though the house-made chorizo is a worthy contender. Match it with a flinty red like the Walsh and Sons syrah for maximum effect and then switch to an albarino and prepare to fight it out with your dining partner over an entire crisp-skinned yellow flounder with a fiery fennel and jalapeno accompaniment. It'll be the most fun you've had in a shed in a long time.

Ask if there's anything new going by the glass in addition to what's on the wine list – the attached bottle shop is a winner

Open	L Fri; D Tue–Sat
Price	$$
Cards	AE MC V eftpos
Chef	Ben Milgate, Elvis Abrahanowicz
Website	bodegatapas.com

Open	L D Daily
Price	$$
Cards	MC V eftpos
Chef	Joel Humphreys
Features	Bar, licensed, wheelchair access
Website	bodega1904.com

Bondi Trattoria

BONDI
34B Campbell Parade
02 9365 4303

citi 🍷

ITALIAN   **14.5/20**

It may be 30 years old, but the food has never been better

Bob Hawke was Prime Minister when The Tratt, as it's affectionately known, opened. That means it's been serving Italian food for three decades, which, in Sydney dining years, makes this beachside restaurant a bazillion years old. Last year chef Joe Pavlovich (ex-Glass Brasserie) took over, and brought with him a feeling of freshness and energy. There were a couple of small changes made to the space, but the real excitement is the new menu. An entree of plump roasted Balmain bugs and dollops of buffalo mozzarella in a garlic and chilli butter is simple, but thrilling (order a side of bread, it's way less embarrassing than using a spoon to eat the sauce) while the pizza (go the spicy salami, potato, garlic, rosemary and mascarpone number) is cushiony and perfectly layered. The service can be clunky and overly familiar at times, but the staff know the menu. It's great to see this long-standing venue hitting its stride once again.

BYO jumper – that sea breeze can get chilly

Open	B Sat–Sun; L D Daily
Price	$$
Cards	AE MC V eftpos
Chef	Joe Pavlovich
Features	Licensed, outdoor seating, wheelchair access, BYO
Website	bonditrattoria.com.au

Boronia Kitchen

HUNTERS HILL
152 Pittwater Road
02 9817 0666

🍷

CONTEMPORARY   **14.5/20**

An overqualified all-day local diner that's an instant hit

Sightings of family-friendly, neighbourhood restaurants are becoming increasingly rare as suburbs are ravaged by feral fast food chains. So Boronia Kitchen shines like a beacon on this stretch of Pittwater Road. Chef Simon Sandall and co-owner Susan Sullivan have left their former high-end (Aria and Chiswick) roles behind to go casual, local and downright neighbourly. By day, they serve up bacon and egg roll breakfasts, prawn spaghetti lunches, and takeaway soups and sausage rolls. At night, things get a little more glam, as the bustling kitchen and revolving rotisserie get a workout. There's a genius prawn toast that crackles with crusty sesame seeds, and silky house-smoked salmon with crisp rye bread, creme fraiche and pickled cucumbers. Rotisserie chicken is the big order for young and old, and spit-roast, herb-scented pork belly encircled by crackling. How good to see a bustling suburban restaurant that's not only alive and well, but over-delivering on top produce, high detail and hospitality.

Make sure what's goes around on the rotisserie comes around

Open	B L D Tue–Sun
Price	$$
Cards	AE MC V eftpos
Chef	Simon Sandall
Features	Licensed, outdoor seating, wheelchair access
Website	boroniakitchen.com.au

Botanic Gardens Restaurant

SYDNEY
Mrs Macquaries Road
1300 558 980

CONTEMPORARY **14/20**

The closest you'll get to dining in a tropical rainforest in Sydney

It's easy to dismiss some venues as tourist haunts but don't let the harbour views (and yes, the tourists) deter you from this garden oasis. Capitalising on its leafy Australiana setting, the menu pays homage to Mother Nature with colourful produce-driven dishes. A salad of heirloom tomatoes, buffalo mozzarella and avocado in a basil vinaigrette is bursting with just-picked greenness. There's confit WA octopus gleaming in anchovy caper butter – so tender you'll be damned if you don't poach all your seafood in oil from now on. Steak tartare is given a sustainable Aussie twist with kangaroo tenderloin. One dip of your potato crisp into the creamy, herby, not-too-gamey 'roo will make a solid case for the most devout Francophiles. Steamed mussels arrive in a classic white wine sauce with house-baked focaccia to make the most of those cooking juices. Finish with the 'sweet addiction', a reworked mint slice replete with mint ice-cream and chocolate 'soil' – a timely reminder to look up and smell the wisteria.

A balcony table is mandatory, as is a stroll through the gardens afterwards

The Bridge Room

SYDNEY
Ground floor, 44 Bridge Street
02 9247 7000

CONTEMPORARY **17/20**

Meticulous globe-hopping fine dining

Meet the prettiest crab dish in Sydney. A ring of sweet spanner crab is bound with coconut and wears a finger lime, kaffir leaf, pork fluff and petal crown like it's going to Coachella. Or perhaps you'd like chef Ross Lusted's meticulously sourced, pickled and grilled winter veg for scooping up mellow artichoke dip and whipped olive oil, or a chawanmushi-ish scallop pudding dressed with abalone, corn and mushroom, all confident subtlety? The influences are broad here – dinner could as easily be matched with a bright Slovenian ribollo, sancerre or oolong tea – but Lusted has a rare talent for execution. Every EA should have this place on speed dial. There's total security in service that's smooth, sedate and utterly rigorous, in a comfortable, minimal room. And there's faith that masterstock-poached quail served in a rhubarb wrap like a tart, savoury roll-up, or a banging dessert of long pepper ice-cream with guava and zingy lime ash will be impeccably produced.

Always work in the cheese course

Open	B Sat–Sun; L Daily
Price	$$
Cards	AE DC MC V eftpos
Chef	Matthew Fletcher
Features	Licensed, outdoor seating, private dining, wheelchair access
Website	botanicrestaurant.com.au

Open	L Thu–Fri; D Tue–Sat
Price	$$$
Cards	AE MC V eftpos
Chef	Ross Lusted
Features	Bar, licensed, wheelchair accessible
Website	thebridgeroom.com.au

Buffalo Dining Club

DARLINGHURST
116 Surrey Street
02 9332 4052

ITALIAN   **14/20**

Italian importer confident it has the goods

Think of Buffalo Dining Club as that friend who always jumps in to order for the whole table. It's convenient for you and allows them to show off a little. How else to explain this intimate Italian joint limiting main courses to just two pastas and a special? Chutzpah, that's what it is, and it's served up continuously. Cheese is the main event and Buffalo goes to great lengths to serve it – fresh mozzarella comes from Italy, nutty yet slightly bitey sheep cheese is shipped in from France and the cacio e pepe pasta is a spectacle served out of a wheel of pecorino. Other produce doesn't hide in the shadows. Bresaola is peppery with horseradish while pecorino-crumbed eggplant gives the juicy vegetable the slightest sharp-tasting coat – like an Italian tempura. Ricotta-stuffed gnocchi soaked in napolitana sauce is helped down by a full-bodied, juicy red. Choose Buffalo and let them take care of the rest.

Have to wait? Buffalo's crew also own wine bar Johnny Fishbone around the corner

Buon Ricordo

PADDINGTON
108 Boundary Street
02 9360 6729

ITALIAN   **15.5/20**

A landmark Sydney restaurant injected with the flavour of Naples

A restaurant like this is all about perspective. In Sydney 2018, its terracotta tiles and floral upholstery may look like a bit of a living museum. But place the Paddington fine diner in Rome or downtown Naples, and this 31-year-old stalwart looks positively contemporary. Founding chef-owner Armando Percuoco may have recently left the building but menu staples remain. Start with pizzetta napoletana – a perfect miniature sphere of fried dough covered in juicy fresh tomato and torn mozzarella. And finger-scorchingly good fritto misto – thinly-sliced, salty, crisp-fried vegetables. Waiters in white dinner jackets call specials such as a deeply golden chicken broth bulked up with bitter greens and ricotta gnudi. Plates of fettuccine al tartufo land with a whole truffled egg yolk resting on a nest of pasta, ready to be mixed through at the table. Richness to the power of funk. The level of fun here really does rest on the deepness of your pockets. Loosen those purse strings and say aaaah.

Saturday lunches here are legendary. Strap in for the ride

Open	L Wed–Sat; D Tue–Sat
Price	$$
Cards	AE MC V eftpos
Chef	Peter Kypreos
Features	Licensed, outdoor seating
Website	buffalodiningclub.com.au

Open	L Thu–Sat; D Tue–Sat
Price	$$$
Cards	AE MC V eftpos
Chef	David Wright
Features	Licensed, private dining
Website	buonricordo.com.au

Capriccio

LEICHHARDT
159 Norton Street
02 9572 7607

citi

ITALIAN   **14/20**

Simple southern Italian cooking with great respect for tradition

Change is slow in this Italian suburb and, although it opened in 2016, Capriccio continues to stand out among the tried-and-true pizza and pasta joints. The menu is fresh, honest fare, centralised around the wood oven. Thin slices of complex-flavoured ox tongue are finished here after the meat is poached until tender. Meaty swordfish is also wood-fired, finished with a dense bagna cauda – a buttery anchovy and garlic-laced sauce. Pasta dishes feature familiar combinations such as sage and brown butter, squid ink spaghetti is served with morsels of sweet blue swimmer crab. Wines are nearly exclusively Italian, and house wines by the carafe – red from Tuscany, white from Piemonte – are excellent value. A menu made for sharing, it pays to remember that many hands make light work. You'll be glad of the help when you're still keen for dolci, such as a cigar of crisp pastry folded around mellow pistachio cream. Take a crowd and dig in.

For a convivial, lively atmosphere, sit downstairs. On a date, upstairs is more intimate

Catalina

ROSE BAY
Lyne Park
02 9371 0555

CONTEMPORARY   **15/20**

Sun-drenched long lunching, yacht-club style

Every atom of this place exudes stellar wattage, thanks in no small part to the wrap-around views of shimmering Rose Bay and the storied family behind the business – hospitality stalwarts Michael and Judy McMahon. The dazzle, thankfully, translates to the plates with a star-studded line-up of producers on show. Western Australian marron is handled with finesse, its flesh grilled just to the point of opaqueness, marrying with the sweet soft tang of citrus butter – the flourish of avruga is an excess (but it's that kind of crowd). Snapper is brilliant in its simplicity: pan-fried to textbook tenderness with the glow of silky lemon-caper butter alone. As is the house-made mushroom ragu tagliatelle – al dente ribbons, brightened with tarragon. Service can be friendly or formidable, but put your trust in their hands when it comes to navigating the binder of a wine list, and let the sun set with an admirable Valrhona chocolate mousse, with jaffa ganache and marmalade ice cream.

When the sun's out, ask for a table on the deck, usually reserved for regulars

Open	L Fri–Sun; D Tue–Sun
Price	$$
Cards	AE MC V eftpos
Chef	Nicole Bampton
Features	Bar, licensed, outdoor seating, private dining, BYO
Website	capriccio.sydney

Open	L Daily; D Mon–Sat
Price	$$$
Cards	AE DC MC V eftpos
Chef	Mark Axisa, Alan O'Keeffe
Features	Licensed, outdoor seating, private dining, wheelchair access
Website	catalinarosebay.com.au

CATALINA

Chaco Bar

DARLINGHURST
238 Crown Street
02 9007 8352

Chat Thai
Circular Quay

CIRCULAR QUAY
Gateway Shopping Centre,
L05/1 Macquarie Place • 02 9247 3053

JAPANESE   **14.5/20**

Elevated yakitori dining in a casual setting

Pass it on a dark night and you're likely to think not much of this pocket-sized restaurant. It isn't exactly fancy to look at, but that doesn't mean anything to the loyal diners who keep the tables full and the atmosphere buzzy. They're here to smash a bunch of grilled meats on sticks, cooked expertly by chef Keita Abe and his team on the bincho and gidgee charcoal-fuelled grill – everything from ox tongue to chicken heart, gizzards and liver served pink in the middle. There is, of course, the likes of chicken thigh and pork belly and the must-order umami-rich silky eggplant skewers that are generously covered in miso. Don't miss the gyoza, which are juicy, plump parcels of salty pork that come to the table sizzling. And for its delicious simplicity, the asparagus that's been wrapped with thick slices of pork and then cooked on the grill. Round it all out with a half litre of Yebisu for maximum refreshment.

Chaco Bar turns into a ramen restaurant on Monday nights and at lunch Wednesday to Saturday

THAI   **14/20**

Thai canteen zinging with flavour and fun – perfect for a pre-show feed

Thai boxing is all about balance and power. One bite of Chat Thai's sublime steamed calamari with its one-two-three sucker punch of garlic, lime and chilli and you'll feel like your mouth has gone three rounds with one of Bangkok's best. Superb balance is also on display in a fragrant and creamy red duck curry – the generous fat chunks of roast bird offset with sweet lychee and pineapple. A crisp turmeric crepe stuffed with prawn mince, tofu, coconut and pickled cucumber could be matched with a glass of decent sauv blanc – but a refreshing iced watermelon slushy does the job even better. There are a couple of swing-and-misses – a charred eggplant, prawn and chicken salad seems underwhelming, and service can be a little haphazard, but the classic sticky rice with mango and coconut ice-cream is right on the money. It's food court noisy and a bit chaotic, but great value and totally delicious – there's that excellent balance on display once again.

Be sure to book ahead to skip the ever-present queue if you have an Opera House show

Open	L Wed–Sat; D Mon–Sat
Price	$$
Cards	MC V eftpos
Chef	Keita Abe
Features	Licensed, BYO
Website	chacobar.com.au

Open	L D Daily
Price	$$
Cards	AE MC V eftpos
Chef	Amy Chanta
Features	Licensed, wheelchair access
Website	chatthai.com.au

Chin Chin

SURRY HILLS
69 Commonwealth Street
02 9281 3322

THAI   **15/20**

This newbie mod-Asian hotspot makes itself heard

You hear Chin Chin before you see it. *Addicted to Bass* and *Black Betty* thump through the glass of Surry Hills' historic Griffiths Teas building. You'll probably have to queue, but once you're inside the whitewashed warehouse space, things happen quickly. Much of the menu has been transplanted from the original Chin Chin in Melbourne, from the zesty kingfish sashimi with lime, to the (kind of underwhelming) spicy Isaan-style duck larb. A new addition, and the hands-down highlight, is the prawn and bug tail egg noodle stir-fry with garlic chives and hellfire chilli oil – it's sweet and spicy and spongy and delicious. Pork belly from the rotisserie is so tender you can cut it with a bamboo chopstick, served with a pickle and scud chilli 'death' sauce that really creeps up on you. It's just as well the attentive waitstaff refill your glass before you even realise you've drained it. If your senses aren't overloaded yet, dessert could be the silky-meets-crunchy iced coffee panna cotta – like the rest of Chin Chin, it'll leave you buzzing.

The 'feed me' selection is good value for those daunted by the 50-strong menu

Open	L D Daily
Price	$$
Cards	AE DC MC V eftpos
Chefs	Graeme Hunt, Benjamin Cooper
Features	Bar, licensed, private dining, wheelchair access
Website	chinchinrestaurant.com.au/sydney

China Doll

WOOLLOOMOOLOO
Shop 4, 6 Cowper Wharf Road
02 9380 6744

MODERN ASIAN   **15/20**

Flavour-packed fine dining with a sparkling city view

Nothing whets the whistle quite like a cocktail tribute to 1980s pop. So pack your parachute pants and order a fruity concoction of China Girl or When Doves Cry at this Finger Wharf fine diner. Hair-metal rockers might instead opt for the Toko Martinez chart-topper of Japanese sake, London gin and Italian vermouth, which kung-fu kicks like a mule. The kitchen is an equally multinational brew of chefs from Korea, Indonesia, Nepal, China, Bangladesh and beyond. Frank Shek (who cut his teeth in his family's Chinese takeaway in suburban Scotland) has this waterside restaurant humming with a lively medley of Asian cuisines. Sweet-and-sour prawn and green bean dumplings are so ripped with flavour they could be on steroids. Crisp beef rice paper parcels are tender and truffly, with a tongue-tingling hit of chilli. Wok-fried Western Australian marron goes all Willy Wonka – candy-red in colour and so plump, gingery and rich that you can skip dessert (but perhaps not the dentist).

Don't be shy in asking for a doggy bag – serves are super generous

Open	L D Daily
Price	$$
Cards	AE DC MC V eftpos
Chef	Frank Shek
Features	Licensed, outdoor seating, private dining, wheelchair access
Website	chinadoll.com.au

CHIN CHIN

China Lane

SYDNEY
2 Angel Place
02 9231 3939

🍷

CHINESE   **14.5/20**

Inner-city laneway dining where the dumplings deliver

The faster-paced and friendlier little sister of China Doll, with a slightly sexier menu, is tricky to find but worth it when you do. There's a small but perfectly formed wine list for the meandering menu that ranges through raw and snacks, steamed, wok and fried. Crisp pig's ear make for an ugly-delicious place to kick off proceedings, alongside flavourful chicken wings packing a Sichuan pepper punch. The wagyu beef massaman comes with sweet potato and cardamom, and duck pancakes are perfectly juicy. Then there are those dumplings, plump, soft, little parcels made fresh that day, with a roaming selection of fillings (prawn, sugar snap and water chestnut is a winner) and served with Sichuan chilli oil and Chinese red vinegar. Overcome your full belly to order dessert. There's a lot to love, including an outrageously rich chocolate mousse with house-made peanut butter ice-cream and hits of dehydrated mandarin, ginger and honeycomb.

Arrive on foot so you can stroll down the lanes. You could (almost) be in Melbourne

Open	L Mon–Fri; D Mon–Sat
Price	$$
Cards	AE MC V eftpos
Chef	Kristian Vale
Features	Licensed, outdoor seating, private dining, wheelchair access
Website	chinalane.com.au

Chiswick

WOOLLAHRA
65 Ocean Street
02 8388 8688

🍷

CONTEMPORARY   **14/20**

Paddock-to-plate dining in verdant surrounds

If you stand back and imagine hard, you can almost see Chiswick's original incarnation as a horse stable. Inside, it feels more like an English conservatory, with French doors offering views of the manicured Chiswick Gardens out the front as well as the compact kitchen garden down the side. The seasonal menu takes full advantage of what's ready to harvest. There's even a marked garden map so you can pinpoint the specific garden bed in which your wood-fired eggplant or zucchini flower with goat's curd was grown. Expect light and clean flavours plated with whimsical rustic prettiness – even the fried spatchcock chicken has a dainty elegance. Moran family-reared lamb shoulder is the signature dish here but the barramundi-in-the-bag is a parcel worth unwrapping, beautifully juicy with fresh peas, twice-podded broad beans and fresh watercress, straight out of the garden. Sweets? Luxuriate in the Paris-Brest choux pastry sandwiched with fresh strawberries and cream.

The sheltered terrace area is ideal for casual drinks and snacks with friends

Open	L D Daily
Price	$$
Cards	AE DC MC V eftpos
Chef	Matt Moran, Tom Haynes
Features	Bar, licensed, outdoor seating, private dining, wheelchair access
Website	chiswickwoollahra.com.au

Chiswick at the Gallery

SYDNEY
1 Art Gallery Road, The Domain
02 9225 1819

CONTEMPORARY   **14/20**

A sunny, smart-casual space where the produce shines as brightly as the art

The artsy sibling to Chiswick Woollahra makes a solid case for dining in public spaces. Following the same ethos as their original kitchen garden-driven restaurant, Chiswick at the Gallery's menu spans seasonal fast snacks for gallery-goers to more substantial fare for long-lunchers. Enjoy floor-to-ceiling views over Garden Island as you start with Sydney rock oysters in a playful Bloody Mary granita. Other Chiswick favourites are here, too, like those butter-soft crab sliders, plus more seasonal plates such as silky Australian burrata bedded in with tomatoes, olives and basil. The tomatoes could sometimes be sweeter and the service faster but all is forgotten by the time a crisp-skinned snapper arrives jutting up to salty capers, green olives and witlof that's been charred to the point of caramelisation. Linguine tangled with pipis, garden peas and chilli explodes with sweetness and serves as a lesson in balance. A global-roaming wine list will please all, as will a deconstructed cheesecake, if you don't mind the wait.

Dining in a group? Order the chef's collective menu for some of the season's best bounty

Open	L Daily; D Wed
Price	$$
Cards	AE DC MC V eftpos
Chef	Matt Moran, Tim Brindley
Features	Bar, licensed, private dining, wheelchair access
Website	chiswickatthegallery.com.au

Cho Cho San

POTTS POINT
73 Macleay Street
02 9331 6601

JAPANESE   **15.5/20**

New-wave Japanese izakaya in a concrete cocktail bunker

If poor little Cho-Cho-san's illegitimate son with the unfaithful Lieutenant Pinkerton grew up and ran away to Sydney, this is the elegant, modern izakaya he would open. The long concrete bar and pegboard walls set the stage for high drama with plenty of twists. So edamame come not in pods but roughly crushed like mushy peas, with seaweed crisps for dipping and diving. Sashimi salad is piled sky-high with shredded daikon and cabbage, laden with kingfish, salmon, tuna and the Tokyo-pop of flying fish roe. Whole prawns swimming in kombu butter might turn up overcooked, but who knew 'charcoal chicken' would mean such sensationally juicy spatchcock, skewered and grilled, on a swirled pool of sesame yoghurt and soy, like a (Middle) Eastern robata? Applause, please, for the intelligent evolution of Japanese drinking food. And whether you choose the green tea tiramisu or the black sesame ice-cream mochi, it'll be a happier ending than Puccini ever gave Madame Butterfly. *Sob*

You can add a flight of three seasonal sakes to your meal for $30

Open	L Fri–Sun; D Daily
Price	$$
Cards	AE MC V eftpos
Chef	Jonathan Barthelmess, Nicholas Wong
Features	Bar, licensed
Website	chochosan.com.au

Chon

BALMAIN
300 Darling Street
02 9810 7826

THAI   **14/20**

Modern Thai bursting with colour and freshness in the heart of Balmain

All the hallmarks of a suburban Sydney Thai joint are accounted for at this feel-good restaurant, where locals love to get comfortable with an exceptional braised lamb shank massaman curry and Barossa shiraz. Prawn pad see ew is present too, of course, but owner-chef Pacharin 'Air' Jantrakool's skills with balancing flavour and spice transcend top-line versions of the classics. North-east-style minced duck salad has sustained heat thanks to its chilli and lime dressing, with wedges of iceberg lettuce on hand to calm the fire. Hard-boiled quail egg is wrapped in prawn mince and deep-fried in a spindly noodle basket for satisfying crunch, while a chicken peanut dumpling hand-carved to resemble a butterfly-pea flower is almost too pretty to eat. It's a bonafide savoury hit anointed with black vinegar, however, and you should probably order a plate of them. Friendly staff offer takeaway containers for anything untouched, so order with your eyes and nose and enjoy.

The bottleshop two doors down has a respectable wine selection for your BYO needs

Open	D Tue–Sun
Price	$$
Cards	MC V eftpos
Chef	Pacharin Jantrakool
Features	Licensed, outdoor seating, private dining, BYO
Website	chonthai.com.au

Chula

POTTS POINT
Shop 7, 33 Bayswater Road
02 9331 0126

MEXICAN   **14/20**

Mescal madness and regional Mexican delights hit the Cross

Ah, Kings Cross, where else would you find diehard mescal geeks and Mexican expats mingling with rowdy 'anything but tequila' party girls? The fun doesn't stop at the bar, either. Chef Alvaro Valenzuela's seafood-heavy menu packs the kind of a zingy punch well attuned to flowing margaritas. Dishes like snapper aguachile are bright and clean with an energising wallop of lime and jalapeno, while tostadas topped with a generous jumble of prawn, octopus and clam make sharing a messy but rewarding experience. Tart up your tinnie michelada-style for an extra $2 and try the tlayuda, a traditional Oaxacan street food featuring a beer-friendly combo of crisp tortilla, pinto bean puree and Oaxacan cheese. Passionate bar staff are a wealth of knowledge when it comes to mescal, tequila and anything in between. Ask to see the 'bible' – an epic list of agave spirits featuring single varietal and wild harvested mescals, raicilla, tutxi, and other beverages you've never heard of.

The dessert menu isn't published, but don't forget to ask

Open	L Sat–Sun; D Tue–Sun
Price	$$
Cards	AE MC V eftpos
Chef	Alvaro Valenzuela
Features	Bar, licensed, outdoor seating, wheelchair access
Website	chula.com.au

Cirrus

BARANGAROO
23 Barangaroo Avenue
02 9220 0111

SEAFOOD   **16/20**

Next-level seafood cookery by some of the best in the biz

You'll want to order a whole crab. And a round of oysters. And a bottle of cold white wine. And some chips. This is a Brent Savage and Nick Hildebrandt joint (they of The Bentley Bar, Monopole and Yellow), dedicated to all things fish. Which means there's a whole lot of paddling going on below the surface. A tartare of trevally hides under an avalanche of rye and nori crumbs, finished with whorls of avocado puree and surf herb nibs. Thick slices of bonito are gently torched and dressed in macadamia, refreshed with thin rounds of cucumber. But oh, that crab. That massive, juicy mudcrab with its sweet fleshy striations smothered in spiced butter and garlic chives served with a side of fried bread. Phwoar. The room, designed by architect Pascale Gomes McNabb, is beautiful enough to forget you're down on the streets of Barangaroo, and while service can be up and down, the kitchen delivers consistently.

The bathrooms are shared with several other Barangaroo restaurants. Time your visit accordingly

Clareville Kiosk

CLAREVILLE
27 Delecta Avenue
02 9918 2727

CONTEMPORARY   **14.5/20**

Laidback seaside dining serving fun, flavourful food

It's hard not to relax when you're greeted with sparkling Pittwater, house-cut salt and vinegar kipfler crisps and bread ferried to you with a side of Vegemite-whipped butter by a smiling waiter in shorts and sneakers. But it all works beautifully – even that salty butter, which offers more flavour than your average pinch of rock salt. If you're worried about filling up on the free stuff, don't – dishes are well-sized. Barely roasted baby zucchini is bound by soft stracciatella and peppered with salty olive specks. Fraser Island spanner crab is given a subcontinental makeover with hints of chilli and mango, finished with grated macadamia and fine pappadum crisps. A pink, tender wagyu rump cap sits on roesti with snow peas, onions and mushroom sauce, offering polished nods to a classic counter meal. When the affable waiter returns with dessert – a palm-sized baked custard tart with shortbread crumbs – it's your turn to smile.

Visit on a Wednesday or Thursday to BYO, and catch the stunning sunset

Open	L D Daily
Price	$$$
Cards	AE MC V eftpos
Chef	Brent Savage, Tony Schifilliti
Features	Licensed, outdoor seating, wheelchair access
Website	cirrusdining.com.au

Open	L Fri–Sun; D Wed–Sat
Price	$$
Cards	AE DC MC V eftpos
Chef	Tom Gillett
Features	Bar, licensed, BYO
Website	clarevillekiosk.com.au

Clove Lane

RANDWICK
19 Clovelly Road
02 9326 3573

citi

CONTEMPORARY   **14/20**

A charming neighbourhood bistro full of friends you haven't met yet

One of the treats at Clove Lane is observing Emile Avramides and Michael Tran cooking, concocting and cajoling behind the long, low pass that commands the dining room. With natural light streaming in and a sea breeze coming through via the kitchen garden out back, it's all too easy to enjoy the show and for the visit to turn into a long, lazy lunch. And why not? The menu has a few quirks (duck liver parfait would be better teamed simply with bread than chicken skin crackers) but there's plenty of technique on display in the bistro fare with a twist. Slow-cooked wagyu rump cap is sublimely pink, dressed in a tarragon emulsion that adds a welcome acid to the protein while Champagne lobster and black garlic risotto is a playfully plated and boozy feat that's made for photography. It's a peach melba though, bejewelled with macadamia and honeycomb, each part a perfect complement to the other, that's the best trick of all.

Try a Sunday lunch to max the relax – Friday and Saturday nights can get hectic

Open	B Sat–Sun; L Fri–Sun; D Tue–Sun
Price	$$
Cards	AE MC V eftpos
Chef	Emile Avramides, Michael Tran
Features	Bar, licensed, outdoor seating, wheelchair access
Website	clovelane.com.au

Continental Deli Bar and Bistro

NEWTOWN
210 Australia Street
02 8624 3131

EUROPEAN   **15.5/20**

A savvy blurring of cocktail bar, bistro and smallgoods grocer

It's a case of anchovy, aperitif and choose-your-own-adventure at this sun-dappled patch of Australia Street. Nice guy Mikey Nicolian commands a marble counter with house-canned cocktails (Martinnies! Canhattans!) and there's only one question after the day's first daiquiri: stay at the bar for boccorones or hit the bistro upstairs? Wildflowers and soft lighting create a cosy vibe on the first level and tables sure make it easier to share Jesse Warkentin's super seasonal dishes. Spindles of calamari and fresh peach are married by macadamia dressing, while cos wedges become a retro hit topped with spanner crab and avocado. Kurobuta pork chop is a good time of sweet barbecued flavours, with heritage tomato salad to cut through the fat. Also check those blistered roman beans and tangle of lightly pickled fennel, all mixed with lovage and a thin peanut pesto. Amaro back at the bar is the right way to finish, especially after rum baba covered in enough chantilly to make a friesian cow blush.

Lunchtime special sandwiches showcase the best of LP's Quality Meats wurst

Open	L D Daily
Price	$$
Cards	AE MC V eftpos
Chef	Jesse Warkentin, Elvis Abrahanowicz
Features	Bar, licensed, outdoor seating, private dining, wheelchair access
Website	continentaldelicatessen.com.au

Coogee Pavilion

COOGEE
169 Dolphin Street
02 9114 7321

CONTEMPORARY **14.5/20**

Relaxed beachside eats ideal for groups and families

Swing chairs, ping pong tables and giant Connect Four? The multi-zoned Coogee Pavilion feels more like a funhouse for kids and adults. It's easy to see why this is such a hit with families, cleverly designed so tykes to teens can make a ruckus in the rear playroom dining area without disturbing distinct sections for casual drinking and sit-down diners. Dive into bubbly-edged wood-fired pizza, cooked Naples-style so they're thin and floppy, scattered with toppings like smoked buffalo mozzarella, roast potatoes and Italian sausage. The expansive menu runs from tender flash-fried cuttlefish with garlic, chilli and lemon to Mediterranean-style whole grilled sardines to a hefty hanger steak served with a turret of stickily rich roasted bone marrow. Sweets? Flashback to childhood with their take on the Golden Gaytime – a dome of butterscotch ice-cream coated in chocolate and biscuit crumbs.

Escape the kid-friendly downstairs zone by heading to the adults-only rooftop bar

Open	B L D Daily
Price	$$
Cards	AE MC V eftpos
Chef	Jordan Toft
Features	Bar, licensed, outdoor seating, wheelchair access
Website	merivale.com.au/venues/ coogeepavilion

Cottage Point Inn

COTTAGE POINT
2 Anderson Place
02 9456 1011

CONTEMPORARY **15.5/20**

A waterside fine diner that doesn't rest on the laurels of its location

Bushland rings with birdsong and cradles a weatherboard-clad dining room where confident staff recommend spot-on wine matches and welcome guests arriving by seaplane, private yacht or Palm Beach ferry. It's easy to forget the city is only 45 minutes away by road. Chef Kevin Solomon isn't one for subtle flavours and dishes punch hard with Japanese and Australian ingredients. Case in point, a lustrous fillet of mirror dory supercharged by caramel miso and native coastal herbs. Cured yellowfin tuna is draped over green beans and dressed with a lick of umeboshi oil, while a side of submissive roast pumpkin proves a highlight thanks to creamy kombu sauce. It complements tajima wagyu rump-cap, peppered by mustard greens and perfect with a glass of Bordeaux. Strawberries fragrant with the herbaceous warmth of fresh thyme are a refreshing finish, and especially delicious with burnt butter panna cotta hiding in the bowl. A boatshed turned destination restaurant that only gets better with age.

Take a load off with a dinner and onsite accommodation package

Open	L Daily; D Fri–Sat
Price	$$$
Cards	AE MC V eftpos
Chef	Kevin Solomon
Features	Licensed, outdoor seating
Website	cottagepointinn.com.au

Culina et Vinum

ELIZABETH BAY
Shop 1, 19-23 Elizabeth Bay Road
02 9356 8307

citi 🍷

MODERN EUROPEAN   **14/20**

European technique applied with passion to local seasonal produce

Slow food is a kitchen-wide philosophy here. Jars of house-made preserves rest quietly in one corner. A dry-aged meat cabinet sits in the other. The temperature-controlled fridge (usually set at 1.7 degrees) might hold fat-marbled lamb tomahawks one day. Two weeks later, you'll find a whole suckling pig. There's an intimate relationship with local suppliers at this neighbourhood restaurant. The dining room blackboard lets you know the source of most menu produce. Start with Tasmanian octopus, smoky eel pâté with charcoal crisps or an expansive charcuterie board that includes burrata, chutney and house-made pickles. The roast spatchcock (from the Upper Hunter Valley) is blanketed with jammy garlic cloves and young witlof leaves. Otherwise hunker down with a slab of Byron Bay pork belly with celeriac and peaches. 'Grandma's scones' is a clever twist on strawberry shortcake, flipping Chef Lowry's Nan's scone recipe into a chunky crumble on top of fresh strawberries and ricotta mascarpone.

Breakfast in the sun in the glassed-in terrace

Open	B Sat–Sun; L D Tue–Sun
Price	$$
Cards	AE MC V eftpos
Chef	Naomi Lowry
Features	Licensed, outdoor seating, wheelchair access
Website	culinasydney.com.au

Da Mario

ROSEBERY
36 Morley Avenue
02 9669 2242

🍷

ITALIAN   **14/20**

Home to more than just some of Sydney's best pizza

Everyone comes for their near-perfect pizza, but it's easy to forget that this family friendly Rosebery institution has entire sections of their menu dedicated to food of the non-pizza variety. Ease yourself into the carb-fest with a plate of tender calamari, fried crisp, lifted with a squeeze of lemon. If you can resist the Italian staples of caprese and carpaccio, thin slices of sour marinated swordfish beneath pink onion and peppercorns makes for a top-notch pesce marinato. Of course, those aren't the slices everyone visits Da Mario for. The pizza here is charred and puffed, chewy and topped with a mess of mozzarella and cured meats. The always-changing menu gives you many reasons to return, not that you need many besides how good that pizza is. It's fun to watch the friendly staff rattle off the specials of the day, knowing that no matter how impressive they are, almost every diner is going to order that pie instead.

Don't fill up on pizza when there's a spectacular tiramisu on the dessert menu

Open	L Fri–Sun; D Tue–Sun
Price	$$
Cards	AE MC V eftpos
Chef	Raffaele Bartiromo
Features	Licensed, outdoor seating, wheelchair access
Website	damario.com.au

THE a2 MILK COMPANY®

a2

FEEL THE DIFFERENCE®

Full cream

The milk that's ALL A2®

2L

Believe in better.

Da Orazio Pizza and Porchetta

BONDI
Shop LG09, The Hub, 75-79 Hall Street
02 8090 6969

ITALIAN   **14.5/20**

Fast and flashy pizzeria that's ahead of the pack

Fast food doesn't always mean mass-produced meals, a pile of preservatives and halfhearted service. This concrete-clad joint is industrial (there's not a soft surface in sight) and industrious, pumping out flavour-packed pizza and pasta faster than your next full-body spray tan. Life moves pretty fast – if you don't stop and look around you could miss it. So linger a moment longer over the richness of risotto al granchio, with sweet chunks of blue swimmer crab, saffron and peas. Bufalina pizza is pared back to highlight the freshness of basil, creamy buffalo mozzarella and San Marzano tomatoes on a precisely cooked base that's naturally risen for 48 hours. Better still is the juicy tagliata di manzo – grilled Angus striploin that's served bloody-as-hell alongside lightly truffled pecorino and rocket leaves. Sure, it arrives at the same time as entrees, but to heck with primi and secondi. When the food's this good, why dilly-dally?

Rock up on Fridays for some late-night pizza and disco action

Dead Ringer

SURRY HILLS
413 Bourke Street
02 9331 3560

citi 🍷

CONTEMPORARY   **14/20**

A sweet old Surry Hills terrace is given new life as a bar-restaurant

For a bar-focused restaurant in the beating heart of the great Darlinghurst/ Surry Hills divide, there's a real emphasis on homeyness here. Out the back, plush leather booths and forgiving lighting is dating catnip. Out the front on the wide balcony, big groups take up the outdoor furniture, more interested in what's on the drinks menu than what they'll be eating. Unless it's the weekend. That's when everyone's going for the set brunch menu with bottomless mimosas. The food menu, by chef Jamie Irving (ex-Est and Berta), is a share-friendly amalgamation of on-trend ingredients (surf herbs, 'nduja, curds) but with a firm pitch in casual ease. Juicy roast chicken, say, dressed in a marsala-spiked pan juices and a Mediterranean mix of capers, roast capsicum and onion petals. Add a perfectly dressed green salad on the side for some brightness. Happy to stay in the comfort zone? Finish off with a wodge of sticky toffee pudding with a scoop of chantilly cream.

Like the cocktail work here? Take a spin at their sister venue, Bulletin Place

Open	L Sat–Sun; D Daily
Price	$$
Cards	AE MC V eftpos
Chef	Josh Carrick, Monty Koludrovic
Features	Bar, licensed, outdoor seating, wheelchair access
Website	daorazio.com

Open	B L Sat–Sun; D Daily
Price	$$
Cards	AE DC MC V eftpos
Chef	Jamie Irving
Features	Bar, licensed, outdoor seating
Website	deadringer.wtf

Dear Sainte Eloise

POTTS POINT
5/29 Orwell Street
02 9326 9745

ITALIAN   **14/20**

This isn't just a wine bar, thanks to the Peruvian-Australian young gun making great vino-friendly snacks

It's a place where everyone is welcome from vino noobs (the staff are ultra friendly and non-intimidating) to wannabe-sommeliers (every night they pour a mystery red – guess the grape and region correctly and the glass is on the house). From red-blooded carnivores (the hanger steak is flavourful) to die-hard plant-fans (the ever-changing menu always includes a few thoughtful vego dishes). On our visit the vegetarian star sees fried brussels sprouts zhuzhed up with kimchi and just-sweet cashew cream. If you're happy to eat both plants and faces, make sure to try the carbonara – the combo of fresh-made spaghetti with a just-split yolk, salty pancetta and gentle seasoning is a winner. It's simply executed and sits beautifully with a glass of San Leonino Chianti. The best wines transmit their terroir and great chefs execute delicious things to go with those drops. Here at this intimate Potts Point wine bar, you can nab both. Praise be.

Nab a seat on the street to feel a little more European while drinking a glass or three from 400-plus strong list

Open	L Fri–Sun; D Daily
Price	$$
Cards	AE MC V eftpos
Chef	Hugh Piper
Features	Bar, licensed, outdoor seating, wheelchair access
Website	dearsainteeloise.com

The Dining Room

THE ROCKS
7 Hickson Road
02 9256 1234

CONTEMPORARY   **14/20**

Postcard-perfect views matched with an Aussie/French menu

It's rare to dine with floor-to-ceiling views over both of Sydney's harbour jewels, so you'll feel like you've stumbled on your own secret hideaway when you reach the far end of the ritzy Park Hyatt. A quieter alternative to the perpetually humming Barangaroo just around the corner, it's here you can feast on French classics brought to life with Aussie produce. Grab a waterfront table and start with perfectly ripe marinated heirloom tomatoes, crisped-up olives and organic farro. Poached blue-eye trevalla is brought to life by a salty slash of bottarga, sharpened by a lush lemon myrtle mousseline. The slow-roasted corn-fed chicken is licked by a classic mustard bearnaise and finished with rye crumbs. Plates may border on fussy but the general standard is a refreshingly far cry from the fare of a restaurant in digs such as these. Recharge the palate with the mandarin sorbet, cremeux and orange jelly – a fun web of textures and temperatures.

Come for the two-course midweek lunch – $62 includes a glass of wine and valet parking

Open	L Mon–Fri; D Daily
Price	$$
Cards	AE DC MC V eftpos
Chef	Etienne Karner
Features	Bar, licensed, private dining, wheelchair access
Website	diningroom.com.au

District Brasserie

SYDNEY
Lower ground floor, 2 Chifley Square
02 9230 0900

CONTEMPORARY　　　**14.5/20**

Getting the business of dining right

Puritanical bosses and a tightening of tax rules may have eroded the tradition of a long lunch, but not for the worker bees buzzing around District Brasserie at midday. Tables are swiftly filled and wine glasses topped up as befits a restaurant that draws on French dining traditions. The menu is diverse and focuses on local produce. Sydney rock oysters are hard to resist but there's also the perfect balance of raw kingfish with macadamia milk, fennel, blood orange and lemon myrtle. The duck liver parfait is a study in beautiful plating, here served with rhubarb chutney and a mache salad. Making money is hungry work and District's charcoal oven is designed to fill office workers' stomachs with steak frites and lamb rump. On a lighter note, the steamed snapper is fragrant with lemongrass and ginger. District has a bright, airy atmosphere with an open kitchen that adds to the industrious air while ensuring the chefs don't act like Gordon Ramsay. No kitchen nightmares, here.

Beyond lunch, District dishes up breakfast and has a bakery serving Single O coffee and organic pastries and sourdough

The Dolphin Hotel

SURRY HILLS
412 Crown Street
02 9331 4800

ITALIAN　　　**15.5/20**

An anything-goes pub for natural wine and pizza while watching the footy

If you're still on the fence regarding pineapple on pizza, the salumi anton pie at Maurice Terzini's nuovo pub wonderland will show you the light. Berkshire leg ham and smoked pineapple is married with mozzarella on a hand-stretched base – it's even better with something chilled and orange poured by party time sommelier Marie-Sophie Canto. Hitting the wine room for snacks is an ace way to begin – LP's mortadella, say, or fluffy polenta chips, before a knees-up in the dining room with Monty Koludrovic's Italo-Oz menu. Orecchiette bounces with sweet spring lamb, fresh peas and a punch of smoked garlic, while the char-grilled flavours of a boneless rib-eye are honed with red wine vinaigrette and bitter radicchio. Lemon pudding is a warming treat, wood-fired and topped with creme fraiche and a fistful of pistachios. And in spite of all the ropes, whitewashed walls and adventures in calico, The Dolphin is still a pub with counter-lunch sandwiches and a true-blue bottle shop. Enjoy.

The Sunday aperitivo series guest stars Australia's best chefs and winemakers

Open	B L Mon–Fri; D Tue–Fri
Price	$$
Cards	AE MC V eftpos
Chef	Mark Knox
Features	Bar, licensed, wheelchair access
Website	districtbrasserie.com.au

Open	L Fri–Sun; D Daily
Price	$$
Cards	AE MC V eftpos
Chef	Monty Koludrovic, Daniel Medcalf
Features	Bar, licensed, outdoor seating, wheelchair access
Website	dolphinhotel.com.au

EST.

Est.

SYDNEY
252 George Street
02 9114 7312

CONTEMPORARY

🍷

♖♖
17/20

Pampered dining as its finest

Legendary chef Peter Doyle may have left the building, but otherwise it's business as usual at Merivale's most lavish fine diner. Waitstaff hover and buzz around the grand dining room, rattling the Champagne trolley and suggesting expensive Coravin pours from a blockbuster wine list. Ornate pillars soar above double-clothed tables and the kitchen sends out elegant creations with a lightness of touch. Doyle protege Jacob Davey now helms the whole shebang, and although the chef's full menu is still to launch at the time of writing, new dishes signal delicious times ahead. A little salad of baby artichoke and peas sharpened by Heidi gruyere is a refreshing way to start, before venison tartare hits with the sustained hum of fermented chilli. Moreton Bay bug tails are long flavoured with shellfish butter, burnt carrot and a slash of harissa, and aged pork loin is harmonised with soft apricots and crisp cavolo nero. Finish with a passionfruit souffle for all time and sink into the plushest banquette in Sydney.

A side of wagyu fat potato batons are like posh hash browns – do it

Open	L Mon–Fri; D Mon–Sat
Price	$$$
Cards	AE MC V eftpos
Chef	Jacob Davey
Features	Bar, licensed, private dining, wheelchair access
Website	merivale.com/venues/est

Ester Restaurant

CHIPPENDALE
46–52 Meagher Street
02 8068 8279

CONTEMPORARY   **16.5/20**

Where there's smoke, there's good food and good times

Is this Sydney's most delicious way to carb-load? Some of the tastiest dishes exiting the wood oven are of the genus 'bread'. Tossing up between piping hot potato bread cooled by yuzu-bright dashi, kefir cream and trout roe or Ester's upscale democracy snag (a spongy house-made white slice topped with a blood sausage)? Order both and regret nothing. Then push on with ruby snapper shrouded with cabbage, its edges crisped by fire, and an unexpectedly subtle bonito butter, or hanger steak under a thatch of softened onion given an umami wallop with anchovy and black garlic. Mat Lindsay's cooking is full of light and shade, a play of powerful flame-licked flavours, delicate textures and smart ideas. Cover maximum territory by ordering the $88 set menu. It's a small room thrumming with activity, hard stools hugging a bar down one side, tightly packed tables in the centre, and a busy wood oven at the back providing the thrust. Get amongst it.

At weekends, they take lunch bookings as late as 4pm

Open	L Sat–Sun; D Mon–Sat
Price	$$
Cards	AE MC V eftpos
Chef	Mat Lindsay, Nathan Brindle
Features	Bar, licensed, wheelchair access
Website	ester-restaurant.com.au

Farmhouse Kings Cross

RUSHCUTTERS BAY
4/40 Bayswater Road
0448 413 791

CONTEMPORARY   **14.5/20**

A wealth of farm-fresh produce ensures you won't leave hungry

For a tiny speck of a restaurant, Farmhouse delivers abundance. There's the pyramid of golden vegetables, the full and falling-apart beef cheeks, the big, juicy field mushrooms on pumpkin puree, and the creamy cucumber condiment – and that's just the main course. Before that there's bright green falafel with pops of pomegranate and mustard seeds, and sea bream with burnt butter and breadcrumbs. Afterward, there are still two desserts, including the cake of the day. For a $60 set menu, that's a lot of bang for your buck. But it's not just the servings that are hearty – there's a warm and fuzzy atmosphere. Inside, there's just one long communal table which, along with the mismatched chairs, low-hanging lights and chipped Italian crockery, works to create a relaxed dinner party vibe. A jazzy playlist hums in the background and the chefs look cool, calm and collected in the open kitchen. It's laidback and unpretentious – you might even feel comfortable enough to undo the top button on your jeans.

Book the outside window seat if communal dining's a turn-off

Open	L Sun; D Wed–Sun
Price	$$
Cards	AE MC V eftpos
Chef	Mike Mu Sung, Juliana Miyamoto, Jordan Stronghan
Features	Bar, licensed, outdoor seating, private dining, wheelchair access
Website	farmhousekingscross.com.au

Felix

SYDNEY
2 Ash Street
02 9114 7303

FRENCH   **15.5/20**

A slice of Paris beneath the skyrise

Felix yells Parisian brasserie loud and
proud. We're talking subway tiles,
chandeliers, rattan bistro chairs with
a striking iced seafood bar parading
a bounty of oysters and crustaceans.
An affirmative nod to the old-school
shines through well-executed classics
like garlic prawns and Berkshire pork
terrine, but chef Nathan Johnson isn't
afraid to pare things back at times to
let produce shine. When it comes to
the steak frites, there's no Cafe de Paris
butter in sight, letting a superb sirloin
of Rangers Valley black Angus do its
thing. A vast wine list will placate the
wine nerd at your table, but a solid
by-the-glass selection makes things
manageable for the rest of us. The
corporate crowd come for the plat du
jour during the week, but at weekends
punters gather to relive their last
Parisian getaway or prep for the next,
because, let's face it, this is the place to
dust up on your high school French.

**Check for daily specials from
the rotisserie. An excellent option
if sharing**

Firedoor

SURRY HILLS
23-33 Mary Street
02 8204 0800

CONTEMPORARY   **16/20**

The power of heat harnessed by sharp technique

At this slick and soft-lit restaurant
where wood-whispering chef Lennox
Hastie fires beautiful Australian
produce on an asado-style grill, there's
one question every time: to beef
rib or not to beef rib? Sliced with a
bandsaw to order, the steak will likely
be dry-aged for more than 150 days
to take on flavours of parmesan, old
sherry and mushroom. Cooked over
grapevine, it's tremendous stuff and
yours for around $170 to share. Of
course, you might prefer to spend
that coin on delicately grilled seafood
such as deboned garfish enhanced
with a parsley party of bagnet vert,
or a tail-end of Murray cod featuring
creamy fat sharpened by rainbow-chard
pickle. Meanwhile, a tartare of rose veal
heart and beetroot is sweet and earthy
and wonderfully scarlet. Oh, to heck
with decisions – commandeer a long
table with mates and order it all. A
smart wine list will happily carry you
from school prawns brushed with chilli
oil to that all-time-great steak. Bombe
alaska caramelised with blue flames
at the table is essential, too.

**A fireside spot at the counter is the
hot ticket when there are two of you**

Open	L Mon–Fri, Sun; D Daily
Price	$$-$$$
Cards	AE MC V eftpos
Chef	Nathan Johnson
Features	Bar, licensed, outdoor seating, wheelchair access
Website	merivale.com.au/felix

Open	L Thu–Fri; D Tue–Sat
Price	$$$
Cards	AE MC V eftpos
Chef	Lennox Hastie
Features	Bar, licensed, wheelchair access
Website	firedoor.com.au

FIREDOOR

The Fish Shop

POTTS POINT
22 Challis Avenue
02 9114 7340

SEAFOOD **14.5/20**

A fish shop you wish was your local serving sophisticated versions of old classics

There's something so familiar and easy about dining at The Fish Shop. Perhaps it's because the space is cosy and inviting, and because most of the clientele are locals, it feels relaxed. The fact it's rarely an issue to secure a table also helps. Then there's the menu – a hit list of dishes showing off fresh, locally caught and sustainable seafood, prepared simply. The fish and chips are expertly cooked golden crisp, while Jezza's crumbed barramundi, bacon and chilli burger – named after the late chef Jeremy Strode – is a must-order thanks to its crunch, heat and pillowy bun. Same rule applies to the crunchy salt cod croquettes. It's not all about the classics, though. There are also prawn and cauliflower dumplings in a delightful prawn and chilli broth. A list of easy-drinking wines rounds out the neat menu offerings and many are the perfect fried food foil – especially when it comes to those irresistible salty potato scallops.

Don't miss Dan Hong's Famous Cheeseburger. Before burgers became ubiquitous, it was Sydney's go-to

Open	L D Daily
Price	$$
Cards	AE MC V eftpos
Chef	Ben Fitton
Features	Bar, licensed, outdoor seating, wheelchair access
Website	merivale.com.au/venues/thefishshop

Flying Fish

PYRMONT
Pier 21, Lower Deck, Jones Bay Wharf,
19-21 Pirrama Road
02 9518 6677

SEAFOOD **14.5/20**

Harbourside dining with peerless seafood made for long lunching

"All the views, half the crowds," could easily be the tagline for Jones Bay Wharf. Here the razzle-dazzle Harbour Bridge views, the sweeping panorama of Barangaroo point, a luxury superyacht or two, impress, but it's the storied heritage of the timber and steel shore shed that houses Flying Fish that supersizes the offer. Here, seafood shines bright, steered towards the punched-up flavours of Asia, with indigenous ingredients in focus. The tang of desert limes and sea blite and the umami-hit of seaweed butter complement the briny sweetness of just-grilled king prawns. The juicy crunch of beach banana and pickled quandong elevate cubes of yellowfin tuna sashimi with tomato ponzu. WA marron gets flash-fried in a crunchy (but heavy) tempura coating, then tossed in an addictive black pepper and curry leaf glaze. Well-versed waitstaff are at the ready with bibs, hand towels and spot-on wine recommendations, and a knowing nod to close the deal with a not-too-sweet milk chocolate ganache and tonka bean ice-cream.

Factor time for waterside pre- or post-prandial drinks on the outdoor lounges

Open	L Tue–Sun; D Mon–Sat
Price	$$$
Cards	AE DC MC V eftpos
Chef	Gavin Carfax-Foster, Peter Kohler
Features	Bar, licensed, outdoor seating, private dining, wheelchair access
Website	flyingfish.com.au

Folonomo

SURRY HILLS
370 Bourke Street
02 8034 3818

CONTEMPORARY   **14/20**

**A food-for-good initiative with
a lively setting and tasty snacks**

Folonomo, or 'for love not money',
as it stands for, is a buzzy restaurant
where 100 per cent of the profits
(after expenses and running costs) are
donated to charity. It's a great initiative
and it's hard not to feel good when you
order that second glass of wine from
a list that respects biodynamic and
sustainable farming principles.
Go hard on the entrees – it's where the
restaurant shines. Order the haloumi
croquettes, which are surprisingly light
and textural thanks to the tapioca/
cheese mix, and the toast topped with
sobrasada (cured sausage made with
ground pork and paprika) and shavings
of manchego. The orecchiette with
mushroom, spinach and dried ricotta
isn't a revolutionary interpretation, but
you're likely to run your finger across
the plate so you don't miss any sauce.
A couple of dishes may fail to hit the
mark, such as the lamb rump and the
chocolate ganache, but when you're
making the world a better place, you
can let that slide.

**If you prefer a quieter dining
experience, sit in the courtyard
or on the street**

Open	D Tue–Sat
Price	$$
Cards	AE DC MC V eftpos
Chef	Vinicius Oliveira
Features	Licensed, outdoor seating, wheelchair access, BYO
Website	folonomo.org.au

Fratelli Paradiso

POTTS POINT
12-16 Challis Avenue
02 9357 1744

ITALIAN   **15.5/20**

**A trattoria with style and substance at
any time of the day. Un posto vero**

Oh, Frat Paz, has it really been 18 years
already? You've had a fine-tune – new
tobacco leather booths made for
lingering longer and more teeny tables
squished in to make the no-bookings
policy less of a kerbside crush – but
keeping up with the Russos, thankfully,
you're not. The tightly edited chalkboard
menu is as familiar and dependable as
the welcoming chime of "buonasera"
from the sassy, swift-of-foot, black-on-
black clad staff. It offers just enough
choice to make you feel like you may
not order the lasagnetta bolognese or
scampi spaghetti or puddly risotto or
cloud-like tiramisu – again. But who
are you kidding? Tonight's vongole
chitarra, though – strands bright with
egg yolk and coated in fermented chilli,
is a no-regrets kind of dish. As is the
bresaola, lively with pickled onion and
pecorino cream. The wine list treads
naturally – Italian, of course – but
there are easy-drinking pours (read:
non-PE socks) to be had. You are
our kind of vintage.

**The custard bombolini sell out by
9am on weekends. Rise earlier**

Open	B L D Daily
Price	$$
Cards	AE DC MC V eftpos
Chef	Akira Urata
Features	Licensed, outdoor seating, wheelchair access
Website	fratelliparadiso.com

FRED'S

Fred's

PADDINGTON
380 Oxford Street
02 9114 7331

CONTEMPORARY **16/20**

A produce-driven Provencal-inspired kitchen where simple is the new luxe

The large, high-ceilinged open kitchen is the heart and soul of Fred's, from the glowing coals of the golden stone hearth to the breads baking in the wood-fired oven. Even the leg of lamb roasting over the brazier and the bowls of broad beans look happy to be here. Fitting, then, that Chez Panisse-trained Danielle Alvarez's cooking is so uncompromisingly seasonal, local, and almost cultishly simple. If she has rich, ripe figs, they may be paired with local buffalo mozzarella, peppery rocket and prosciutto. Zucchini might star in a fresh delicate tagliolini with a handful of its own tiny golden blossoms. Sweetcorn accompanies a meaty chunk of steamed bass grouper with charred greens, and tangy blood plums come encrusted in sugar-dusted pastry with a smooth, wild fennel ice-cream. It's not cheap, but add accommodating service and a living, breathing wine list with daily specials and house wine from monthly changing single-producers, and Fred's is the most joyful place to dine in the eastern suburbs.

Order the freshly baked Provencal fougasse with butter and olive oil

Frenchies Bistro and Brewery

ROSEBERY
The Cannery, 6/61–71 Mentmore Avenue
02 8964 3171

FRENCH **14.5/20**

Smart French fare in a buzzing back block location

If you haven't ventured down to the Cannery in Rosebery, you're fast running out of excuses. There are food choices for days, a cooking school, one of Australia's finest gin and vodka distillers in Archie Rose and this slick French-inspired beer hall banging out brews and clever bistro-flavoured plates. It's a family friendly affair, too – a packed long table of all ages setting to work on neat slabs of meaty pate en croute and dipping toasted brioche in equally airy and delightful prawn terrine. It all works with the crafty selection of house-brewed beers, of course, but there's similar pride in the wines and gems like an unfiltered, wild fermented pazzo by KT reward a taste for adventure. John Dory with steamed mushrooms is light and subtly earthy, while pink lamb saddle is bedded down with firm Israeli couscous, all signs that what really makes this place French is not slavish adherence to classic dishes but a devotion to quality and technique at every turn.

Frenchies Feast happens Thursday nights – a big communal table and plenty of good cheer

Open	B Sat; L Fri–Sun; D Tue–Sun
Price	$$$
Cards	AE DC MC V eftpos
Chef	Danielle Alvarez
Features	Bar, licensed, wheelchair access
Website	merivale.com.au/freds

Open	L Tue–Sat; D Tue–Sun
Price	$$
Cards	AE MC V eftpos
Chef	Thomas Cauquil
Features	Bar, licensed, wheelchair access
Website	frenchiesbistroandbrewery.com.au

Fujisaki

BARANGAROO
Shop 2, 100 Barangaroo Avenue
02 9052 9188

JAPANESE   **14/20**

Modern Japanese in a large format fine diner

Gleaming Barangaroo still feels a little too close to Darling Harbour, but Lotus Dining group seeks to distinguish Fujisaki with two awarded chefs, a dark, sleek fitout, and a serious wine room. Chui Lee Luk, ex-Claude's, is on the robata grill and her popular Angus beef comes with a black pepper sauce that sits cleverly between French, Japanese and Chinese. But perhaps salted duck with muntries better demonstrates her considerable skill. A mushroom tempura lacks the same precise touch. Sushi is served last, from the hand of master Ryuichi Yoshii. His five-piece nigiri is selected daily, and it's good. Eyes around the restaurant – CBD workers on date night, mostly – close on first mouthfuls. Minds turn to the possibility of returning for the omakase sushi degustation. The signature dessert, a white-chocolate-crafted wasabi root, is no match for the hint of freshly grated wasabi in the nigiri, and it's the memory of those perfect morsels you'll carry into the night.

Sit inside or book the tatami room – the outdoor view is of passing traffic

Open	L D Daily
Price	$$
Cards	AE MC V eftpos
Chef	Chui Lee Luk, Ryuichi Yoshii, Joey Ingram
Features	Bar, licensed, outdoor seating, private dining, wheelchair access
Website	lotusdining.com.au/restaurant/ fujisaki

The Gantry

WALSH BAY
11 Hickson Road
02 8298 9910

citi

CONTEMPORARY   **15/20**

Innovative food, pretty enough to compete with the harbour views

Dining on and over water never gets old and sleek design brings this historic fisherman's wharf very much up to date. The handsome wooden interior is elegant and warm, and a fun mismatch to the resort-style pier sporting faux turf, lush foliage and festoon lights. There's nothing mismatched about the food, though, with every carefully constructed element adding a certain zing, snap or phwoar. Wallaby is served with earthy grains and beetroot, complemented by bitter nettle and sweet blackberries. Pair this with harbourside views and suddenly you're feeling quite proud to be Australian. Menu descriptions are brief, so when quail lands on the table with a dollop of foam you find yourself asking what that amazing puree is, or where that hint of cinnamon comes from. Thankfully staff are total pros and can talk you through it in detail. Tap on chocolate with caramelised milk to crack it open like a decadent gift. It's a rich man's Mars Bar, and so much better.

Enjoy a pre-meal splash in the summer pop-up pool, complete with private pontoon

Open	L Wed–Sun; D Daily
Price	$$
Cards	AE DC MC V eftpos
Chef	Thomas Gorringe
Features	Bar, licensed, outdoor seating, private dining, wheelchair access
Website	thegantry.com.au

FUJISAKI

Glass Brasserie

SYDNEY
Level 2, 488 George Street
02 9265 6068

CONTEMPORARY   **15/20**

A suave city setting with unpretentious food and amazing wine

With high ceilings, walls of heavy hitting wine and super-sized windows framing the QVB, this place sure has X factor. Add that international hotel vibe and you've got the perfect action movie set – the hero crashes through every last window, mirror, bottle and glass, saves the day then sips from a magnum of Veuve Clicquot (which acts as decoration throughout). Opulence aside, the food is simple with a diverse menu offering subtle Asian flavours alongside classic dishes off the grill. Ramen noodle broth with Moreton Bay bug is homey yet refreshing, while steamed mulloway is drizzled with a light truffled pecorino sauce that packs just enough punch. The ever-popular steaks are simply presented with sauce on the side and grilled broccolini – not to mention a hefty bill that's often picked up by a corporate card. It's easy to get a taste of chef Luke Mangan, be it his brand of olive oil, mustard or even wine. Better yet, grab him for a selfie.

There are 3500 wines on display, so get a head start at the bar

Gogyo

SURRY HILLS
52-54 Albion Street
02 9212 0003

JAPANESE   **14/20**

Ramen reveals its dark side

We've eaten ramen here before, when it was the funky, Tokyo-pop Salaryman designed by Sydney's Paul Kelly. Now it's the communal-tabled, crowd-pleasing Gogyo, again designed by Paul Kelly, but this time set up by the global Ippudo group to give Sydney its first taste of the scarily dark kogashi (burnt miso) ramen. First, lard is heated to a zillion degrees, then miso is added, and the whole thing catches fire before being doused with chicken broth. Then comes cabbage, soft-yolked egg, tender chashu pork, naruto fish cake and magnificently al dente, medium-thin wheat noodles. It might look like the black lagoon, but it tastes clean, rich, smoky and deep. Beyond the ramen, there are fat spring rolls filled with wagyu sukiyaki, beautifully engineered and thin-skinned gyoza and fresh, clean sashimi gohan tumbled over a bowl of warm steamed rice. Stay for the taiyaki, Japan's much-loved sweet batter cake shaped like a sea bream, so you can tell everyone you had fish for dessert.

Wear black and not white, if you're going for the charred ramen (bibs available)

Open	B D Daily; L Mon–Fri
Price	$$$
Cards	AE DC MC V eftpos
Chef	Luke Mangan, Peter Cassidy
Features	Bar, licensed, private dining, wheelchair access
Website	glassbrasserie.com.au

Open	L D Daily
Price	$$
Cards	AE DC MC V eftpos
Chef	Daisuke Kobayashi
Features	Bar, licensed, wheelchair access
Website	ippudo.com.au/gogyo

Golden Century

HAYMARKET
393-399 Sussex Street
02 9212 3901

CHINESE **14.5/20**

The late-night restaurant where worlds collide, deliciously

When it comes to late-night haunts that attract big names none delivers such a heady good time, every time, the way Golden Century has been doing since 1989. But what makes it a magnet for the Queen of Morocco, Rod Stewart, David Chang and Tetsuya Wakuda? Is it those pipis, sauteed in house-made XO sauce, stickily coating a bed of noodles? Could it be the green beans sauteed with pork mince and black olive? Maybe it's the fresh live prawns lightly cooked by lamplight at the table in shao hsing wine, the meat so sweet and tender you'd just about eat them raw. Or that off-menu number of Chinese doughnut sticks stuffed with prawn mince, then deep-fried and finished with chilli flakes. Maybe it's the extensive wine list, made to be dug into with a side order of Peking duck. The room, for the GC uninitiated, doesn't leave much to the imagination. It's pretty much designed to be spill-proof. Again, that's part of its charm.

Golden C now does daily yum cha from noon

The Grounds of the City

SYDNEY
500 George Street
02 9699 2235

CONTEMPORARY **14/20**

Old-world bistro charm provides respite from the wild frontier of George Street

Staff dart around with astute precision and confidence at the Grounds' empire's city outpost. The place is tailored to umpteenth degree – custom dainty floral ceramics, studded maroon leather chairs, stained glass windows and a big band soundtrack – somehow, it's simultaneously somewhere you could take your Nan for a tea or a client for a steak. Here they'll grill you a wagyu tri tip – it comes juicy and thick and the compound butter and crunchy roast potatoes make it a brasserie-inspired knockout dish. Or get around the sweet meat of split Yamba prawns, which come charred with a rounded chilli, citrus and a zesty ponzu dipping sauce. There are also salads, sandwiches and coffee to go all day served smartly from an adjoining kiosk outside. There's a lot going on here – from free-wheeling dessert carts to an in-house shoe shiner to boot – but the Grounds executes it all with finesse.

For once, you don't need to save room for the dessert – you can order up to 12 pastries and they'll pack them up for you to take back to the office

Open	L D Daily
Price	$$
Cards	AE DC MC V eftpos
Chef	Ho Li
Features	Licensed, private dining, wheelchair access, BYO
Website	goldencentury.com.au

Open	B L Daily; D Tue–Sun
Price	$
Cards	AE MC V eftpos
Chef	Paul McGrath
Features	Bar, licensed, wheelchair access
Website	thegroundscity.com.au

Hartsyard

NEWTOWN
33 Enmore Road
02 8068 1473

CONTEMPORARY   **15/20**

A new, more serious Hartsyard grows up and eats its vegetables

Is there life beyond fried chicken? Gregory Llewellyn and Naomi Hart think so, having surgically removed the fried chicken – and the deep-fryer – from their heaving Enmore Road diner. The menu refresh sees the installation of a charcoal grill, more plant-based dishes, and a focus on the holy trinity of smoking, dehydrating and fermenting. Cheese puffs dusted with pastrami spices taste like a vegetarian reuben, and a scampi and prawn tartare brightly paired with saffron rouille and tobiko roe come with a sensational side-serve of potato crisps, punchy with freeze-dried vinegar. A gnarly, roasted head of cauliflower is peppered with crunchy fried capers, and in place of fried chicken, there's brined and rolled pork neck or duck, cooked low and slow. Dessert harks back to the old, more rambunctious Hartsyard, as busted waffle, cherry ice-cream, poached cherries, labne and wild fennel pollen get together for a party on a plate. It's still high-energy, and flavour-first – just a little less deep-fried and meaty.

There's fried chicken on the menu up the road at sister diner Wishbone

Hello Auntie

MARRICKVILLE
278 Illawarra Road
02 8068 8200

VIETNAMESE   **14/20**

Spend a little extra for a lot more fun

It might be a few extra bucks more than dinner at one of the many Vietnamese institutions on Illawarra Road, but there's a genuine flair in the kitchen that you won't find elsewhere in Marrickville. Chef Cuong Nguyen adds a touch of modernity to the Southeast Asian staples on the menu, cooking with significantly better ingredients than any of the nearby pho joints. Bring a friend or three and share a serve of the fried chicken wings marinated in a fermented tofu funk, then move on to the seldom-seen-in-Sydney banh khot: pikelets of coconut and turmeric with prawns and smelt roe. It'd be easy to just order another round of wings and pikelets but the hearty bo ssam is worth a look-in, too. Some of the more adventurous attempts at fusion on the dessert and drinks lists don't always work out but it's hard to stay mad at somewhere as fun and friendly as this.

Remove the pressure of choice by signing up for the $55 banquet

Open	D Tue–Sat
Price	$$
Cards	MC V eftpos
Chef	Gregory Llewellyn, Jarrod Walsh
Features	Bar, licensed
Website	hartsyard.com.au

Open	L D Wed–Sun
Price	$
Cards	MC V eftpos
Chef	Cuong Nguyen
Features	Bar, licensed, wheelchair access
Website	hello-auntie.com.au

Hotel Centennial

WOOLLAHRA
88 Oxford Street
02 9114 7349

CONTEMPORARY   **15/20**

Grown-up dining in a grown-up dining room

After buying this Woollahra institution, just 600 metres away from its popular pub, The Paddington, the Merivale Group can practically divvy up the entire eastern suburbs between them. While the Paddo packs in a young, spirited, noisy crowd, the Centennial is more your parental version, with its deeply comfortable seating, natural light and striking photographic art. Head chef James Evangelinos works with Merivale's Ben Greeno and Danielle Alvarez to deliver an inviting Mediterranean menu built around the restaurant's wood-fired oven. Almost everyone orders steak frites with mustard butter, but you'd be silly not to do the seafood. Flash-roasted fresh squid with aioli and roasted tomatoes is all scorch and sizzle while a whole, meaty, wood-fired yellow-belly flounder with seaweed salsa verde is a joy. Follow it with a roasted whole nectarine and beautifully smooth, creamy vanilla ice-cream. If your idea of a good time is being able to see your food and hear yourself think, with cooking you understand, you're in the right place.

Check out the red and white wines listed under 'Interesting'

Open	L D Daily
Price	$$$
Cards	AE DC MC V eftpos
Chefs	Ben Greeno, James Evangelinos
Features	Bar, licensed
Website	merivale.com/venues/hotelcentennial

House of Tong

NORTH RYDE
North Ryde RSL Club, 27-41 Magdala Road
02 9878 4766

CHINESE   **14.5/20**

Simple, honest and authentic Cantonese cooking

The team that once made Sea Treasure famous is back, with Tong Lau carving the Cantonese roast ducks out the front and his brother Wah in the kitchen. It's worth navigating through the Ryde RSL to find all the Cantonese favourites cooked with real care. The white cut chicken is partially deboned and comes with a textbook perfect ginger and shallot dressing. Giant Pacific oysters are steamed until just warm. Of course there are pipis with wok-fried vermicelli. King prawns coated in salted egg yolks will be welcomed by lovers of Cantonese food, even if the taste is a bit unusual. Live parrot fish is steamed, and plated at the table (go for the fish lips and cheeks). There's even a good sweet and sour pork, without the garish red colour many people are used to seeing. The mango pancakes could be the best in Sydney. And if it's not on the menu, ask Tong. Chances are the kitchen will oblige.

If you're after something special, go straight to the cellarmaster's suggestions for some keenly priced classic reds

Open	L D Tue–Sun
Price	$$
Cards	MC V eftpos
Chef	Lau Yui Wah
Features	Licensed, wheelchair access
Website	northrydersl.com.au

Icebergs Dining Room and Bar

BONDI BEACH
1 Notts Avenue
02 9365 9000

ITALIAN   **16.5/20**

Where to go when you want to show off Sydney

"I was surfing right there this morning," says the waiter, pointing down to the pounding surf below. "And my mother wants to know why I won't go back to Sicily." Bondi Beach has that effect on people, especially from a double-clothed table in this softly glowing dining room, negroni in hand. Sydney's most Sydney restaurant draws a razzle-dazzle, A-list crowd with its intoxicating blend of vistas, meticulous service and refined cooking, showcasing ever more meticulously sourced ingredients. This is the place to go big. Six sea-sweet WA scampi tails mix it with a bevy of poached baby radishes. Hand-rolled spinach twirls of pici are laced with nuggets of tender lamb, juniper and eggplant. Uncompromisingly fresh crisp-skinned trumpeter is grounded by cime di rapa and kipfler potatoes cooked in anchovy butter. Finish on a pink atomic cloud of meringue, whipped mascarpone, beetroot and grapefruit sorbet. The mercurial Maurice Terzini has kept Icebergs fresh for 16 years – and counting.

Hail the magnificent digestivi trolley after – or instead of – dessert

Open	B Sun; L D Daily
Price	$$$
Cards	AE DC MC V eftpos
Chef	Monty Koludrovic, Alex Prichard
Features	Bar, licensed, outdoor seating, private dining, wheelchair access
Website	idrb.com

Indu

SYDNEY
Basement, 350 George Street
(enter via Angel Place)
02 9223 0158

INDIAN/SRI LANKAN   **14/20**

Indian classics and modern magic served in a bustling basement.

There's something enjoyably clandestine about Indu. Maybe it's the laneway entrance down a nondescript staircase. Or perhaps the discreet lighting and odd mirror for checking over your shoulder. Catch a glimpse of dosa charring on the front grill and the secret is blown – you're in for a subcontinental adventure. The dining room is all hustle – squad up and go for a dining nook and you'll be rewarded with more privacy. But there's no wrong choice – or no choice that can't be eased with one of the signature gin and tonics. Spiced spanner crab and salt cod wrapped in a crunchy fresh betel leaf makes a moreish starter before moving on to devilled pumpkin heady with coconut and ginger warmth, or a Kashmiri lamb curry skewered by a shin bone full of marrow and drenched with fresh chilli. Swing back to cocktails for dessert and try the gin and tonic cheesecake – four perfect parcels sitting on a pistachio-crusted glass – and then it might be time to slip your tail and vanish into the night.

Do not, repeat, do not miss the cheesecake

Open	L Mon–Fri; D Mon–Sat
Price	$$
Cards	AE MC V eftpos
Chef	James Wallis
Features	Bar, licensed, private dining, wheelchair access
Website	indudining.com.au

Intermezzo

SYDNEY
Ground floor, 1 Martin Place
02 9229 7788

ITALIAN **14/20**

Traditional Italian food with a great respect for authentic ingredients

Intermezzo adheres to the motto "tried and true". That doesn't mean boring – it means the menu is full of beautifully executed, traditional Italian dishes. Punchy entrees such as buffalo mozzarella wrapped in prosciutto served with tart pickled beetroot awakens the palate for the pasta course. House-made pappardelle tossed with mushrooms and ricotta, punctuated with fragrant black truffle oil, say. The main event can go light or heavy. Choose between a delicate ocean trout fillet with tomatoes baked en papillote (sealed in parchment paper) or tender veal osso buco. For dessert, the panna cotta is pretty and texturally complex, served with crunchy bits of honeycomb and a scoop of creamy buttermilk gelato. The ornate drama of Martin Place's GPO Building setting is matched by the wine collection housed in an eight-metre-tall temperature-controlled glass tower. White-jacketed staff run up and down the stairs, fetching bottles that are a good representation of Italy and Australia's best wine regions. Settle in for a good time, and a long time.

For best results, let your waiter guide you through the long wine list

Open	B L D Mon–Sat
Price	$$
Cards	AE DC MC V eftpos
Chef	Craig Ferrier
Features	Licensed, outdoor seating, wheelchair access
Website	gpogrand.com

Izakaya Fujiyama

SURRY HILLS
Shop 9, 38-52 Waterloo Street
02 9698 2797

JAPANESE **15/20**

Super-fun flavours with a smashing soundtrack and sake

When was the last time you chowed down on smoked fish with salted caramel popcorn? If you haven't eaten at this Japanese joint, the answer is probably never. The dim-lit drinking den puts the looney back into tunes – which here career from hip-hop to jazz, rockabilly and the blues (the soundtrack was crafted with the help of regular diner Jimmy Barnes). The menu is equally eclectic, starting with hand-scrawled specials that might feature seared bonito served on super-crunchy sweet potato chips with (a little too much) chickpea hummus and caramelised popcorn, which tastes a bit like eating a fish at the movies. Grilled octopus with crisp-fried potato and candied grapefruit is fresh, vibrant and slightly more sensible, while tender smoked 'Tokyo duck' with pear and pickled green tomatoes is on song with sweet and sour flavours and textures. The sake bottles and plastic figurines lining the walls are perfect drinking companions for a wonderfully nutty night out, particularly with some Hibiki Harmony whisky jet-packing around your gums.

Save space for dessert – the pina colada ice-cream is a cracker

Open	D Mon–Sat
Price	$$
Cards	MC V eftpos
Chef	Kenji Maenaka, An Hyek
Features	Licensed, wheelchair access
Website	izakayafujiyama.com

Jonah's

PALM BEACH
69 Bynya Road
02 9974 5599

CONTEMPORARY   **15.5/20**

It's like dining at the edge of the world, armed with a very good martini

This is Type A Sydney dining, where the largest problem you're likely to face is where to park the Porsche Cayenne. A martini to start might seem excessive if you were anywhere but here, where you'll take your cocktail out in the cliffside garden. The only thing separating you from the sea is a very sheer drop and mindful waiters. It's full service, with wines for each course displayed tableside on thick linen a declaration of intent. And really, lunch is The Thing. Start with the royale – a goat's cheese custard hidden under shavings of macadamia with savoury tang from a little pine cone bud syrup. Squid ink linguine is outrageously luxe – black pasta woven with salmon roe and chives relax over a bed of reggiano with rich, sticky, bittersweet and briny results. And while lamb neck cooked in hay seems like a secondary cut compared with Patagonian toothfish with miso and capers, the treatment, as with everything here, is primo.

Book well in advance for weekend lunch – this is wedding-central, especially in the warmer months

Katsumi

MORTLAKE
58 Tennyson Road
02 8385 4940

JAPANESE   **14/20**

Mortlake Japanese where East (almost) meets West

So you're drinking lychee gin and tonics, capturing excellent tempura prawn sushi rolls with your chopsticks, and listening to Van Morrison's *Into the Mystic*. Welcome to the new Mortlake. Katsumi opened in 2017 with a Japanese interior, private dining room and long, low fish tanks serving as steps to a raised dining level. Former Koi sushi chef, Yang Wu presides over a menu that gives equal time to classic and fusion dishes. Anything raw is the place to be: his mixed nigiri is meticulous, the fish generously draped over hand-warmed rice. Lightly seared Hokkaido scallops with brown butter, soy, and salmon caviar, are a treat. The fusion main courses are interesting but ultimately less convincing – a char-grilled lamb rack with carrots, brussels sprouts and sweet miso mint sauce is like Sunday roast in a ryokan. Sushi, sashimi and sake on the terrace overlooking the street sounds like an excellent way to spend a summer evening.

Sushi and sashimi are highlights

Open	L D Daily
Price	$$$
Cards	AE DC MC V eftpos
Chef	Matteo Zamboni
Features	Bar, licensed, outdoor seating, private dining, wheelchair access
Website	jonahs.com.au

Open	D Tue–Sun
Price	$$
Cards	AE DC MC V eftpos
Chef	Yang Wu
Features	Licensed, outdoor seating
Website	katsumi.com.au

Kepos and Co

WATERLOO
Shop 5, Casba, 18 Danks Street
02 9690 0931

citi   MIDDLE EASTERN   **15/20**

Rocking the Casba with Middle Eastern delights

Found in the aptly named Casba complex in a room decorated like old Tel Aviv, chef Michael Rantissi aims to showcase his memories of classic Middle Eastern cuisine. He succeeds brilliantly. There's obvious pride in the produce and considerable craft on show. Warm hummus is finished at your table in a mortar and pestle and comes with za'atar-flecked flatbread direct from the wood-fired oven. The bitterness of radicchio is perfectly balanced by a slightly sweet dressing and thinly sliced haloumi. Snapper comes under a thick pavement of walnuts and tahini and a classic brisket is transformed by the use of wagyu and a surprisingly spicy harissa, which brings waves of heady, complex flavours. Even the humble bombe alaska is elevated by a tangy, concentrated pomegranate granita and labne ice-cream. These are pure Israeli tastes, so different to the average Middle Eastern restaurant, as is the elevated service from waiters who look after their guests from za'atar to halva.

Dine early to avoid the inevitable Tel Aviv party atmosphere

Open	B Sat–Sun; L Tue–Sun; D Tue–Sat
Price	$$
Cards	AE MC V eftpos
Chef	Michael Rantissi
Features	Licensed, outdoor seating, wheelchair access
Website	keposandco.com.au

Kepos St Kitchen

REDFERN
96 Kepos Street
02 9319 3919

citi   MIDDLE EASTERN   **15/20**

The corner store we wish was on our corner

KSK may offer breakfast and lunch, and be housed in an unpretentious corner setting but don't let that stop you frocking up for a dinner visit to Kepos. In fact, adding a dash of panache to your threads means you'll fit right in, or at the very least hold your own with the handsomely dressed staff. The plates, unsurprisingly, are similarly styling. Crisp-shelled falafels are so picturesque they could accompany the encyclopedia definition of the dish, and looks don't deceive. A pot of blush pink chicken liver pâté is housed under a roof of sweet pomegranate jelly, generously sized and perfect in its simplicity with charred bread and fresh figs. Quail is another hit, bursting with fragrant Iranian rice, scents of nutmeg and fresh parsley giving way to tender, juicy bites of perfectly pink bird. It's confident, comforting food and worth finishing with knafeh, its crisp top giving way to salty-sweet cheese and syrup so moreish that you'll want to drink it straight.

If the weather plays nice, try and score an outside seat for a bit more elbow room

Open	B L Daily; D Wed–Sat
Price	$$
Cards	AE MC V eftpos
Chef	Michael Rantissi
Features	Licensed, outdoor seating, private dining, wheelchair access
Website	keposstkitchen.com.au

Khao Pla

CHATSWOOD
Shop 7, 370 Victoria Avenue
(entry via Anderson Street)
02 9412 4978

THAI   **14/20**

The best (and spiciest) reason to visit a Westfield shopping centre

It's been a big year for head chef Pla Rojratanavichai, who just opened his second Khao Pla inside Macquarie Shopping Centre and began renovations at his Chatswood location, expanding to fit even more diners desperate to chow down on some of Sydney's most fun Thai food. The sweet and sour tamarind pork ribs are the stuff of legend – crisp, fatty and perfect with a beer on the side (or something from the organic wine and sake list that'll be added once renovations are done), and there's some serious heat coming from the wok section, like the fried pork belly with chinese broccoli and scud chillies. A salad of shredded chicken and grapefruit provides a quick escape from the spice before your inevitable return. Service is fun and frantic, the mix of families and first dates only adding to the atmosphere of the best place to go in Chatswood for a great night out.

The black sticky rice is a must order, if only for that scoop of Thai milk tea ice-cream

Open	L D Daily
Price	$
Cards	MC V eftpos
Chef	Pla Rojratanavichai
Features	Licensed, outdoor seating, private dining, wheelchair access, BYO

Kid Kyoto

SYDNEY
17–19 Bridge Street (entry via Bridge Lane)
02 9241 1991

JAPANESE   **14/20**

Japanese gets a retro remix at this high-concept rock 'n' roll izakaya

Down the alley near the ever-packed Mr Wong, this quirky izakaya is inspired by alternative '90s music. No joke. That means Nirvana is on high rotation, 'Smells Like Mixed Spirits' is a section of the menu, and a neon sign shines 'Come As You Are' across the industrial concrete room. On the whole, the food lives up to the gimmick, with creative dishes offering big flavours in stylish ways. A glass lid is lifted from a plate of Japanese peppered salmon in a pool of smashed wasabi peas, filling the air with perfumed smoke. Chicken tsukune patties arrive with a just-set onsen egg in a 'bird's nest' of crisp onions. Crunchy Japanese fried rice is charged with bone marrow and kimchi, perfect for scoffing alongside a herb-loaded bowl of Cloudy Bay clams in viscous broth. Desserts are more mainstream, the salty sweet fondant cake with caramelised miso proving a fittingly rich encore. It's a very now mix of recent nostalgia and 'grammable food that never takes itself too seriously.

The lunchtime Punk Drunk bento box ($35) features the greatest hits of the menu

Open	L Mon–Fri; D Mon–Sat
Price	$$
Cards	AE MC V eftpos
Chef	Justin Lee
Features	Bar, licensed, private dining, wheelchair access
Website	kidkyoto.com.au

KID KYOTO

Kindred

DARLINGTON
137 Cleveland Street
02 8937 0530

ITALIAN   **14.5/20**

The neighbourhood local you wish you had

Order the carrot triangoli. Trust us. And get a serve of the house-made sourdough, too. The puree of carrot – roasted to a deep sweetness – inside each triangular raviolo is impressive but the burnt butter sauce is amazing. Soak up that deep, nutty richness with crusty bread and thank us later. With a fine-tuned menu, friendly staff and a sense of cosy intimacy in this converted Irish restaurant (it was called Mulligan's, and they employed their own after-dinner fortune teller as part of the experience) we can see why this tiny corner restaurant is busy every night. Owner chef Matt Pollock (ex-A Tavola) proves a deft hand with pasta, all house-made. Grilled eggplant and fresh mozzarella lace parsley reginette, a wide ribbon pasta with frilly edges. Bucatini strands are smothered in a rich and spicy tomato sauce fortified with cured pork jowl. It's not all pasta. Take your pick from flank steak, market fish and a good selection of salads. Meringue with fresh cream, lemon curd and mango sorbet provides the perfect finish.

Coeliacs rejoice – house-made gluten-free pastas are available

Open	L D Tue–Sat
Price	$$
Cards	MC V eftpos
Chef	Matt Pollock, Gus Santosa
Features	Licensed
Website	kindredrestaurant.com.au

Lankan Filling Station

EAST SYDNEY
58 Riley Street
02 8542 9936

SRI LANKAN   **15/20**

Sri Lankan home cooking for the here and now

The tables are set with fork, spoon and pencil. But really, you only need the pencil for the fiendish tick-the-box menu. This is food to eat with your hands, tearing off bits of crisp-edged hopper to dip in curries and load with fiery sambols. After two years of market stalls and pop-ups, O Tama Carey's hoppers (bowl-shaped pancakes made from fermented rice flour and coconut) at last have a home – a bunker-chic space of polished concrete and dark wood lined with spice jars. Go for a set of one plain and one egg hopper and load up on curries, perhaps a nicely judged mild snapper curry or a hot-but-not-too-hot chicken curry with flavour to burn. String hoppers – lacy little nests of steamed noodles – come with sambol and kiri hodi, a gentle comforting gravy with a slurry of onion. It's a pleasure to deep-dive into jaggery or a coconut sorbet after the spicy warmth of Sri Lankan home cooking at this sweet and super-casual spot.

When in doubt, go for the $60 a head banquet menu

Open	L Tue–Sun; D Tue–Sat
Price	$$
Cards	AE MC V eftpos
Chef	O Tama Carey, Jemma Whiteman
Features	Bar, licensed
Website	lankanfillingstation.com.au

La Rosa The Strand

SYDNEY
Level 2, The Strand Arcade,
133/193 Pitt Street
02 9223 1674

ITALIAN   **14/20**

A haven for classic Italian dishes hiding amid the glitz of the Strand

It may be buried in the CBD but somehow the ambience of this trattoria transports you well out of the harbour city to somewhere that feels decidedly more established. La Rosa's menu delivers all the big recognisable Italian hits: bruschetta, salumi, seafood, pasta, risotto, pizza and a Roman grill. The lasagne is glistening and meaty with clearly defined slabs of pork, veal, napped in a truffled chanterelle sauce. The bruschetta comes deconstructed, allowing you to assemble the dish yourself and recognise just how how good lightly pickled fennel can be. Similarly, the DIY tiramisu arrives in separate shot glasses of espresso, marsala, silky mascarpone and an Italian lady-finger biscuit that is perfectly crisp on the outside and fluffy on the inside. Having all the elements to taste individually reminds you of how genius the balance of this classic Italian dessert is. And at the end of the day, that's what La Rosa is all about – respecting the classics.

The bruschetta is a must-order

Open	L D Mon–Sat
Price	$$
Cards	AE DC MC V eftpos
Chef	Joseph Giuffre, Pablo Tordesilles, Nino Zoccali
Features	Licensed, private dining, wheelchair access
Website	larosathestrand.com.au

Long Chim

SYDNEY
Corner Pitt Street and Angel Place
02 9223 7999

THAI   **14.5/20**

A temple of smashable Thai street eats

If your super smiley waitperson says, "Don't even look at this part of the menu, it's Thai-hot," your response falls in either of two camps: mouth starts watering or body tenses in fight-or-flight. Those in the latter camp can (slightly) settle knowing that the (well-intentioned) warning is overdone. It's really only the Chiang Mai chicken larp that is eye-wincingly hot. Go for the minced duck larp, smoky with roasted chillies and rice, instead. The hot and sour seafood soup is a jab to the mouth, fragrant with turmeric and galangal. The fall-off-the-bone lamb ribs, dry-crusted with cumin and coconut cream, rips with flavour, while the mashed prawn curry is the final sucker punch – a rich Southern coconut milk curry exploding with kaffir lime and krachai (wild ginger). The tapioca pudding, steamed in banana leaves with slivers of fresh young coconut, is a refreshing textural delight. Though the servers may be hard to flag down in the cavernous space, they're swift of foot and have a big Bangkok heart.

Well-crafted cocktails go head-to-head with the heat

Open	L Mon–Fri; D Mon–Sat
Price	$$
Cards	AE MC V eftpos
Chef	David Thompson, Meena Throngkumpola
Features	Bar, licensed, private dining, wheelchair access
Website	longchimsydney.com

Longrain

SURRY HILLS
85 Commonwealth Street
02 9280 2888

THAI **14/20**

A Surry Hills stalwart serving mod-Asian comfort food

While some newcomers on the Sydney mod-Thai scene trade on a more raucous approach to menu and venue styling, this stalwart has the comfort market cornered. Built for all comers – parents keeping their kids fed and watered, first dates and the midweek work crowd – there's something to be said for the broader approach. Longrain's signature betel leaves deliver sour, sweet, fresh hits – a mild punch if you don't want nuclear-grade snacking. Tender stir-fried squid, scored finely, hits that Thai trinity of salty, hot and sweet with welcome freshness thanks to basil and snake beans. Northern Thai lamb curry offers more of that comfort – deep and rich, it's at the milder end of the spectrum – the meat shreds at the pull of a fork, the fat cut with pickled garlic and fresh ginger. Longrain isn't for those with a hardcore, even sadistic attitude to heat, but is for those who want the hum of a communal table and and a familiar comfort.

A limited by-the-glass wine list – by the bottle works for those looking for something beyond dependable or predictable

Open	L Fri D Daily
Price	$$
Cards	AE DC MC V eftpos
Chef	Griff Pamment
Features	Licensed, private dining, wheelchair access, BYO
Website	longrain.com/sydney

LP's Quality Meats

CHIPPENDALE
12–16 Chippen Street
02 8399 0929

CONTEMPORARY **15/20**

If there was ever time to bust out a Canadian tuxedo, this would be it

Not everyone can pull off double denim, but at Luke Powell's North American-style diner, everyone can pull off a delicious dinner. It's a menu that, while meat-centric (want to order a kilo T-bone steak? You can), lends itself to some serious vegetarian scope. Check out that eggplant parmigiana with its crumbed, golden edges peeking out under a light sugo. We'll leave it to you to fight over who splits open the entire knot of burrata resting on top. There's corn on the cob, slick with what tastes like butter sweetened with smoked maple syrup. And while roast pumpkin lacks a little oomph (the concentrated flavour you might get from roasting it in small pieces is lost when delivered as a giant hunk), the signature smoked-then-fried chicken (yes! meat!) is as juicy as ever. And sure, you could finish with the Quebecois glory that is the pouding chomeur but the lightness and elegance of a perfect, unadorned creme caramel is just as bon.

Love that chicken, but can't dine in? Call ahead, and it's available to take away

Open	D Tue–Sat
Price	$$
Cards	MC V eftpos
Chef	Luke Powell, Shannon Debreceny
Features	Bar, licensed, wheelchair access
Website	lpsqualitymeats.com

Lucio's

PADDINGTON
47 Windsor Street
02 9380 5996

ITALIAN   **16/20**

The art of hospitality is alive and well and living in Paddington

Lucio's is a true family restaurant, run by Lucio and Sally Galletto for an awe-inspiring 35 years. And now, son Matteo and daughter Michela have joined as restaurant managers. But there's another family as well, of regular diners – including a busload of famed Australian artists (Olsen, Shead, Storrier etc) whose work features in the restaurant's dazzling art collection. Family favourites such as the long-serving salt-baked snapper, green tagliolini with crab in a homey tomato sugo, and the dramatic black handkerchief pasta with seafood never leave the menu. If you're going to stray, however, try the magnificent Codesa Cantabrian anchovies with bruschetta and tomato butter or the spirograph of finely sliced, rosy-red beef carpaccio with cured egg yolk and hot chilli. Chef George Kohler turns slow-cooked lamb neck with buttermilk and garlic emulsion into comfort food with a pile of barberry-studded grains. And yes, of course you can over-indulge in the cone-shaped cassata ice-cream studded with candied fruit. You're family, after all.

Chat up sommelier Dirk Bromley for his instinctive food and wine matching skills

Open	L D Tue–Sat
Price	$$$
Cards	AE DC MC V eftpos
Chef	George Kohler
Features	Licensed, private dining
Website	lucios.com.au

Luke's Kitchen

WATERLOO
8 Danks Street
02 9002 5346

CONTEMPORARY   **14/20**

Warehouse chic gets a Luke Mangan makeover

Luke Mangan is everywhere. He's on ships (P&O), planes (Virgin), in hotels (Hilton Sydney), at the airport (Chicken Confidential), and in Singapore and Tokyo (Salt Grill). Now, he's in Waterloo, handing out Iggy's bread and chatting to locals at his recently landed restaurant and event space. The former pop-uppish Mojo Bar now has added comfort, soft lighting, flowers, and a menu designed to please. There's everything from high-end seafood to a comfort-zone truffled cheese toastie, with truffled mushroom paste, mozzarella, cheddar and truffled pecorino, the lot topped with soft-poached duck egg. WA marron with a red wine and shallot butter and frazzled figs shows serious intent, and the signature dish sees Inglewood chicken breast filled with a mousse-like farce, then pan-roasted. Part of the fun is the tableside trolley service – especially a with-the-works Rocky Road dessert, which is a bit like eating all the showbags at the Royal Easter Show. Not that there's anything wrong with that.

It's a good spot for an eggy weekend brunch – especially with bloody marys made tableside

Open	B L Sat–Sun; D Wed–Sat
Price	$$
Cards	AE DC MC V eftpos
Chef	Luke Mangan, Matt Leighton
Features	Bar, licensed, private dining, wheelchair access
Website	lukeskitchen.com.au

LUCIO'S

LuMi Dining

PYRMONT
56 Pirrama Road
02 9571 1999

CONTEMPORARY   **17.5/20**

Is this the best-value degustation dinner in Sydney?

Since opening in 2014, this luminous glass box of a restaurant on a Pyrmont pier has evolved from One To Watch into One Not To Miss. Federico Zanellato's fusing of Italian and Japanese flavours is as precise, creative and transformative as those whose degustations are twice the price.
The 'wow' moments come thick and fast – like the 'Italian gunkan' battleship sushi of Italian rice, milky stracciatella and fat, sweet lobes of sea urchin. Wow. A finger of impossibly tender wagyu karubi (from near the brisket) with shishito peppers. Wow. A crisp, delicate seaweed tart loaded with Moreton Bay bug, finger lime and karkalla. Double wow. Pasta here is always a thrill. This time, superfine agnolotti with a peppery cheese filling that is at once delicate and grandmotherly. Crisp meringue with blackcurrant and salted geranium ice-cream sustains the excitement right to the end. With its walk-in wine cellar and newly comfortable interior, LuMi is one of Sydney's most lively, polished and confident big nights out.

Book an early table so you can watch as the daylight outside fades and the nightlights inside take over

Mark and Vinny's Spaghetti and Spritz

SURRY HILLS
G08, 38–52 Waterloo Street
02 9007 7789

ITALIAN,   **14/20**

New York's Little Italy invades Surry Hills with a vegan twist

The shelves are lined with Campari and Aperol. Pink neon sings "Fly Me To the Moon", Little Italy's Sinatra and Dino are in the air. Mark Filippelli and Vince Pizzinga, two Aussie Italians who met up in LA, have hit the ground running at this cute, tall-ceilinged but still squeezy 45-seat spaghetti and spritz joint. Be prepared for blue tagliatelle (coloured with spirulina) and ruby red spaghettini (beetroot), and some wicked puns ('gnoc.gnoc.gnocchi on heaven's door'). There's a distinct vegan vibe that runs from a surprisingly satisfying caprese salad with soy mozzarella to zucchini flowers with smoked almond curd and romesco. Then there are hearty pork, veal and mortadella meatballs in rich tomato sugo, and rigorously al dente macaroni Calabrese with beef rib – carnivore-friendly islands in a meat-free sea. Throw in a 20-plus list of spritzes, and Mark + Vinny's has everything millennials require from a dining experience – clean eating options, lower alcohol drinks, 'gram-friendly, no preachy sermons, and a sense of fun.

Say yes to the comped, pre-batched, vermouth-based digestivo

Open	L Fri–Sun; D Wed–Sun
Price	$$$
Cards	AE MC V eftpos
Chef	Federico Zanellato
Features	Bar, licensed, wheelchair access
Website	lumidining.com

Open	L Fri; D Mon–Sat
Price	$$
Cards	AE MC V eftpos
Chef	Connie Billie
Features	Licensed, outdoor seating
Website	markandvinnys.com

Marta

RUSHCUTTERS BAY
30 McLachlan Avenue
02 9361 6641

citi 🍷

ITALIAN   **14.5/20**

A smart Roman diner offering bold flavours in easy surrounds

Once upon a time, this used to be a restaurant called Popolo, inspired by the flavours of the Basilicata and the wines of Sardinia, co-owned by restaurateurs Flavio Carnevale and Fabio Dore. It's now a Roman restaurant run solo by Carnevale (you'll find Dore at Balmain's One Ford Street), and it's here you'll order silky rounds of mortadella dressed with olive oil and crushed pistachios served with just-charred focaccia to make your own mortadella sambos. Or gnocchi fritti – little puffs of dough, fried until golden and covered in a mountain of pepper and pecorino. Maybe it'll be one of the daily specials (Sunday is lasagne day!), a midweek bowl of cacio e pepe. Or maybe you'll lay it all down and order a perfectly seasoned veal chop, burnished and finger-scorching, with a side order of bitter greens. For dessert, there's a sour cherry tart or just go for a regionally specific digestivo – Carnevale's importing the lion's share himself.

Go for Sunday brunch, Roman style

Matteo

DOUBLE BAY
29 Bay Street
02 9327 8015

🍷

ITALIAN   **14/20**

Excellent pizza hits this well-heeled Sydney 'burb

Double Bay is out in full feather tonight. It's Gucci as far as the eye can see. And where the Gucci stops, the Vuitton begins. All punctuated with a healthy dose of carelessly rumpled linen. The room reflects similar of soft comfort – outside on the deck, it's white cane and canvas. Inside, buttery caramel banquettes and tables weighed down with pizza from chef Orazio D'elia. Here, you'll find bases that are slightly charred, puffed and bubbly. The bufalina (think of it as the margherita's slightly richer, fancier cousin, topped with buffalo mozzarella, San Marzano tomatoes and basil) sits alongside a rich, salty and sweet mix of nduja, fior di latte, capsicum, black olives and caramelised onion. Abruzzese-style lamb skewers – tiny pieces of lamb, wood-fired and served with a cheek of lemon – make for a very good thinking snack. Gnocchi doused in an anchovy tinted silky broccoli sauce would actually be enough if you weren't into the pizza. But then, why else would you be at Matteo?

Drink a spritz at one of the outdoor tables and watch the human traffic

Open	B L Sun; D Tue–Sun
Price	$$
Cards	AE MC V eftpos
Chef	Claudio Barzano
Features	Bar, licensed, outdoor seating, wheelchair access
Website	marta.com.au

Open	L Fri–Sun; D Daily
Price	$$
Cards	AE MC V eftpos
Chef	Orazio D'elia
Features	Bar, licensed, outdoor seating
Website	matteosydney.com

Mekong

CHIPPENDALE
Level 2, 14 Kensington Street
02 9282 9079

citi

SOUTH-EAST ASIAN   **14/20**

A spicy south-east Asian taste tour

If you're dining at Mekong, you'd better have your bags packed. The menu metaphorically floats down the restaurant's namesake river. Thai and Vietnamese are the menu's hardest-working influences, but chef Tiw Rakarin has shrugged off the need to impress with old favourites and instead embraces Cambodia, Laos and Burma, offering up lesser known fare like the amok curry. Pipis and prawns star in this warm peppery seafood curry built on a zesty base of lemongrass and galangal that is native to Cambodia. The upstairs room is Thai villa-esque, with lush green walls and wooden light fixtures (although it is in desperate need of a dimmer). Sizzling seafood crepes perfectly set the restaurant's tone: lightly fried egg and sweet soy, loudly punctuated with plenty of chilli, fragrant herbs and a bit of crunch in the form of mung beans and coconut shards. The grilled pork neck salad rides high on fresh mint and red onion but is burn-your-gums spicy, as the two chilli menu marker (out of a possible three) hints. Hey, no one said travelling is easy.

Chef Rakarin teams up with Sydney breweries for monthly curry and craft beer degustations

Open	L Sat–Sun; D Daily
Price	$$
Cards	AE MC V eftpos
Chef	Tiw Rakarin
Features	Bar, licensed, wheelchair access
Website	mekong-restaurant.com.au

Momofuku Seiobo

PYRMONT
The Star, Level G, 80 Pyrmont Street
02 9657 9169

CONTEMPORARY   **18/20**

Gutsy flavours meet sharp technique at this Sydney star

Anyone who suggests you should sit anywhere but the bar at chef-restaurateur David Chang's Sydney outpost is huffing a little too hard on the restaurant's house-fermented chilli paste. That bar, which circles the open kitchen where head chef Paul Carmichael and his crack team work the pans, is the perfect vantage point to watch the show. Crisp cassava crackers are spread with pepper sauce butter sandwiching rich, silky lobes of cooling uni. There's a luxurious take on rice and beans – elevated comfort food inspired by Carmichael's Barbadian upbringing. Live marron wrestling each other in a cast-iron pot are brought over for a viewing before they're taken off to be grilled and smothered in chilli paste, served with a side of puffy coconut buns to make the most of the sweet, juicy remains. Bombastic flavour and messy fun with all the fine dining trimmings? Truly, this is a restaurant that thrives as a sum of its delicious parts.

The ever-changing bar menu is just as much (if not more) fun as the restaurant

Open	D Mon–Sat
Price	$$$
Cards	AE MC V eftpos
Chef	Paul Carmichael
Features	Bar, licensed, wheelchair access
Website	seiobo.momofuku.com

Monopole

POTTS POINT
71A Macleay Street
02 9360 4410

CONTEMPORARY   **16/20**

A wine-fuelled magnet for date-nighters, terroir lovers and Potts Points sophisticates

Sydney can never have enough versatile venues like Brent Savage and Nick Hildebrandt's slim-lined bar and restaurant featuring one of the most compelling wine lists in the country. Black-clad locals line the low-lit counter, snacking on house-cured charcuterie with a glass of something single-vineyard and delicious. You can join them for sardines on toast bolstered by lardo, and a chablis too, or settle into a banquette for the arresting flavours of Brent Savage's menu. An open kitchen sends out chubby prawns covered in brown-butter crumbs zapped with fruity yuzukoshu bisque, before hunks of fresh zucchini arrive invigorated by spiced yoghurt under a canopy of their own flowers and pea shoots. Dry-aged-then-roasted duck breast with grilled endive is elevated by a Sichuan pepper glaze, with blackcurrant jus providing sweetness. Sommelier Glen Goodwin leads a confident floor team happy to talk through the top-line cheese selection or praise the majesty of Chartreuse to finish. All class.

Half the space is always reserved for walk-ins should you be in the area

Open	L Sat–Sun; D Daily
Price	$$
Cards	AE MC V eftpos
Chef	Brent Savage, Chris Benedet
Features	Bar, licensed
Website	monopolesydney.com.au

Mr Wong

SYDNEY
3 Bridge Lane
02 9114 7317

CHINESE   **16/20**

Modern Cantonese in a slick, clubby setting

Roast duck fragrant with star-anise. Deep-fried ice-cream channelling Australian-Chinese bistros. Wok-fried XO mud crab and chilled chablis. Over two no-expense-spared levels of London nightclub via old Hong Kong, Mr Wong does a lot of things and it does them very well. Yum cha is a relaxing way to spend Saturday, with impeccable shumai cradling scallop and prawn, and pork xiao long bao barely containing its hot soup. Dinner calls for sharing large plates – the sweetness of char siu-style barbecued pork lacquered in honey is tempered by a side of spinach braised with garlic and chicken oil. Shandong-style Angus short rib is roasted until it's soft and submissive but still carries enough vigour to be held with chopsticks and swiped through a light chilli and soy dressing that lets the beef's natural flavour shine. Fried ice-cream is hard to go past, of course, but there's refined pleasure in a milky sponge cake enriched by yuzu cream and green tea anglaise.

A no-bookings policy for parties fewer than six on Friday and Saturday nights warrants a drink at Palmer and Co. nearby when you need to wait for a table

Open	B Sat–Sun; L D Daily
Price	$$
Cards	AE DC MC V eftpos
Chef	Dan Hong, Kohmingyuan Mingyuan
Features	Bar, licensed, private dining, wheelchair access
Website	merivale.com/venues/mrwong

Ms.G's

POTTS POINT
155 Victoria Street
02 9114 7342

ASIAN   **14.5/20**

Young, hip, boisterous house party with crushable Mod-Asian snacks

Culinary mash-ups live their best life here at Ms.G's. Case in point: cheeseburger spring roll. Exactly what it sounds like, down to the melty American cheese, mustard and pickles. It's a signature for good reason. The plates-without-borders approach means steak tartare gets funked up with fish paddy herb and fish sauce and served with prawn crackers, Filet-o-Fish is reinvented with a banh mi pickle boost, and fried chicken is by way of Bangkok with a spiced up sambal-cum-marie rose sauce. The in-your-face flavours are as loud as the Tupac soundtrack, and what could have been cheap dude food thrills in less expert hands are, instead, fight-to-the-last-bite kind of dishes executed with swag. The haphazard waitstaff in denim hotpants, assault-on-the-senses interiors and Contiki-crowd hangs may not be everyone's flavour, but the well-matched booze list and seasonal dig-in desserts sure are: bring on the kopi-o-ice cocktails and the yuzu cream and sago-filled cream puffs.

Book a sunset table for bubble-tea-style sundowners with a 'gram-worthy harbour view

Open	L Fri–Sun; D Daily
Price	$$
Cards	AE DC MC V eftpos
Chef	Dan Hong, Mat Swinhoe
Features	Licensed, bar
Website	merivale.com/venues/msgs

Nel.

SYDNEY
75 Wentworth Avenue
02 9212 2206

citi
CONTEMPORARY   **14/20**

High-wire cooking in a chic CBD basement

Eaten off a log lately? If you haven't – and you're keen – chef Nelly Robinson might be able to facilitate the experience at his swanky city bunker of high-octane, modernist cooking. Sorrel emulsion is blanketed by New Zealand venison, sliced carpaccio-style and honed by pickled riberries with toasted breadcrumbs for crunch. Served on a lacquered log (because, well, why not?), it's a balanced bit of easy-going fun, much like Robinson's barley flatbread hosting a garden party of pickled pumpkin, radish and coriander, sharpened with mahon cheese, jalapeno dust and a wild chive mayonnaise. Fold. Squish. Eat. Enjoy. Maremma free-range duck – dry-aged for two weeks, juniper-rubbed and smoked in hay – is strikingly plated with salsify root, oxalis and a beetroot sauce providing an earthy counterpart for the duck's perfectly rendered fat and crisp skin. Rich and fruity flavours finish the tasting menu with ethereal flakes of Daintree chocolate swathing creamy coffee, marsala and hazelnut crumble.

Keep an eye out for winter Sunday roast specials featuring Yorkshire puddings and a generous amount of gravy

Open	L Fri; D Tue–Sat
Price	$$
Cards	AE MC V eftpos
Chef	Nelly Robinson
Features	Bar, licensed, wheelchair access
Website	nelrestaurant.com.au

MEET, EAT, AND DRINK

WITH MARRIOTT INTERNATIONAL

It all began with a root beer stand in 1927. Founder J. Willard Marriott and his wife, Alice, got their young business off the ground by quenching people's thirst during Washington D.C.'s hot, muggy summers.

Good food and good service became a guiding principle for Hot Shoppes restaurants... and for Marriott International. It still is.

Explore our venues at MeetEatDrink.com.au

marriott.com.au

Nilgiri's

CREMORNE
Shop 3, 283 Military Road
02 9909 0063

INDIAN   **14.5/20**

Regional Indian classics given a very original spin

There's no doubt that Nilgiri's is a bit pricier than your local suburban Indian. But the moment the adraki murg tikka lands in front of you, it all makes sense. The level of care applied to this juicy ginger and palm sugar-laced chicken entree says everything about why Nilgiri's is beloved in the area. Chef and owner Ajoy Joshi was originally trained in Chennai and has set out to put his own spin on several regional classics. Nilgiri's signature dish, a braised and diced leg of lamb called gosht saag, has just the right amount of heat but never overwhelms the cocktail of fragrant spices and the structure of the meat itself. A side-plate of korma green beans (ordered in an attempt to be virtuous and healthy) tastes, well, virtuous and healthy. But no one will be talking green beans after the desserts arrive. The gulab ki kulfi is a rose-flavoured dome of ice-cream wreathed with pistachios, crunchy home-made honeycomb and cardamom seeds.

If the meal isn't enough, Nilgiri's also offers a range of cooking classes dedicated to regions and spices

Open	D Tue–Sun
Price	$$
Cards	AE DC MC V eftpos
Chef	Ajoy Joshi
Features	Licensed, private dining
Website	nilgiris.com.au

No.1 Bent Street

SYDNEY
1 Bent Street
02 9252 5550

CONTEMPORARY   **14/20**

A buzzy eatery with a focus on fresh ingredients and creative cooking

The casual ethos of Mike McEnearney's dining style translates well in this sleek CBD restaurant. A favourite with the lunchtime corporate crowd, at night No.1 Bent Street morphs into a youthful eatery with communal tables and bass-heavy music you'll need to raise your voice to talk over. Whether McEnearney has jumped on the 'designed to share' bandwagon or he's in the driver's seat whipping the horses (we think it's the latter), it's a blessing for anyone seeking a diverse feed. The menu is indeed diverse. Tender beef skirt tataki is seasoned with a citrus-salty ponzu and horseradish. A buttery collection of mushrooms and tofu makes such an authentic hot pot, you might look around for chopsticks. The words 'tiger's milk' might give you pause, but it's the fragrant coconut and lime liquid that cures the John Dory for a classic ceviche. There are nice service touches – the rich chicken liver pâté is scooped like gelato at the table – but a more formal approach to serving would refine the dining experience.

Sit near the back of the room to watch the theatre of the wood-fired oven

Open	L Mon–Fri; D Mon–Sat
Price	$$
Cards	AE MC V eftpos
Chef	Mike McEnearney, Jeffrey De Rome
Features	Bar, licensed, wheelchair access
Website	onebentstreet.com.au

Nomad

SURRY HILLS
16 Foster Street
02 9280 3395

MODERN AUSTRALIAN   **15/20**

A buzzy restaurant where the wood-fire rules

Ringside is where you want to sit – where you can feel the heat of the wood-fire oven and be among the hubbub of the open kitchen. The counter seats have the advantage of helping you pinpoint what to order from a menu that's jammed with dishes you'll want to order. Order the tinned anchovies served with house-made ricotta, pickled peppers and baguette. Oh, and a serve of the charred focaccia so you can slide it through the dollops of salty-sweet black garlic paste and the wedges of jersey yoghurt that comes with the grilled eggplant (get a half-serve if you're a small group). Throw in the empanadas – cute golden pastry parcels of smoked brisket that are served with a house-made chilli sauce – and the barbecue lamb. It's tender and given a lift by the accompanying pine nut agrodolce, adding a sweet/sour layer to the rich dish. Get your sommelier to suggest something from the well-curated wine list, and you're game, set and snack.

Like the wine? Join their wine club to get curated drops sent to you monthly

Open	L Wed–Sat; D Mon–Sat
Price	$$$
Cards	MC V eftpos
Chef	Jacqui Challinor
Features	Bar, licensed, private dining, wheelchair access
Website	nomadwine.com.au

Nour

SURRY HILLS
Shop 3, 490 Crown Street
02 9331 3413

citi

MIDDLE EASTERN   **14/20**

Vibrant Middle Eastern fine dining with a touch of glam

Don't come to Nour expecting stock-standard Lebanese fare like tabouli or kofta. While there are nods to classics – bright fattoush salad and hummus with za'atar smoked goat – you'll have more fun sharing their zanier Middle Eastern experiments. Charcoal octopus with harissa oil, olives and thin strips of fennel is modern art on a plate, but that tender tentacle is as delicious as it is pretty. Less successful is kingfish bastirma that's almost overpowered by grassy dill gazpacho. That crucial balance of style and substance is better in larger dishes – you taste every melting minute of effort in a sous-vide lamb shoulder finished in a wood oven. Chunks of roast chook scattered with spicy sujuk sausage stuffing show that somewhere between the glitzy bar and pastel decor is a chef who knows how to mix traditional ideas with modern flair. The Lebanese bombe alaska might be made for Instagram, but its sour cherry heart is in the right place.

Vegans rejoice – they'll happy look after you on all menus with a bit of notice

Open	L Thu–Sat; D Tue–Sat
Price	$$
Cards	AE MC V eftpos
Chef	Roy Ner, Riyad Seewan
Features	Bar, licensed, outdoor seating, private dining, wheelchair access
Website	noursydney.com

Nu Bambu

HURLSTONE PARK
Canterbury-Hurlstone Park RSL,
20-26 Canterbury Road
02 9559 0088

MODERN ASIAN   **14.5/20**

Forget everything you thought you knew about RSL club restaurants

Grilled Champagne lobsters with confit sambal butter might not be your usual RSL club fare, but then, the Paul Kelly-designed Nu Bambu is not your usual RSL club restaurant. A steamy, open kitchen runs down one side of the room, while an eye-catching 10-metre silk sculpture floats overhead. Former Longrain chef Freddie Salim has installed a pan-Asian menu running from a handful of different steamed buns to a rich, red curry of Cape Grim brisket with wild ginger. Those Champagne lobsters are split and grilled over coconut charcoal to spectacular effect, while a dramatic free-standing, deep-fried snapper makes great pickings of crunchy skin and soft giving flesh. Spectacular sorbets are on show, too, when it comes to a restrained dessert of three smooth whorls of charcoal coconut, mango lychee and a sharp yuzu passionfruit. Nu Bambu could have been a step too far, had it been fancier and more formal, but the clever menu manages to please both the crowd and the connoisseurs.

Take ID so you can sign in as temporary member of the club

Open	L Fri–Sun; D Daily
Price	$$
Cards	AE DC MC V eftpos
Chef	Freddie Salim
Features	Bar, licensed, wheelchair access
Website	nubambu.com.au

O Bar and Dining

SYDNEY
Level 47, Australia Square,
264 George Street
02 9247 9777

CONTEMPORARY   **14/20**

Dress-circle views for a special night out

Position, position, position. O Bar certainly satisfies this holy trinity on its 47th floor eyrie, slowly revolving as day becomes night. Fifty-one years after opening, the Sydney Tower still lords it over much of the changing cityscape. Couples, tourists and special occasion diners in dimly lit, tiered seating recline with cocktails as the floor show of the Harbour Bridge and Opera House moves by. It's a hell of a view. The menu has a focus on the healthy eating philosophy of its owner, chef Michael Moore. King salmon is glazed and torched, its richness offset by crisp radish, puffed rice, tatsoi, white miso and smoked soy. Pork cheeks are lean, if firm, with blanched fennel and pickled koshu. Yearling lamb rump on a slick of caramelised cashews needs more green leaves to make it a meal, despite its grilled eggplant slice and just-balanced acid-forward jus. Peanut curd, black sesame sponge, banana miso, scorched meringue dessert triumphs.

Enjoy the same view from the bar, with seasonal cocktails and well-priced bar food

Open	L Fri; D Daily
Price	$$$
Cards	AE DC MC V eftpos
Chef	Michael Moore, Darren Templeman
Features	Bar, licensed, private dining, wheelchair access
Website	obardining.com.au

Olio

CHIPPENDALE

Level 2, The Old Rum Store,
2-10 Kensington Street
02 9281 1500

ITALIAN **14/20**

Sicilian fare that marries the traditional with a modern twist

Does anybody do free bread baskets anymore? Olio does, a carb-loaded welcome of sourdough, focaccia and pane carasau flatbread with as much olive oil – from Chef Lino's family farm in Sicily – as you like. Then the complimentary amuse bouche arrives. All this before you've even put a fork into your entree. It's an incredible level of generosity, supporting a menu of Sicilian classics like arancini and bucatini with sardines and raisins. Things get a little fancier with the calamari, char-grilled until smoky and served with fine shavings of fennel and charred corn that are arranged around the edge of the plate. House-made squid ink tonnarelli (a square-edged spaghetti enriched with egg) provides a dramatic contrast to chunks of sweet Queensland spanner crab and spiced 'nduja (decidedly Calabrian rather than Sicilian but delicious all the same). Desserts range from the timeless tiramisu and cannoli to a walk on the wild side with a semolina parmesan cheesecake with toasted rice gelato.

Ask for a table by the window for maximum privacy

Open	L Fri–Sat; D Mon–Sat
Price	$$
Cards	AE MC V eftpos
Chef	Lino Sauro
Features	Licensed, outdoor seating, private dining, wheelchair access
Website	olio.kensingtonstreet.com.au

One Ford Street

BALMAIN

1 Ford Street
02 9818 4232

ITALIAN **14.5/20**

A little bit of sun-kissed southern Italy hidden behind a pub

Unless you get lost on the way to the bathroom and end up in the gaming lounge, there's no way you would know this charming trattoria is attached to an otherwise unremarkable pub. Heck, you wouldn't even know you're in Balmain. A secluded courtyard with just the right amount of sun sneaking through the foliage is made for lazy weekend lunches of house-made pasta and super fresh produce. Tomato, basil, cucumber and stracciatella shine in a panzanella sharpened with pickled red onion, and twists of casarecce are engineered to ferry the long flavours of pork and fennel sausage ragu. Rosy pink swordfish is perfectly pitched with oregano and the sweetness of bullhorn pepper while the kitchen's Sardinian love is showcased in toasty fregola brimming with calamari, cuttlefish, prawns and clams. Attentive Italian staff are always ready to fill your glass and extra kudos to a wine list full of organic and native grapes from The Boot.

The $70 set menu is great value for celebrations with the whole famiglia

Open	L Fri–Sun; D Wed–Sat
Price	$$
Cards	AE MC V eftpos
Chef	Stefano Gaspa
Features	Bar, licensed, outdoor seating, private dining
Website	onefordstreet.com.au

One Penny Red

SUMMER HILL
2 Moonbie Street
02 9797 8118

CONTEMPORARY   **14.5/20**

A favourite neighbourhood haunt that raised Summer Hill's dining game

One Penny Red is so beloved among locals, a weekend booking made late might land you upstairs in a compact antechamber to Vernon's Bar. Don't worry. Stellar service – knowledgeable, anticipatory – will have you feeling as special as those eating in the open dining room downstairs. The wine and food are as good as the people who serve them. Start with raw yellowfin tuna served with explosively tart cubes of kanzi apple jelly. Some dishes are downright exciting such as the crisp-skinned barramundi with pipis and delicate crab broth. Others like the hearty lamb shoulder perform as expected: belly-filling. The modern menu is in contrast with the setting, a grand columned post office building that's been part of the neighbourhood since 1900. Not quite as long-lived but just as lovely are the beignets, soft doughnuts filled with salted caramel and banana. They've been on the menu since One Penny Red opened and should never be refused.

If you think you can do better than the sommelier, the last Tuesday of every month is BYO

Open	L Wed–Sun; D Daily
Price	$$
Cards	AE MC V eftpos
Chef	R.J. Lines
Features	Bar, licensed, outdoor seating, private dining, wheelchair access
Website	onepennyred.com.au

Ormeggio at the Spit

MOSMAN
D'Albora Marinas, Spit Road
02 9969 4088

MODERN ITALIAN   **17/20**

Modern Italian dining with views custom made for long lunching

One of the Restaurants Most Likely is in one of the Most Unlikely locations, hidden out the back of a boat shop, jutting off a marina. But therein lies its charm. Chefs Alessandro Pavoni and Victor Moya combine their strengths to create a series of menus that are at times reserved, but never shy. A tender, raw mussel arrives on a bed of seaweed, topped with the tiniest dice of sweet pickled vegetables. A perfect pasta button filled with liquid parmigiano reggiano and garnished with a sliver of fresh truffle explodes on impact like an umami bomb, set to stun. The cooking here is assured, balanced, and smart from the lightly acidic kingfish crudo to the rich, salty wallop of a piece of char-grilled wagyu licked with fermented garlic. The menu add-ons of 'premium' wine matches, extra snacks and supplements don't feel too hospitable but the wine service is truly outstanding. Settle in for lunch, and stay for sunset.

Window seat an absolute must? You can request one for an extra $20 per head

Open	L D Thu–Sun; D Wed
Price	$$$
Cards	AE MC V eftpos
Chef	Alessandro Pavoni, Victor Moya
Features	Licensed, outdoor seating, wheelchair access
Website	ormeggio.com.au

Oscillate Wildly

NEWTOWN
275 Australia Street
02 9517 4700

CONTEMPORARY **16/20**

A progressive fine diner with the heart of a neighbourhood bistro

This pocket-sized Newtown jewel keeps on kicking goals. Under chef-restaurateur Karl Firla (ex-Est), the menu reaches new heights of pared-back elegance. There's the welcome snack of a miniature caesar salad. House-made sourdough, malty and chewy with a burnished crust, comes with a little pot of whipped, rendered pork fat in place of butter. An avocado cheek is simply sliced to fall in waves and dressed with finger lime caviar. There are lots of tricks on show here, but they tend to be for the eye, not for the tongue. Food here is genuinely delicious, with a firm grounding in great produce treated with care. There are missteps, sure (wine pairings don't always hit the mark, and why does a dish of ocean trout roe, carrot puree and marigold leaves taste like raw cake batter?) but who can argue with pieces of raw scampi tail and thin shavings of butternut pumpkin gently poached in a perfect lobster bisque? No one.

Split a wine pairing if you'd like to taste everything without rolling out the door

Osteria di Russo and Russo

ENMORE
158 Enmore Road
02 8068 5202

ITALIAN **14.5/20**

Modern Italian cooking that's not afraid to step outside the box

This Enmore Road tratt delivers a menu that's experimental, surprising, but assured – a fine line to tread, but one it does successfully. Dishes combine owner Marc Russo's Italian heritage and Australian native bush ingredients with great success. Creamy burrata is married with crunchy amaranth and the tartness of quandong. A silken tri-tip steak is brought to life by a busty anchovy sauce and char-grilled Victorian alpine trout is finished with lemon myrtle and nashi pear-textured riberries. If the menu is a fusion of Italian and Australian, the wine list is the opposite. It's almost all Boot, and covers the length and breadth of regions from Veneto to Campania. The service is skilful and attentive, but it's a lucky night if you get the affable, funny owner as your waiter. The restaurant is truly a family affair. Russo senior, Pino, is co-owner and among framed images of the old country, baby photos of Russo junior hang on the wall. Aw, bless.

The 'ultra bene' degustation with matched wines is excellent value

Open	D Tue–Sat
Price	$$$
Cards	AE MC V eftpos
Chef	Karl Firla
Features	Licensed, private dining, wheelchair access
Website	oscillatewildly.com.au

Open	D Tue–Sun
Price	$$
Cards	AE MC V eftpos
Chef	Arkin Barretto
Features	Bar, licensed, private dining, BYO
Website	russoandrusso.net.au

Otto Ristorante

WOOLLOOMOOLOO
Area 8, 6 Cowper Wharf Road
02 9368 7488

citi 🍷

ITALIAN   **15.5/20**

Sydney's hottest-property harbourside Italian, hands down

Otto is all about the magic of the long, water-fringed Finger Wharf, the sunshine (and sunset), the well-heeled people and the rich and glossy food, fresh from the wood-fired grill. It's very Italian, from the soft white-peppery mortadella with pickles and peppers, to the golden zucchini flowers filled with ricotta and pecorino. But it's also very Australian, with its Sydney rock oysters, Mooloolaba swordfish and wood-grilled eastern rock lobster – not to mention the sulphur-crested cockatoos wheeling overhead. Chef Richard Ptacnik knows just how to spruce up a twirl of bucatini in fresh, light, tomatoey juices with a tumble of sweet Moreton Bay bug meat or a mighty 300-gram black Angus scotch fillet with giant onion rings and bone marrow butter. His desserts are now show-stoppers, like a polished creation of lemon meringue and citrusy sudachi sorbet. Otto has always been a big night out for Sydney, but right now, there's a little more magic in the mix.

Get there in time for sunset drinks and watch the city skyline fade to black

The Paddington

PADDINGTON
384 Oxford Street
02 9114 7329

🍷

CONTEMPORARY   **14.5/20**

Rotisserie chicken and rollicking good times in a reimagined pub

Chicken rules the roost at Merivale's jumping Paddo pub – roasting on the custom-built rotisseries, stuffed into brioche buns with jalapeno dressing, and turned into spring rolls to have with a drink. Even your glass is etched with a rather fetching chook. That doesn't mean the lamb chops are not worthy, as three thick chops of fine flavour and solid bite get chummy with a nutty romesco and warm, fruity peppers; nor the plate-sized barramundi with its characteristic soft flesh, roasted whole with fennel and sweet confit lemon. Warning: the crab tartine has shrunk to a canape (save up for the one at The Centennial up the road instead). The elbow-to-elbow tables run from after-school family teas to girls' nights out – all tucking in to Ben Greeno's Bannockburn roast chicken, cos salad and fries. There's no chicken on the dessert menu, so you'll just have to have a sweet little preserved cherry and cream cheese tartlet with cherry sorbet instead. No hardship.

Hit The Chicken Shop next door for take-home roast chicken and chips

Open	L D Daily
Price	$$$
Cards	AE DC MC V eftpos
Chef	Richard Ptacnik
Features	Bar, licensed, outdoor seating, private dining, wheelchair access
Website	ottoristorante.com.au

Open	L D Daily
Price	$$
Cards	AE DC MC V eftpos
Chef	Ben Greeno
Features	Bar, licensed, private dining, wheelchair access
Website	merivale.com.au/thepaddington

Paddo Inn Dining Room

PADDINGTON
338 Oxford Street
02 9380 5913

PUB DINING · **14/20**

Honest, pared-back cooking in stylish pub surrounds

There's nothing pubby about this dining room, in a very Paddington pub kind of way. Much like the unofficial Local's Code to Getting Dressed (weekend linen and boat shoes), the smart backspace at the Paddo Inn touts a very deliberate brand of elegant casual. The menu follows suit with a blend of bistro classics and pub staples, tweaked to match the digs. Salt-and-pepper squid receives a Mediterranean makeover with pickled red peppers, radicchio and kalamata olives, while tuna tartare is reworked with a bloody mary inspired twist. 'Less is more' is the attitude from the grill, letting high quality produce speak for itself. Jack's Creek sirloin is grilled on the bone and served with nothing but lemon and a chunk of cos lettuce. Confronting simplicity seems part of the shtick, but it works. Young staff are learning the ropes and portion size is slightly askew at times, but in the end, a pub lunch doesn't get much better than this.

Great for groups, the private dining room is a stunner

Open	L Fri–Sun; D Daily
Price	$$
Cards	AE DC MC V eftpos
Chef	Mark Holland
Features	Bar, licensed, private dining, wheelchair access
Website	paddoinn.com.au

Paper Bird

POTTS POINT
46a Macleay St
02 9326 9399

MODERN ASIAN · **15/20**

East Asian eats with a less-is-more approach to all-day dining.

There's a quiet creativity flowing from the kitchen team, riffing on flavours from Korea, China and Japan with a thoroughly modern, restrained touch. Don't be put off by unfamiliar food words (the switched-on waitstaff have their fave recommendations) or unheard-of varietals on the tightly edited wine list (co-owner Ned Brooks has got your back). Order whatever bap (a Korean rice bowl) is on, perhaps soy-cured abalone with nori or a toasted rice dolsot (hot stone) bibimbap with clams and iceberg. And anything doughy, like the bulgolgi pork and zucchini tart (it's sweet and salty, with just a small breath of burnt chilli), or the shallot and shiitake fried pancake, a crisp, pull-apart treasure. And look the elephant in this big jade-green basement bunker in the eye and just order the fabled shrimp-brined fried chicken, with its Jurassic-crumb coating gleaning with salty maple soy syrup. You may as well go all out and order the signature cloud-like Japanese cheesecake, too.

Run to brunch for miso caramel peanut shortbread, pandan lamingtons, black sesame-wattleseed cookies

Open	B L Sat–Sun; D Mon–Sat
Price	$$
Cards	AE MC V eftpos
Chef	Eun Hee An, Ben Sears
Features	Licensed, outdoor seating, wheelchair access, BYO
Website	paperbirdrestaurant.com

Pheast

WAVERLEY
302 Bronte Road
02 9387 6020

CONTEMPORARY   **14.5/20**

Globally inspired cuisine that's well worth coming home for

In life, as in love, it's the little things that matter. The mint-on-the-pillow moments that linger long after all else fades. Pheast is forged on such small flourishes. Chef Amanda Gale's unassuming bolthole is a personal affair. Black-and-white botanical sketches on the wall are copies of prints she picked up in Provence. The 'chocolate nemesis' flourless chocolate cake – that River Cafe classic – is a call-back to her weakness for bitter-sweet treats. Pheast's eclectic menu speaks to Gale's 16 years' spent living and working overseas, from the back hills of Bhutan to the streets of LA. Crunchy zucchini blossoms coated in spiced flour look for all the world like a serve of fries in a Californian diner. Lush spiced eggplant with nutty farro salad taps its hat to the Middle East. Rose-pink slivers of pickled onions and radishes atop smoky lamb cutlets might just be the prettiest darn things you'll see. On such modest moments are great meals made.

Give your liver a break and order a sweet and spry elderflower spritz

Open	D Tue–Sat
Price	$$
Cards	MC V eftpos
Chef	Amanda Gale
Features	Licensed
Website	pheast.com.au

Pilu at Freshwater

FRESHWATER
End of Moore Road
02 9938 3331

ITALIAN   **16.5/20**

Beachside dining with views all the way to Sardinia

"It's a gift," says Giovanni Pilu, of the views of sun, sea, sand and surf from the open window of his 'beach house' dining room. And it comes gift-wrapped, with an exciting and often dramatic three-course menu from Pilu and head chef Jason Saxby that explores the distinctive flavours of modern Sardinian cooking. Fat, saffron-stained spaghettoni is richly sauced with braised duck under a black olive crumb, an inky squiggle of licorice sauce highlighting the anise in the ragu. Little butterflies of roast capsicum farfalle perch among gently cooked mussels, spicy 'nduja and creamy stracchino. And while Melanda Park's roast suckling pig has its own long-term fan club, we think the handsome, crisp-skinned fillet of Cone Bay barramundi, rising from a smoky ham consomme amid crunchy coastal succulents, should have one, too. Engaging floor staff and an award-winning wine list with a seriously Sardinian accent add to the experience – as does the little drama-queen dessert of chestnut mousse, candied citrus and sweet pumpkin sorbet.

Availability of the famous roast suckling pig can be limited – get your order in fast

Open	L Tue–Sun; D Tue–Sat
Price	$$$
Cards	AE DC MC V eftpos
Chef	Giovanni Pilu, Jason Saxby
Features	Bar, licensed, outdoor seating, private dining
Website	pilu.com.au

Poly

SURRY HILLS
74-76 Commonwealth Street
02 8860 0808

CONTEMPORARY **15.5/20**

Ester gets a sister and Surry Hills gets a barstaurant

Is it a natural wine bar, a casual restaurant – or a barstaurant? Er, yes, probably. Mat Lindsay is the sort of quiet chef who just cooks what he likes, and ends up changing the world. He did it at chef-canteen Ester, and now he's done it again with this cool, semi-subterranean space in Surry Hills. The punk kitchen glows with grills (all coals, no gas) and the bold flavours are carried by buttery sauces, ferments and duck fat. Garlic bread is warm, puffy and stuffed with a green mulch of young garlic. Blood pie, heir apparent to Ester's renowned blood sausage sanga, is a tennis ball of earthy black pudding wrapped in dark, malty pastry – ridiculously good. A single king prawn is split, grilled, and slathered with buttery, cured duck egg yolk, and a genius Brillat-Savarin cheese course is all triple-cream squish and bitter orange marmalade under crisp witlof. Poly is whatever you like, really, as often as you like.

Drop in for a late-night cheese course and a drop of something interesting

Porteno

SURRY HILLS
50 Holt Street
02 8399 1440

ARGENTINIAN **16/20**

Old-school/new-school Argentinian grills with thrills

What a lovely restaurant this is. The six o'clock queues at the door may have gone, and there's less hysteria around getting a table, but Porteno now feels comfortable and settled in its tiled and bottle-lined Holt Street digs. Chefs Ben Milgate and Elvis Abrahanowicz are still very much on active grill duty, and hospitable bar staff vie with waist-coated co-owner and sommelier, Joseph Valore, to let you know what's new and exciting on the wine list. Porteno's much-loved crisp brussels sprouts and cauliflower gratin really hit the spot, but it's the meat you have signed up for, from a whole side of Berkshire pig stretched out over the firepit, to the meltingly tender barbecued wagyu skirt steak with its green roof of hand-chopped chimichurri. Calamari comes straight off the parilla with a lush green jalapeno sauce, and the coffee cream on the custardy, caramelly flan is enough to make you think you started at the wrong end of the menu. (You didn't.)

Pop in to their next door wine bar Wyno, for befores or afters

Open	L Sat-Sun; D Daily
Price	$$
Cards	AE MC V eftpos
Chef	Mat Lindsay, Isabelle Caulfield
Features	Bar, licensed, wheelchair access
Website	polysurryhills.com.au

Open	L Fri; D Tue-Sat
Price	$$$
Cards	AE MC V eftpos
Chef	Ben Milgate, Elvis Abrahanowicz
Features	Bar, licensed, private dining, wheelchair access
Website	porteno.com.au

Public Dining Room

MOSMAN
2A The Esplanade
02 9968 4880

citi

CONTEMPORARY   **14/20**

Relaxed and refreshing seaside haven, no matter the weather

Every day's a holiday by Balmoral Beach, where the water is always fine and even the poodles have Instagram accounts. If you've never needed a mortgage to pay for parking, you haven't lived. The Public Dining Room is a refreshing break from so much excess and activewear. The terrace deck feels like your favourite beach shack, with wood floors, bench seats, a salty sea dog's menu and the sun streaming through the branches of a Moreton Bay fig. The ocean's so close you can smell it. Opt for a light and lovely kingfish carpaccio with delicate yuzu dressing and smoked salmon roe, or a pretty little plate of char-grilled scampi with punchy lime and chilli butter and a delightfully simple salad of shaved baby fennel, eschalot and daikon. Crisp-skinned Cone Bay barramundi with spiced cucumber veloute and a rich and creamy brandade croquette is well worth lingering over. Moor the superyacht and step ashore for a perfectly pleasant lunch by the sea.

Bring the kids along to enjoy the impressive 'young adults' menu

Open	B Sat–Sun; L Daily; D Mon–Sat
Price	$$$
Cards	AE MC V eftpos
Chef	Joel Turpin
Features	Bar, licensed, outdoor seating, private dining, wheelchair access, BYO
Website	publicdiningroom.com.au

Quay

THE ROCKS
Overseas Passenger Terminal
02 9251 5600

citi

CONTEMPORARY   **19/20**

Soft punches land hard at the new-look Sydney all-star

Finally Peter Gilmore has a restaurant worthy of his food. Thanks to a multi-million dollar makeover, the jewel in the Fink Group's crown is unrecognisable as the restaurant that once was. The early thousands' nightclub decor has been turfed in favour of sleek, intimate spaces micro-managed by brigades of attentive floor staff, led by Jeremy Courmadias and Amanda Yallop. The six- or 10- course menu is a letter of intent from a viscous miso bagna cauda hiding under a bed of sweet raw heritage peas to a whole sand crab claw, shelled and gently poached in butter. An individual rockpool of hand-harvested seafood sees luscious scallops bed down with cockles and baby octopus tentacles finished with flecks of fermented seaweed and the pop of lotus seeds.And if eating a malted barley crumpet spread with butter hidden under a shower of shaved truffle while listening to Townes Van Zandt isn't the very definition of stupid, beautiful luxury, then we don't know what is.

Did we mention those baked goods are served in a custom-made Tasmanian timber crumpet tray? Yeah. They are

Open	L Fri–Sun; D Daily
Price	$$$
Cards	AE DC MC V eftpos
Chef	Peter Gilmore
Features	Licensed, private dining, wheelchair access
Website	quay.com.au

THE Store
BY FAIRFAX

THESTORE.COM.AU

Queen Chow

ENMORE
Level 1, 167 Enmore Road
02 9114 7333

CHINESE   **15/20**

A steamy Hong Kong hangout serving dumplings and dreams above an Enmore pub

Follow the stairs up the back of the old Queen Vic Hotel and discover a slinky speakeasy dishing nostalgic Cantonese to the real cool kids of the inner-west. The lush greenhouse terrace could star in a technicolour Wes Anderson movie, with sharp service and a spot-on drinks list adding to the party vibe. A tightly edited menu is all killer, no filler. Gorgeous dim sum platters of steamed or fried dumplings are non-negotiable – have your chopsticks at the ready, these will vanish fast. Graduate to share-centric dishes from glossy sang choy bau to tender slivers of salt and pepper squid or smoky, sweet pork ribs. Flavours are turned up to maximum volume to match the soundtrack, including fiery duck Hokkien noodles shot with dried chillies, perfect XO pipis or numbing, creamy chicken salad with plenty of Sichuan zing. Desserts recall the suburban lazy susan with retro fried ice-cream or an updated pavlova, but it's a long way from the daggy local pub Chinese.

A second QC location has opened at the old Papi Chulo site in Manly

Raita Noda Chef's Kitchen

SURRY HILLS
Suite 1, 222 Riley Street
02 8093 9807/0451 068 815

JAPANESE   **14/20**

Three hours of Zen kitchen with 10 courses of Japanese cuisine

It's omakase only here at chef Raita Noda's 10-seat restaurant, where he and his apprentice/son, Momotaro, execute a three-hour tasting menu. Sit at the counter and be enchanted by Momotaro's sweet service as Raita slices and dices with deft precision. Daily offerings from the fish market may include scampi mille feuille, fried compressed flesh forming crisp leaves with a hit of kaffir and finger lime aioli. Or a pristine sashimi collection encased in a dome of smoke. Tuna tartare continues to be cleverly served in a sealed tin, with an orb of mozzarella slightly dominated by the accompanying dehydrated soy sauce-roasted soybeans, as does a sensational Cajun-spiced soft shell crab taco – a hit for texture and flavour. Wagyu is roasted on salt with fried brussel sprout halves. Strawberry shortcake is a beautiful contrast of fresh and dried berries and mascarpone mousse.

Try the omakase beverage matching including wine, sake and green tea

Open	L Fri–Sun; D Daily
Price	$$
Cards	AE DC MC V eftpos
Chef	Patrick Friesen, Christopher Hogarth, Eric Koh
Features	Bar, licensed, wheelchair access
Website	merivale.com/venues/queenchow

Open	D Mon–Sat
Price	$$$
Cards	AE MC V eftpos
Chef	Raita Noda
Features	Licensed, wheelchair access
Website	raitanoda.com.au

ReccoLab

ROZELLE
Shop A4–A7, 120 Terry Street
02 9555 1706

ITALIAN   **14.5/20**

A carb and curd dreamland with regional Italian flare

Bakery, cafe, bar, restaurant. ReccoLab is the kind of all-day neighbourhood favourite that keeps the locals flocking in. They're all here for the focaccia col formaggio, a specialty from the small coastal city of Recco in northern Italy. Here, it's two ultra-thin, almost pastry-like layers of dough, filled with stracchino and blistered mercilessly at high heat. It comes out bubbling, molten and delicious. Be careful, finger burns await the impatient. There are also pizza, pasta, and other comfort food favourites. A muddle of warming eggplant parmigiana is the kind of ugly/delicious that goes a treat mopped up with the excellent house-baked breads adorning every table. But don't get too comfortable – you'll be kept on your toes with reworked classics like a caprese salad served, unexpectedly, with a vibrant tomato and basil emulsion. Every ounce of buffalo mozzarella is coated in the flavour of summer. Again, bread mopping is obligatory. One more, and it's a trend.

Still dreaming about the focaccia? You can get it to take away

Open	B L Wed-Sun; D Tue-Sun
Price	$$
Cards	AE DC MC V eftpos
Chef	Antonio Zambarelli, Alfredo Amendolare, Francesca Iacono, Jacopo Bosello
Features	Bar, licensed, outdoor seating, wheelchair access
Website	reccolab.com.au

Red Lantern

DARLINGHURST
60 Riley Street
02 9698 4355

VIETNAMESE   **14/20**

In a city that loves Vietnamese food, Red Lantern's star shines on

Don't forget that great Vietnamese food is tucked away at the dead end of Riley Street. Others haven't, and this buzzing French-colonial-inspired dining room is full on a weeknight, no doubt in part thanks to the immense charisma of restaurateur Luke Nguyen on our screens. But it's the food and service that determines repeat visits, not a Luke sighting. On that count, service is attentive when you've got someone's attention. 'Aunty 5's rice cakes' are delightful, though hidden under a heavy shroud of pork floss that may prove too much of a good thing. The banh xeo is crisp and fresh by comparison, the rice flour crepe filled with juicy tiger prawns and topped with generous handfuls of herbs. The sublime coconut and lemongrass curry that coats pan-fried mulloway demands extra rice – don't let anyone take that sauce away – and the special of grilled Jack's Creek sirloin with papaya salad is a reminder of why Sydney's modern Asian food is just so good.

Red Lily bar out the back has closed, now a fun private dining room instead

Open	L Fri; D Tue-Sun
Price	$$
Cards	AE DC MC V eftpos
Chef	Mark Jensen
Features	Bar, licensed, outdoor seating, private dining, wheelchair access
Website	redlantern.com.au

Regatta

ROSE BAY
594 New South Head Road
02 9327 6561

CONTEMPORARY   **14/20**

Pier-side dining among the superyachts

DJs and deckhands come and go, unloading equipment and cases of Champagne, while glamorous 20-somethings totter down the pier in stilettos to board boats the size of four-bedroom homes. Front-row seats like these are hard to find. Soak up the harbour views as the frivolities of yacht life unfold pier side. Damien Pignolet may have taken shore leave, but Lucio's veteran Logan Campbell is having no problems keeping things shipshape. With the water literally lapping up against the side of the dining room, ordering seafood seems natural. There's the house 'frutti di mare' for those on a superyacht budget, or go for lighter options like king crab and avocado salad, served with squid ink crisps and plated daintily, making for enjoyable DIY mixing destruction. Gigantic grilled Mooloolaba prawns highlight the quality of produce on offer, while market fish courses like perfectly grilled skate with Jerusalem artichoke and oyster mushroom offer an interesting alternative to some of the safer dishes on the menu.

Make a day out of it and catch the ferry – the wharf is conveniently close by

Open	L Tue–Sun; D Tue–Sat
Price	$$$
Cards	AE DC MC V eftpos
Chef	Logan Campbell
Features	Bar, licensed, outdoor seating, private dining
Website	regattarosebay.com

Restaurant Hubert

SYDNEY
Basement, 15 Bligh Street
02 9232 0881

FRENCH   **16/20**

A grown-up restaurant in an atmospheric basement

At the foot of a snaking timber-panelled staircase, you'll find this romantic restaurant and supper club gussied up like a 1940s French jazz club with red velvet drapes, fringed lampshades and twirling fans. All that's missing is the cigarette smoke. Bartenders in bowties and long aprons mix martinis. A pianist is tickling the ivories. Sommeliers are shimmying up ladders fetching wine from overhead shelves. And in the warren of small private rooms, revellers can be glimpsed braying for rounds of oysters. The time-warping food leaps from the pages of *Larousse* then takes a jump to the left. Gnocchi parisienne catches choux pastry dumplings in a crisp, lacy web. Tender escargots dabble in a buttery XO sauce. And oeufs en gelee is a pretty jewelled thing capturing three kinds of egg (caviar, salmon roe, bonito) in jelly. Fitout, service, food and drinks form such a seductive package that if Restaurant Hubert didn't exist, it would have been necessary to invent it.

Lunch bookings of any size are available on Thursday and Friday and for groups of six or more at dinner

Open	L Thu–Fri; D Mon–Sat
Price	$$$
Cards	AE MC V eftpos
Chef	Dan Pepperell
Features	Bar, licensed, private dining
Website	restauranthubert.com

RESTAURANT HUBERT

Restaurant Moon

DARLINGHURST
346 Liverpool Street
02 9357 6084

citi

THAI   **14/20**

Thai cliches bite the dust at this new Darlinghurst local

Thai food is changing, and one of the people changing it is Aum Touchpong Chancaw, a former Longrain chef bringing a few European kitchen smarts to traditional Thai cooking. He and former Koi Dessert Bar frontman, Jackie Park, have flipped the long-running Onde into a smart but simple dining room of battleship grey walls, local artists' works, wooden banquettes and low stools. Deep-fried chicken ribs coated with spices and dry-roasted rice spark and fizz like electricity, panang confit duck curry is thick, rich and glossy, and a clever surf and turf comes as a wreath of crisp, fried basil leaves over confit octopus and stir-fried sirloin, framing a fried egg. Moon's signature braised beef rib is a glorious thing – slow-cooked sous-vide for 72 hours on the bone, smothered in tamarind glaze, then flash-grilled in a Big Green Egg ceramic barbecue. And when all you need is something refreshing, passionfruit sorbet with lychee granita and syrupy hibiscus flowers will do it with style.

Braised beef rib is the signature dish for good reason

Open	L D Tue–Sun
Price	$$
Cards	AE MC V eftpos
Chef	Aum Touchpong Chancaw
Features	Licensed
Website	restaurantmoon.com.au

The Restaurant Pendolino

SYDNEY
Level 2, Strand Arcade,
412-414 George Street • 02 9231 6117

citi

ITALIAN   **15/20**

Upmarket Italian with service as polished as the cutlery

There's something almost daring about entering a closed shopping centre after dark, as if you're privy to a secret upstairs club. Particularly when you're greeted by suited staff at a low-lit gold counter, guided to a handsome table then promptly presented with a Champagne cart. Another waiter appears with water, another with bread and a detailed description of your three-part olive oil tasting. All this before you even spot a menu. Salmon and scallop tartare comes as a delicate salad with creamy lemon mascarpone. A 'wild weed' seafood spaghetti is simple and finessed, or go bolder pastas such as mushroom pappardelle with truffle oil (why?) and porcini salt. Main courses such as slow-cooked beef are generous and rich, but don't be afraid to opt for a second pasta instead. Quality olive oil is a key focus here, with the menu listing oils used in place of matching wine suggestions. For that, there's the knowledgeable sommelier, at your service before you even think to ask.

Buy a premium olive oil gift pack to go

Open	L D Mon–Sat
Price	$$$
Cards	AE DC MC V eftpos
Chef	Nino Zoccali, Dean Worthy
Features	Licensed, private dining, wheelchair access
Website	pendolino.com.au

Rising Sun Workshop

NEWTOWN
1C Whateley Street
02 9550 3891

MODERN ASIAN   **15/20**

All-day inner-city cafe for fine diners and easy riders everywhere

There are five million stories in Sin City, and here's one of them. Sydney got bigger and space got smaller. Backyard sheds vanished faster than free parking spots. So some motorbike-riding food fanciers found a fix. Rising Sun Workshop is part-restaurant, part-communal repair shop. Dining and tinkering are two components of the one machine. And chef Nick Smith (who owns a 1987 Royal Enfield Bullet 500) is a dab hand at both. Lunch is all about the light and darkness of ramen. Dinner kicks things up a notch: crunchy crumbed shiitake mushrooms pickled in soy, ginger and sherry, with Japanese spices and Kewpie mayo; grilled broccolini with braised fungi, Marrickville-made stracciatella and Argentinian chilli oil, or charred mackerel with a rainbow of roasted sweet beets. Tonight's shellfish dish is full-throttle fresh: purple scallops fished that morning off Kangaroo Island, warmed over charcoal and swimming in rich koji butter and smoked vinegar. They're top gear. And just one of the stories behind this supercharged social enterprise.

Pop in for a pre-dinner 'afternoon delight' drink from the all-Australian natural wine list

Open	B L Daily; D Wed–Sat
Price	$$
Cards	AE MC V eftpos
Chef	Nick Smith
Features	Bar, licensed, wheelchair access
Website	risingsunworkshop.com

Rocker

NORTH BONDI
Shop 5, 39–53 Campbell Parade
02 8057 8086

CONTEMPORARY   **14/20**

North Bondi is home to Darren Robertson and Cam Northway's breezy do-it-all diner

This beachside eatery swings between tapping out beetroot lattes in the AM, excellent jaffles at lunch and house-made pasta in the PM. Just before dusk is the time to visit, so you can settle into one of the soft chestnut leather banquets and explore the wine, cocktail and snack list with more consideration. Periwinkle blue table tops are the stage for plates that play with nostalgia (the crunchy Welsh rarebit bites deliver just enough bitey mustard tang to make them feel grown up), produce-centred simplicity (citrus-fuelled, yoghurt-laden charred broccoli) and pasta (order the hearty lamb ragu which sees shreds of slow-cooked meat tossed through ribbons of al dente tagliatelle). None of the menu screams 'beachside' and sometimes feels a little uncertain of direction, but if you approach each plate with a well-shaken margarita or a glass of textural Em Soleil pinot gris and a relaxed attitude, you'll still be in for a rockin' time.

Head in for locals' pasta night – a fettuccine party with a glass of wine for $39

Open	B L Wed–Sun; D Tue–Sun
Price	$$
Cards	AE MC V eftpos
Chef	Stuart Toon, Darren Robertson
Features	Bar, licensed, outdoor seating, wheelchair access
Website	rockerbondi.com.au

Rockpool Bar and Grill

SYDNEY
66 Hunter Street
02 8099 7077

STEAKHOUSE   **16/20**

Sydney's glamorous cathedral of steak, wine and seafood

The sprawling menu at Neil Perry's Deco-era steak temple has been stressing choice-a-phobes for the past 10 years. Cape Grim vintage rib-eye or David Blackmore Mishima rump? Lobster thermidor or pearly snapper from the charcoal oven? A sazerac to start or straight into the broad wine list? So many decisions! Straight-up, simple dishes are taken to the next level with world-class ingredients, such as juicy Redgate Farm partridge cooked over fire and sweetened with apricot cheeks, or hand-cut fettuccine basking in a wagyu bolognese that's rounded, smooth and an essay in comfort. The service isn't as polished as it once was but the kitchen flexes its considerable muscle to treat exceptional steaks with the respect they deserve – wood-fired to showcase deep, gamey flavours developed over a lengthy time dry-aging. Finishing with date tart surrounded by marble columns remains one of the finest moments of post-prandial zen in town.

The bar's full-blood wagyu burger is still sensational value for a business lunch or casual dinner

Ron's Upstairs

REDFERN
133A Redfern Street
02 9699 2018

CONTEMPORARY   **14/20**

It's *Muriel's Wedding* in looks, and echoes of Ester in taste

Well, it's happened. Redfern's hit peak excellence with this newbie from the team behind the small bar around the corner, Arcadia Liquors. Walk up a set of stairs that may or may not lead you to an illegal gambling den. Or at the very least, the sort of place where '80s politicians would slide a few briefcases under the table. It looks like the latter (bunches of plastic grapes, fairy lights and furniture that looks like it fell off the back of a truck) but on the plate it's something much different. There's Iggy's bread and salty butter to start, then lightly fried calamari to eat while you think about what to order for dinner. Pipis cooked in white wine and dressed in burnt butter are a maybe, but juicy roast chicken rubbed in chilli and paprika with Lebanese-style garlic sauce is a definite. Especially with a side of crisp roast potatoes. A bowl of sugared doughnut holes to end? It'd be impolite not to.

Walk-ins are welcome – if you can't get a table straightaway, hang at the bar

Open	L Mon–Fri; D Daily
Price	$$$
Cards	AE DC MC V eftpos
Chef	Corey Costelloe, Neil Perry
Features	Bar, licensed, private dining, wheelchair access
Website	rockpoolbarandgrill.com.au/sydney

Open	D Tue–Sat
Price	$$
Cards	AE MC V eftpos
Chef	Damir Mujanic
Features	Bar, licensed
Website	ronsupstairs.com.au

Rosetta Ristorante

SYDNEY
118 Harrington Street
02 8099 7089

ITALIAN   **15.5/20**

Classy southern Italian seafood in the heart of the city

For an Italian restaurant run by non-Italians, Rosetta does a damn fine job of making you feel you're holidaying on the Amalfi Coast instead of dining in this elegant, split-level space overlooking Grosvenor Place. It's the seafood that does it. Australia's finest and freshest is sent out in a celebratory antipasto of finely sliced calamari; fresh-picked crab; diced tuna; pipis in the shell; king prawn and scampi, and fresh pasta gets the luxury treatment with grilled marron or spanner crab. It's the vast Italian wine list as well, with its focus on textured whites from the Italian islands. And the meat, too, from a salumi misti with lush mortadella, aromatic prosciutto San Daniele with crisp gnocco fritto (fast becoming our favourite salumi accompaniment) to a no-frills, all-thrills grill of long-boned, meaty Cowra lamb cutlets with just a cheek of lemon and rosemary and chilli salsa. And bravi, you non-Italians, for the molto Italiano tartufo of chocolate ice-cream and cherries.

Aperitivo hour on the sunny terrace runs Monday to Friday from 4-6pm

Open	L Mon–Fri; D Daily
Price	$$$
Cards	AE DC MC V eftpos
Chef	Neil Perry, Richard Purdue
Features	Bar, licensed, outdoor seating, private dining, wheelchair access
Website	rosettarestaurant.com.au

Sagra

DARLINGHURST
62 Stanley St
02 9360 5964

ITALIAN   **15/20**

An osteria serving up homespun Italian fare that you want to eat every day

Such is the hospitality at Sagra and intuition of their clientele's needs that a negroni and olives hit the table first, followed by water second. This no-frills dining room buzzes with the chat of locals, eating here weekly without fatigue. A noteworthy achievement when you consider the menu: highly curated, with only a few antipasti, four primi and four secondi, which means *every* dish needs to be really likeable. And they are. Like the house-rolled tagliatelle with prawns, saffron and chilli. Or the braised Hawkesbury squid, a sticky delicious mess, relying on nothing more tricky than carrot, onion, celery, potato and red wine melding together over time. Patagonian toothfish is allowed to shine with the simplicity of a fennel puree and caper sauce. The less-is-more philosophy continues through to the Italy-focused wine list and onto desserts – Amedei chocolate mousse with a honeycomb crunch. Although owner-chef Nigel Ward has handed over the reigns, the osteria still crackles with old traditions.

Travel around Italy via their monthly regional dinners

Open	L D Mon–Sat
Price	$$
Cards	AE MC V eftpos
Chef	Michael Otto, Edward Saxton
Features	Licensed, outdoor dining
Website	sagrarestaurant.com.au

Sails on Lavender Bay

MCMAHONS POINT
2 Henry Lawson Avenue
02 9955 5998

CONTEMPORARY   **14.5/20**

A north-side heavy-hitter serving the well-heeled with views to match

It's that typical flash Sydney restaurant on the harbour, but this time with a difference – these stunning Opera House views are from the north side of the bridge. Despite the filthy rich waterviews, white tablecloths, and mod-Oz food with a slight French twist, once you're seated it's entirely unpretentious. Here, you'll find families with teen boys in their best collared shirts, and contented couples, sunsetting on generous nest eggs. Service is friendly and professional and pacing is excellent. They're best at the classics – fresh-baked sourdough, crisp potatoes, bouncy cos lettuce salad. In the rich and luxurious pie, four (count 'em) different types of mushrooms thrive under a light pastry lid, though it's the onion lyonnaise that's the star of the show. It's never a bad idea to order seafood here, such as snapper balanced nicely with thin-sliced calamari, plum sauce and olives. From here, there's little to do but settle in with another glass of wine.

Parking is tricky – Uber, use the $10 valet service or (even better) catch the ferry

Open	L Tue–Sun; D Mon–Sat
Price	$$$
Cards	AE DC MC V eftpos
Chef	Saro Derderyan
Features	Bar, licensed, private dining, wheelchair access
Website	sailslavenderbay.com

Saint Peter

PADDINGTON
362 Oxford Street
02 8937 2530

SEAFOOD   **16.5/20**

Forging new frontiers in fish cookery and crumpets

There are few menu constants at this modest Paddo hotspot where Josh Niland cooks seafood with talent and integrity. Sweet South Coast oysters are a given, served naked and fat. Broadbill belly cured into a kind of fish bacon will likely feature, too (pan-fried with brussels sprouts as a side, maybe), and either custard or lemon tart is a must. Niland's commitment to high-quality produce, however, means the carte is an ever-changing adventure spotlighting Australia's best ocean catch. Dusky flathead, fresh that day and served with slippery jack mushrooms, or yellowfin tuna aged in-house for intense, complex flavour. Flaky fleshed Corner Inlet King George whiting is sharpened with barbecued zucchini, preserved lemon and chilli, while stinging nettles and ink sauce provide Port Albert calamari with a beautiful savoury undertone. Brunch is a fun time at the weekend, especially when Julie Niland is flipping golden crumpets topped with sea urchin. It's a restaurant like no other in Australia – possibly the world.

Niland's Fish Butchery is a few doors up selling seafood and cracking fish and chips

Open	Brunch Sat–Sun; L Fri–Sun; D Tue–Sun
Price	$$
Cards	AE MC V eftpos
Chef	Josh Niland
Features	Licensed
Website	saintpeter.com.au

Sake Restaurant and Bar

DOUBLE BAY
33 Cross Street
02 8017 3104

JAPANESE **15.5/20**

Fine dining with polish and precision never gets old

Everything old is new again at Sake, from spruced-up signature dishes to the dermal-filled faces of Double Bay diners. This schmick eastern suburbs inpost is more polished than a 20-something with a property portfolio. In a city infatuated with the new, it's right on the money. The Neil Perry-infused set menu of 'chef's new classics' gives a nip-and-tuck to old favourites, such as pairing Hiramasa kingfish with sweet ponzu and spicy lime and jalapeno paste. A la carte options feature "new style sashimi" arranged like a flower in bloom, with glistening salmon, snapper and a fat, fresh scallop lightly seared with hot oil. Crisp cubes of agedashi tofu come with dried bonito flakes that dance and shimmy in a rich broth. Tajima wagyu arrives at the table on a teeny charcoal grill and topped with lively kombu-nori salt and dried chilli. It's tender, silky and cut neater than a deck of cards. Who said you can't teach an old dog new tricks?

Ladies who lunch can kick up their heels over the Champagne set menu

Sake Restaurant and Bar

THE ROCKS
12 Argyle Street
02 9259 5656

JAPANESE **14/20**

A pumping venue for party-goers who love to eat

Between the bars, booths, communal tables and multiple private dining rooms, there are plenty of dark corners to suggest a date night. But there's really only one way to embrace the Sake experience – invite a big group of your best-dressed guests, drink up, spend big and overorder on the shared food. Raw, fresh or fried, go-to options include sushi and sashimi sets, the famed popcorn shrimp or steamed prawn shumai, light-as-air dumplings dripping in ponzu, and noodles. The more innovative dishes aren't always so crowd-pleasing – mushroom ceviche is on the acidic side, while crisp-skinned chicken is a little one-dimensional. But then there's gyoza and chicken karaage, plus impressive desserts mixing Western classics with all manners of matcha, miso and green tea. Keep in mind this restaurant opens onto a pumping nightlife venue – expect heavy base, scatty service and a line outside the bathroom. Embrace the kickass sake collection and cocktails, and it'll all be part of the fun.

Go in a group and order tried-and-tested favourites to share

Open	L D Daily
Price	$$
Cards	AE DC MC V eftpos
Chef	Jungbae Cho, Shaun Presland
Features	Bar, licensed, private dining, wheelchair access
Website	sakerestaurant.com.au

Open	L D Daily
Price	$$
Cards	AE DC MC V eftpos
Chef	Chi Ung Kim, Shaun Presland
Features	Bar, licensed, private dining, wheelchair access
Website	sakerestaurant.com.au

Sasaki

SYDNEY
Shop 102, 21 Alberta Street
02 8068 9774

Sean's Panaroma

BONDI BEACH
270 Campbell Parade
02 9365 4924

♔

JAPANESE   **14.5/20**

CONTEMPORARY   **15/20**

The hole-in-the-wall restaurant that transports you to regional Japan

Sasaki is, quite literally, a hidden gem. It's buried in the lane out the back of the Australian Federal Police building, concealed behind waving Japanese curtains. Step inside and you're instantly transported to Shimane, Japan. Chef Yu Sasaki deals in precision and specificity. Each of his daily creations stems from his childhood memories growing up on the remote prefecture on Honshu Island. The sparse menu reads like a shopping list ('Beef, Cauliflower, Spice') but Sasaki delivers technical marvels without becoming overly cerebral. Take the seemingly innocuous blue swimmer crab emerging out of a bright, silky capsicum gazpacho. It may be a cold soup but it writhes with heat, sharpness, sweetness and a salty edge. The tempura asparagus is so meaty and firm you'd have a hard time being convincing it wasn't cleverly shaped beef on its way to a vegetarian-themed dress-up party. And when you do actually get to the 'Beef, Cauliflower, Spice' that perfect caramelised meat melts in the mouth.

The desserts are almost comically tiny so don't be afraid to order everything and then refuse to share it with anyone

Settle back at a classic beachside setting built for comfort

Outside, it's blowing a gale strong enough to blow the budgie smugglers from a Bondi bum. Inside, all is calm and warm. Watching the waves from a window seat at Sean Moran's mainstay is a fine way to spend a day. This beachside local feels like an old friend. Family photos, preserving jars and worn books (*Kidnapped, The Boy Who Harnessed the Wind*) line the shelves. Fresh produce from Moran's Blue Mountains farm bolsters the blackboard menu, which is regularly rewritten with understated seasonal fare. Today's offerings include a shimmery serve of Hiramasa kingfish tartare with salmon roe and popping-candy finger limes. Or a rich vein of blood pudding with seared radicchio and chunks of sweet tomato chutney. House-made ravioli with earthy rainbow chard and olives is just a tad too al dente. But a retro goblet of blackberry jelly with dark chocolate ice-cream finishes the meal with a flourish. We're happily home and hosed, no matter the weather.

For the full Sean's experience, book a visit to the Farm Panaroma

Open	D Mon–Sat
Price	$$
Cards	MC V eftpos
Chef	Yu Sasaki, Kensuke Yada
Features	Licensed, private dining, wheelchair access
Website	sasaki.com.au

Open	L Sat–Sun; D Wed–Sat
Price	$$
Cards	AE MC V eftpos
Chef	Sean Moran, Sam Robertson, John Hicks
Features	Licensed, outdoor seating, BYO
Website	seanspanaroma.co

SEAN'S PANAROMA

Sixpenny

STANMORE
83 Percival Road
02 9572 6666

SIXPENNY

citi 🍷
CONTEMPORARY   👑👑👑 **18/20**

A little restaurant with big ideas

It doesn't have million-dollar views, massive wine cellars, legions of staff or a centre-of-the-universe location, but Sixpenny is The Perfect Small Restaurant. A place where the chefs care so much about the food they bring it to the table themselves. Where the constantly evolving menu is informed by the seasons and by small-scale growers such as Pocket City Farms. Where there's a sense of grace about the act of wining and dining, in a spare, elegant corner dining room with civilised space between tables. Where the food from Dan Puskas is balanced and precise, from the barrage of opening snacks to the silky mead vinegar custard with strawberry consomme. There are plays on both texture (Ballina spanner crab with clam butter, salmon roe and turnip leaves) and temperature (warm rye-poached potato with oyster and coins of mushroom). There's provocation, too. At a certain point, almost every dish does a handbrake turn, tyres spinning, as a second wave of flavour comes through. Clever Sixpenny.

The leisurely weekend lunches are among the country's finest

Open	L Sat–Sun; D Wed–Sat
Price	$$$
Cards	AE MC V eftpos
Chef	Daniel Puskas
Features	Licensed, private dining
Website	sixpenny.com.au

Sokyo

PYRMONT
Level G, The Darling, The Star,
80 Pyrmont Street
02 9657 9161

`citi` 🍷   🍽

JAPANESE   **15/20**

**Party-time Japanese with
superlative sushi**

It feels as if everyone at this
glamorously dark restaurant has
something to celebrate, be it second
date, family get-together, anniversary,
birthday or winning streak at the casino.
If the crowd is there for a good time,
then so too is Chase Kojima's mix-and-
match Japanese menu. Good things
come from the robata – skewers of
grill-marked chicken are an easy crowd-
pleaser, and wagyu tenderloin is bravely
teamed with cubes of smoked eel and
crisp blue ghost kale. Hand-shaped
dumplings envelop a mix of snapper,
lobster and prawn that is so finely
minced it simply tastes of seafood. But
the big drawcard here is always the
sushi bar, run by the talented Takashi
Sano. His touch is elegant, his knife
skills exemplary and his respect for fish
such that entry-level nigiri is as thrilling
as the silky, lightly torched ocean trout
ikijime nigiri; meltingly sweet Japanese
scallop or translucent sea bream on a
crisp mat of high-grade nori. Yet more
reasons to celebrate.

**Surprisingly, there's also a dedicated
vegetarian menu**

Open	B D Daily L Fri–Sat
Price	$$$
Cards	AE MC V eftpos
Chef	Chase Kojima, Brian Logan
Features	Bar, licensed, private dining,
	wheelchair access
Website	star.com.au/sokyo

Sotto Sopra

NEWPORT
G04 The Palms, 316–324 Barrenjoey Road
02 9997 7009

`citi` 🍷   🍽

ITALIAN   **15/20**

**Relaxed, rustic trattoria serving
old-school fare with style**

Of the various things one might
enjoy topsy-turvy (handstands, yoga,
small motor maintenance), eating
pasta is not among them. But Sotto
Sopra (or "upside down" in Italian)
takes a different perspective. The
industrial-chic beach shack sits on a
floodplain, so everything mechanical
has to be 1.5 metres or more above the
floor – including the kitchen. Up there
you'll find the busiest wood-fired oven
this side of the Spit, busting a gut on
bullish fare such as buttery Khorasan
sourdough or whole heads of broccoli.
Roasted eggplant ravioli with ginger
butter and citrusy zucchini is smooth,
rich and unashamedly rustic. Traditional
tagliolini allo scoglio is stripped back
to let the flavours of mussels, prawns,
garlic and lemon shine. Simpler still
are slivers of raw kingfish and watermelon radish on light and lush pistachio
cream. But save room for a top-notch
sweet potato jam tart with semifreddo
lime meringue and basil sorbet. With
desserts like this, everything's looking
up – no matter which way you're facing.

**Take home a tub of pastry chef Flavia
Beniamini's superb sorbet**

Open	L Fri–Sun; D Wed–Sun
Price	$$
Cards	AE MC V eftpos
Chef	Mattia Rossi
Features	Licensed, wheelchair access, BYO
Website	sottosopra.com.au

Spice Temple

SYDNEY
10 Bligh Street
02 8078 1888

CHINESE **15/20**

Hot and heady spice den deep in the city

Neil Perry's the food equivalent of the Marvel multiverse, serving up blockbusters faster than you can say "By the hoary hosts of Hoggoth!" Furthering his deep-seated desire to take over the planet, one restaurant at a time, is this dark-lit subterranean lair. Kick things off with a Chinese zodiac-themed cocktail ("Daily horoscope: You are warm, generous and lack self-control. Hangover ahead!") before moving to the main menu, which is lit up with red-hot dishes. Firm and super-fresh prawn wontons come with treacly aged black vinegar and chilli oil for added punch. Silken Sichuan salt-and-pepper fried tofu is bolstered by a spicy salad of salted chilli and coriander. 'Fish drowned in heaven facing chillies and Sichuan peppercorns' dials up the heat to I-can't-feel-my-face-anymore, with pearly white leather jacket submerged by a thick layer of chilli and hot peanut oil. It's bright, light and fiery as hell. With food this full-on and flavoursome, you won't want to wait for the sequel.

Order half-size dishes to make the most of the regional Chinese menu

Open	L Mon–Fri; D Daily
Price	$$$
Cards	AE DC MC V eftpos
Chef	Neil Perry, Andy Evans
Features	Bar, licensed, private dining, wheelchair access
Website	spicetemple.com.au

Spring Yunnan

HAYMARKET
215A Thomas Street
02 9280 4537

CHINESE **14/20**

A casual (and delicious) introduction to Yunnanese cuisine

A bright and cheery new addition to Chinatown, this is a celebration of the mountainous Yunnan province of China and the diverse cuisines that can be found there. Highlights of the 'little bit of everything' menu can be seen in photo form on the outside wall of the restaurant, calling out to the hungry with a colourful mix of noodles, soup and the threat of chilli. Start by plonking a great big plate of cold rice noodles with Diane flavour sauce in the middle of your table and making your way through the mountain of chewy starch soaked in a savoury sauce of pork, cucumber and carrot. Spring Yunnan's specialty is guoqiao, a hot broth served with raw meat and eggs to be cooked yourself in that said broth, but if you're feeling lazy there's no shortage of fried meats and stir-fries to choose from instead. Begin or finish your meal with some Yunnanese dim sum – shortbread buns filled with ham or rose petals.

The drinks menu is especially Yunnanese, featuring plum juice, soy milks and pu'er tea

Open	L D Daily
Price	$
Cards	MC V eftpos
Chef	Frank Feng
Features	Wheelchair access, BYO
Website	spring-yunnan.business.site

St Claude's

WOOLLAHRA
10 Oxford Street
02 9331 3222

FRENCH   **14/20**

Relax – you're eating French among friends

Cracking the door of St Claude's reveals starched linen tablecloths, grey-green walls and moody lighting that suggests a night of serious dining to come. And although the kitchen sticks to the script of traditional French cooking, and in fact does this quite well, the vibe in this two-storey skinny terrace is far more laidback than first impressions suggest. Clusters of old friends are engrossed in conversation, not paying too much attention to entrees such as the sweet, moussey chicken liver parfait. A steak tartare could do with some punch, but Ortiz anchovies on toast dissolve on the tongue in a delightful salty, oily mashup. Steak is served without fuss. Confit duck a l'orange combines sweetness and tang underneath crisp skin and rests on homey vegetables. Given main courses nudge the $40 mark they lack some wow, but maybe that's part of St Claude's allure. In food, as in fashion, it is hard work to get everything right while keeping it relaxed.

A prix fixe menu ($68 for three courses) covers favourite dishes

Stanbuli

ENMORE
135 Enmore Road
02 8624 3132

TURKISH   **15/20**

Channelling the meyhanes of Istanbul

"You can get it at any kebab shop," says our waitress as she takes away an empty plate of what was iskender, one of Turkey's most famous dishes, wiped enthusiastically clean with bread. "I would hope ours is better," she adds. She needn't worry – Stanbuli's is significantly better, made with skirt steak (it also includes ripped pieces of bread all smothered in a rich tomato sauce). Like the beautifully tiled meyhane (or tavern in Turkish) – disguised behind a 1950s hairdressing salon facade – it's refined and elevated by produce that's more restaurant than street. It's there with the sigara borek, too – a fried golden pastry cigar filled with prawn and feta. That upmarket vibe is echoed by the jovial, efficient service and a drinks list that encourages sipping rather than throwing back raki, although you can if your night calls for it. Head to Stanbuli if you want a good rendition of a modern Istanbul restaurant, but don't want to fork out for a plane ticket.

Book a table downstairs – the room is prettier and the vibe more exciting

Open	D Daily
Price	$$
Cards	AE MC V eftpos
Chef	Matt Barnett
Features	Licensed, private dining, BYO
Website	stclaudes.com.au

Open	D Tue–Sat
Price	$$
Cards	MC V eftpos
Chef	Ibrahim Kasif
Features	Bar, licensed, private dining, wheelchair access
Website	stanbuli.com.au

Sushi e

SYDNEY
Level 4, Establishment, 252 George Street
02 9114 7314

JAPANESE   **15/20**

Come for the sushi, stay for the show

Make sure you sit at the bar. Specifically
positioned behind the chefs, who you'll
spend your entire meal watching in
silence as they expertly slice through
fish with one hand and roll seaweed
around rice with the other. You can
order exclusively from the sushi and
sashimi being prepared directly in
front of you, but you don't want to
miss out on the food being cooked in
the kitchen, like the delicate and sweet
charred toothfish with radish and finger
lime, or an absolute knockout dish of
soba noodles piled high with a generous
helping of king crab in dashi, butter and
bottarga. This is one of Merivale's most
effortlessly classy dining experiences,
save for the awkward walk through
Establishment to get to your seat,
although that will be quickly forgotten
once you sit down and start to watch
the sushi theatre in front of you. Raise
a glass of red rice sake and enjoy the
performance.

**An $80 a head signature menu features
all the greatest hits**

Tetsuya's

SYDNEY
529 Kent Street
02 9267 2900

JAPANESE   **17/20**

A classic fine-dining temple of poise, grace and good humour

"Please enjoy these truffles from
Penrith," says a suited waiter presenting
crimson-pink Black Onyx beef
tenderloin under a canopy of kalettes,
fragrant perigords and morel jus.
Penrith truffles, hang on, what? "Just
kidding, they're from Manjimup in
Western Australia." Aha. After almost
30 years, Tetsuya Wakuda's benchmark
restaurant is still a place of warm
humour, linen tablecloths and straight-
edge Japanese dishes threaded with
French technique. The arc of confit
ocean trout over a little thicket of apple
crowd-pleases with its savoury kombu
hit, and there's further big-flavoured
joy in a steamed spanner crab tian laced
with sea urchin cream and balanced by
a crown of avruga. Later, sticky plum
sauce marries barley and duck breast
dry-aged two weeks for a clean and
complex taste. There's no background
music but views to the Japanese garden
provide all the relaxing vibes you need.

**Best double-down on your comfort
level with another helping of malt
bread and a black truffle butter
that's definitely not from western
Sydney either**

Open	L Mon–Fri; D Mon–Sat
Price	$$
Cards	AE MC V eftpos
Chef	Michael Fox
Features	Bar, licensed, wheelchair access
Website	merivale.com/venues/sushie

Open	L Sat; D Tue–Sat
Price	$$$
Cards	AE DC MC V eftpos
Chef	Tetsuya Wakuda, Josh Raine
Features	Licensed, private dining
Website	tetsuyas.com

Three Blue Ducks

BRONTE
143 Macpherson Street
02 9389 0010

CONTEMPORARY   **15/20**

The neighbourhood diner where every face is a friendly one

Early birds have long crowed about this beachside eatery's breakfast offerings, but night owls are not forgotten by the team at Three Blue Ducks, which transforms at sunset from breezy cafe to intimate restaurant. Couples rule the roost at night. Sweethearts coo at each other over sirloin steak and fillets of crumbed John Dory. The menu is concise, dispensing with florid prose for simple dish descriptions. Plump scallops are pleasingly accompanied with seaweed butter and wood ear mushrooms, while kaffir lime and pickled ginger provide a delicate balance to crab served on betel leaves. Main dishes are generous, earthy and well executed. The delicate flavours of a lemongrass, green mango and chilli salad contrast with the rich texture and flavour of braised beef ribs. The roast lamb tomahawk looks like a weapon, but tastes like a dream on a bed of parsnip puree. The conviviality extends to the bright-eyed, enthusiastic waitstaff, explaining dishes and recommending drinks from an eclectic drinks menu.

Duck away from your dining companion to admire the restaurant's garden

Open	B L Daily; D Wed–Sat
Price	$$
Cards	AE MC V eftpos
Chef	Darren Robertson, Mark La Brooy, Lauren McKenna
Features	Licensed, outdoor seating, wheelchair access
Website	threeblueducks.com

Three Blue Ducks

ROSEBERY
1/85 Dunning Avenue
02 9389 0010

CONTEMPORARY   **14.5/20**

Smart, clever earthy food delivered with a great vibe

The cavernous Rosebery shed sits in a clutch of local food and drink icons: Archie Rose distillery, Black Star bakery and Da Mario pizza. The 'Ducks pulses with life from the regular live music playing to the plants growing from the ceiling. Though this is a much-loved breakfast joint, the dinner options really sing. Keep an eye out for the risotto with smoked ricotta. It's clearly not a share plate but you're going to want to force-feed your guests just to make them truly understand how good this chive-rich rice dish is when it's laced with the smoky ricotta. Similarly, the generous platter of octopus is inviting, but it's the gelatinous, salty squid ink sauce that takes it to the next level. Both generous share plates and individual dishes are on offer but there's not a lot of communication around which is which. Double-check what you're ordering lest you're stuck with a massive barbecue chicken all to yourself.

Make sure you get the eggplant chips as an entree

Open	B L Tue–Sun; D Wed–Sat
Price	$$
Cards	AE MC V eftpos
Chef	Andy Allen, Mark La Brooy, Darren Robertson
Features	Licensed, wheelchair access
Website	threeblueducks.com

Toriciya

CAMMERAY
18 Cammeray Road
02 9904 2277

JAPANESE **14/20**

Small inn much favoured by the local Japanese community

There are three ways to order here. The lazy way – the chef's menu at $75 is sure to be good but you'll need to convince the chef you're up to some of the more unusual delicacies. The usual way – the main menu is heavy with yakitori grilled chicken parts. Also enjoy simmered ox tongue or Okura risotto, which turns out to be a thin congee made slick in a most delicious way thanks to the fresh okra. And then there's the adventurous way – the long list of specials is loaded daily on the website, but only in Japanese. Here is the best seafood from the market or rare home-style dishes. Urchin sashimi has the pure taste of the ocean, 'carpaccio' is in fact lightly seared and grilled eel that has the smoky breath of the grill. Impress the chef and order the fish head. Desserts maintain the flavour hit with excellent green tea ice-cream.

It's easy to make the $50 minimum charge by indulging in some fine sake

Uccello

SYDNEY
Level 4, Ivy, 320 George Street
02 9114 7309

ITALIAN **15.5/20**

A rooftop gem where the sun always shines, no matter the weather

The Ivy's overhanging garden is starting to look like a post-apocalyptic *Planet of the Apes*, when foliage and simians reclaim the Earth. Upstairs, the scene by the rooftop pool is more *Miami Vice* meets *Under the Tuscan Sun*. Lunches are smart suits and share portfolios, dinners are bubbles with your mortgage broker. Away from the cabanas, the focus is on classic Italian cooking stripped back to let the produce shine. Fresh and firm skillet-fried southern calamari comes with sweet and smoky blistered chilli and the simple delights of garlic, lemon and parsley. Scampi risotto damn near dubsteps off the table with flavour, the pearl-white flesh and rich, buttery rice hitting more high notes than the poolside DJ. The wood-fired oven is on song for shredded suckling pig slow-cooked with fig jam and served with a crisp pork chop. Finish with cleansing pistachio gelato and cookie dough-like brittle before settling back in the sun. When Armageddon comes, where else would you rather be?

Pack your swimmers and shades for a sojourn by the swimming pool

Open	D Daily
Price	$$
Cards	AE MC V eftpos
Chef	Miya Tatsuya, Hiroya Yamaguchi
Features	Licensed, private dining, wheelchair access
Website	toriciya.com.au

Open	L Mon–Fri; D Mon–Sat
Price	$$$
Cards	AE MC V eftpos
Chef	Ben Sitton
Features	Bar, licensed, outdoor seating, wheelchair access
Website	merivale.com/venues/uccello

The Unicorn

PADDINGTON
106 Oxford Street

CONTEMPORARY   **14/20**

Come for the pub grub, stay for the good times

It's difficult to eat barbecue corn here. The dish – juicy cobs covered in a slick of chilli, pecorino and a hint of citrus – is not the problem. Blame the Friday night resident piano man who rolls out '90s rock ballads, keeping patrons singing along instead of eating. The team behind this pub are some of Sydney's good times kings – Porteno, Mary's and Young Henrys – so fun and flavour are served equally. The menu is recognisable pub fare, but quality is next-level. Chicken parmigiana has a macho coating of crumb but the breast is perfectly juicy within. The Mary's burger is a rich, slightly charred patty in a sweet bun with crunchy hand-cut chips. Silver service it is not. Ordering is from the bar for every course or top up. But you'll be happy to get another glass of the Ochota Barrels pinot noir, made especially for the venue. If there was a hat for vibe, The Unicorn would wear it jauntily.

The Unicorn skirts the lockout law zone, so dinner can be late (up to 11.30pm)

Open	L Thu–Sun; D Daily
Price	$$
Cards	DC MC V eftpos
Chef	James Garside
Features	Bar, licensed, outdoor seating, wheelchair access
Website	theunicornhotel.com.au

Via Alta

NORTH WILLOUGHBY
197 High Street
02 9958 1110

citi 🍷

ITALIAN   **14/20**

Charming suburban diner where waitstaff make you feel a million bucks

Brought to you by the same group as Italian fine diner Ormeggio, this suburban bambino is all about flavourful regional Italian, largely from the north of the Boot, and charming, flirtatious waiters. It also ticks the box for consistency: more than four years on, the restaurant hasn't succumbed to a reinvention or moved widely away from its staples. The seasonal menu changes daily, with an emphasis on simple cooking of whatever's fresh. High points are the juicy prawns, grilled simply with lemon and rosemary, sea lettuce and chilli. The pasta sees plump tortelli packed with apple, sage and dressed in burnt butter. Or there's the aromatic beef bresaola, its brininess complemented by pecorino and baby beetroot. Like the food, the decor is simple and homey. There's a little alcove out the front, and a crowd of mostly distinguished and well-dressed older couples, all here for the neighbourhood vibes.

Check out their well-priced, Alessandro Pavoni-hosted monthly regional feasts showcasing different regions of Italy

Open	L Tue–Sun; D Daily
Price	$$
Cards	AE MC V eftpos
Chef	Damiano Ottaviani
Features	Licensed, private dining, wheelchair access, BYO
Website	viaalta.com.au

The Welcome Hotel Dining Room

ROZELLE
91 Evans Street
02 9810 1323

ITALIAN   **14/20**

A taste of Italy in the unlikely backstreets of Rozelle

You'd be hard-pressed to find many other establishments summed up by the common experience of elegant Italian dining and leaving the venue with a meat tray under your arm, but at the Welcome Hotel it's pub night in the front and date night at the back. Despite the rear dining space's markedly more 'styled' appearance, you're thankfully never too far from the action. Attentive service quickly sets the tone. When it comes to understanding the nuances of obscure regional pasta varieties, staff are more than happy to retrieve a sample from the kitchen for some tableside training. The menu traverses regional Italy with a soft spot for Sardinian classics. Crisp, wafer-thin shards of flatbread help to tame a bounteous platter of antipasto, while a humble bowl of malloreddus (tiny pasta shells sometimes known as Sardinian gnocchi) with wild boar ragu highlights the efficacy of simplicity and patience. Overall good value and an approachable wine list of mostly Italian varietals will keep you wishing this was your local.

Pasta and a pint? Some restaurant dishes can be found on the front bar menu

Open	L Wed–Sun; D Wed–Sat
Price	$$
Cards	AE MC V eftpos
Chef	Kristjan Oplanic
Features	Bar, licenced, outdoor seating, wheelchair access, private dining
Website	thewelcomehotel.com.au

Wyno

SURRY HILLS
Shop 4, 50 Holt Street
(enter via Gladstone Street)
02 8399 1440

CONTEMPORARY   **14.5/20**

Wine service that vies with the food for top billing

Much more than a pocket-sized waiting room for Porteno, Wyno is an opportunity to dive into the mind of co-owner Joe Valore, who's dispensing some of the best booze around. Seated at the long tasting bar, you may find yourself reliving a Sicilian holiday through a native variety, leftfield drops from our own Granite Belt, or regaled with the story of a 90-year-old Patagonian vineyard and Valore's own travels. Food is simple but ever so appropriate: salt cod dumplings with an acidic salsa verde; mortadella; crunchy school prawns that hit you with a pungent coastal note before they've even reached the counter. Salty, hit with paprika and lemon, a quick dip into aioli – they're a near-perfect bar snack. Offal is hardly brave these days but Cape Grim beef tongue, laid out long and unmistakeable, is a bold plate. Tender but firm, it's accompanied by pickled eggplant, a Porteno original. Wyno finds that perfect balance between the glass and the plate.

Don't feign wine knowledge. Surrender and discover

Open	D Tue–Sat
Price	$$
Cards	AE MC V eftpos
Chef	Ben Milgate, Elvis Abrahanowicz
Features	Bar, licensed, wheelchair access

Yan

WOLLI CREEK
19 Arncliffe Street
02 9599 8712

MODERN ASIAN   **15/20**

White-hot charcoals, fresh ideas and smoked treats make this a dining destination

When it comes to barbecue, Yan manages to take multiple cultural cues while still doing its own thing. This tiny Asian smokehouse is all about charcoal meats. King prawns are served cold – peeling off the delicate shells is a task, but it also imbues your fingers with a sublime woody smokiness that complements the sweet meat. Blackened lamb rib-ends merge into tender meat and pockets of rendered down fat, which are rescued from the brink of This Is Too Much by a fresh chilli-loaded chimichurri-cross-prik nam pla. Even the crumb on tender chicken katsu gets a faint whisper of charcoal, which takes it from Japanese comfort food to Yan's own forward-thinking signature dish. Sydney has far too many restaurants rendered homogeneous by their attempts to execute pan-Asian food, but Yan manages to punch out Asiatic flavours in new and inventive ways that make it equal parts welcoming, flavoursome, familiar and totally new.

It's almost impossible to save room for dessert but a $5 matcha cream cheese and red bean doughnut is worth a look

Open	L Sat–Sun; D Wed–Sun
Price	$$
Cards	AE MC V eftpos
Chef	Raymond Lim
Features	Licensed, outdoor seating, wheelchair access
Website	yanrestaurant.com.au

Yellow

POTTS POINT
57 Macleay Street
02 9332 2344

VEGETARIAN   **16/20**

Progressive plates that just happen to be vegetarian

It's vegetables but not as you know them. The veg-centric plates here are as thoughtfully crafted as any protein, leaning on fermentation, pickling, dehydration, smoking and sous vide to create complex layers of flavour and textural depth. It's alchemy. Wafer-thin cones of celeriac flirt with oozy stracciatella, banana powder and plantain oil for a cross-eyeballed explosion. Baby corn charred in the husk, pepped up by miso and the crunch of milk crumb, and a salad of just-picked broad bean shoots, puffed rice praline and turnip-coffee puree continue the head-scratching, 'Oh my gosh' wonder. As does some of the best savoury-edged desserts in town. Witness the sheep's milk yoghurt sorbet with licorice honeycomb and yuzu meringue. The en-pointe waitstaff channel a warmth that grounds the produce-driven concept, turning it from something experimental to a neighbourhood joint worth dropping into regularly, if only to perch at the bar and drink from the excellent Old World meets Young Gun minimal-interventionist wine list.

Gong for 'Breakfast Worth Getting Out of Bed For' goes to the poached eggs, kohlrabi and mushroom broth

Open	L Sat–Sun; D Daily
Price	$$
Cards	AE MC V eftpos
Chef	Brent Savage, Chris Benedet
Features	Licensed, outdoor seating
Website	yellowsydney.com.au

YELLOW

CONTINENTAL DELI BAR BISTRO

TOP 20 SYDNEY BARS

By Callan Boys

Archie Rose

85 Dunning Avenue, Rosebery
02 8458 2300 • archierose.com.au

It's exciting times ahoy for Sydney's first
independent distillery in more than 150 years,
as its initial batch of aged whisky waits to be
released in mid-2019. Meanwhile, head
of hospitality Harriet Leigh runs a tight
cocktail game at the bronze-on-timber
bar, well-suited to an Archie Rose
G&T and sardines with Iggy's bread.

Bar Topa

4 Palings Lane, Sydney • 02 9114 7368
merivale.com.au/bartopa

It's been an age since Sydney had tapas to be
excited about, so kudos to Justin Hemmes for
bringing the sunny flavours of San Sebastian to
the CBD. Chefs Lauren Murdoch and Jordan
Toft have collaborated on a simple menu
featuring pipis, sweet peppers and a steak
sandwich a la plancha. Tables and chairs? No.
Miniature three-sip martinis? Absolutely.

The Baxter Inn

152–156 Clarence Street, Sydney
02 9221 5580 • thebaxterinn.com

Australia's number-one whisky bar thanks
to more than 800 single malts, blends and
ryes, plus a crack team of staff who know
what they're pouring and do it with panache.
Whether you're jonesing for a rare Speyside,
rich stout or perfect Manhattan, Baxter
knocks it out of the basement every time.

Bentley Restaurant + Bar

27 O'Connell Street, Sydney
02 8214 0505 • thebentley.com.au

Do you like cult wine and nifty snacks such as
angasi oyster heightened with finger lime and
scampi caviar? Do you like drinking balanced
cocktails in a beautiful setting? If yes, then
come on down to Bentley's refurbished bar,
now featuring drinks boss Bobby Carey on
martini duty.

Bondi Beach Public Bar

180 Campbell Parade, Bondi Beach
02 9132 5777 • bbpb.com.au

It could probably pass for a streetwear store
if you replaced the fridge of pre-batched
cocktails and sustainable wine with a clothes
rack, but Maurice Terzini's tribute to surf rock
and '80s pub culture is a thong-friendly Aussie
boozer all the way. Squish burgers and white
russians – the new taste of Sydney summer.

Bulletin Place

Level 1, 10-14 Bulletin Place, Sydney
02 8006 8833 • bulletinplace.com

Daily changing cocktails made with market-
fresh fruit are the drawcard at this tiny bar
straddling the CBD and Circular Quay,
though expert-level bartenders also sling
pitch-perfect classics and suggest long-
forgotten drinks. Arrive early and settle into a
comfy banquette that's very hard to leave.

Charlie Parker's

Basement, 380 Oxford Street, Paddington
02 9114 7332 • merivale.com.au/charlieparkers

This sandstone-walled bar beneath Fred's
is big on the gospel of local, seasonal and
botanical. Fruit-forward cocktails might
feature strawberry gum, toasted wattleseed
or bee pollen, but a good bottle of red is all
you need to enjoy the homey space. Maybe
some wood-fired flatbread and whipped
lardo, too. The Bird is indeed the word.

Continental Deli Bar Bistro

210 Australia Street, Newtown • 02 8624 3131
continentaldelicatessen.com.au

Can we have a neo-trad delicatessen and
cocktail bar like this on every leafy Sydney
street, please? Bartender Michael Nicolian
leads Team Porteno's tinned martini and
sandwich hotspot, and the Hawaiian-shirt-
sporting top bloke can fix you any drink fit
to be poured under the Newtown sun.

The Dolphin Hotel

412 Crown Street, Surry Hills
02 9331 4800 • dolphinhotel.com.au

Chef Monty Koludrovic leads the Aussie-
Italo kitchen at this funland of natural wine,
beautiful hand-stretched pizzas and $2 ponies
of ice-cold beer. Head sommelier Marie-
Sophie Canto is 100 per cent committed
to every guest having a cracking time and
the ongoing aperitivo series showcases
the most exciting chefs cooking today.

Earl's Juke Joint

407 King Street, Newtown

How great are old Russian butcheries
repurposed for serving tinnies and New
Orleans-inspired tinctures? Swamp rock and
hip-hop pump at this good-time bolthole
where owner Pasan Wijesena's tikis have
been the cause and solution of inner west
hangovers for the past five years. Now with
bonus Radikon and pet-nat.

Jacoby's Tiki Bar

154 Enmore Road, Enmore

The Earl's team double-down on their zombie love at Sydney's only dedicated tiki bar named after a *Twin Peaks* psychiatrist. Try the Scorpion Bowl – a boozy basin of cognac, rum, gin and citrus, served on fire with a rainbow of straws. The rattan-walled room packs out at the weekend so arrive early to claim a table.

Love, Tilly Devine

91 Crown Lane, Darlinghurst
02 9326 9297 · lovetillydevine.com

A national treasure since it opened in the old Best Cellars stockroom in 2010, LTD is a cheerful patchwork of old bricks, hanging pot plants and cheese. A soft relaunch in 2017 saw a renewed focus on thirst-quenching, fist-pumping, Australian wine with new-wave producers knocking bottlenecks with classic labels.

Maybe Frank

417-421 Bourke Street, Surry Hills
02 9357 3838 · maybefrank.com

A pizzeria, yes – and a very good one at that – but this margherita-spinning eatery also delivers bittersweet Italian cocktails that warrant a visit in their own right. Now also in Randwick and rocking all-you-can-eat pizza nights every Tuesday. Get on your bicicletta pronto.

Monopole

71A Macleay Street, Potts Point
02 9360 4410 · monopolesydney.com.au

Nick Hildebrandt's otherworldly talent for sourcing rare and exceptional wine is on full display at Bentley Group's sophisticated bar where terroir is king. This mood-lit meeting hub for locals and grape boffins also provides house-cured charcuterie and a full menu of smart share plates if one glass becomes two magnums.

PS40

Shop 2, 40 King Street, Sydney
ps-soda.com

The 'PS' stands for Pop Soda, you know. Wattleseed, cola nut and Australian ginger find their way into house-made craft sodas, which in turn find their way into the bar's 'cellar door' and aromatic cocktails. Whisky and lemonade is a bracing time, the latter smoked by LP's Quality Meats.

Ramblin' Rascal Tavern

199 Elizabeth Street, Sydney
ramblinrascaltavern.com

The original home of 'shit tinnies' and top-shelf cognac. The Rascal heroes can also mix a killer classic and the dive bar-channelling boozer gets rowdy with live rock 'n' roll every Thursday. Mary's delivers fried chicken on request, which is exactly what you want to eat spread out in a booth with Emu Export and brandy.

Restaurant Hubert

Basement, 15 Bligh Street, Sydney
02 9232 0881 · restauranthubert.com

New York's 1930s Cafe Society lives on at this party-time bunker of French wine and caviar in the financial district. Start with a 'roe boat' above the velvet-draped dining room before hitting the bar for Languedoc, steak frites and all the pastis. A champion service team pulls out all of the stops, all of the time.

Shady Pines Saloon

Shop 4, 256 Crown Street, Darlinghurst
0405 624 944 · shadypinessaloon.com

Sydney's premier julep-muddling honky-tonk hoedown house. Sundays are a boot-scootin' belter when live country music kicks in and you can sink boulevardiers surrounded by vintage Marlboro signs and taxidermied moose heads the size of Texas.

The Unicorn

106 Oxford Street, Paddington
theunicornhotel.com.au

A prototype pokie-free pub that's all about great-value food showcasing producers such as Rangers Valley beef and Borrowdale free-range pork. There's a beaut beer garden with shady spots suited for smashing natural Aussie wine and a pub schnitzel that sets a national standard. Dessert is a game of darts.

Wyno

Shop 4, 50 Holt Street, Surry Hills
02 8399 1440

As much a holding pen for neighbouring Porteno as it is a standalone bar, Elvis Abrahanowicz and Ben Milgate's snacks at the former 121BC site are full of powerfully seasoned deliciousness that loves chilled and textured wine. It's a good thing there's plenty of refreshing grape juice available to drink in or take home.

ดู๋ดี๋ ป้ายแดง
DO DEE PAI DANG
THAI NOODLE BAR & CAFE

DO DEE PAI DANG DRINK

DODEE PAIDANG

TOP 20
SYDNEY
CHEAP EATS

By Andrew Levins

Afran Lebnan Bakery

29 Good Street, Granville • 02 9760 2099

Pizza for breakfast usually suggests cold leftovers – but at one of Sydney's many Lebanese pizza joints, you can start your day with a hot manoush topped with za'atar. This is one of the best. Their lahm bi ajeen manoush is amazingly crisp and topped with a spicy mix of lamb mince and tomatoes.

An Restaurant

27 Greenfield Parade, Bankstown
02 9796 7826 • anrestaurant.com.au

Few arguments get as heated as naming the best bowl of pho in Sydney, but An is a contender. The broth has incredible depth (and a touch of sweetness), piled high with herbs, onions and a generous amount of good-quality raw beef slices.

Aria Persian Fast Food

1 Iron Street, North Parramatta
02 8626 8956

You can't take five steps without running into a new burger spot in Sydney, but how many of them offer a decent burger for under a tenner? Aria's is just $6.90 for grilled kofta, vegetables and special sauce in a soft bun. If you're not satisfied by that bargain, try their sheep's brain and tongue sandwich instead.

Belly Bao

184 King Street, Newtown • bellybao.com

The classic slow-braised pork belly bao is top-notch, although fried chicken and tofu options give it a run for its money. The star of the show, though, is the $13 "baoger" – one of Sydney's best (and most reasonably priced) cheeseburgers, served in a special bao.

Chat Thai

Shop 1, Lower level, The Galeries
500 George Street, Sydney
02 9283 5789 • chatthai.com.au

Boasting a bain-marie full of ever-changing Thai curries, stir-fries and more, $12 will get you a plate piled high with rice and your choice of two dishes. You could come back every day for a month without eating the same thing twice.

Chatkazz

Shop 4–6, 14–20 Station Street East,
Harris Park • 02 8677 0033
chatkazz.com.au

The undisputed king of Indian street snacks in Sydney, Chatkazz in Harris Park is massive, colourful and almost always completely full of diners tucking into classics like biryani and roti alongside bizarre (and delicious) takes on Western snacks such as club sandwiches and pizza. Possibly the most fun vegetarian eating experience in Sydney.

Dodee Paidang

Shop 9, 37 Ultimo Road, Haymarket
02 8065 3827 • dodee.com.au

Are you game enough for level seven? Dodee Paidang serves up small bowls of tom yum soup with levels of chilli varying from a neutral zero to a fiery seven, which will make you see through time. Cool things down with a simple bowl of vinegary boiled rice and barbecue pork.

El Jannah

4–8 South Street, Granville
02 9637 0977 • eljannah.com.au

This Granville institution (it's also hatched four other locations) must go through thousands of charcoal chickens a week, and while the chicken alone is worth the visit, it'll be the addictive garlic sauce that's served with it that'll have you coming back.

Faheem Fast Food

194–196 Enmore Road, Enmore
02 9550 4850

This late-night Indian/Pakistani restaurant is a favourite for many Sydney cabbies, and one bite of the bright orange fish tikka is all you'll need to see why. Order everything on the tandoor menu – anything pulled from that red-hot fire pit is worth your time.

Happy Chef

Shop F3, 401 Sussex Street, Haymarket
02 9281 5832

There are many reasons to visit Chinatown's excellent food courts, and while some nominate Sussex Centre as the pick of the bunch, it's largely because of the legendary Happy Chef. The adventurous will be rewarded with noodles topped with offal, and those less so should try the Dried Spicy Beef Noodle (number 37).

Khao Pla

Shop 7, 370–374 Victoria Avenue, Chatswood
02 9412 4978 • khaopla.com.au

Sydney's best Thai restaurant outside of
Thainatown, Khao Pla's menu is a mix of
straight-up classics and unique spins on
standards. Come with a group and order
as much as you can, especially the
tom-yum-flavoured fried chicken wings and
the irresistibly sticky tamarind pork ribs.

Khushboo

38 Railway Parade, Lakemba • 02 9750 6600

Bangladeshi restaurants now outnumber
the many Middle Eastern restaurants in
Lakemba. Start by ordering a plate of
fuchka, hollow balls of crisp chickpea wafer
filled with boiled egg, potatoes and tamarind,
then move on to a whole fried fish with
an intensely spiced gravy.

KK Bakery

Shop 2, 85 John Street, Cabramatta
02 9755 0656

Marrickville Pork Roll may be the undisputed
home of Sydney's best pork roll, but the best
chicken banh mi can be found here. What
makes these rolls so special? They slow-roast
chicken marylands in master stock and shred
the meat for each order, stuffing it inside a hot
bread roll with ample pâté, mayo and huge
pieces of pickled daikon.

La Paula

9 Barbara Street, Fairfield • 02 9726 2379

Sometimes you just feel like eating a hotdog,
and this is one of the few places in Sydney
serving good ones. Their completo is a work
of art - avocado, tomato and mayonnaise
on a frankfurt, in a house-made bun that's
borderline impossible to fit in your mouth.

Lao Village

29 Dale Street, Fairfield • 02 9728 7136

The Lao-style fried rice at this humble family
restaurant is one of Sydney's must-try dishes,
a crunchy mix of deep-fried rice balls, herbs,
ham, peanuts and coconut. It goes well with
the fried quails and lemon pepper, or the fatty
sausages and barbecue ox tongue.

New Star Kebab

15 Auburn Road, Auburn • 02 9643 8433
newstarkebabrestaurant.com.au

You'll know you're in Auburn when you see
the smoke billowing from the many Turkish
kebab joints on Auburn Road. New Star
Kebab is the best of the bunch, serving
succulent skewers of lamb, chicken and
kofte alongside freshly baked bread and
pickled vegetables.

Phu Quoc

Shop 11, 117 John Street, Cabramatta
02 9724 2188

A great all-rounder, this Vietnamese
restaurant serves a stack of classics,
including the best sugar cane prawns
and spring rolls you'll find in Sydney.
There's nothing better than coming with
a group, ordering a few serves of both
and spending an hour making your own
rice-paper rolls with sugar cane prawn.

Tan Viet Noodle House

209 Rowe Street, Eastwood • 02 9858 5167

The skin on the fried chicken is just that little
bit more crisp at the Eastwood location than
at the Cabramatta location of this fantastic
Vietnamese noodle restaurant. Keep your
order simple: fried chicken with dry noodle,
soup on the side.

Vatan

65 Auburn Road, Auburn • 02 9649 4450

There are several Persian restaurants in the
Auburn area but Vatan rises to the top thanks
to their beautifully round and puffy discs of
proper Persian bread, which is wonderful
when torn and submerged in any of their
dishes, be it a grilled eggplant dip, a stew of
lamb with kidney beans, spinach and lime,
or a slow-cooked lamb shank with buttery
saffron rice.

Xi'an Eatery

183D Burwood Road, Burwood
02 8056 4600

Opt for anything on the menu with 'signature'
in the description, including but not limited
to the signature cold noodles, the signature
biang biang noodles and last but not least, the
fabulously fatty signature pulled pork burger.

CORNERSMITH

TOP 20
SYDNEY
CAFES

By Angie Schiavone

The Alchemist Espresso

8 Carter Street, Cammeray • 0418 977 082
thealchemistespresso.com.au

Here's the formula for the perfect community cafe. It's one part excellent coffee, one part crowd-pleasing food (the smashed avo is on Bread and Butter Project's rye, topped with cherry tomatoes, feta, mint and a heap of tender kale), one part service-with-a-smile, and one huge communal table. Science.

Barbetta

2 Elizabeth Street, Paddington
02 9331 0088 • barbetta.com.au

Part cafe and espresso bar, part food store, part Italian cooking school, Barbetta is a marvel of old-fashioned booth seating, chrome-edged tables, high-sheen wood and glass. Familiar Italian dishes get a brekkie twist – think carbonara recast as scrambled eggs on toast. Allora.

Boon Cafe

Shop 1, 425 Pitt Street, Haymarket
02 9281 2114 • booncafe.com

One of Sydney's original East-meets-West cafes. Toast with pandan custard, matcha-tea-flavoured ices, Thai coffee and tea, fried chicken with fiery green papaya salad in a burger, bowls of rice noodles topped with greens, herbs, fried crab and prawn cake – that's just scratching the surface.

Bread & Circus Wholefoods Canteen

21 Fountain Street, Alexandria
0418 214 425 • breadandcircus.com.au

Who knew pink paint and pumpkins could play a role in a long-lasting love affair? But that's the case with this wholefoods canteen. Added appeal is from colourful, crunchy salads, assorted sandwich boxes, an extensive tea selection and Daylesford milk kefir and Marvell Street coffee.

Circa Espresso

21 Wentworth Street, Parramatta
circaespresso.com.au

Circa just keeps getting bigger and better. Seating now extends to the neighbouring terrace, giving more people the chance to try the small batch roasted coffee, and A-grade food. 'Ottoman' poached eggs come with crumbed eggplant, garlic labne, burnt chilli and sage butter.

Cornersmith

88 View Street, Annandale • 02 8084 8466
cornersmith.com.au

Leading the game in ethical and sustainable practices at its two cafes and picklery. The Annandale locale, with its sunny courtyard and parkside position, is all-veg, with a penchant for ferments and pickles. Shop the range of Cornersmith cookbooks and pantry products to bring the goodness home.

Cuckoo Callay (Surry Hills)

413 Crown Street, Surry Hills • 02 8399 3679
cuckoo-callay.com.au

There's an extensive bar, excellent coffee (by Reformatory Lab), and playful dishes such as Pimp Mi Goreng, a crunchy noodle-encrusted chicken thigh on a burger with house-made kimchi, maple bacon, avo and coriander aioli. An annual Bacon Festival showcases the fine offerings of Marrickville's Black Forest Smokehouse.

Devon Cafe (North Sydney)

36 Blue Street, North Sydney • 02 8971 0377
devoncafe.com.au

The third Sydney outpost features a menu that's very-Devon with a few healthier additions such as linguine with blue swimmer crab, chilli, and cherry tomatoes. Sandos on soft white bread feature (panko-crumbed prawns, cabbage slaw and tom yum mayo is a crunchy, creamy delight), along with the classic soft serve and chips combo.

Double Tap

54-56 Smith Street, Marrickville
0404 475 430 • doubletapcoffee.com.au

It's no surprise the coffee's great, given the owner is former Coffee Alchemy head barista Daniel Karaconji. And the food is simple but satisfying – sandwiches stuffed with saucy home-made meatballs, pesto, parmesan and rocket are a popular special. Keep your eyes peeled for nostalgia-inducing cakes, too.

Edition Haymarket

60 Darling Drive, Haymarket
editioncoffeeroasters.com

The OG Darlinghurst location remains a favourite, joined now by this larger Edition. Dishes range from butter-poached prawns and crunchy puffed tapioca senbei, to pork katsu milk bun burgers.

Good Fella Coffee

Unit 7, 5 Celebration Drive, Bella Vista
0424 868 274 • goodfella.co

This high-caffeine, high-carb escape from the hub has a mini-amphitheatre setup that puts the baristas centrestage. From the kitchen come properly boiled then baked bagels with plenty of toppings to choose from – perhaps simple house-made cream cheese and chives, or boiled egg, ham, gremolata mayo, rocket and tomato relish.

The Lookout

1 Ithaca Road, Elizabeth Bay • 0415 945 651

Estate agents would just about pass out spruiking the 'location, location, location' of this new cafe at Elizabeth Bay Marina. The smoked trout hash with roasted carrot and sweet potato, crisp potato rounds and a poached egg hidden under seeded mustard hollandaise is good enough that the location fades into the background.

Matinee

23-29 Addison Road, Marrickville
02 9519 7591 • matineecoffee.com

Looking as retro-flash as the flashest old-school cinema foyer, Matinee is a show in itself. This bright, sprawling space is a feast for the eyes, and dishes such as cumin, quinoa and coriander falafel with grilled vegetables and smoky baba ganoush are full of flavour. It's licensed, too, and coffee is a custom blend.

Meet Mica

Shop 5, 492-500 Elizabeth Street
Surry Hills • 02 8018 7370 • meetmica.com.au

At this bright cafe, where chef Lee Li (formerly Tetsuya's) cooks with a distinct Japanese accent, patrons set records for the longest time between receiving their meal and eating. Why? So many snaps to take! The aerial of confit duck with green tea buckwheat noodles! Close-ups of croissants with crab and scrambled egg! Lobster congee!

ONA Marrickville

140 Marrickville Road, Marrickville
onacoffee.com.au

While the aim at the first Sydney outpost of Canberra's esteemed ONA Coffee is to deliver a 'coffee experience', the food is no afterthought. Dishes such as a kingfish smorrebrod with pickles, lemon aioli and capers are simple and vibrant. Short Stop doughnuts and Butterbing biscuits feature, too.

Paramount Coffee Project

80 Commonwealth Street, Surry Hills
02 9211 1122 • paramountcoffeeproject.com.au

The coffee at PCP is exceptional, with vast choice in beans and brewing methods. Bonus: the food more than holds its own, with dishes including coconut chowder with prawn, smoked barramundi, and crisp baked chat potatoes, aromatic with lemongrass and fresh herbs.

Queenside

Shop 1, 727 New Canterbury Road
Dulwich Hill • 02 8054 5998
queensidedulwichhill.com

Of the many new developments along this busy road, this small, understated cafe is surely the one locals are happiest about. Chess playing (hence the name), coffee-loving owner Jim Papadakis has years of experience as a barista and roaster and has created the house blends under his own label, Wonderlust Workshop.

Rising Sun Workshop

1C Whateley Street, Newtown
02 9550 3891 • risingsunworkshop.com

Lunch at this motorcycle workshop/multi-level cafe a block back from Newtown's main drag means ramen and katsu burgers alongside filter coffee. It's a good mix and a convivial vibe. Brekkie is more wide-ranging with bibimbap, granola, simple toasts and sweets (and a brekkie cocktail from 10am).

Ruby's Diner

173-179 Bronte Road, Waverley

Yep, we're still loving the $2.50 piccolo, made with Single O's Killerbee blend, but honestly, what's not to love about Ruby's? The coffee and tea offerings are vast, right down to the 'dark and stormy' ginger beer-espresso combo, and food takes cafe classics off the beaten track.

Son of a Baker

301 The Grand Parade, Sans Souci
02 9529 3335

Roman Urosevski grew up making Balkan burek pastries and now they're a star attraction at his small, smart-looking cafe. The burek pastry is prepared in view of customers and the end result is golden, crisp and flaky. A more extensive menu features the likes of lobster tail benedict.

♔♔

Biota Dining
Fleet
Muse Restaurant
Paper Daisy

♔

The Argyle Inn
Bistro Molines
Bistro Officina
The Byron at Byron Resort
Caveau
Clementine
Fumo
Harvest
Lolli Redini
Margan Restaurant
Muse Kitchen
Pearls on the Beach
Restaurant Mason
Shelter
St. Isidore
The Stunned Mullet
Subo
The Zin House

New
South Wales
regional

The Argyle Inn

TARALGA
80 Orchard Street
0448 402 008

CONTEMPORARY   **15/20**

Farmer-owned country inn with local, seasonal comfort food

Holmbrae Chicken's Hugh Wennerbom and Bannaby Angus beef farmer Keith Kerridge have brought life to this once-rundown, 113-year-old Taralga main street inn. They have also brought roast chicken, chook pie, and scotch fillet to the popular bar menu, prepared by former Bentley Bar and Restaurant chef Brenden Gradidge. But the big deal here is the six-course, set menu Saturday dinner, held in the Grand Dining Room and warmed by log fires in winter. It might kick off with the clean, lactic tang of crumbed Meredith goat's cheese, before velvety potato gnocchi sauced with a beautifully judged kangaroo ragu under a shower of parmesan. There's no seafood – because they are not near the sea – but there might be crisp-skinned Goulburn River trout with fruity, ruby red cabbage and beetroot, or sliced, house-smoked duck breast paired with wonderfully feudal slow-roasted potatoes. An old-school baked custard with a dollop of stewed rhubarb is fittingly unpretentious yet delicious. The place is a joy, for both locals and blow-ins alike.

Stay overnight in one of six comfortable guest rooms upstairs

Open	L Fri–Sun; D Fri–Sat
Price	$$
Cards	AE MC V eftpos
Chef	Brenden Gradidge
Features	Bar, licensed, outdoor seating, private dining, wheelchair access, BYO
Website	theargyleinn.com.au

Babyface Kitchen

WOLLONGONG
Shop 1, 179 Keira Street
02 4295 0903

CONTEMPORARY   **14.5/20**

Seafood-focused diner with strong Japanese and Korean influences

How do you make a bite-sized warm crumpet more delicious? By loading it up with sweet honey-mustard Moreton Bay bug. How do you make a crisp potato scallop even better? By roasting it in smoked pork fat and dunking it in tangy rhubarb ketchup. How do you have a great night out in Wollongong? Head to Babyface Kitchen. Horse-sized Mooloolaba prawns come in a splash of thick cultured butter sauce, spiked with prawn head stock and kombu. It's a rich umami puddle perfect for a slice of sourdough. Two fat cigars of perfectly pink David Blackmore wagyu rib blade arrive with what must be the 'Gong's greatest roast potatoes. Don't expect the quiet hush and linens of fine dining – this place is more about laid back good times and generous pours of natural wines. The seafood is sustainable, the floor staff are chatty and the playlist is full of Four Tet. More of this please.

The tasting menu is generous and excellent value. They'll happily adjust to include your favourites

Open	L Thu–Sat; D Tue–Sat
Price	$$
Cards	AE MC V eftpos
Chef	Andrew Burns
Features	Licensed, BYO
Website	burnsburyhospitality.com.au

THE ARGYLE INN

Balcony Bar and Oyster Co

BYRON BAY
Corner Lawson Street and Jonson streets
02 6680 9666

CONTEMPORARY   **14/20**

A nautical boho fantasy that feels like the beating heart of the town

Perched above Byron Bay's busiest intersection is a bastion of style and comfort, if you're the type of person who finds comfort in platters of cold oysters and pitchers of spicy bloody marys, that is. Named for the wide, plant-adorned balcony that overlooks the street, it's casual and affable, with friendly staff clad in Hawaiian shirts and sporting scruffy beards. The menu is so broad that you might fear the mediocrity that often arises at something-for-everyone establishments, but simple, straightforward cooking and above-average ingredients stave off that pitfall. Seafood is the strong suit, whether it's a giant bowl of moules mariniere – fat, fresh mussels swimming in creamy broth dotted with slivered garlic and shallots – or a crisp-skinned grilled kingfish cutlet served with miso hollandaise. This is a wonderful place to while away an afternoon, nibbling on crunchy school prawns served with habanero mayonnaise and drinking from the wine list that – like everything here – is easy, breezy and immensely approachable.

The private function room is one of the loveliest party locations in Byron

Open	B Sat–Sun; L D Daily
Price	$$
Cards	AE MC V eftpos
Chef	Sean Connolly
Features	Bar, licensed, outdoor seating, private dining
Website	balcony.com.au

Bills Fishhouse

PORT MACQUARIE
Shop 2, 18–20 Clarence Street
02 6584 7228

SEAFOOD   **14/20**

Fresh fish and good drinks, served with finesse

A seaside holiday isn't worth its salt without a good fish dinner. Almost everything on the menu at this lively bistro is hauled out of the sea by a local fishing trawler. Pull up a stool, order a rhubarb sour – the vanilla and fennel-spiced fruity cocktail is the perfect foil for the salty tang of limed sardines with squid ink from the snack menu. Sized to share, you could happily dine out on a selection of entrees alone – the roast pumpkin with local Ewetopia haloumi is practically a meal – but then you'd miss out on daily catches of local snapper with a foamy mustard sabayon and sweet onion soubise, or cod with tomatoes and spiced lentils that is full of flavour but still tastes purely of the sea. Desserts are simple – the dark chocolate mousse is so rich it's best shared, while the sheep's yoghurt panna cotta crumbed with pistachio is more delicate. There's no ocean view and noise levels hit a high as the night wears on, but the seafood's the best in town.

These guys also run the Salty Crew Kiosk on Port Macquarie's Town Beach

Open	D Mon–Sat
Price	$$
Cards	AE MC V eftpos
Chef	Peter Cutcliffe
Features	Bar, licensed, outdoor seating, wheelchair access
Website	billsfishhouse.com.au

Biota Dining

BOWRAL
18 Kangaloon Road
02 4862 2005

citi

♛♛

CONTEMPORARY   **16/20**

Southern Highlands produce in an Instagram-pretty setting

When late afternoon sun and woodsmoke drift into this dining room of sisal carpet, chalky walls and timeworn timber tables, all seems right with the world. Particularly if there's a 'G and Tea' (a cooler-than-it-sounds combination of gin, lavender and earl grey) at hand. What the chefs don't forage, owner/chef James Viles grows himself or sources from nearby producers for a tasting menu that rolls with the seasons. Crusty bread in a kangaroo fur merkin and snacks such as gougeres with dory roe taramasalata, and pear leather cigars piped with ewe's milk blue, might lead into an autumnal rosette of smoked blood plum slices bejewelled with garlic chive flowers and nasturtium buds, then a charry tile of Angus short rib that cuts like butter, served with a tart salad of small potatoes grown in seaweed. Onsite accommodation comes with a bonus: an outstanding breakfast of baked eggs with cream, chilli oil and smoky bacon in the leafy courtyard.

Guests can hire bikes and take a picnic lunch for $85

Bistro Molines

MOUNT VIEW
749 Mount View Road
02 4990 9553

♛

FRENCH   **15/20**

An ode to all things fine and French in the Hunter

This is a verandah with a view you could sit and gaze at for hours. Add a glass of Tallavera Grove shiraz and some gentle French warbling in the background and you have a fine afternoon on your hands. Inside it's all farmhouse chic – copper saucepans, dripping candelabras and the scent of slow-roasting meat. An entree of homegrown baked figs stuffed with blue cheese, wrapped in soft ribbons prosciutto dressed with gorgonzola cream lets you know this isn't diet food, but it's well worth the indulgence. Puy lentils, caramelised with niblets of speck, quietly shine underneath pink-centred quail and fat slices of sausage. A main course of twice-roasted duckling, lacquered deep mahogany with sweet orange glaze has its richness tempered by tart red cabbage. Room for dessert? Perhaps something on the lighter side like bright honey and pistachio parfait with thick blood plum slices. Farewelling that view is hard, but a mouthful of blackberry financier eases the blow.

Diners get a nifty little discount at the adjoining Tallavera Grove cellar door

Open	L D Thu–Mon
Price	$$
Cards	AE MC V eftpos
Chef	James Viles
Features	Bar, licensed, outdoor seating, private dining, wheelchair access
Website	biotadining.com

Open	L Thu–Mon; D Fri–Sat
Price	$$$
Cards	AE MC V eftpos
Chef	Robert Molines, Garreth Robbs
Features	Licensed, outdoor seating, wheelchair access
Website	bistromolines.com.au

Bistro Officina

BOWRAL
6 David Street
02 4861 7787

ITALIAN   **15/20**

Wood-fired Italian mountain refuge hiding in a southern highlands boutique hotel

Italian-born Nicola Coccia is a chef with fire in his belly – and just about everywhere else in his open kitchen. Flames, smoke and charcoal add life to everything on his heartfelt menu, while a log fire warms the art-lined dining rooms. Even the hand-churned butter that comes with the wood-fired bread is smoked. To start, impeccably fresh, raw slices of Hiramasa kingfish are bathed in a chilled, smoked fish broth that is both delicate and deep-flavoured (but don't miss out on the zesty, punchy taramasalata with its gnarly house baked crisps). Next, order anything from the grill – a magnificent 450g marron, perhaps, for a messy hands-on feast, or 10-week, dry-aged rib-eye grilled over ironbark or yellow box. Or pig out on wood-roasted porchetta wrapped in its own crisp, blistery crackling, served with a smoked apple sauce and baby smoked onions. This is gutsy, romantic, character-laden cooking deeply immersed in its southern highlands setting – a dream dining destination for that weekend away.

Six- and eight-course tasting menus deliver the whole experience

Open	B Sat–Sun; L Fri–Sun; D Wed–Mon
Price	$$$
Cards	AE MC V eftpos
Chef	Nicola Coccia
Features	Bar, licensed, wheelchair access
Website	bistroofficina.com.au

Bombini

AVOCA BEACH
366 Avoca Drive
02 4381 1436

ITALIAN   **14.5/20**

Polished Italian experience a little off the beaten path

After driving past for the third time while hurling abuse at your GPS system, the palm-laden oasis that awaits is a calming reminder that sometimes the best places are hard to find. Perched among the palms sits a charming bungalow cottage where chef Cameron Cansdell dishes out refined Italian fare to locals and those in the know. Tender Fremantle octopus comes smoky from the grill, matched with potato, lemon, black olive and mayonnaise. As you'd expect, pasta is taken seriously here. The supple texture of house-made linguine works wonders with a rich ragu of rabbit and basil. Blushing roast suckling lamb is served simply with golden garlic and charred chicory plucked straight from the bountiful vegetable garden you may have spotted on the way in. It's a good idea to finish on gelato, which is made from jersey cream, churned daily and flavoured with whatever is at its seasonal best. Truly, places like this are worth searching for.

Feeling a little more casual? Bombini does pizza on a separate menu in the garden

Open	L Sat–Sun; D Wed–Sun
Price	$$$
Cards	MC V eftpos
Chef	Cameron Cansdell
Features	Bar, licensed, outdoor seating, private dining, wheelchair access
Website	bombini.com.au

The Byron at Byron Resort

BYRON BAY
77-97 Broken Head Road
02 6639 2111

CONTEMPORARY　　　**15/20**

A luxury resort with elevated dining on the edge of the ocean

This restaurant and resort are conclusive proof that this once-sleepy beach hamlet has morphed into an elite playground. You can sit in the large glassed-in dining room or on the luxurious patio that overlooks the pristine swimming pool and is warmed by firepits at night. Service is exactly formal enough – waiters have an old-school deference, but a twinkle in the eye and a good dose of humour when it's needed. Get the night started with a bottle of Champagne and a platter of oysters, expertly shucked, cleaned and served perfectly chilled. There is the requisite Asian-ish raw tuna entree, or an $18 serving of nuts and olives. But this place is all about the mains: big hunks of expensive, expertly cooked beef, or caramelised duck with parsnips, pears, gizzards and local sorrel. A dessert of coconut milk and vanilla rice pudding rounds out the meal, with a tropical loveliness appropriate to the lush surroundings.

The resort offers 'gourmet' packages that include accommodation, breakfast, dinner, yoga, and guided outings to the farmers' market

Open	B L D Daily
Price	$$$
Cards	AE MC V eftpos
Chef	Matthew Kemp
Features	Bar, licensed, outdoor seating, private dining, wheelchair access
Website	thebyronatbyron.com.au/restaurant

Caveau

WOLLONGONG
122-124 Keira Street
02 4226 4855

CONTEMPORARY　　　**15.5/20**

Inspired fine dining with an ultra-local philosophy

Plenty of chefs and fisherman are more than familiar with the Aussie mullet (fish, not hairstyle), but not many of them treat these locals to the brainspiking treatment usually reserved for prize tuna and the like. Served with mussel broth, succulents and seaweeds, the result is a revelation. Simon Evans and Tom Chiumento's commitment to local, sustainable produce is extreme. The menu is best experienced in a tasting menu format. An assembly of tiny snacks appears on arrival, featuring playful combinations like magpie goose ham with grissini and gruyere, or smoked eel cannelloni with finger lime and sea lettuce. An elegant slice of blushing pink Thirlmere duck breast is heightened by the sweet/sour/bitter union of beetroot, Illawarra plum and radicchio. The local focus extends to the wine list and if you're curious about provenance, on most nights one of the boys will check in on the tables for a proud chat about the farmers, fisherman and foragers who make all of this possible.

The space is quiet and probably not the best place for a rowdy birthday dinner

Open	D Tue–Sat
Price	$$
Cards	AE MC V eftpos
Chef	Simon Evans, Tom Chiumento
Features	Licensed, private dining, wheelchair access, BYO
Website	caveau.com.au

CLEMENTINE

Clementine

YASS
104 Meehan Street
02 6226 3456

EUROPEAN   **15/20**

Convivial, rustic dining in a weatherboard cottage

Foraged sorrel. Upside-down nasturtium. Edible flowers for reasons unknown. Clementine wants nothing to do with these or any other gimmicks common to destination restaurants in country towns. This is a relaxed place of honest cooking focused on flavour. The warmer months warrant a spot on the verandah with views to muttering trees and a proud old church while winter calls for a fireside table and Yass cabernet shiraz (it's local wine only here, right down to the fizz). Attentive staff keep glasses full and offer extra sourdough for a cassoulet rich with confit duck leg, pork sausage and lardons the size of a thumb. Crisp-fried kalettes cling to braised veal shank sticky with ossobuco sauce while squiggly house-made spaghettini ferries a calamari and chorizo ragu. How else would you want to eat in the bush? Finish with baked apple and gingerbread sponge housing soft, sweet rhubarb and sink into throw cushions brighter than any garnish you'll find on a plate.

A pantry stocks olives, sourdough and chutney for your picnicking needs

Cupitt's Kitchen

ULLADULLA
58 Washburton Road
02 4455 7888

CONTEMPORARY   **14/20**

A prime location for lively lunching with a view

With a stunning outlook over the Budawang Range, it's not hard to see why securing a table on a sunny weekend in wedding season can be tricky. This gastronomic wonderland also boasts a brewery, cheese room and winery cellar door. The large, handsome restaurant has an inside/outside feel and has no problem catering for large groups. Kick things off with a beer made on site while you soak it all in. But don't be fooled, there's a clear distinction between restaurant and beer garden here. Chef Russell Chinn's food is polished and thoughtful. A dish of sashimi tuna and kingfish is heightened by zingy citrus pearls and the subtle charred flavours of puffed rice. There's plenty of technique on show at times, with main courses such as confit duck leg, smoked breast, pork and prune with seasonal mushrooms. To finish, it's hard to look past a selection of estate cheeses, and don't forget to pick one up for the road.

A pre-meal wine tasting in the cellar door makes matching a breeze

Open	L Fri–Sun; D Thu–Sat
Price	$$
Cards	AE MC V eftpos
Chef	Adam Bantock
Features	Licensed, outdoor seating, wheelchair access
Website	clementinerestaurant.com.au

Open	L Daily; D Fri–Sat
Price	$$
Cards	AE MC V eftpos
Chef	Russell Chinn
Features	Bar, licensed, outdoor seating, private dining, wheelchair access
Website	cupitt.com.au

Darley's Restaurant

KATOOMBA
5-19 Lilianfels Avenue
02 4780 1200

🍷

CONTEMPORARY   **14.5/20**

Pampered dining in old-world surrounds

This charming fixture of Echo Point sets the comfort levels to maximum with chandeliers, double linen and ornate leadlight windows. Take a spot in a butter-yellow velvet armchair by the marble fireplace and there's every chance you might doze off, especially after a sweet and fragrant peach cheek loaded with pastry cream. Only the odd crying child might jolt you back, or a waiter loudly explaining the menu to guests possessing limited English – a resort restaurant two-minutes walk from the Three Sisters is a magnet for tourists. New chef Roy McVeigh furnishes rustic cooking with modern flair in dishes such as sous vide Berkshire pork striploin, pan-fried and finished with prunes and a puree of daily-baked gingerbread. Watermelon rind is glazed in honey and stout to sweeten Flinders Island lamb rack to delicious effect, but candied violet on hay-smoked carrots and grapefruit curd takes the sugar hit too far. Sink into the cushions with red meat and cool-climate cabernet for the most gratifying time.

There's an extensive cheese list to accompany a fireside whisky

Open	D Tue–Sat
Price	$$$
Cards	AE MC V eftpos
Chef	Roy McVeigh
Features	Bar, licensed, private dining, wheelchair access
Website	darleysrestaurant.com.au

Dogwood, BX

BATHURST
87 Keppel Street
06 3312410

🍷

AMERICAN   **14/20**

It's all American, all the time at this rollicking bar-restaurant

The party's already rolling when you walk into the American saloon style bar/restaurant. The fried pickles are a great start. They're crunchy hot and salty, with a smooth chipotle mayo. Lip smackers just like the next act, smoked rib croquettes. You'll be told, "Trust us, just get 'em", by one of the friendly waitstaff. And they're right. You should. The tender short rib is rich and smoky, perfectly paired alongside brussels sprouts with bacon and maple. Countering the festival of Americana is the fish of the day – on this visit it's red emperor, which is clean and sweet, lightly spiced and nestled on a base of creamed corn, surrounded by sweet clams. There are all the sides to accompany all the meats, cooked over the fire pit in the kitchen. It's perfect if going large with a bunch of pals is on the cards. Finish off with a whisky (bartender/owner Evan Stanley is a pro – take his lead) and sharp cherry tart.

It's as much bar as it is restaurant, tended by one of the best bartenders in the biz

Open	L Fri & Sun; D Thu–Sun
Price	$$
Cards	AE MC V eftpos
Chef	John Mannion
Features	Bar, licensed, outdoor seating, wheelchair access
Website	dogwoodbx.com.au

EXP. Restaurant

POKOLBIN
1596 Broke Road
02 4998 7264

CONTEMPORARY   **14.5/20**

A progressive Hunter dining experience that champions Aussie ingredients

Halfway between the Tesla charging port, and test tubes of fennel and plum palate-cleansing cordial is the realisation this isn't the Pokolbin of yore. Instead you're in a futuristic Hunter Valley restaurant-cum-laboratory serving the most adventurous bites this side of Cessnock. Snacks to start – perhaps a thick slice of emu pastrami or diamond clams with pickled radish. Fingers crossed rare kangaroo with delicate shavings of butternut pumpkin, macadamia nuts and brown butter chicken jus is also on this week (because what's better than a night devouring the Australian coat of arms?) Floorstaff match the kitchen's intensity, but also give each plate context and approachability, success-fully pairing duck tongue in a crisp kale leaf with the 2015 Oakvale chardonnay but trust them. Buttery sponge cake topped with the pop of finger lime and goat's milk ice-cream for a final flourish, then Vegemite marshmallows and caramelised carrot to nibble while the bill is sorted. Yes, the future is a fun place to be.

Keep an eye out for regular collaborations with local producers and chefs

Open	L Wed–Sun; D Wed–Sat
Price	$$
Cards	AE MC V eftpos
Chef	Frank Fawkner, Josh Gregory
Features	Licensed, outdoor seating, wheelchair access
Website	exprestaurant.com.au

Fins

KINGSCLIFF
shop 5, 6 Bells Boulevard, Salt Village
02 6674 4833

SEAFOOD   **14/20**

Seafood stalwart that's still going strong

Steve Snow's fish-focused restaurant was one of the first restaurants to offer quality, forward-thinking dining on the North Coast and the tradition continues 26 years on. Once upon a time it was a little diner next to the Brunswick River. Now, find Fins in Salt Village – a sort of upscale, ungated community. The indoor/outdoor patio dining room has a tropical colonial vibe, with wooden slatted shutters flanked by palms and hanging plants. Hot and cold sashimi piles a whole lot of Asian fusion onto one plate, with hunks of tuna sashimi, avocado, seaweed mayonnaise, ginger crisps and warm chilli lime oil. The real strength here is in the local line-caught fish of the day, served in one of five preparations, which range from Portuguese to Javanese to Indian-ish. Or there's the lovely straightforward version called 'Snowy's fish', served seared over potatoes and green beans with a sauce of riesling and lemon. Dig into the wine list for best results.

The indoor bar area serves as a rotating pop-up with a completely different menu

Open	L Fri–Sat; D Mon–Sat
Price	$$$
Cards	AE MC V eftpos
Chef	Steven Snow
Features	Bar, licensed, outdoor seating, wheelchair access
Website	fins.com.au

Fleet

BRUNSWICK HEADS
Shop 2, 16 The Terrace
(entrance via Fingal Street)
02 6685 1363

CONTEMPORARY   **17.5/20**

The little restaurant that could makes bold cooking look easy

Is Fleet Australia's most likeable restaurant? You can make a case for Brunswick Heads' 14-seater as wildly original and refined as it is fun. In one sitting your mind is blown by the faith-leap miracle of gently warmed oysters, sheep's curd and shaved macadamia (so mineral, tart, round), then the perfect execution of prawn oil, pure crustacean sweetness, lubricating squid curls and shaved squash and by the straight-up boss move of that squishy fried sweetbread sanga as mid-course served with a tinnie of fruity lager. Yep, chef Josh Lewis and service gun Astrid McCormack have killer instincts. The good times flow with ease from mini-yet-mighty wine list of left-field producers to dishes that surprise but never posture. See crisp lamb with kale given great surprise depth from sardine garum, and the closing whodathunkit brilliance of licorice ice-cream nesting on onions fried to sweet crisps. Weird? Sure, but no discomfort. Fleet breaks the rules in just the right way.

Join the wait list if you miss a booking. Tables come up

Open	L D Thu–Sun
Price	$$
Cards	AE MC V eftpos
Chef	Josh Lewis
Features	Bar, licensed, outdoor seating, wheelchair access
Website	fleet-restaurant.com.au

Fumo

BLACKHEATH
33 Govetts Leap Road
02 4787 6899

CONTEMPORARY   **15/20**

Modern comfort cooking for long lunches in the mountains

It's a testament to chef Joe Campbell's dessert skills that even when it's five degrees above freezing in Blackheath, Fumo's bombe is so good you might consider another slice. A cross-section of blackberry sorbet, praline, lavender and sour cream ice-cream, it's elegantly layered and perfectly balanced. One doesn't pilgrimage to the old Vulcan's site just for sweets, though, and the workhorse oven that legendary chef Philip Searle once commanded still heats the cosy dining room and wood-fires comforting dishes rendered in contemporary style. Slow-braised beef oyster blade is giving and fragrant in an earthy mushroom sauce freshened by galangal, lemongrass and kaffir lime. A side of nutty roast potatoes is essential. Searle's bush landscapes share wall space with ukiyo-e prints and the Blue Mountains-via-Japan theme carries through to the cooking. Sake-steamed mussels are glossy with kimchi butter, while local carrots add crunch to house-made green tea noodles in a deeply savoury miso broth. Book well ahead during the holiday season – no one wants Fumo FOMO.

A new breakfast menu features crab omelette, croissants and yuzu granola

Open	B L D Fri–Sun
Price	$$
Cards	MC V eftpos
Chef	Joe Campbell
Features	Licensed, outdoor seating, wheelchair access
Website	fumorestaurant.com.au

Harvest

NEWRYBAR
18-22 Old Pacific Highway
02 6687 2644

CONTEMPORARY   **15/20**

House-grown produce and organic smiles

You can't taste much of the tea-tree in the dressing on your fresh-picked greens, but it sets the hyper-local tone for the menu at this heritage whitewashed weatherboard. No dish escapes without something house-grown, baked or foraged from the Hinterland wilds. And those embellishments work. It's an all-local sausage party on the charcuterie board, served with chewy sourdough baked in Harvest's amazing deli next door. Pretty shaved beets come with a cheesy cultured cream. A braised sugarloaf cabbage quadrant is all sherry vinegar tang and bitey parmesan, and the bone slips clean from a lamb leg, bedded on freekeh-turned-stew with juices and curry-leaf fragrant sweet onion soubise. Is tangy hibiscus granita the best foil for rich chocolate ganache? Maybe not, but it's otherwise a fresh old time on that sunny deck, linens in laps, drinking negronis made with Australian Campari substitute Okar, beers probably brewed in the shed (or close anyway), and natural-leaning Aussie wines.

Stock up on cheese at the deli

HARVEST

Open	B Sat-Sun; L D Daily
Price	$$
Cards	AE MC V eftpos
Chef	Alastair Waddell
Features	Bar, licensed, outdoor seating, wheelchair access, BYO
Website	harvestnewrybar.com.au

Lochiel House

KURRAJONG HEIGHTS
1259 Bells Line of Road
02 4567 7754

CONTEMPORARY   **14.5/20**

Asian flavours and scones in an old bush setting

A fireside table is hot property anywhere in winter, but especially at this charmer, built in an old coach house on the Blue Mountains' slopes. Mercifully, you'll be toasty wherever you sit thanks to three roaring hearths. Owners Nathan Parker and Tayla Smith have done a beautiful job revitalising this historic site (those fireplaces are almost 200 years old) where ancient floorboards creak under the footsteps of friendly staff and happy day-trippers. Outside, chickens cluck at sunflowers in the kitchen garden while their yolks cap steak tartare marinated in lemon juice with spring onion and fried shallots for texture. Ricotta gnocchi is pan-fried with guanciale, sage and brown butter for a powerfully savoury time sharpened further by grana padano, while the sweet notes of char siu-style pork are supported by white soy dressing enhanced with compressed celery. Finish with fresh-baked scones heaped with chantilly cream and jam – all the better if the sun's out and you can take tea in the courtyard.

Ask about the onsite accommodation for a weekend of breakfasts in bed

Open	B Sat–Sun; L Thu–Sun; D Thu–Sat
Price	$$
Cards	MC V eftpos
Chef	Nathan Parker, Maddison Willett
Features	Licensed, outdoor seating, wheelchair access, BYO
Website	lochielhouse.com.au

Lolli Redini

ORANGE
48 Sale Street
02 6361 7748

CONTEMPORARY   **15/20**

Perennially popular restaurant that's refined but relaxed

"One should always be drunk. That's all that matters." When the menu kicks off with a bawdy quote (from a French poet whose muses included a hussy nicknamed 'Squint-Eyed Sarah', no less), you know you're in for a rollicking good time. And this local legend doesn't disappoint. The soft furnishings are so comfy you'll want to stay the night. And there are plenty of reasons to linger, from the polished but personal service to the award-winning wine list and flavour-packed French and Italian food. Every meal should start with souffle, especially now Lolli's has expanded its range. The St Agur blue cheese and fig souffle is surprisingly light and lush. A rotolo of roasted pumpkin, feta and buffalo mozzarella with brown butter sauce is so gloriously rich you'll regret not ordering it as a main. For more heft, there's slow-cooked beef brisket with heirloom carrots and house-made horseradish cream. Order another bottle of wine and settle back for a spell. That's all that matters, after all.

The restaurant opens for Sunday lunch and dinner on long weekends

Open	L Sat; D Tue–Sat
Price	$$
Cards	AE DC MC V eftpos
Chef	Simonn Hawke
Features	Licensed, outdoor seating, wheelchair access
Website	lolliredini.com.au

Margan Restaurant

BROKE
1238 Milbrodale Road
02 6579 1317

CONTEMPORARY   **15/20**

Ethical, sustainable and delicious vineyard garden wine and dining

At the bottom of each Margan menu is what looks like a farmers' market shopping list, from eggs and honey right through to choko, elderflower and yacon. It's actually a rundown of ingredients directly produced onsite. Everything they can't pluck from the soil or raise on the farm is sourced within 100 miles. But it's what this luxe Tuscan-style food and wine citadel does with that garden-fresh produce that's extraordinary – from intensely sweet pea puree underneath an entree of melting confit pork belly (and a splinter of perfect crackling) to fresh bursts of zucchini basil mousse piped around a main of ridiculously juicy swordfish and capers. Surrender yourself to a relaxed meal with plenty of handy hints from the sommelier, drink in the stunning Brokenback Range vineyard view and save space for a light finish of citrus curd with blood orange granita and shards of meringue. Don't forget to peek at that whopping cheeseboard – it alone should make you go for Broke.

Ask about the 100-metre meal – you can literally see where everything on the plate comes from

Muse Kitchen

POKOLBIN
Corner Hermitage and Deasys roads
02 4998 7899

EUROPEAN   **15/20**

Zero pretense – just good honest food and a courtyard full of sunshine

It's all a bit breezy and relaxed at Muse Kitchen, which is a wonderful counterpoint to the stuffiness of a few of the Hunter's swankier establishments. The almost beach cafe-like vibe belies serious restaurant food – like sharp fermented chilli dripped over a sweet puddle of corn veloute and sea-fresh snapper brandade. Soft nuggets of pan-fried gnocchi with zucchini flowers and an intensely umami parmesan cream are also a winner, with a hint of chardonnay vinegar to cut through all that richness. Chef Sean Townsend has taken over the reins, with a passion for local ingredients. Milk for his house-made ricotta comes from a 72-year-old dairy farmer mate up the road. It's dolloped over pecan-smoked pulled goat, sweetened with purple baby carrots and a hint of fig. This casual contrast to its big sister Muse Restaurant has deft service and a standout wine list but it's proof you don't need starched linen to put the fine into fine dining.

You can try before you buy plenty of the wine list at the Tulloch's cellar door

Open	L Fri–Sun; D Thu–Sat
Price	$$
Cards	AE MC V eftpos
Chef	Thomas Boyd, Lisa Margan
Features	Bar, licensed, outdoor seating, private dining, wheelchair access
Website	margan.com.au

Open	L Wed–Sun; D Fri–Sat
Price	$$
Cards	AE MC V eftpos
Chef	Sean Townsend
Features	Licensed, outdoor seating, wheelchair access
Website	musedining.com.au

Muse Restaurant

POKOLBIN
Hungerford Hill Winery, 2450 Broke Road
02 4998 6777

citi 🍷   ♕♕

CONTEMPORARY   **17/20**

Bells-and-whistles fine dining with the best wine in the Hunter

A raft of striking snacks might begin proceedings at NSW's premier wine country restaurant – poached and potted kingfish with miso dressing and seaweed crackers, say, or sweet mirin-sprayed nasturtium flowers plucked from owner-chef Troy Rhoades-Brown's garden – but Port Stephens oysters are essential. Paired with house-baked brown bread, butter and Lake's Folly chardonnay (the cult Hunter wine is available by the glass), it is a moment of long-lunching perfection beneath a soaring glass ceiling in the sparkling dining room. Sebago potato noodles nest cured yolk crowned with seared black-lip abalone, and wood-fired Redgate Farm quail is joined by dashi-poached cauliflower, romanesco and buttery orbs of beurre bosc pear. An all-star service team ferries the signature Muse coconut mousse to every second table, but there's more dessert joy found in warm creme caramel and red miso invigorated by frozen blood orange. Exit via the Hungerford Hill cellar door and gift shop if it's open.

A courtesy shuttle will return guests to anywhere within a five-kilometre radius of the restaurant after lunch or dinner

Open	L Sat–Sun; D Wed–Sat
Price	$$$
Cards	AE MC V eftpos
Chef	Troy Rhoades-Brown, Mitchell Beswick
Features	Licensed, wheelchair access
Website	musedining.com.au/restaurant

The Painted Horse Cafe

SOFALA
27 Denison Street
02 6337 7092

CONTEMPORARY   **14/20**

Historic Sofala is booming again thanks to this new cafe

Kate Geale and Nicole Mcilwaine have created a cafe that's fast become the beating heart of this tiny colonial gold rush town. The formidable team, with a culinary past that includes Sydney's Centennial Hotel, cater for both the stream of fussy tourists, and the Sofala locals. Classics change with the seasons. Local figs are good anyway, but when plucked fresh from the tree down the road, roasted and plated with prosciutto, blue cheese and balsamic glaze, they're exceptional. The flathead and chips play all the right salty/crunchy notes and the pan-fried prawns are generously tumbled through a Thai-style green papaya salad. It would be rude to stop there and not have one of the handmade sweets that Mcilwaine has become known for, such as lemon curd tart and locally made vanilla ice-cream. Sofala, the oldest surviving gold town and the most painted streetscape in Australia, has once again struck it lucky.

Take a camera, talk to the locals and don't miss the ice-cream

Open	B L Thu–Sun
Price	$$
Cards	MC V eftpos
Chef	Nicole Mcilwaine
Features	Outdoor seating, wheelchair access, BYO

Paper Daisy

CABARITA BEACH
21 Cypress Crescent
02 6676 1444

CONTEMPORARY   **16/20**

A dreamy ocean-side fantasy in a refurbished retro hotel

The whitewashed walls, the chevron-striped cane chairs, the ocean breeze, the twinkling lights – there may be no better example of the beachy breezy fantasy life possible on northern NSW's coast. Lunch and dinner are both degustation-only, but this may be the most flexible tasting menu ever, with a choice of whichever four or five dishes you want from the diverse menu. ("You can literally have four desserts if you'd like" – a member of the standout service team.) Chef Ben Devlin is a fan of layering flavour: sea urchin is nestled under a cap of thinly shaved yellow squash with lime and chickpeas. Grilled cauliflower comes in a drift of crumbs spiked with the sharp surprise of watercress, which hide a treasure of saline-sweet smoked oysters. Mains are more traditional but no less delicious. Roast chicken with poached fennel sounds straightforward enough, but put it over a swoosh of pine nut puree and throw in some smoked red grapes? Life altering.

For a taste of the magic, the bar has both an enchanting view of the ocean and a short and sweet menu

Pearls on the Beach

PEARL BEACH
1 Tourmaline Avenue
02 4342 4400

CONTEMPORARY   **15/20**

A slice of shore-side paradise

Take a seat on the verandah under the Norfolk pines and soak up some of the best seaside views around. The atmosphere is relaxed and the service noticeably unobtrusive, making way for a soothing soundtrack of lapping waves and children playing in the distance. Chef Scott Fox works up flavours as big as the view. Take the silky tortellini filled ricotta and pea tortellini that's amped up with rich mushroom broth – umami for days – or the boldness of cashew cream, kimchi and wakame, handled with just enough delicacy not to overpower a dish of perfectly seared sea scallops. Larger plates, such as roast chicken, skin crisp and golden, served simply with seasonal vegetables, are perfect for sharing. Desserts like dark chocolate and roast pumpkin terrine, meanwhile, teeter into a more experimental realm with solid technique to pull it off. The pacing of dishes can be a little slow at times, but with a view like this, who's in a rush?

The dining room is cosy, but the verandah is where it's at

Open	B L D Daily
Price	$$$
Cards	AE MC V eftpos
Chef	Ben Devlin
Features	Bar, licensed, outdoor seating, wheelchair access
Website	halcyonhouse.com.au

Open	L D Thu–Sun
Price	$$$
Cards	AE MC V eftpos
Chef	Scott Fox
Features	Licensed, outdoor seating
Website	pearlsonthebeach.com.au

PAPER DAISY

Pipeclay Pumphouse

MUDGEE
Robert Stein Vineyard, 1 Pipeclay Lane
02 6373 3998

CONTEMPORARY   **14/20**

Paddock-to-plate dining in a classic country setting

No restaurant is complete without fresh produce, fine wine and a vintage motorcycle museum. Here you get to enjoy all three, starting with the collection of classic bikes, from a Douglas Dragonfly to a 250CC single cylinder once fancied by "lady postmen". The rustic restaurant next door puts the corrugated back into iron, from the farm-shed rooftop to the bizarro metal sculptures (giant foot, Ned Kelly) around the dam. The menu is more conventional, focusing on locally sourced fare with loads of flavour and little fuss. Rich pork rillettes and slivers of salami on the cracking charcuterie plate are sourced from the swines grazing by the vines. Tender spiced lamb backstrap comes with caramelised cauliflower from the vegie garden by the cellar door. Better still is a perfectly simple bowl of roasted zucchini, with lemon and brown butter. Service can be a little patchy but there's always another glass of chocolatey Robert Stein cab sauv at hand. And you can always ask to ride pillion home.

Park by the cellar door for some shade on a summer's day

Racine

NASHDALE
42 Lake Canobolas Road
02 6365 3275

CONTEMPORARY   **14.5/20**

Creative fare with a fine view to boot

Rumour has it that Racine once stopped serving a wine from Bathurst because customers wouldn't stomach such a foreign drop – even one from only 55 clicks away. People here are geographically precise in their love of local wine, food and flavours. And the expansive view of vineyards and rolling hills from this relaxed restaurant is a reminder of why. The wine list is a tribute to local tipples, from pinot gris through to a sweet sticky riesling. There's award-winning winemaker Philip Shaw sitting at a nearby table, hooking into a charcuterie plate. His vibrant Pink Billy saignee goes down a treat with smoky shredded ham hock, pea puree and puffed pork scratching. Switch it up for tender slow-cooked lamb saddle with caramelised onion puree and pickle, or crisp, pressed duck with rich roast beetroot. Parsnip cake is already perfectly paired with smooth goat's cheese mousse and maple gel. It's no wonder no one wants to stray. Everything you need is right here.

Try wallet-friendly Thursday nights, when apprentices are in charge of the kitchen

Open	B Sat–Sun; L Thu–Sun; D Thu–Sat	
Price	$$	
Cards	MC V eftpos	
Chef	Andy Crestani	
Features	Licensed, outdoor seating, wheelchair access	
Website	pipeclaypumphouse.com.au	

Open	L Thu–Sun; D Thu–Sat
Price	$$
Cards	AE MC V eftpos
Chef	Shaun Arantz
Features	Licensed, outdoor seating, private dining, wheelchair access
Website	racinerestaurant.com.au

Restaurant Botanica

POKOLBIN
555 Hermitage Road
02 6574 7229

CONTEMPORARY **14.5/20**

Pretty perfect for a long, lazy lunch or dinner among the vines

Chef Matthew Bremerkamp's philosophy is that good chefs must be good gardeners – and that garden to plate attitude is evident in every bite. Apparently, this year's crop of corn was stellar. It pops up sweetly pureed with miso in a truly exquisite entree of just-seared fat scallops alongside dots of pickled ginger gel and house-made leek kimchi. Raspberries you can still spot down the hill on bushes turn up in dessert as a zingy sauce alongside deeply rich chocolate mousse, crunchy honeycomb and a scoop of malted Jerusalem artichoke ice-cream we would gladly eat by the tub. Say yes to all three courses, to the cauliflower veloute amuse bouche, to the charming waitstaff and to perfectly pink duck with orange sabayon and hazelnuts. Book a table on the balcony overlooking the vines, order a glass or two of the (excellent) local Vinden Estate semillon and let your own garden grow long for a weekend as you come eat from this one.

Sunday lunches are accompanied by a rotating roster of outstanding acoustic artists

Open	L Sat–Sun; D Wed–Sun
Price	$$
Cards	AE MC V eftpos
Chef	Shayne Mansfield
Features	Licensed, outdoor seating, wheelchair access
Website	spicersretreats.com/spicers-vineyards-estate/dining

Restaurant Mason

NEWCASTLE
Shop 3, 35 Hunter Street
02 4926 1014

CONTEMPORARY **15/20**

Reliable and refined dining for special occasions and long business lunches

Since it opened in 2011, this Steel City bolthole has provided Novocastrians with the most assured cooking in town. Chef Chris Thornton doesn't rely on gels and foams to impress his well-paying guests, just premium local produce enhanced with beautifully balanced sauces and focused technique. Local Swansea mackerel is flame-grilled and brushed with tonkatsu sauce to cut through its natural oils. Steamed barramundi is elevated with a Japanese accent too, graced by a wonderfully savoury dashi and topped with crisp-fried shiso, while smoked and roasted Berkshire pork neck is big flavoured main, served with bitter grilled Morpeth cabbage and sweet cider puree. Triple-cooked chips supercharged with black garlic salt are valuable players on the side. Baked yoghurt cheesecake crowned with lemon sorbet is a zesty finish and although the dining room can feel like a function centre in the evening (beige chairs next to beige curtains on beige walls), a confident, smiling floor team keeps the vibe warm and bright.

Visit Reserve wine bar nearby beforehand for an exceptional selection of classic Hunter Valley drops

Open	L Thu–Sat; D Tue–Sat
Price	$$
Cards	AE MC V eftpos
Chef	Chris Thornton
Features	Licensed, outdoor seating, private dining, BYO
Website	restaurantmason.com

Rick Stein at Bannisters

MOLLYMOOK
191 Mitchell Parade
02 4455 3044

SEAFOOD   **14.5/20**

A British chef's Aussie homage to all things piscine in a seaside setting

Rick Stein's name on Bannisters' title isn't hubris. It says "Trust me, I love fish." The menu reflects the British TV chef's travels around the globe, and the menu covers just about every way you can cook fish, with more than 30 dishes on offer, plus sides and specials. There are dishes from Cambodia, California, Sri Lanka. There's fish 'n' chips, lobster thermidor, fish pie, and ceviche. The dishes that showcase the quality of the produce work best. Local oysters are opened to order, Ulladulla snapper cooked in paper with roast tomatoes and a tarragon mayo demonstrates just how great this fish can be. Barramundi is firm-fleshed, crisp-skinned, napped with a porcini and sweet onion sauce. In a beach pavilion setting, the unusually high staff-to-guest ratio ensures attentive service. Raisin ice-cream, Pedro Ximenez and an espresso shot hit the spot from the long and tempting dessert menu. And yes, that is Mr Stein at the table over there.

Get a room – there's a lot on the menu and wine list to try

Ruby's Mount Kembla

KEMBLA HEIGHTS
39 Harry Graham Drive
02 4272 2541

CONTEMPORARY   **14.5/20**

Ten minutes from the motorway, 100 years from care

As you leave the motorway and wend your way up the mountain you relax. In 10 minutes you find yourself in a huddle of heritage-listed cottages. Park, breathe in, and take your seat in a gracious, spacious, uncluttered, wooden-floored, weatherboard-walled, century-old, high-ceilinged room. Ceiling fans turn over wide spread tables. It's degustation only – small plates that add up to a satisfying meal. Water, wine, and an amuse bouche of pumpkin soup arrive. There are curls of sashimi snapper, garlic chive flowers. A twice-cooked goat's cheese soufflé is balanced with apple and walnuts. Chef Scott Woods teases braised pork cheek into a yielding, gelatinous pleasure, served on a lentil and shredded oxtail ragu. This is classic cooking, the flavours distinct and clean. Hunks of venison are served alongside radicchio braised in honey and balsamic, followed by bright cherry sorbet, gingerbread and roast grapes. Salted caramel petit fours are savoured and glasses are raised to Ruby, postmistress and wicketkeeper, Kembla Ladies' Cricket Team, 1931.

The matched wines are very good value

Open	L Fri–Sun; D Wed–Sun
Price	$$$
Cards	AE MC V eftpos
Chef	Paul Goodenough
Features	Bar, licensed, outside seating
Website	bannisters.com.au

Open	L Sun; D Fri–Sat
Price	$$
Cards	AE MC V eftpos
Chef	Scott Woods
Features	Licensed, outdoor seating, private dining, wheelchair access
Website	rubysmtkembla.com.au

Shelter

LENNOX HEAD
41 Pacific Parade
02 6687 7757

CONTEMPORARY   **15/20**

A beachside cafe that doubles as one of the area's most exciting new restaurants

On a sleepy stretch of ocean front road in Lennox Heads lies that greatest of Australian inventions: the all-day cafe that doubles as a serious restaurant. The scene at Shelter is almost too beautiful to behold: walls of windows thrown open to the sea breeze. Sunlight streaming in over polished wooden tables and jugs of native flowers. A direct line of sight to the ocean. Effortlessly stylish patrons drinking natural wine. Settle in for a full meal of beautifully sourced ingredients used to stunning effect. Raw fish sits on cultured cream with cucumber and succulents – subtle and fresh and lovely. Line-caught mullaway comes over a hearty paste of almonds with broccoli and peas. Shelter's version of brussels sprouts with mustard and more of that cultured cream will reignite any lost love for the divisive green. There's a subtlety to this cooking, and an aesthetic that gets close to health food but never loses sight of pure deliciousness.

Monday to Friday, Shelter runs a cracker midweek lunch special: for $35 get two courses and a glass of wine or tap beer

Open	B L Daily; D Thu–Sat
Price	$$
Cards	MC V eftpos
Chef	Dennis Baker
Features	Licensed
Website	shelterlennox.com.au

South on Albany

BERRY
Shop 3, 65 Queen Street
02 4464 2005

CONTEMPORARY   **14.5/20**

A no-nonsense celebration of local produce in the heart of Berry

Modest decor and warm, enthusiastic service set the tone for relaxed weekend dining – a welcome break from the touristy bustle of Berry's main drag. The kitchen adopts an obsessively local philosophy to drive home honest, simple flavours that deliver the goods. Local Southern Highland extra virgin olive oil infused with parmesan rinds, rosemary and garlic highlights thrifty ingenuity in the kitchen. Ultra-fresh and seriously crunchy baby carrots from Buena Vista Farm in Gerringong are lightly pickled and served with a dainty side of salad cream. Mains delve into heartier territory with generous dishes like confit duck maryland, rhubarb, parsnip puree and a hazelnut-flecked cabbage slaw. Fish of the day is a highlight. Locally caught snapper on this occasion, is cooked perfectly and served with a luscious olive oil mash, local corn grilled in the husk and a parsley white wine veloute. Comfortingly simple stuff with the precise technique to match.

The wine list features plenty of NSW producers, so be sure to try some local gems

Open	L Sat–Sun; D Wed–Sat
Price	$$
Cards	MC V eftpos
Chef	John Evans
Features	Licensed, outdoor seating, wheelchair access, BYO
Website	southonalbany.com.au

St Isidore

MILTON
89 Croobyar Road
02 4455 7261

CONTEMPORARY   **15/20**

Smart dining with plenty of rural charm

With sliding doors, a view of the vegetable patch and Aerogard cans at the tables, St Isidore is like an ultra-elegant version of your classic Aussie patio. A sense of place also runs through the menu, as chef Alex Delly draws on multicultural influences to showcase the best local and seasonal produce. Start with casual bites like Russian-style crisp-fried rabbit croquettes or creamy taramasalata with bottarga and warm focaccia. Moreish dumplings made from yesterday's sourdough, and served in a cheesy jumble of pumpkin puree, pecorino and super ripe taleggio may just be the ultimate guilty pleasure. Sharing is encouraged, but you won't want to. Roast hapuka with slow-cooked oxtail gracefully straddles the line between rich and light perfumed by refreshing lemongrass to brighten the surf and turf mood. Service is friendly and informative, though the pacing can be a little erratic at times. But we'll blame the buzz from the diners – it's Milton's hot ticket, mozzies and all.

Drop in on a Thursday for locals night, featuring a $60 set menu

The Stunned Mullet

PORT MACQUARIE
24 William Street (opposite Town Beach)
02 6584 7757

CONTEMPORARY   **15.5/20**

A class act that never misses a beat

It's been six years since this unpretentious restaurant overlooking Town Beach earned its first hat, and it shows no sign of being the town's first and only hatted diner for granted. The views steal the show during lunch. At night the quiet, softly lit room is fanned by sea breezes. Service is spot on, the wine and drinks list the best for miles, the food uncomplicated but creative. Despite the name, it's not just about fish – and the flavours are a worldly mix. Deboned wagyu ribs are sticky and sweet, with a tangy hit of kimchi. A silky sformata of Jerusalem artichoke comes dressed with hazelnuts and purple carrot chips, punched up with a chilli parsley sauce. A chicken breast goes Japanesey with kombu butter and bacon dashi. Pomegranate tabbouleh and za'atar give a piece of locally caught bass groper Middle Eastern zing. Desserts like the pumpkin gelato fortified with date, burnt orange and coffee crumbs offer unexpected combinations and are a bittersweet end to a slick night out.

Spend some time studying the gin and whisky list and you'll find some rare treasures

Open	L Fri–Sun; D Thu–Sat
Price	$$
Cards	MC V eftpos
Chef	Alex Delly
Features	Licensed, outdoor seating, private dining, wheelchair access
Website	stisidore.com.au

Open	L D Daily
Price	$$$
Cards	AE MC V eftpos
Chef	David Henry, Michael Urquhart
Features	Licensed, wheelchair access
Website	thestunnedmullet.com.au

Subo

NEWCASTLE WEST
551D Hunter Street
02 4023 4048

CONTEMPORARY   **15.5/20**

A modest little restaurant with assured and creative cooking

Beau and Suzie Vincent have provided Novocastrians with the city's most progressive dining since cutting the ribbon on Subo's sharp lines and soft lighting in 2011. The husband-and-wife team captain a charming ship with Suzie leading a professional floor team and pouring wild-ferment chardonnay to match Beau's chawanmushi. That savoury Japanese custard is a heady treat, fragrant with a soy-braised mushroom party of morels, shiitake and trumpets, while buttery scallop carpaccio is punctuated with jamon, XO and beer-battered nori. The kitchen knows that few things are more warming than a slow-cooked rib and here Cape Grim beef is braised overnight in Guinness and red wine for flavour that lasts. Served with beef fat-enhanced bagna cauda and lifted with yuzu-dressed celeriac, it's one of the more civilised times you can have in grungy Newcastle West. Banana cream pie proves the highlight, though, with spot-on shortcrust, a scattering of tonka beans and bonus banana slices macerated in icing sugar for extra sweetness.

Head in a little early and enjoy a boulevardier at Koutetsu cocktail bar next door

Open	D Wed–Sat
Price	$$
Cards	MC V eftpos
Chef	Beau Vincent
Features	Licensed, private dining
Website	subo.com.au

Three Blue Ducks at the Farm

EWINGSDALE
11 Ewingsdale Road (via Woodford Lane)
02 6684 7795

CONTEMPORARY   **14/20**

Glamorous farm or cafe? You decide

When it comes to choosing a cult to join in Byron Bay, there are plenty. But this one's the most Instagrammable. More lifestyle theme park than eatery, the cafe-slash-restaurant is girt by a bakery, produce store and florist. There's a hitching post and gratitude bench. But drink that wellness Koolaid. Mark LaBrooy and Darren Robertson's smart, sharp cooking style where everything is farm-plucked, fresh or fermented was born for this backdrop. These guys literally wrote books (buy them here!) on the likes of caramelised pumpkin slick with hummus and crunchy pepitas, crackle-perfect porchetta stuffed with herbs from the gardens outside or fire-roasted rib-eyes electrified by acid-bright herb blitz chimichurri. Smash a sunny egg into a warm, gingery rubble of cauliflower, broccoli and quinoa, or watch dudes who never miss leg day eating fat brioche rolls stuffed with bacon, lacy fried eggs and mustard-sharp relish while basking in the sun.

It can be a hot mess at weekends – prepare to wait

Open	B L Daily; D Fri–Sun
Price	$$
Cards	MC V eftpos
Chef	Mark LaBrooy, Darren Robertson, Sam Morton
Features	Bar, licensed, outdoor seating, wheelchair access
Website	threeblueducks.com/byron

Tonic

MILLTHORPE

Corner Pym and Victoria streets
02 6366 3811

CONTEMPORARY **14.5/20**

Bold seasonal flavours in a picture-perfect setting

While watching the human traffic pass by the wide windows of this quaint corner restaurant, certain truths become evident. Walking while drinking a hot beverage is a profoundly disappointing experience. A mobile phone is your best friend. Old men dress like trees in the dead of winter. A table at Tonic is the perfect possie for people-watching in this picturesque village. The ever-changing view is more enjoyable still when served alongside a pretty little plate of roasted quail with nutty black rice and earthy wild mushrooms. Pan-fried snapper with king oyster mushrooms and fresh radicchio is crisp, juicy and plump in all the right places – despite the mismatched accompaniment of sweet corn ravioli. Sichuan-peppered Mandagery Creek venison gets things back on track with a beautiful blend of flavours and textures, featuring golden cauliflower gratin, sweet poached rhubarb and smooth duck liver parfait. Service can be a little slipshod. But there's plenty to see outside to pass the time.

Time your trip to coincide with Millthorpe's massive biannual markets

Open	L Sat–Sun; D Thu–Sat
Price	$$
Cards	AE MC V eftpos
Chef	Tony Worland
Features	Licensed, private dining, wheelchair access
Website	tonicmillthorpe.com.au

Town Restaurant and Cafe

BANGALOW

33 Byron Street
02 6687 1010

CONTEMPORARY **14.5/20**

A cheery daytime cafe morphs into a serious degustation-only restaurant at night

Sure, you can pop in for a coffee or a ham baguette daily. But on Thursday, Friday and Saturday nights, head up the steep staircase at the back of the cafe where the gracious staff serves a full-blown degustation menu. You might start with an intense mushroom broth, speckled with chives, before heading into an elegant sliver of cured salmon accompanied by a dollop of miso almond cream. Asian ingredients are used alongside classic European technique to create elegant contrasts – silver-skinned snapper sits in a broth that's rich with ginger, and beef with Jerusalem artichoke is bolstered by the addition of shiso. The cross-cultural juxtapositions are particularly alluring once you make it to sweets, including pear sorbet showered with parmesan cheese, and pineapple nasu dengaku with vanilla custard and miso ice-cream. Don't expect a fast ride – this is the place to treat yourself to a long night of delicious food and quiet conversation.

To take full advantage of the carefully chosen wine list you'll want to stay nearby; Bangalow Guesthouse is a lovely option

Open	B L Daily; D Thu–Sat
Price	$$$
Cards	AE MC V eftpos
Chef	Karl and Katrina Kanetani
Features	Licensed

Vine and Tap

BATHURST
The Brooke Moore Centre
142 William Street
02 6358 0875

ITALIAN   **14/20**

A cosy corner of town to enjoy contemporary Italian sharing plates

This cosy heritage brick building with its leafy courtyard outside, is smack bang in the middle of Bathurst, and pulses with all walks of life. Chef Chris Brooks (ex-Albert and Sydney, in Melbourne's Fitzroy) offers up Italian-style antipasti and primi while keeping things as local as possible. Golden beetroot mousse with bee pollen is a delicate start – especially with a glass of prosecco, which they serve on tap. Wild mushroom arancini are perfectly fragrant and great with the recommended sauvignon blanc (again, on tap) from Veneto. The brisket and marrow meatballs are rich in flavour and texture, finished in a shower of pecorino. There's a pause before dessert, cooked a la minute and worth the wait. Sfogliatelle – a shell-shaped ricotta pastry, is here filled with Nutella cream – and the result is an eye-rolling sweet dream. This is a fine showcase of local produce and wine for both locals and visitors alike.

Rolling with a group? Take the thinking out of it, book the courtyard and order pizza

Open	L D Wed–Sun
Price	$
Cards	DC MC V eftpos
Chef	Chris Brooks
Features	Bar, licensed, outdoor seating, wheelchair access
Website	vineandtap.com.au

The Zin House

MUDGEE
329 Tinja Lane
02 6372 1660

CONTEMPORARY   **15.5/20**

Warm welcome and fresh seasonal fare in a classic country setting

The short stroll to the Zin House passes grapevines and garden beds of biodynamic berries, vegies and flowers in bloom. Much of the set-course seasonal menu travels only the same hop, step and jaunt to the plate. Might this be the most carbon-neutral meal on the planet? Certainly, it's one of the most relaxed. Unbuckle your belt, drop your voice to a drawl and settle in for some smart country cooking that's bursting with flavour. Food this fresh doesn't need tarting up. Served on the farmhouse tables might be crisp cucumber cubes with a light and lemony oyster mayonnaise, or zingy tomato tagliolini with fresh garden herbs and shaved gruyere. Slender slices of beef from the Zin House's own herd are well-matched by a colourful tangle of zucchini and an earthy shiraz from Lowe Wines, which is only an amble away. Some diners instead opt for a kip in the clover between courses. So lie back, relax and stay awhile.

Take a guided garden walk as part of the open kitchen lunch on Mondays

Open	L Fri–Mon; D Fri–Sat
Price	$$
Cards	AE MC V eftpos
Chef	Kim Currie
Features	Licensed, outdoor seating, private dining, wheelchair access
Website	zinhouse.com.au

Northern Territory

Hanuman

DARWIN
93 Mitchell Street
08 8941 3500

INDIAN/THAI   **15/20**

**All the flavours of a tropical
night market rolled into one
breezy restaurant**

Darwin's reputation as a melting pot
of cultures and languages precedes it
(the weekend markets are legendary),
so it's no surprise that the city's most
popular spot for a fancier night out
(i.e. no thongs) skips merrily across
Asia, picking from the best of Indian
and Thai flavours. Nuggets of juicy
chicken grilled inside pandan leaves
and swiped through a sticky sweet chilli
sauce could be straight out of Bangkok,
but the fish tikka is a unique chimera,
with meaty, spiced barramundi portions
marinated in ginger, garlic, chilli, garam
masala, black mustard paste and rose
petal. Order the Hanuman prawns,
a glut of shelled crustaceans and
snappy green beans in a rich, fragrant
curry sauce humming with ginger and
makrut lime. In texture it's a cousin of
a satay, but it pairs better with a fluffy
naan than the buttery triangles of roti.
Happily everything goes with a cold
beer on the terrace under the banks
of fans going full throttle in the
tropical heat.

**Hit two Darwin icons at once:
Hanuman caters the Deckchair
Cinema two nights a week**

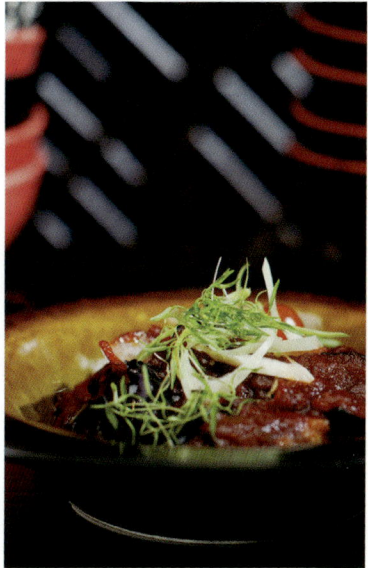

HANUMAN

Open	L Mon–Fri; D Daily
Price	$$
Cards	AE DC MC V eftpos
Chef	Syed Nainar, Ali Muhammed
Features	Licensed, outdoor seating, wheelchair access
Website	hanuman.com.au

NU NU

Queensland

Aria
Otto
Stokehouse Q

1889 Enoteca
Blackbird Bar and Grill
E'cco Bistro
Gauge
Gerard's Bistro
GOMA Restaurant
Montrachet
Tartufo
The Wolfe

Brisbane

1889 Enoteca

WOOLLOONGABBA
10-12 Logan Road
07 3392 4315

ITALIAN   **15.5/20**

The laidback wine-forward Roman hero Brisbane needs

Given half the restaurant is a specialist wine shop, the clues are clear on how to nail dinner. That's by ordering as many of the Roman trattoria staples as your table can hold – ricotta-stuffed zucchini flowers in the finest lacy batter, vitello tonnato with a luxurious pool of properly funky tuna mayo and the tiniest capers – plus extra spaghetti for luck. Then, throw yourself on the mercy of the well-versed Italian staff and let them pour anything and everything from wine importer owner Dan Clark's almighty collection of left-field Italian and natural wines. This is everything you want an Italian restaurant to be. It's sticky, salty, sharp cacio e pepe, the aged pecorino and pepper tossed with spaghetti at table alongside eggy carbonara with the crispest slips of guanciale. It's gilded mirrors and bareback tables and big accents on everyone and everything, from the lemony sauce drenching juicy veal fillets in crisp prosciutto jackets to the glass of skinsy Dinavolino.

Go big on grappa with mates in the private cellar downstairs

Open	L Tue–Fri, Sun; D Tue Sat
Price	$$
Cards	AE MC V eftpos
Chef	Matthew Stubbing
Features	Bar, licensed, outdoor seating, wheelchair access
Website	1889enoteca.com.au

Aria

BRISBANE
1 Eagle Street
07 3233 2555

CONTEMPORARY   **17/20**

A powerhouse combination at the northern outpost of Matt Moran's plush fine diner

Take that view looking out over the Brisbane River and Story Bridge. Add the wine stylings of sommelier Ian Trinkle (the *2018 Good Food Guide* Sommelier of the Year) who's as happy pouring from Healesville as he is Burgundy. Then throw head chef Ben Russell in the mix. That's a three-punch combination, right there. The important thing is to do what you feel. So from the menu, that could look like an entree of fresh-picked spanner crab mingling with lightly pickled cucumber and crunched up with puffed wild rice over a silken avocado puree. Or a piece of roast duck sporting a perfectly even rosy blush, offset by wood ear mushrooms. Or it could easily look like a piece of Rangers Valley chuck tail, salted and charred with a squeeze of lemon and a little cress salad. And for the mack move, elect to try every sauce on offer from the condiment tray, from Bearnaise to hot English. Killer style from go to whoa.

This is a restaurant made for long lunches. Take the boss's black Amex for a spin

Open	L D Tue–Sat
Price	$$$
Cards	AE DC MC V eftpos
Chef	Matt Moran, Ben Russell
Features	Bar, licensed, private dining, wheelchair access
Website	ariabrisbane.com.au

E'CCO BISTRO

Blackbird Bar and Grill

BRISBANE
123 Eagle Street
07 3229 1200

CONTEMPORARY   **15/20**

Louche lunching on the riverside

What was the brief for this room
of royal red and blue banquettes,
bird-adorned gold wallpaper and
armchair-girt table surrounded by
glitzy drapes? Arabian boudoir?
Having a little money can really
enhance your time here. You'll be
able to upgrade your caviar service
from salmon roe (delicious) to $220
scampi jewels, though either is good
with warm blinis and finely chopped
trim. You could also chase with an
outrageous grilled tomahawk, starting
at $270. But Blackbird, while built
for louche lunching, isn't all steak and
Selosse. Chef Jake Nicolson's Lake
House credentials means there's also
impressively supple chestnut-showered
rabbit tortellini in silky thyme-rich jus,
kangaroo loin with a riberry and tail
meat pie, and Dutch cream potatoes
cooked in clay shells and drowned in
parmesan butter. Are you drinking
Bordeaux? It's the place, but there's
also fun natural juice from Brash
Higgins – the ultimate high/low mix.

**Check out the selection of Coravin
wines by the glass**

E'cco Bistro

NEWSTEAD
Haven Complex, 63 Skyring Terrace
07 3831 8344

CONTEMPORARY   **15.5/20**

The reliable city bistro has slick new digs and tricks

You'd never know this bistro had
22 years on the clock. The brand new
spot in Newstead helps – all blond
woods and buffed concrete, an open
kitchen with parilla grill – but the rest
of the package is just as here and now
(aside from pushing black pepper with
everything). Tight martinis are made
on craft gins. Silky scallop and scampi
crudo is all vibrant heat, dressed with
chilli oil, pink peppercorns and ginger.
Roast baby carrots have their sweetness
offset with stracciatella and pickled
walnut, while that grill gets worked out
on pink duck breast freshly countered
with figs and more walnut, whipped
up in a tart, garlicky tarator. Sommelier
Mia McIntyre brings a interesting
Aussie wines to this party from
Shobbrook and Murdoch Hill, making
it as appealing to hit the bar solo and
snack, or bring pals for whole snappers,
skin blistered and slathered in harissa.
Either way, bring it home with the
DIY ganache-slathered chocolate
ice-cream sanga.

The $89 set menu is great bang for buck

Open	L D Daily
Price	$$
Cards	AE MC V eftpos
Chef	Jake Nicolson
Features	Bar, licensed, wheelchair access, private dining
Website	blackbirdbrisbane.com.au

Open	L D Tue–Sat
Price	$$
Cards	AE MC V eftpos
Chef	Philip Johnson, Gert Pretorius
Features	Bar, licensed, wheelchair access
Website	eccobistro.com

Gauge

SOUTH BRISBANE
77 Grey Street
07 3638 0431

CONTEMPORARY   **15/20**

Experimental cooking in a sleek diner setting

If serving a blood taco stuffed with mushrooms enriched with bone marrow on a busy road in Southbank isn't a sign of the times, we're not sure what is. Of course, once you add in a serve of chicken skin crisps, it also reads less like dinner and more like a ritual sacrifice on paper. This cafe by day, fun diner by night, delivers big flavour in small dishes. Chestnut tortellini filled with Jerusalem artichoke puree covered in a layer of raw button mushrooms veers into boiled dumpling territory when it comes to the starch-factor but still, it's very comforting. Slips of raw squid dressed in fennel oil and elevated with shavings of fresh horseradish is a perfect balance of cool and really weird vegetal heat. Singular, assured, delicious. Yup, it's envelope-pushing stuff, and it doesn't always work. But that doesn't really matter – the fact chef Cormac Bradfield and team refuse to play it safe is exactly why we'll keep coming back.

Start with a perfectly unadorned negroni to get the evening started correctly

Open	B Tue–Sat; D Wed–Sat
Price	$$
Cards	AE MC V eftpos
Chef	Cormac Bradfield
Features	Bar, licensed, wheelchair access
Website	gaugebrisbane.com.au

Gerard's Bistro

FORTITUDE VALLEY
Gerard's Lane, 14/15 James Street
07 3852 3822

MIDDLE EASTERN   **15.5/20**

An elegant spin on some well-loved Middle Eastern classics

Everyone pause for this crumpet-related Public Service Announcement. Chef Ben Williamson has created a falafel-crumpet hybrid, dressed it in taramasalata and bejewelled it with a scattering trout roe. Whether you think of it as breakfast for supper or supper for breakfast, it's a wonderful thing. This Valley bistro does a fine line in Middle Eastern classics with a contemporary Australian spin. A single octopus tentacle is grilled and dressed in a sauce of fermented chilli and butter, and finished in crisp, semi-sour green strawberries and shavings of almond. There's certainly some interesting stuff going on here on paper, even if there are a few notes missing when it comes to depth of flavour. King quail, served claw-on (very cool) and dressed in its own juices, could spend more time on the grill (some pieces are blackened on the outside and all but raw inside – eek) but a beautifully simple dessert of lemon myrtle meringue, strawberry ice-cream and mountain pepper-fragrant whipped cream pulls everything back into focus.

Take a post-prandial stroll through some of the area's new and very excellent boutiques

Open	L Tue–Sun; D Daily
Price	$$
Cards	AE MC V eftpos
Chef	Ben Williamson
Features	Licensed, outdoor seating, private dining, wheelchair access
Website	gerardsbistro.com.au

GOMA Restaurant

SOUTH BRISBANE
Stanley Place
07 3842 9916

CONTEMPORARY   **15.5/20**

Edible art in one of Brisbane's most striking settings.

There really is nowhere in Brisbane that competes with GOMA when it comes to the luxury lunch. The striking modern glassed-in room. The sweeping view of the William Jolly Bridge and Brisbane River. The huge white plates with ingredients laid out like, well, art. The compact drinks list is one of the few places anywhere to showcase some of the fascinating wines coming out of Queensland, and that dedication to a sense of place extends to the food offerings as well. Bay lobster comes meticulously plated with macadamia, riberry and finger lime. A crisp strip of suckling pig reduces the meat to its pure essence, the pleasure of which is only heightened by the pop of grapes and the crunch of pecans. Spring lamb is served in two thick juicy slices, with both leeks and yoghurt presented as textural changelings. Just when you think things are getting too self-serious, a whisky frose arrives, bringing a cooling whoosh of whimsy along with it.

For early week lunch or a less lavish expenditure, the downstairs cafe offers a similar view and smart fresh (affordable) cooking

Open	L Wed–Sun; D Fri
Price	$$$
Cards	AE DC MC V eftpos
Chef	Douglas Innes-Will
Features	Licensed, outdoor seating, private dining, wheelchair access
Website	qagoma.qld.gov.au/visit/eat-and-drink

Montrachet

BOWEN HILLS
1/30 King Street
07 3367 0030

FRENCH   **15/20**

A deep-cellared, classic French bistro for closing deals

This 15-year-old home to big Burgundies and hot buttered steaks may have moved to a fancy strip mall, but it's still bringing the bistro vibes. The deep booths, white linens, pressed maroon ceilings and obligatory framed absinthe ads and Rue de Somewhere street signs unite with waistcoated waiters, kir royales (Champagne-topped cassis liqueur) and some pretty classic dishes that imply France perfected cooking years ago, so back off, son. This is duck liver parfait (slightly too chilled but it comes to life on hot brioche), and supple smoked salmon with boiled egg dressing and paper-fine pickled onions. But it's not all hot buttered snails and suits flexing bicep by out-ordering each other with impressive vintages. Bronzed scallops with a three-way party of fresh, pureed and baby corn swaddled in hot lardo keeps things in the here, now and delicious before you get back to the old school with a comte course before (or instead of, if you don't go in for complex creations) dessert.

Go big on breads – they have their own bakery attached

Open	L Tue–Fri; D Tue–Sat
Price	$$
Cards	AE MC V eftpos
Chef	Shannon Kellam
Features	Bar, licensed, outdoor seating, private dining, wheelchair access
Website	montrachet.com.au

Otto

BRISBANE
Level 4, 480 Queen Street
07 3835 2888

citi ♥

ITALIAN   ♕♕ 16/20

Relaxed Italian dining in light-filled surrounds

There's nothing more pleasing than seeing other tables have a really good time in a restaurant. Especially when they're splitting a magnum of Champagne between four. It's little wonder, though, in this light-filled room overlooking the river where lunch could spill very happily into dinner. Everything about this tightly run Sydney offshoot nudges you to exhale and relax. Service is attentive, but not overly so, only appearing when needed with more wine/extra house-made focaccia/another napkin after you've wrestled the ultra-cheesy cacio e pepe with firm house-made pici. From the grill, a free-range Gooralie pork cutlet is served just cooked through, caramelised and on the bone. It's joined by slices of grilled pear and pumpkin puree, all dressed in burned butter. But if you really want to up the extravagance factor, there's a scoop of house-made gelato, churned with Manjimup truffle resting on a rubble of hazelnut praline covered in (more) shaved truffle, all finished with a flutter of gold leaf. YOLO.

There's a strong selection of Coravin wines – a perfect way to try something rare without breaking the bank

Open	L D Mon–Sat
Price	$$$
Cards	AE MC V eftpos
Chef	Will Cowper
Features	Bar, licensed, private dining
Website	ottoristorante.com.au

Stokehouse Q

SOUTH BANK
1 Sidon Street
07 3020 0600

♥

CONTEMPORARY   ♕♕ 16/20

Sun-soaked, water-fronted surf-and-turf dining at its best

You can still get the most luxurious fish and chips in the land at South Bank's waterfront hero but chef Richard Ousby doesn't rest on the laurels of a good view. This is contemporary surf and turf pushing into bold places. There'll always be grass-fed steaks, possibly with truffle butter, but in citrus season maybe raw WA scampi framing a dark, spicy sauce starring chilli and lime skin that'll push you to the bitter edge. Or barbecue pork ribs, smoky and deboned, amped by warm, pickled brassicas and bush lemon jam. Ousby sometimes pushes you right over the edge (shaved persimmons with ricotta and bitter mandarin accents is a challenge) but counters with comfort. Soak your baked chocolate bread and stout ice-cream with chocolate cream. Deep dive into the glorious, global wine list, as fun by glass or bottle and known inside out by staff. Oyster and Champagne up. Here's the place.

Hit Stoke Bar for a drop-in drink and quick-fire crab spaghetti

Open	L D Daily
Price	$$
Cards	AE MC V eftpos
Chef	Richard Ousby
Features	Bar, licensed, outdoor seating, private dining, wheelchair access
Website	stokehouseq.com.au

Tartufo

FORTITUDE VALLEY
1000 Ann Street
07 3852 1500

ITALIAN   **15/20**

Fortitude Valley's all-occasions pizza-pasta party

Welcome to Brisbane's outrageously outfitted answer to any dining situation. Fairy-light-festooned palms and red carpet leads into a red-boothed ristorante on the left, tiled pizzeria on the right, all bathed in red neon. You can go big with a wine list that's all Italy by glass, but offers multiple grand cru vintages and stacks of vermouths. Then again, the biggest draw is Tony Percuoco's Naples-style pies. All hail a purist, OG marinara. Sweet tomato liquor, oregano and olive oil over an excellent, foldable, blistered base. Beyond, it's a broad menu of classics slightly tizzed up. Vitello tonnato featuring salty anchovy-spiked tuna mayo and pickles tastes like the best bits of a roast beef sandwich. Ultra buttery linguine tangles with braised leeks and bug meat, and tender, peppery spatchcock with skin seared by a hot brick comes with jus-soaked grilled cos that's far better than usual. The scene is set for glam times or plain good times. You decide.

Book for the pizzeria side to get the best of both menus

The Wolfe

EAST BRISBANE
989 Stanley Street
07 3891 7772

CONTEMPORARY   **15.5/20**

A quiet neighborhood gem that outshines the competition

The Wolfe is that restaurant many chefs fantasise about opening: a small storefront in a quiet but hip neighbourhood, an intimate dining room with a marble-topped bar, ambitious food that nonetheless feels personal and approachable. Since opening in early 2016, chef Paul McGivern has been living this dream, serving European-leaning food with plenty of contempo-Australian touches. There's a charming old-fashioned feel to the place – the napkins are heavy, the glassware is fine, you're not instructed to share your food. Which is good, because you won't want to. Calf's liver with crumbles of black pudding gets a fresh snap from cos lettuce, and beautifully cooked duck breast comes with kohlrabi and daubs of carrot ketchup. For dessert, an elegant shortbread-like frangipane tart is crisscrossed with sweet/tart rhubarb. This is a place that knows how to deliver, then leave you in peace to enjoy the rewards.

On Tuesday and Wednesday nights, you can BYO wine

Open	L D Daily
Price	$$
Cards	AE MC V eftpos
Chef	Tony Percuoco
Features	Bar, licensed, wheelchair access
Website	tartufo.com.au

Open	L Thu–Fri; D Tue–Sat
Price	$$
Cards	AE MC V eftpos
Chef	Paul McGivern
Features	Bar, licensed, BYO
Website	thewolfeeastbrisbane.com.au

THE WOLFE

TOP 10
BRISBANE
BARS

By Daniela Sunde-Brown

Brooklyn Standard

Eagle Lane, Brisbane City • 07 3221 1604
brooklynstandard.com.au

The basement bar neon says "If the music's
too loud, you're too old" and the regular
cavalcade of blues, country and funk bands
do their best to prove it. Don't come to chat
with friends. Do grab a cocktail or beer and
try not to spill it as the dancefloor fills.

Cobbler

7 Browning Street, West End
cobblerbar.com

The 400-strong whisky list feels like you
need to scan your library card to take a look.
If the dimly lit speakeasy is quiet, pull up a
bar seat and chat to the friendly staffers.
If it's busy, give a price point and trust
their recommendation.

Gerard's Bar

13a/23 James Streett, Fortitude Valley
07 3252 2606 • gerardsbar.com.au

Maybe there's something about seriously
top-notch cheese and charcuterie boards
that keeps the pink polo shirts away. The
backstreet star of Brisbane's boutique
shopping strip has the least pretentious
crowd and serves the best vino and cocktails.

The Gresham

308 Queen Street, Brisbane City
0466 726 593 • thegresham.com.au

This historic former 19th century bank has
cemented its place as one of Brisbane's
standouts for an after-work wine, a late-
night whisky sour or a cheeky XXXX tin of
Queensland's finest. With great liqueur and
smarts behind the bar, saying "Surprise me" is
a delightfully safe option.

Jack Rabbits

Level 1, 23 Logan Road, Woolloongabba, 07
3891 2316 • electricavenuejr.com.au

Open the wardrobe and step into the
rabbit hole. Cleverly hidden within
Electric Avenue, this whisky den filled
with cuckoo clocks, masks and jazzy
hits emphasises the prohibition aesthetic.
Snacks veer wildly from classic fries
to classy chicken liver parfait.

Lefty's Old Time Music Hall

15 Caxton Street, Petrie Terrace
leftysoldtimemusichall.com

Friday night at Lefty's – with whisky apples
flowing freely and a rockabilly band firing
on the tiny stage – is a raucous, crowded
good time. It's some of the best fun you
can have with your pants on or off – an
important qualification given the venue's
shady strip club past.

Maker

9 Fish Lane, South Brisbane

No word better describes Maker than
intimate. Pull up one of a dozen chairs in
this tiny, black cocktail bar. Lights hanging
over the long brass bar illuminate a seriously
creative drinks menu – but it's more fun for
everyone if you ask them to whip something
up just for you.

Netherworld

186 Brunswick Street, Fortitude Valley
0424 156 667 • netherworldarcade.com

Ga-ling! Ga-ling, ga-ling! Damn good beer,
deliciously weird wine, tasty vegan snacks, and
enough classic pinball, Galaga, Mario and card
games to make your inner 12-year-old scream.
Finish him! Netherworld brings pub vibes and
hours of fun for a fistful of gold coins.

Savile Row

667 Ann Street, Fortitude Valley
savilerowbar.com.au

It's worth going here just to marvel at
how beautiful a towering wall of 900
glistening booze bottles looks. This
cocktail bar takes cues from older
sibling Cobbler but adds gin, rum, vodka
and more to the dark speakeasy vibe.

The Valley Wine Bar

171 Alfred Street, Fortitude Valley
07 3252 2224 • thevalleywinebar.com.au

What it lacks in naming creativity it makes
up for in wild wine choices and strong
cheeseboards. Find around 20 by the
glass and 400 or so interesting drops lining
every wall. Crack a bottle there or take
one home for less. Simple.

TOP 10 BRISBANE CHEAP EATS

By Daniela Sunde-Brown

Ben's Burgers

5B Winn Lane, Fortitude Valley
07 3195 3094 • bensburgers.com.au

The best NBA games of the '90s screen against a backdrop of the decade's best hip hop. Don't dare ask for alterations to one of three burgers or the monthly special. Beer is great but the house-made ginger ale is straight-up excellent, especially when spiked.

Bird's Nest Yakitori Bar

Shop 5, 220 Melbourne Street, South Brisbane and 702 Ann Street, Fortitude Valley
07 3844 4306 • birdsnestrestaurant.com.au

Hungry salarymen perched solo at the counter wash down a barrage of chicken skewers with Asahi schooners. Hearts, thigh, liver, skin – all charred over Japanese charcoal. Few spots provide a better dining experience for one, and on Monday all sticks are $3 each.

Cheeky Poke Bar

63 Skyring Terrace, Newstead
07 3625 0467 • cheekypokebar.com.au

It's hard to tell if these heavily sauced raw fish Hawaiian rice bowls have all the health benefits touted on Instagram, but we're not worried. A full bar list and fried-wonton tacos show this slick poke palace is not just for Newstead's lycra-wearing health nuts.

Greenglass

336 George Street, Brisbane City
0403 966 671 • greenglasswine.com

Top steak frites and excellent boutique Aussie vino are the only guarantees at Greenglass. A daily changing menu of four or five French-inspired dishes should give you change for a lobster at lunch. Arrive early, visit often.

Happy Boy

East Street, Fortitude Valley
0413 246 890 • happyboy.com.au

Big spicy flavours, a buzzing dining room and unusual wines – there's a lot to like at this truly excellent Chinese restaurant's newer, bigger location. Hot and sour Sichuan broth with fillets of tender white fish deserves applause, as does the duck fried rice.

Izakaya Kotobuki

93 Albert Street, Brisbane • 07 3061 2152
sushikotobuki.com.au

Fresh sushi or cheap sushi – you don't have to pick here. Kotobuki's extensive list of made-to-order rolls, bentos and Japanese fare will leave you will change for a draught pour or three of Asahi. By night the yakitori grill flicks into action, too.

Ol' School

58 Hope Street, South Brisbane
0402 360 432 • olschool.co

A wave of hungry hands dives into the scoop of crunchy hand-cut fries dumped on brown paper at the table centre. Ol' School has refreshed the classic fish 'n' chips shop with daily fish specials, house-made sauces and proper hospitality. Don't skip the fish dim sim.

Pho Queue

9 Cracknell Road, Annerley • 07 3195 6915
phoqueue.com.au

Keep it classic with tripe, tendon and meatballs in a huge bowl of southern-style broth, or treat yourself to a Darling Downs wagyu eye fillet pho. This BYO specialty Vietnamese soup and dessert kitchen is from the same stock as Cafe O Mai, with a massively expanded selection.

Taro's Ramen

Level 2, 480 Queen Street, Brisbane City
07 3839 4840 • taros.com.au

The rich Bangalow sweet pork tonkotsu broth for the ramen takes two days to cook. The noodles are handmade using locally milled unbleached flour. Free-range eggs come from the Darling Downs. Producing the perfect bowl of ramen is an obsession for owner Taro Akimoto, whose four Brisbane stores serve some of Australia's best ramen.

Wandering Cooks

1 Fish Lane, South Brisbane • 07 3844 6000
wanderingcooks.com.au

Enter the cage into Wandering Cooks for a food safari. This warehouse tucked down Fish Lane rotates three food vendors through its kitchens and has one of the city's better-stocked bars. Order Peruvian snacks, a vegan laksa and red curry dumplings for a beer garden meal beneath the stars.

TOP 10 BRISBANE CAFES

By Daniela Sunde-Brown

Felix For Goodness

50 Burnett Lane, Brisbane City
07 3161 7966 • felixforgoodness.com

Fresh dishes and wholesome salads
accompany Parallel coffee at this hidden
laneway cafe. It seems right to keep the doors
of this hip, slightly ramshackle, building open
after 5pm for fresh tagliatelle and a natural
Aussie vino or two.

Freja's

3/1 MacGregor Street, Wilston
0458 159 945

Scandi vibes meet brunch classics refined
beyond recognition as head chef Nathan
Dunnell (formerly Stokehouse Q) takes
every dish upscale. Pastry chef wife Freja
Rasmussen makes sweet treats daily and
flies in French croissants to enjoy with
Seven Miles coffee.

Gauge

77 Grey Street, South Brisbane
07 3638 0431 • gaugebrisbane.com.au

Gauge pushes cafe fare forward with a casual
but creative, produce-driven day menu and
Marvell Street coffee. Adventurous types can
try raw beef with sambal, toasted wheat and
a fried egg, while a high-end bacon sanga will
keep everyone happy.

King Arthur

164C Arthur Street, Fortitude Valley
07 3358 1670 • kingarthurcafe.com

Local farmers, producers and friendly
neighbours are key to King Arthur's
seasonal menu. LOOP Growers' small farm
north of Brisbane provides the vegetables
and retrieves the scraps, a few regulars
exchange backyard produce and coffee
comes from Sunday Coffee Co.

The New Black

694 Ann Street, Fortitude Valley
0410 195 459

Dishes like mushrooms with a parmesan
veloute and and a kimchi egg scramble
with salmon push food boundaries in the
right direction. The narrow laneway space
runs Gold Coast roasters' The Black Lab
Coffee Co's house blend, single origin
roasts and coffee-tasting plates.

Parallel Roasters

Shop 3, 50 Hudson Road, Albion
0434 025 700 • parallelroasters.com

Coffee is the focus for this Brisbane roaster
but dishes like house cornbread with roasted
spiced carrots and salsa verde mean you
shouldn't skip breakfast. Espresso comes
on the house blend or two rotating single
origin roasts, along with two batch brew
and a pourover option.

Pearl

28 Logan Road, Woolloongabba
07 3392 3300
Amid a deluge of turmeric lattes and
buddha bowls, Pearl sticks to house-made
butterscotch milkshakes and rustic homestyle
cakes. Allpress coffees are passed over the
counter, while modern Euro dishes – made
lovingly with full-fat cream - land on brass-
rimmed bistro tables.

Putia Pure Food

4/17 Royal Parade, Banyo • 07 3267 6654
putiapurefood.com.au

Deep in the suburbs, chef Dominique
Rizzo's Mediterranean cafe is big on
heart and flavour. Drawing on her Sicilian
heritage, home-grown garden produce
and local ingredients are used to make
wholesome pastas, salads, cakes, relishes,
jams and supply the cooking school.

Sourced Grocer

11 Florence Street, Newstead • 07 3852 6734
sourcedgrocer.com.au

On busy days locals spill over every step, seat
and bench to lap up rays of sun and cups
of Marvell St coffee at this grocer and cafe
institution. Cabbage pancakes and house-
made rye crumpets with local honey both
typify the creatively healthy menu.

Wild Canary

2371 Moggill Road, Brookfield
07 3378 2805 • wildcanary.com.au

Chef Glenn Barratt's local food obsession
defines this eatery sprawled in a suburban
nursery. The mammoth kitchen garden
supplies fresh greens, avos are from down the
road and edible flowers turn cakes into art.
Bunya nuts, finger limes and rosella feature
heavily in-season.

♟♟
Wasabi Restaurant and Bar

♟
The Fish House
Hellenika
Homage
Kiyomi
The Long Apron
Nu Nu
Rick Shores
Rickys
Spirit House

Queensland
regional

The Fish House

BURLEIGH HEADS
50 Goodwin Terrace
07 5535 7725

SEAFOOD   **15/20**

Seafood and stars a stone's throw from the sea

The name says it all: this is a steakhouse for fish, from the dry-aging room to the wide range of cuts, creatures and cost. The chefs mostly keep out of the way, letting high-quality seafood shine, with the exception of the fried baby snapper wallowing in sweet nam jim. Small additions such as fennel pollen lift baby calamari to new heights. Tiny bottomless bowls of salad, greens and potatoes accompany the fish mains. Splashes of white linen tumble from tablecloths and well-heeled guests' shirts. The sound of crashing waves rolls in through panoramic windows as locals sling back oysters by the dozen. Warm waitstaff sometimes struggle to keep up when busy and a request for refills of those lovely side dishes leaves the kitchen as our dessert menu lands. But long lunches by the beach should never be rushed. Keep calm, order more wine and dig a spoon into a sticky apple tarte Tatin.

Bring flexible friends and investigate sharing a whole fish from the daily specials menu

Open	L D Daily
Price	$$$
Cards	AE MC V eftpos
Chef	Damien Styles
Features	Licensed, wheelchair access
Website	thefishhouse.com.au

Hellenika

NOBBY BEACH
2235 Gold Coast Highway
07 5572 8009

GREEK   **15/20**

A stylish Greek hotspot from the former owner of the Fish House

How could you not enjoy a meal with a giant pop art portrait of Zach Galifianakis overlooking your table? The aesthetic at Hellenika is enough to endear any design-obsessed diner, but all this style comes with a generous side of substance. Simplicity is the name of the game – a perfectly fried triangle of saganaki, say, accompanied only by a slice of lemon. Fat prawns are grilled and so fresh the flesh is almost creamy. The menu is taken up with a whole page of daily fish specials, the preparations ranging from raw to fried to grilled, along with a couple of classic Greek 'village dishes', like braised John Dory with potatoes and olives and herbs. All the fan favourites are present, but upgraded considerably: you may think you know all about dolmades, but wait until you try them made with veal and fistfuls of herbs, wrapped in silverbeet, and served with tzatziki so thick it's downright decadent.

The rooftop bar has a vibe like the Mediterranean meets Miami, and the beautiful people to match

Open	L Sun; D Wed–Sun
Price	$$
Cards	AE MC V eftpos
Chef	Douglas Keyte
Features	Bar, licensed, outdoor seating, wheelchair access
Website	hellenika.com.au

Homage

GRANDCHESTER
617 Grandchester Mount Mort Road
1300 179 340

citi 🍷   ♙
CONTEMPORARY   **15.5/20**

Daring paddock-to-plate country dining with heart

In an old homestead overlooking a
4,800-hectare property, the saddleback
pork arrives enticingly pink after
12 hours over coals – a paddock-to-
plate journey of about 50 metres. In the
kitchen, chefs contrast the building's
country charm with often daring dishes.
Thankfully flavour is never forsaken in
favour of technique. Queenslanders,
hesitant to 'settle' for freshwater fish,
will rue missing out on Murray cod
from a farm down the road. A coiled
black tornado of crisp charcoal-
fermented potato towers over the
bowl, with a tart sauce and soft pieces
of fish to balance the oil and salt in
this fine-dining take on fish 'n' chips.
A pink rose formed of rosewater-soaked
apple slivers is visually striking against
a black plate and, paired with vanilla
bean ice-cream, the taste is pure apple
crumble. With a massive market
garden and Australia's salad bowl
beyond that, the commitment to
local produce is an asset, full of heart
and without gimmickry.

Wander the orchard, 89-bed market garden, preserve room, smokehouse and poultry-filled barn for a meal preview

Open	B L D Daily
Price	$$$
Cards	AE DC MC V eftpos
Chef	Ash Martin
Features	Bar, licensed, outdoor seating, private dining, wheelchair access
Website	spicersretreats.com/spicers-hidden-vale/dining

Kiyomi

BROADBEACH
The Star Gold Coast, 1 Casino Drive
07 5592 8757

citi 🍷   ♙
JAPANESE   **15/20**

Place your bets on ace sushi and sashimi here

Perched above the chaos, diners observe
everything below in all its kitschy and
confusing glory. A man in thongs and
a Surfers Paradise T-shirt walks straight
past students in black tie kicking on
after a university ball. A hen's party
weaves its way down the footpath below
a neon sign: Casino. Echoes of all of
this float up to Kiyomi on the second-
storey terrace, but background noise is
forgivable when the sushi is this good.
The sashimi sampler lands with three
raw dishes bathed in wafts of dry ice.
It is pure showmanship that delights.
Light tempura broccoli and snapper
come out before rolls of soft salmon
belly and thin wagyu sushi, all distinctly
plated, in quick succession. Binchotan
should be the Japanese word for magic.
The white charcoal transforms grilled
wagyu beef into charred melting
moments, finished with foie gras butter.
Soy, wasabi and pickled ginger sit at the
table centre barely touched, a testament
to the balanced dishes on show here.

Portion sizes are small, so order like a high roller or opt for a multi-course tasting menu

Open	D Mon–Sat
Price	$$$
Cards	AE DC MC V eftpos
Chef	Yonge Kim, Chase Kojima
Features	Bar, licensed, wheelchair access
Website	star.com.au/goldcoast/restaurants/kiyomi

The Long Apron

MONTVILLE
68 Balmoral Road
1300 252 380

CONTEMPORARY   **15/20**

A winding drive into the clouds ends at a garden estate

The flower petals scattered on the lawn aren't the product of changing seasons, but the relentless demand for weddings here on the hills overlooking the Sunshine Coast. French doors open onto a wide verandah with lush green views. Service can be slow off the mark but picks up once the ample snacks start dropping. Mushroom caramel holds tiny fronds of licorice leaf to a tree-shaped Italian rye cracker. Snails follow, then house-baked sourdough. Soft slow-cooked pork belly sings sweet rich notes, enhanced by fresh pomelo segments, crunchy crackling and spicy toasted pumpkin seeds. Sadly, sour cream, pickled kohlrabi and a honey and chamomile jelly overwhelm the subtlety of cured scallops. The cheese to finish is not a board but a savoury dessert. Chunks of warm washed rind are scattered between rhubarb jam and linseed crackers. Follow the bone marrow white chocolate truffle (yes, for real) with a stroll through the garden and a hit of croquet for peak *Downton Abbey* vibes.

Thanks to sneaky bonus snacks, the cheaper a la carte is as fun as the tasting menu

Open	B D Daily; L Fri–Sun
Price	$$$
Cards	AE MC V eftpos
Chef	Chris Hagan
Features	Licensed, outdoor seating, private dining
Website	spicersretreats.com/restaurants/the-long-apron

Nu Nu

PALM COVE
1 Veivers Road
07 4059 1880

CONTEMPORARY   **15/20**

Soak up the best Queensland produce by the Coral Sea

Ah, the delights of tropical north Queensland. Rogue crocs, fat mud crabs, wild barramundi, the Reef. And Nu Nu's deck at sunset. They've been serving showstopping muddies next to this flaxen peel of beach for 14 years and it's still hard to keep up with demand from white-skinned tourists fleeing the southern winter. The menu plays to the universal truth that too much seafood eaten under palm trees is never enough, by kicking off with brioche sliders stuffed with lime-spritzed spanner crab and avocado. There's usually barramundi, house-cured, with the pop of orange segments and crunch of toasted hazelnuts. Whey-poached reef fish is napped in a pungent green masala with smoked zucchini and labna. There are, of course, non-seafood options – many with an Asian-accent – like crackling-crowned pork belly, pineapple and turmeric curry. The wine list and floor staff are testament to the two industry pros. Chef Nick Holloway and maitre' d Jason Rowbottom own NuNu as part of their burgeoning Palm Cove mini-empire.

Ask for the table on the beach festooned with fairy lights

Open	B L D Daily
Price	$$$
Cards	AE MC V eftpos
Chef	Nick Holloway
Features	Bar, licensed outdoor seating, private dining, wheelchair access
Website	nunu.com.au

Rick Shores

BURLEIGH HEADS
Shop 3, 43 Goodwin Terrace
07 5630 6611

MODERN ASIAN   **15/20**

Chilled rosé, sun rays and beach days with a spicy kick

It is possible to dine at Rick Shores without trying the fried bug roll. Or so we're told. Plate after plate hits every table in the room, the signature sandwich jamming battered bug, lettuce and spicy mayo between a soft bun. It would be easy to pair four more with cocktails and forget cutlery altogether. From an oceanfront corner table, the sea threatens to take back the whole snapper cooked in burnt seaweed butter finished with Japanese seasoning. It's enough to feed three or four and at home on a menu full of generous, shareable dishes. Staff are all smiles and keep pace in a busy room. Salty sweet potato skin ice-cream (it's weird, but it works) and a brown rice and miso crumb play well with chocolate parfait to round out a lazy lunch. Dressy scenesters drinking rosé dominate what has become a place to see and be seen, for good reason. But board shorts and thongs are just as welcome.

Walk off the beach and onto the patio for a cheeky snack without a booking

Rickys

NOOSA HEADS
2 Quamby Place
07 5447 2455

SEAFOOD   **15/20**

Panoramic water views and a menu made for long lunches

The Noosa River catches every ray of light, sparkling like diamonds. It helps this relaxed restaurant stand out in a town synonymous with long, lazy lunches by the rolling ocean. Seafood anchors the menu. A generous serve of seared yellowfin tuna plays it right with tart pickled cucumber and a substantial hit of green chilli oil. Likewise, a punchy green herb-infused sauce drowns a bowl of pipis in the best possible way, proving too much for the three slices of sourdough toast. Hundred of white triangular 'sails' tinkle in the breeze above tables covered in white linen. The pared-back modern bistro is beginning to feel a little dated, but views like this will never fall out of style. Before long it's time to unwind your thoughts from the endless stream of bobbing boats and clouds passing by the panoramic window. But only after polishing off the whipped baked cheesecake, topped with sweet peach ice-cream, prosecco jelly and crunchy granola – it's a good excuse to linger.

Ditch the car in downtown Noosa and arrive by ferry, water taxi or gondola

Open	L D Tue–Sun
Price	$$
Cards	AE MC V eftpos
Chef	Jake Pregnell, James Brady
Features	Bar, licensed, outdoor seating, wheelchair access
Website	rickshores.com.au

Open	L D Daily
Price	$$$
Cards	AE DC MC V eftpos
Chef	Josh Smallwood
Features	Bar, licensed, outdoor seating, wheelchair access
Website	rickys.com.au

Spirit House

YANDINA
20 Ninderry Road
07 5446 8994

MODERN ASIAN   **15/20**

Embark on an aromatic rumble in the jungle

Upon entry to this tropical hideout/ restaurant, vibrant rainforest and burning incense gives way to punchy, spice-laden entrees and warm, fragrant curries. It really is an all-sensory experience. Lemongrass sambal packs heat on charred kingfish, with a squeeze of lime to lift rather than extinguish. Smoked salmon and aromatic herbs drenched with a silky coconut soup cool the palate. Like a deconstructed dumpling dipped in curry, five huge barbecued Mooloolaba prawns land on a sour pork and turmeric sauce. Melting apart on the fork, duck legs peek out of a green curry, where roasted beetroot runs psychedelic pink swirls through the sauce. At this modern Asian institution, the flora and fauna around the venue are almost as important as those on the plate. Request a table by the pond where water dragons scuttle around your feet vacuuming up crumbs. Order the whole crisp fish to become an instant target. The reptiles know the sweet scent of nam jim.

Extend the journey at Hong Saa Bar with street food snacks and cocktails

Open	L Daily; D Wed–Sat
Price	$$$
Cards	AE MC V eftpos
Chef	Aaron Tucker
Features	Bar, licensed, outdoor seating, private dining, wheelchair access
Website	spirithouse.com.au/restaurant

Wasabi Restaurant and Bar

NOOSA HEADS
2 Quamby Place
07 5449 2443

JAPANESE   **16.5/20**

Refined Japanese dining with pelican-watching potential

Elegantly restrained cooking, crisp linens and tessellated artwork is the perfect antidote to the glitz of Noosa. Chef Zeb Gilbert's nigiri exemplifies the art of helping fish live their best death. Translucent scallops and fleetingly cured tuna loin, caught not too far from the restaurant, are judiciously enhanced by lemon zest or soy-marinated wasabi tops and the gentle warmth of nutty rice. Even better, that minimal interference, maximum impact approach extends beyond fishwork. Binchotan charcoal both filters your water and imparts sweet, smoky char to quail, cleaved and stacked on sweet corn puree amped with the zing of burnt lime powder. But it's the extras bringing it home, like crunchy-shelled onigiri to spread with whipped pork fat, your own wasabi root grated tableside, Ruinart Champagne or brown rice sakes and tableside tea service to close. Spoon that compellingly savoury soba custard showered in strawberry granita.

If you've got the numbers book the low tatami table

Open	L Fri, Sun; D Wed–Sun
Price	$$$
Cards	AE MC V eftpos
Chef	Zeb Gilbert
Features	Bar, licensed, private dining, wheelchair access
Website	wasabigroup.com.au

HENTLEY FARM

♕♕♕
Restaurant Orana

♕♕
Hentley Farm
Magill Estate

South Australia

♕
Africola
Appellation
Bistro Blackwood
Botanic Gardens Restaurant
The Currant Shed
d'Arenberg Cube Restaurant
FermentAsian
Osteria Oggi
The Pot by Emma McCaskill
Press Food and Wine
Shobosho
Stone's Throw
The Summertown Aristologist

Africola

ADELAIDE
4 East Terrace
08 8223 3885

AFRICAN   **15.5/20**

High-octane, free-flowing fun for everyone

It's Southern African food, Duncan Welgemoed style. The taste chord – like the soundtrack – is spicy, sour, hot and loud, and the attitude of the kitchen and the floor staff, if you catch them on a good night, match it with bombastic swagger. Sit at the bar for whisky and natural wine times, or around the kitchen so you can watch as chefs work the wood-fired grill. It's a good time. Not least because even on a Tuesday night the brightly coloured room is packed hip to hip with diners clustered around the open kitchens where chefs blacken peri peri chicken and blister padron peppers, served over a swirl of almond aioli. Pipis, hand harvested from the waters of the Coorong National Park, are bright with fresh lime, the meat tender and sweet, fragrant with ginger, coriander and chilli. A little piece of grilled bread would be welcome to take up the slack, but it's not essential. The tea sandwich of crisp chicken skin and iceberg lettuce on soft white bread is, though.

The wine list is brief, but deep and delicious. Don't know what you're doing? Close the menu and leave it to them

Open	D Tue–Sat
Price	$$
Cards	AE MC V eftpos
Chef	Duncan Welgemoed
Features	Bar, licensed, outdoor seating
Website	africola.com.au

Appellation

MARANANGA
The Louise, Seppeltsfield Road
08 8562 2722

CONTEMPORARY   **15/20**

The kind of high-end dining you visit a celebrated wine region for

They're channelling high-finance elegance at Appellation – the sleek, neutral-toned dining room in the luxurious The Louise retreat in the Barossa Valley. This is the place where service makes you feel like a visiting dignitary and the enthusiasm of your sommelier can bubble over into a dining chair wine tour if you get them on a roll. The produce in your four courses might be locally sourced, but rustic it is not – executive chef Ryan Edwards and his team are aesthetes. Kingfish sashimi with radish, avocado, finger lime and edible flowers is as beautiful as a watercolour, while a creamy tomato soup contrasting with green basil oil surrounds a butter-poached prawn along with a perfect dice of cucumber and salmon roe. It's as if a gazpacho and a prawn cocktail had a royal baby. Just when you think you've got their number, a dish will really surprise you, like the sweetcorn pudding with cinnamon-spiked morcilla and a just-set egg – a cowboy breakfast given a fairytale ending.

Arrive before sunset for a drink at the bar looking out over the vines

Open	D Fri–Tue
Price	$$
Cards	AE DC MC V eftpos
Chef	Ryan Edwards
Features	Bar, licensed, private dining, wheelchair access, BYO
Website	thelouise.com.au/dine

Bistro Blackwood

ADELAIDE
285 Rundle Street
08 8227 0344

CONTEMPORARY **15.5/20**

Jock Zonfrillo's modern Australian bistro has finally hit its stride

This retro-modern bistro beneath one of the country's top fine diners has a certain spark. It might be the blazing fire-pit – the kitchen's weapon of choice – used to char leek and organic banana peppers and smoke potato and pumpkin wedges, the latter of which stars in a smoky-sweet and deeply satisfying vegetable dish that gives Africola's storied cauliflower a run for its money. Or the fire-pit squid gussied up with ruby grapefruit, smoked almonds, fresh herbs and cassava, deep-fried into crisp golden wafers. Then again it might be the vim of rock-star team Jock Zonfrillo, maître d' Greta Wohlstadt and sommelier Jonathan Brook. Or the sparkling Adelaide Hills natural wine on pour. It might be all of the above – Bistro Blackwood hits it on all marks. For too long the casual diner dwelt in the shadow of its elegant sibling, Orana. But after a (second) makeover, it's risen from the ashes a red-hot contender.

If the 40-strong wine list isn't quite enough, order off Orana's 400-bottle menu

Open	L Fri–Sat; D Tue–Sat
Price	$$
Cards	AE DC MC V eftpos
Chef	Jock Zonfrillo, Sam Christopher
Features	Licensed, outdoor seating, wheelchair access
Website	bistroblackwood.com.au

Botanic Gardens Restaurant

ADELAIDE
Adelaide Botanic Gardens, Plane Tree Drive
08 8223 3526

CONTEMPORARY **15/20**

A relaxed fine-diner in the heart of Adelaide's green lung

'Garden to plate' is no trite phrase at this heritage rotunda in the middle of Adelaide's Botanic Gardens. Some 60 ingredients feature on the menu – from anise hyssop to warrigal greens – are harvested from the 51-hectare turf by head chef Paul Baker. Just-picked lettuce is stuffed with crushed walnuts, pecorino and pear. Lovage is crushed into oil and heirloom tomatoes smoked to elevate springwater-raised barramundi fillet. Curry leaves and chive oil enrich a textural, next-level stracciatella with peaches, pickled green tomatoes and quinoa crackers. It's a plate-licker of a dish in less polite surrounds. Dessert wows too, with a rich chestnut mousse sitting in a puddle of syrupy orange marmalade, crowned with banana, raisins, and a jumble of dehydrated flowers from – yep – the garden. It's a knockout. The interior would enjoy a refresh, but with floor-to-ceiling views of native shrubs and towering Moreton Bay fig trees, there's plenty to eye off elsewhere.

Go at lunch for sweeping views of the garden followed by a post-meal saunter

Open	L Tue–Sun; D Fri–Sat
Price	$$
Cards	AE DC MC V eftpos
Chef	Paul Baker
Features	Licensed, outdoor seating, wheelchair access, BYO
Website	botanicgardensrestaurant.com.au

The Currant Shed

McLAREN VALE
104 Ingoldby Road
08 8383 0232

d'Arenberg Cube Restaurant

McLAREN VALE
58 Osborn Road
08 8329 4888

CONTEMPORARY   **15/20**

Out with the dried fruits and in with the long lunches in this historic shed

There are only 12 tables inside this rustic shed in McLaren Vale, because cramped quarters are anathema to a long lunch. The industrial spirit of the building remains in sturdy timber tables and heavy chairs, and the generous spacing between each setting means you can dine in your own conversational bubble. The service team go the extra mile, too – we even get beach recommendations for a post-lunch swim. Local produce hones the seasonal palate of the menu to a keen edge. Early autumn is captured by a bowl of fresh sliced plums, cured cucumber, puffed rice, salmon, crisp fish skin and the faintest flutter of horseradish. Winter's bones will be warmed by golden gnocchi with garden carrots and a nutty dukkah, bound in a creamy smoked ricotta. Dessert and cheese are covered in one fell swoop with a dish of blue-cheese ice-cream, sharp rhubarb, candied walnuts and sweet, crunchy quinoa that tastes better in a dessert than it ever did in a salad.

Save room for the soft, fluffy churros with chocolate sauce that arrive at the end of every meal

CONTEMPORARY   **15.5/20**

It's a little bit of MONA in McLaren Vale

The striking architecture is only the start of the fun at this new jewel on the d'Arenberg estate, with a smellatorium, a top-floor tasting room with views out over the vines and outrageously decorated bathrooms that feel like a hedge maze. Fourth-generation winemaker Chester Osborn's hijinks are matched in the kitchen by Brendan Wessels and Lindsay Durr, serving a perfect single grape made from foie gras encased in a port gel to kick off your 11-course degustation. There are one-bite black pudding doughnuts and smoking charcoal that reveal barramundi fritters with a Vegemite-spiked mayo. Even the butter is a trip, speckled with chicken skin and bonito and extruded from a giant elephant trolley at your table. Has any degustation ever been so much fun? We challenge you to think of a contender as you suck 'nose candy' (acai and goji berry sherbet) up through a rolled note and then eat a 3D-printed riff on lemon meringue.

Arrive an hour before your booking to tour the art and fit in a wine tasting

Open	L Thu–Tue
Price	$$
Cards	MC V eftpos
Chef	Wayne Leeson
Features	Licensed, private dining, wheelchair access, BYO
Website	currantshed.com.au

Open	L Thu–Sun
Price	$$$
Cards	AE DC MC V eftpos
Chef	Brendan Wessels, Lindsay Durr
Features	Bar, licensed, wheelchair access
Website	darenberg.com.au/the-experience/darenberg-cube-experience

FermentAsian

TANUNDA
90 Murray Street
08 8563 0765

MODERN ASIAN **15/20**

Modern Vietnamese with a killer wine list

You don't expect to find an expansive Vietnamese diner in the heart of the Barossa's red-meat-and-wine country. Equally, you don't expect a 92-page wine manifesto, complete with personal essays, in a south-east Asian restaurant. But contradiction is all part of this enduring favourite's appeal. Inside the classic stone building the decor is restrained, but on your plate flavour is given free rein. Caramelised pork mince with toasted coconut finds fresh ballast in a betel leaf wrapper. Humble oxtail is at the heart of tender dumplings at sea in a sweet and spicy ginger and star anise broth. Pork belly with perfect crests of crackling is a comforting classic executed with precision – but the real adventure is found in the snapper flavoured by the trade winds with dill, tamarind, green onion and peanuts. Food comes out of the kitchen at a cracking pace, but that wine list will keep you in your seat for just one more bottle.

Request a table in one of the smaller dining rooms for a quieter evening

Open	L Thu–Sun; D Wed–Sat
Price	$$
Cards	MC V eftpos
Chef	Tuoi Do
Features	Licensed, private dining, wheelchair access, BYO
Website	fermentasian.com.au

Hentley Farm

SEPPELTSFIELD
Corner Jenke and Gerald Roberts roads
08 8562 8427

CONTEMPORARY **16/20**

A culinary joyride inside the restored stone stables

It takes just over an hour to get here from Adelaide, and then it's time to let go of the wheel because, at Hentley Farm, there is no menu. The extremely talented kitchen is going to take you on a culinary joyride that begins with a cocky dessert-first snack of a macadamia cream tart wearing the heart of a golden peach as a hat. A five-hour coal-roasted shallot, puree of burned onion, and a green onion and lemon dressing providing the king's guard to a cold-smoked kingfish. Try not to snatch the pot of blue cheese sauce out of the hands of the young chef as he dresses your rare kangaroo fillet, served with charred cos lettuce. Instead, ask nicely and he will tell you exactly how it's made (mostly butter). This generous attitude characterises everything they do at Hentley Farm, from the exceptionally warm and personable service to a home vineyard wine pairing that includes their famous Beast shiraz.

Request a table in the glassed-in dining room out the back of this ancient stone building

Open	L Thu–Sun; D Fri–Sat
Price	$$$
Cards	AE MC V Eftpos
Chef	Lachlan Colwill
Features	Licensed, private dining, wheelchair access
Website	hentleyfarm.com.au

Magill Estate

MAGILL
78 Penfold Road
08 8301 5551

🍷
CONTEMPORARY   👑👑 **17/20**

Cellar door dining that's all bells and whistles, no attitude

There are few dining rooms that are quite as comfortable, calm and reassuring over a Saturday lunch service. Perhaps that has something to do with the local gin and tonics to start in the plush bar-antechamber. It could be watching the breeze blow gently over the leaves on the vines out the front of the restaurant. Or maybe it's the sheer generosity of the food offering. There's a cavalcade of snacks to start (fingers of baby witlof in a shower of cheese and cured egg, scampi roe tartlets, stuffed and burnished chicken wings, candied gougères, a cooling Chinese-style squid roll). And then it begins. Folds of raw tuna hiding a hen's egg yolk, finished with a quenelle of beluga. Aylesbury duck breast, served perfectly rosy with crisp skin and toasted oats. And if wagyu striploin with the last of the figs and the first of the chestnut isn't a perfect example of the circle of life, we don't know what is.

Book a Penfolds winery tour and see one of the country's last cooperages in action

Open	L Fri–Sat; D Wed–Sat
Price	$$$
Cards	AE MC V eftpos
Chef	Scott Huggins
Features	Bar, licensed, private dining, wheelchair access
Website	penfolds.com

Osteria Oggi

ADELAIDE
76 Pirie Street
08 8359 2525

🍷
ITALIAN   👑 **15.5/20**

New-wave Italian food for new-wave eaters

"Where's *our* Osteria Oggi?" It's what the rest of the country is shouting at their plates right about now, wishing for a gently steamed savoury wobbly flan bathed in a little sausage ragu. Or a hot smoked kingfish toastlet, salsa verde, thinly sliced green chilli and a deft scattering of shallot. Kingfish appears again, this time raw and sliced thinly, brightly acidic with little lumps of pomelo and finished with radish slices and a little black pepper. An interpretive miniature vitello tonnato sees a slip of grilled veal tongue draped in anchovies and fried capers. Very likely, though, you're here for the pasta. And with good reason. Take slender strands of linguine tossed with local mussels, baby zucchini and chilli, lifted with samphire and crunched up with toasted breadcrumbs. Or throw the need to eat for the rest of the day out the window with the agnolotti – noodle parcels filled with roast chicken and pork covered in brown butter and chicken jus and fried sage.

The wine list is a thing of delight, and beautifully written. Pink Champagne! Served in coupettes!

Open	L D Mon–Sat
Price	$$
Cards	AE MC V eftpos
Chef	Andrew Davies, Mimi Rivers
Features	Bar, licensed, private dining, wheelchair access
Website	osteriaoggi.com.au

The Pot by Emma McCaskill

HYDE PARK
160 King William Road
08 8373 2044

CONTEMPORARY **15.5/20**

Naturalist cooking in modernist environs

Here's the thing about Emma McCaskill. She's guided solely by the things in front of her. She doesn't manipulate ingredients, they manipulate her. The gentle char on a welcome bowl of sugar snap peas, say, that pop sweetly on contact with your lips. Or a white peach, just the wink to the season, hidden under a snowstorm of parmesan. Niblets of green asparagus are tossed with black lentils, thin shavings of fennel bulb and topped with a firm lobe of hung and strained yoghurt, its sourness masked by a dusting of burnt leek ash. A whole yellowfin whiting with grilled cucumber and seaweed salad is a nod to the chef's time at Tetsuya's while the whole pork chop served just very slightly pink in the middle with a pineapple relish is the old-school new-school mashup of your childhood dreams. Speaking of which, the spiced cherry jam inside McCaskill's take on the monte carlo really does trigger all the right memories.

It pays to remember this is a hustling, bustling local favourite, which means it also pays to book

Open	L D Tue–Sun
Price	$$
Cards	AE MC V eftpos
Chef	Emma McCaskill
Features	Licensed, wheelchair access
Website	thepotfoodandwine.com.au

Press Food and Wine

ADELAIDE
40 Waymouth Street
08 8211 8048

CONTEMPORARY **15/20**

Seven years on, this lofty all-rounder is an enduring Adelaide favourite

Pork bun? Pithivier? Pappardelle? The border-hopping menu at this lofty two-storey bistro might feel chaotic in lesser hands. But with Simon Kardachi and Andrew Davies at the helm it's (mostly) smooth sailing. A custom char-grill is the setting for a line-up of signature steaks and charred vegetables. But offal is the stuff here. Daring diners are rewarded with inspired riffs on pan-fried lamb brains, wood-grilled ox tongue and sweetbreads. Visually unremarkable but deeply delicious morsels of Spanish blood sausage lifted with zesty kohlrabi remoulade are a rousing start. Add to that, delightful nuggets of wood-grilled sweetbreads, delicate little thymus and pancreas glands cooked just so, served on a slash of cauliflower puree with honey, walnuts and caramelised pear. It'll convert the most timid of eaters. Rolling with a group of pals? The whole-roasted suckling Berkshire pig remains a popular pick. Waitstaff are a little green but very keen. Hey – they have a lot of continents to cross.

Skip the crowd-pleasers here. Daring diners are rewarded at this lofty favourite with the ambition to match

Open	L D Mon–Sat
Price	$$
Cards	AE DC MC V eftpos
Chef	Andrew Davies, Josh Lansley
Features	Bar, licensed, outdoor seating, wheelchair access, BYO
Website	pressfoodandwine.com.au

RESTAURANT ORANA

Restaurant Orana

ADELAIDE
Level 1, 285 Rundle Street
08 8232 3444

AUSTRALIAN   **18/20**

A degustation-only magical mystery tour of Australian ingredients

Never mind the cultural cringe. These are native ingredients as you've never tasted them before. The pitch of Jock Zonfrillo's intimate restaurant is Indigenous ingredients spotlit by the chef's fine dining training. It's storytelling at its most delicious – 20-or-so courses, each with a narrative deeply embedded in a mix of Zonfrillo's personal history and that of the Australian landscape. Start with damper, brought to the table on smouldering coals, skewered on young eucalyptus bushels. Zucchini flowers, served from the neck up, are stuffed with bunya nut, sea grapes and macadamia. Tender pieces of baby squid are dressed in warm aged beef fat, the richness and musk refreshed with native ice plant. All the while, other tables are receiving their damper, so there's a constant smell of woodsmoke in the spare, mid-century dining room. It's immensely comforting. Not quite as comforting, though, as crocodile 'soup soup' – a soothing consomme, fragrant with too many types of myrtle to mention. Sit still, breathe in. This one's a game changer.

One of the most exciting drinks lists in town. Order the matched wines, regret nothing, learn plenty

Open	D Tue–Sat
Price	$$$
Cards	AE DC MC V eftpos
Chef	Jock Zonfrillo
Features	Licensed
Website	restaurantorana.com

Shobosho

ADELAIDE
17 Leigh Street
08 8366 2224

JAPANESE   **15/20**

A slick, modern ode to a traditional izakaya

Chef Adam Liston's clean, serene bleached wood Japanese diner treads that fine line between bustling, rambunctious izakaya and full service restaurant. Where you might be eating chicken tsukune – a silken chicken sausage that's been boiled, then grilled over Japanese coals and served dressed in soy emulsified with a single egg yolk – while drinking sake chilled in a hand-blown glass decanter. Or the titan pork katsu sando, dressed with Kewpie mayonnaise, given a bit of vinegary bite thanks to a layer of pickles and only just held together by slices of soft white bread. This is a three-napkin job and shouldn't be attempted in polite company. Some of the dishes are little more restrained in presentation though no less bombastic in flavour. Liston's take on teriyaki chicken sees the breast and leg of the hen, claw and all, burnished and resting in a light shio broth along with a side of wood-fired bread, that's almost more like a Chinese-style shallot bun.

Try the lunchtime ramen special, with noodles made in-house

Open	L D Tue–Sun
Price	$$
Cards	AE DC MC V eftpos
Chef	Adam Liston
Features	Bar, licensed, private dining, outdoor seating
Website	shobosho.com.au

Stone's Throw

NORWOOD
127 The Parade
08 8333 1007

CONTEMPORARY   **15/20**

A breezy bar and atrium-style dining room made for long lunch

If this large-format bar and restaurant looks vaguely familiar, it's because it is. In a former life, this was Grace the Establishment, pioneers of wine on tap and small plates dining. Not too much has changed, really. Sure, the wine's by the bottle now, and the small plates are now much larger, but it's still geared towards sharing. Really, you could probably begin and end with the congee, packed with gooey eggs, firm tofu, spiced up with blobs of gochujang and finished with sliced green onion and nori crisps – DIY fish sauce for extra umami. Sweet and sour eggplant hidden under a blanket of hummus, finished with crisp-fried chickpeas and the tang of barberries is a perfect party starter, and if you want to keep the whole shindig meat-free there's also grilled broccoli resting on labne, finished with a scattering of puffed rice. Or you could just cut to the chase with the juicy beef rib, braised and served with shiitake mushrooms. Party on.

Take a group, make a feast

The Summertown Aristologist

SUMMERTOWN
1097 Greenhill Road
0477 410 105

CONTEMPORARY   **15.5/20**

A temple to all things natural from plate to vine

The journey is all part of the adventure when it comes to eating at this full-circle restaurant, set in the ultra-pretty Basket Ranges in the Adelaide Hills. Care of winemakers Anton Von Klopper (Lucy Margaux) and Jasper Button (Commune of Buttons) along with Orana's ex-floor boss Aaron Fenwick, the 'Aristologist is all locavore, all the time, from vine to plate in a convivial setting. The menu is made up of things grown, cured, dried, milled and hewn at or near the restaurant. From the open kitchen, that could translate as broccolini draped in lardo from their own pig (which also turns up as two types of French-style cured sausage on a salumi plate). Calamari tendrils, tender and licked with a little heat, are dressed with lime and coriander while many expressions of pumpkin (pickled, gnocchi'd, roasted, seeds) party down with a scattering of crunched up, crisped up kale leaves. Wine? Much like the food, it's a celebration of local and natural.

Take an Uber. There's a whole cellar downstairs that needs your attention

Open	L D Tue–Sun
Price	$$
Cards	AE MC V eftpos
Chef	Quentin Whittle
Features	Bar, licensed, outdoor seating, wheelchair access
Website	stones-throw.com.au

Open	B L D Fri–Sun
Price	$$
Cards	AE MC V eftpos
Chef	Oliver Edwards
Features	Bar, licensed, outdoor seating, BYO
Website	thesummertownaristologist.com

THE SUMMERTOWN ARISTOLOGIST

STILLWATER

The Agrarian Kitchen Eatery
Franklin

Tasmania

Dier Makr
Fico
The Source
Stillwater
Templo

The Agrarian Kitchen Eatery

NEW NORFOLK
11A The Avenue
03 6262 0011

CONTEMPORARY   **16/20**

Light-drenched lunch-only dining hall serving paddock-to-plate dishes

"It's the best restaurant in New Norfolk," a delivery driver in high-vis tells a couple studying the menu posted at the high gates that once confined patients at the former mental hospital. That's the understated Tassie way of saying it's among the country's best. Once a hospital dorm, it's now a vibey, monochromatic dining hall with a huge central fireplace, soaring pressed tin ceilings and aproned waiters deftly steering traffic. As the name says, it's as much agrarian as kitchen, with many of the ingredients grown on the owners' farm. It's worth the 30-minute drive from Hobart just for the potato fritters in a shattery sourdough batter with house-made tomato ketchup. But while you're here, stick a fork into 'last summer's corn polenta', a coarse-textured mash enriched with paper-thin cured pork, shaved cheese and a golden yolk. Or grill-blackened calamari on koshi 'risotto' potent with lime leaf, green garlic and dried mussels. Better yet, settle into the $65-a-head tasting menu and don't ignore dessert.

Bring a designated driver to appreciate the cocktail wizardry and locavore wines

Open	L Thu–Mon
Price	$$
Cards	AE MC V eftpos
Chef	Ali Currey-Voumard
Features	Bar, licensed, private dining, wheelchair access
Website	theagrariankitchen.com

Dier Makr

HOBART
123 Collins Street
03 6288 8910

CONTEMPORARY   **15.5/20**

Impressive degustations from a tiny kitchen

Sit at the kitchen bar with a bottle of something low-intervention from the open cellar, and chances are you'll be watching the team dancing to Annie Lennox plating a fresh and bold eight-course degustation of Japanese-inflected Tasmanian food. Open just over a year, chef Kobi Ruzicka and Sarah Fitzsimmons' restaurant-bar brings the fun. Coming out of a laughably tiny kitchen in a high-ceilinged room, instead of bread it's horseradish-dusted doughnuts filled with creamed raclette, shiitake mushrooms and inky grissini crusted with dehydrated mussels – truly fancy seafood sticks. Raw red cod sparking with elderberry capers, burnt lime dust and angasi oyster celeriac is all rich and fresh. It's an eclectic ride, changing daily, for the bargain price of just $75. Will there be the umami-ful broth washing local winter vegetables? Just-set chawanmushi frosted with flying fish roe and fried leek twigs? You can only hope. Eat your sticky beef rib shrouded in mustardy brassica leaves and grab another bottle off the shelf. The good times are many and easy.

As much a bar, the cocktails are some of the best in Hobart

Open	D Wed–Sun
Price	$$
Cards	AE MC V eftpos
Chef	Kobi Ruzicka
Features	Bar, licensed
Website	diermakr.com

Fico

HOBART
151 Macquarie Street
03 6245 3391

EUROPEAN **15/20**

Characterful, convivial bistro serving punchy Italian-esque dishes

There's an unpretentious warmth that makes relaxing here easy. Its two atmospheric rooms have been decorated with more brio than budget, using potted palms, unmatched tables and artwork by Tom Samek. It's the creation of Oskar Rossi and his Naples-born partner Federica Andrisani, who share the green-tiled kitchen. Personable, well-drilled staff are good for a joke and a recommendation from a wine list big on boutique and biodynamic labels. The menu, by contrast, is a pithy single page that opens with outrageously tasty snacks such as buttery sable rafts freighting leek mousse and comte; brittle, stubby cannoli stuffed with smoked eel and caviar, and creamy brains in a tempura batter blackened with 'vegetable carbon'. But really, if you're not ordering pasta, you're doing Fico wrong. Orecchiette is all crunch (fried breadcrumbs, kale shards) and funk (oyster emulsion). Chilli, salt and butter lift squid ink spaghetti with braised octopus to peak deliciousness. And pork-filled cappelli del preti eat like Chinese dumplings. Order the lot or risk dish envy.

Settle in for a long lunch ($85 a head) on Sundays

Open	L Thu–Sun; D Wed–Sat
Price	$$
Cards	AE MC V eftpos
Chefs	Federica Andrisani, Oskar Rossi
Features	Bar, licensed
Website	ficofico.net

Franklin

HOBART
30 Argyle Street
03 6234 3375

CONTEMPORARY **16/20**

Star of the Hobart dining scene turns up the heat

"I get much more enjoyment out of making everything from scratch these days as opposed to buying in. If we make a pizza, I'm more interested in adding sourdough, milling grains, making cheese, than in making it fancy." So says Analiese Gregory, who took over the kitchen here in mid 2017. The former Quay chef has embraced life on this rugged island – foraging, diving for abalone, making mozzarella. The food is fancy, though. Not through use of gels and hydrocolloids but through delicate layering of deliciousness, masterful use of a show-pony scotch oven and an accomplished, well-travelled hand with spice. Pearlescent perch may come parchment-wrapped, basted in deeply fragrant madras spices. A dish of octopus tendrils ticks every box: sweet and sour from currants, crunch from almonds, smoke from time in that scotch oven. Be led on your sharing plate and natural-leaning-wine choices by chilled but passionate staff, and watch as Gregory quietly commands her open, chicly industrial kitchen with a confident sense of belonging.

Check the revolving program of events, which include visiting chef pop-ups and Sunday sessions

Open	D Tue–Sat
Price	$$
Cards	AE MC V eftpos
Chef	Analiese Gregory
Features	Bar, licensed, private dining, wheelchair access
Website	franklinhobart.com.au

FICO

FRANKLIN

The Source

BERRIDALE
Ether Building, 655 Main Road
03 6277 9904

CONTEMPORARY   **15/20**

Enter MONA's weird art lair-restaurant

As with all things in David Walsh's wacky art museum, dining at MONA's flagship restaurant is like rolling through a sensory tumble dryer. Everything hits your senses, from soaring views of the Derwent to waitstaff who are just the right amount of weird, to the globe-pillaging wine list you could drown in. Unsurprisingly, the international dishes fringed in native ingredients are as wilfully complex. Keep it simple for best results. Order your oysters natural, and the textbook goat's cheese and gruyere souffle thatched with capery herbs. Elsewhere, hold tight. Golden flathead with red curry warmth and a buttery king oyster mushroom doesn't need its nori paste and native flower kunzea. Ditto beautifully sticky braised lamb collar with harissa on a base of soothing spelt – a hailstorm of almonds and saltbush are unnecessary trim. But will you care, eating your cashew and salted caramel parfait, eyes set on the original Olsen in the foyer? Doubtful. This is MONA. Too much is never enough.

In summer, book an outside table where the tabletop is made of grass

Open	B L Wed–Mon; D Fri–Sat
Price	$$
Cards	AE MC V eftpos
Chef	Terry Clark
Features	Licensed, outdoor seating, wheelchair access
Website	mona.net.au/eat-drink/the-source-restaurant

Stillwater

LAUNCESTON
Ritchie's Mill, 2 Bridge Road
03 6331 4153

CONTEMPORARY   **15/20**

The best of Tasmania in a historic riverside flour mill

The 1830s Launceston mill that made flour for bread to sustain the young colony is these days home to one of the city's best restaurants. It's a dining room of rough-hewn timbers, heavy beams and polished but well-worn wooden floors, with paned windows gazing out on the Tamar River. And it's here that chef Craig Will gathers some of the state's best produce – Moulting Bay oysters, Cape Grim beef, Shima wasabi – for confident dishes that pull ideas from East and West. Rags of tender calamari are lightly dusted with dehydrated celery and draped over XO-spiked pickled celery - a gift of complexity and crunch. Tiles of just-seared wallaby, speckled with warm spices, rest on silky truffled celeriac puree. Hapuka bundled in brittle brik pastry like an upmarket Chiko roll is luxed up with avruga and brown butter hollandaise. The drinks list makes a strong case for the local product, ably supported by well-drilled staff.

The Stillwater team also runs Black Cow Bistro in a former butcher's shop

Open	B L Daily; D Tue–Sat (D Wed–Sat in winter)
Price	$$
Cards	AE DC MC V eftpos
Chef	Craig Will
Features	Bar, licensed, outdoor seating, private dining, wheelchair access
Website	stillwater.com.au

Templo

HOBART
98 Patrick Street
03 6234 7659

ITALIAN   **15/20**

A celebration of Tasmanian produce with an Italian twist

This restaurant is a tiny beacon of everything great about Hobart right now. You'd hardly notice it, located as it is on a windswept street behind a barely there shopfront door. Push through though and you are embraced by a vibe you won't quite have encountered before but which immediately makes you feel welcome and certain that good things are happening. You may be at a table so small in this 20-seater you elbow someone as you drink your pet-nat. But that's alright – focus on the blackboard menu above a window into the kitchen and let the dishes roll (a set menu is $65). Golden gnocchetti draped with ruby prosciutto. Silky, squid-ink black fazzoletti sheets encasing smooth mozzarella and sweet tomatoes. Crunchy cotoletta (from local pigs, of course) with a rubble of green olives is simple, elegant and vibrant. Let chirpy staff guide you through the edgy wine list, and relish a restaurant marching proudly to the beat of its own drum.

Book ahead and make new friends at the communal table

TEMPLO

Open	L Sat–Mon; D Thu–Mon
Price	$$
Cards	MC V eftpos
Chef	Matthew Breen
Features	Licensed, wheelchair access, BYO
Website	templo.com.au

citi®

THERE'S A BRAND NEW *WORLD OF FLAVOUR*

Enjoy a complimentary bottle of wine with the Citibank Dining Program.

citibankdining.com.au

The Bridge Room, NSW

Conditions apply

Victoria

👑👑👑

Attica
Minamishima

👑👑

Amaru
Cutler and Co.
Dinner by Heston Blumenthal
Flower Drum
Grossi Florentino Upstairs
Ides
Iki Jime
Ishizuka
Lume
Matilda 159 Domain
O.My
Rosetta Ristorante
Vue de Monde
Woodland House

👑

Anchovy
Atlas Dining
Bacash
Bar Carolina
Bar Liberty
Bar Lourinha
Cafe Di Stasio
Carlton Wine Room
Caterina's Cucina e Bar
Cecconi's Flinders Lane
Centonove
Coda
Cumulus Inc.
Da Noi
Donovans
Elyros
Embla
Ezard
French Saloon
Greasy Zoe's
Highline at the Railway Hotel
Il Bacaro
Kakizaki

Kenzan
Lee Ho Fook
Lesa
Maha
Marion
Miznon
MoVida
Noir
Osteria Ilaria
Pascale Bar and Grill
The Press Club
Ramblr
The Recreation
Rockpool Bar and Grill
Ryne
Saint Crispin
San Telmo
Saxe
Scopri
Spice Temple
Stokehouse
Sunda
Supernormal
Tempura Hajime
Tipo 00
Tonka
Trattoria Emilia
Tulum

Melbourne

Amaru

ARMADALE
Shop 5, 1121 High Street
03 9822 0144

CONTEMPORARY
🏆🏆 **16.5/20**

Moody, intimate and assured Chef's Own restaurant

On a heatmap of Melbourne restaurants, Amaru is glowing. Almost three years after former Vue de Monde sous chef Clinton McIver opened, he's realised his vision. The small, low-lit room of polished concrete walls, wide-set tables, broad seats and open kitchen captures a calm, purposeful energy. Experienced floor staff read diners' needs, fetching a small stool to prop a handbag or suggesting half pours if you hesitate about saddling up for the full wine match, while guiding the journey through a series of small, harmonious and tightly edited compositions on the deg-only menus. Playful snacks riff on the flavours of dim sims or sour cream Pringles. Dry-aged bass grouper, with a frizz of deep-fried black cabbage and a roasted yeast and mead sauce, is an umami bomb. And a tile of kangaroo loin served with hazelnut praline and quince is revelatory, its exterior seared to a crust and interior juicy yet rested. Amaru is gathering steam by the day. Get it while it's hot.

The chef's table is the best place to view the kitchen ballet

Open	L Fri–Sat; D Tue–Sat
Price	$$$
Cards	AE DC MC V eftpos
Chef	Clinton McIver
Features	Licensed, wheelchair access
Website	amarumelbourne.com.au

Anchovy

RICHMOND
338 Bridge Road
03 9428 3526

MODERN ASIAN
🏆 **15.5/20**

Flavour-packed twist on pan-Asian fare puts a tiny restaurant in mighty territory

Cafes and restaurants are crammed in like sardines along this busy stretch of road, but this one stands out. Certainly not because of its size. A tiny shopfront gives way to a modest interior with a Thonet stool-lined bar on one side, grey banquettes on the other. It's what's on the plate that dazzles. Chef Thi Le opened with the desire to make dishes her Mum would love. She takes the food of her Vietnamese heritage, jams it with flavour and funks things up. A lot. Take the signature dish: black pudding doused in a zingy ginger dressing, cloaked in lettuce and Vietnamese herbs. Quail is often on the menu, perhaps cured in a Sichuan pepper spice mix then poached in stock perfumed with cassia bark. There may be brisket pastrami nestled into whipped tofu, crowned by curls of pickled beetroot. Sit up at the bar and chat to the passionate staff about a menu that changes so regularly, it demands multiple visits.

Hours change in the summer months so it is open even more frequently

Open	L Fri; D Tue–Sat
Price	$$
Cards	AE MC V eftpos
Chef	Thi Le
Features	Licensed, outdoor seating, wheelchair access
Website	anchovy.net.au

ANNAM

Annam

MELBOURNE
56 Little Bourke Street
03 9654 6627

VIETNAMESE   **14.5/20**

A storied vision of grill and garden, smoke and chatter

Chef Jerry Mai has a mission. It's to show Melbourne that Vietnamese food isn't (just) what we've been eating in Richmond, Footscray and Springvale all these years. It's the food her parents made in refugee settlements in Cambodia and Thailand. It's the flavours she inhaled in Brisbane, where she'd stand on a crate to wash dishes in her parents' restaurant. It's the festive gatherings around a suckling pig and rice paper. All her experience and energy have culminated here, in this handsome, substantial restaurant in the heart of Chinatown. The grill burns charcoal for heat and ironbark for a fragrant lick of smoke. Octopus tentacle is cooked hard and fast, then turned into a salad with abundant herbs, green mango, cucumber and a garlicky galangal dressing. Thai influences come to the fore in the jungle curry – a spicy, soupy bowl of chicken, eggplant and corn, and house-made sausages. It's the complete package, down to the theatre and aroma aplenty spilling from the open kitchen.

On a date? Bags a booth. On business? There's a private room available

Atlas Dining

SOUTH YARRA
133 Commercial Road
03 9826 2621

FRENCH   **15/20**

An adventurous restaurant that's constantly evolving

Charlie Carrington: wunderkind, chef, globetrotter. His mission? To create a peripatetic dining experience that dishes up a set menu from a different part of the world every four months. Last stop was Peru, next stop is Brazil and tonight, it's France. It's ambitious for anyone, let alone a chef who's just 24. The commitment to the cause is admirable, down to the Laguiole knives in leather cutlery rolls and house-made pastis to start. Even our waitress is French, though she says that's a coincidence. On paper (the skin of the menu is a French passport), dishes read as bistro staples but on the plate, it's technique driven. That onion soup? It's a glossy, concentrated broth punctuated with charred onion cups and a nest of crisp onions resting on top. The parmentier translates as mushrooms cooked down until completely giving, blanketed under a light, silken potato puree and finished with a thicket of matchstick-thin French fries. This is a restaurant in perpetual motion. No standing still here.

The menu changes every four months – that's three different adventures a year

Open	L Mon-Fri; D Mon-Sat
Price	$$
Cards	MC V eftpos
Chef	Jerry Mai
Features	Licensed, private dining
Website	annam.com.au

Open	L Sat; D Tue-Sat
Price	$$
Cards	AE MC V eftpos
Chef	Charlie Carrington
Features	Licensed
Website	atlasdining.com.au

Penfolds®

GRANGE

Vintage 2014

Complex yet balanced.
Traditional yet timeless.

ATTICA

Attica

RIPPONLEA
74 Glen Eira Road
03 9530 0111

🍷
CONTEMPORARY   🍺🍺🍺 **18/20**

It's possum sangas, it's bespoke cutlery, it's the vibe of the thing

"There's no dress code at Attica but most people come dressed smart," says the website of Ripponlea's most thrilling, twisting, narrative-led fine diner. Indeed, most people do, from a table of barolo-swirling international tourists, to a couple celebrating young love with Tasmanian cider. Whether every guest is across the kitsch of a spectacularly savoury 'Vegemite' scroll made with black garlic and miso, or an ant-covered riff on the lamington, is less certain. Ben Shewry spins delicious Australian yarns spanning pre-settlement to post-punk, and unique ingredients star in dishes such as pearl meat poached in coconut oil and hand-dived Port Phillip scallops invigorated by house-made wattleseed soy. Possum (yes) sausage sandwiches are served straight from the barbecue in a courtyard-cum-shrine to the garage rock of Radio Birdman. Service could do with a tune-up, but the extended tasting menu is an immersive experience remembered long after the last lick of bunya nut ice-cream.

Tables are snapped up lightning fast, three months in advance – be ready to book on the morning they become available

Open	D Tue–Sat
Price	$$$
Cards	AE MC V eftpos
Chef	Ben Shewry
Features	Licensed
Website	attica.com.au

Bacash

SOUTH YARRA
175 Domain Road
03 9866 3566

🍷
SEAFOOD   🍺 **15/20**

Piscatorial perfection on Kings Domain

Decades on, flipping flounder for a full house most nights, seafood savant Michael Bacash hasn't changed his mantra. It's all about the quality of the catch. Modest, maybe. But it takes meticulous preparation, skill and precision to pull off perfect fish every time with the clarity of flavour and delicacy in texture in say, Bacash's signature garfish and prawn nori rolls, gossamer-thin battered King George whiting and grilled John Dory in herb-flecked butter. But it's not all fish. Upstairs, doctors talk surgery over juicy grilled quail or chilli-spiked crab salad chased by Cape Grim steak, roast duck breast or Lebanese-style snapper. Downstairs at the coveted window tables with a leafy outlook over Kings Domain, it's whole flounder all round for regular silver-haired old boys. Criss-cross scored, grilled, seasoned and served with lemon, fries and green salad. Tartare sauce and spicy tomato chutney are optional. Why spoil the fish. Dessert? Go for dark chocolate soufflé or coconut sorbet and pineapple. Expert service and a cracking cellar up the ante.

Ask about Fiona Bacash's popular winemaker dinners

Open	L Mon–Fri; D Mon–Sat
Price	$$$
Cards	AE MC V eftpos
Chef	Michael Bacash
Features	Licensed, outdoor seating, private dining, BYO
Website	bacash.com.au

Bar Carolina

SOUTH YARRA
44 Toorak Road
03 9820 9774

ITALIAN　　　　　　　　　　**15/20**

Classy Italian food in a lively setting from experienced operators

It's a scene, but it's a good one. Divorcees gossip over prosecco, power-dressers twirl silky pappardelle, and designer dogs in the rear outdoor nook help their owners decide between wood-roasted eye fillet and lamb rump with sweetbreads. Owner Joe Mammone (Il Bacaro, Sarti) and team work the welcome and the detail, delivering soulful but playful food, mostly Italian wine from an easy-to-navigate list, and a happy buzz that makes it hard to have a quiet natter but easy to feel like you're somewhere. Snack on tapioca crackers topped with juicy snapper and a rethinking of vitello tonnato, the classic Italian poached veal with tuna sauce. Then, excellent handmade pasta or the Toorak ladies' favourite: barramundi baked in herb salt crust – steamed, seasoned and scented all at once. The tiramisu is a showstopper, a white chocolate sphere sitting on wispy liquid nitrogen 'snow'. Smash it to find the coffee, marsala and mascarpone within. It's cheeky fun, just like Bar Carolina itself.

The restaurant is open through the afternoon for stuzzichini and salumi

Open	L Wed–Sat; D Mon–Sat
Price	$$
Cards	AE MC V eftpos
Chef	Paolo Masciopinto
Features	Bar, licensed, outdoor seating, wheelchair access
Website	barcarolina.com.au

Bar Liberty

FITZROY
234 Johnston Street

CONTEMPORARY　　　　　　**15/20**

A tiny wine bar-restaurant punching way above its weight

Is there anything more beguiling than food you get to cut up yourself with scissors? Not in our books. And especially not when it's salty, puffy flatbread with whipped butter curd. Treat Liberty as a bar with a full menu or a very small restaurant with an incredibly impressive drinks list, whether it's a young pet-nat or a heavy-hitting red from the Jura – old world catnip for sommeliers. Pair that flatbread with cured scallops, plump slices of shiitake and sticks of lightly pickled kohlrabi, finished with shavings of hazelnut. Chef Casey Wall's menu is seemingly an ode to midnight snacking, with pipis bathed in XO sauce accompanying a bowl full of Chinese doughnuts. Dip them in one at a time, or throw the lot in the fragrant broth and have yourself a carb party. Flying solo? The ultra-peppery, nicely al dente bucatini alla cacio e pepe will put hairs on your chest whether you want them there or not.

Check out the team's new venue, Capitano, in an old Carlton pub

Open	L Sun; D Daily
Price	$$
Cards	AE MC V eftpos
Chef	Casey Wall
Features	Bar, licensed, outdoor seating, wheelchair access
Website	barliberty.com

CROWN

PROUD SUPPORTERS OF THE
2019 GOOD FOOD GUIDE AWARDS

· BISTRO ·
GUILLAUME   CONSERVATORY

NOBU   KOKO   LONG CHIM   SILKS
MELBOURNE   BANGKOK
              KOKO

Bar Lourinha

MELBOURNE
37 Little Collins Street
03 9663 7890

MEDITERRANEAN   **15/20**

San Sebastian good times in downtown Melbourne

Are you even a Melburnian if you haven't sat at this black counter and coveted the dolphin bottle opener collection displayed above the coffee machine? Go for a casual tempranillo (or syrah, the list isn't Spain-centric) and crunchy jamon-studded croqueta, plonk on a bar stool and survey the giant paellas and bay leaf laurels on the wall. Or settle into a booth under the Good Times sign and take in the full Iberian jaunt: tapas, like the rightly famous yellowtail kingfish 'pancetta' spiked with lemon oil, then segue into raciones such as pull-apart lamb neck, dressed with green olive and mint on cleansing fennel shavings, or pork shoulder, slow-cooked to sticky unctuousness with raw apple cheeks. Churros are compulsory for dulce. Chef Matt McConnell has thought about spreading his wings with other venues, and for a while he did open elsewhere. But this is his 100 per cent focus again, and his passion. Ours, too.

There are usually numerous specials – be sure to ask your waiter

Bar Saracen

MELBOURNE
22 Punch Lane
03 8639 0265

MIDDLE EASTERN   **14.5/20**

Middle Eastern party in an inner-city cave

Cheat's notes on Saracen: order the okra to start and the mamool for dessert. Whatever happens between those bookends at this new broadly Middle Eastern restaurant from industry vets Ari Vlassopoulos and Rumi's Joseph Abboud is a bonus. Those okra are cuminy, crisp and de-slimed thanks to a flash frying. Mamool are buttery shortbread with molten, stretchy hearts of goat's cheese. Order, rinse yourself with a beer, Greek wine or arak and repeat. This cavern-like space used to be comforting Sicilian stalwart Rosa's Kitchen and, aside from adding a front bar and changing nationalities, the ethos lives. Vibrant simplicity and warm service rules. Your welcome is a spliced and salted cucumber sprinkled with nigella seeds. Steamed puffy Egyptian flatbreads can be stuffed with za'atar-rolled labne or silky hummus dressed with chickpeas, garlic butter and lemony baby squid. A basic room belies big flavours, from rich hanger steak contrasted by yoghurt-slicked cucumbers to soft pineapple sorbet with a well of arak to close.

Don't use the bathroom cologne unless you want to smell like a Turkish disco

Open	L D Mon-Sat
Price	$$
Cards	AE MC V eftpos
Chef	Matt McConnell
Features	Bar, licensed, private dining
Website	barlourinha.com.au

Open	L Tue–Fri; D Tue–Sat
Price	$$
Cards	AE MC V eftpos
Chef	Tom Sarafian
Features	Bar, licensed
Website	barsaracen.com.au

Bar Tini

MELBOURNE
3–5 Hosier Lane
03 9663 3038

SPANISH **14.5/20**

MoVida's new bodega packs luxe fish, loads of sherry and good times

MoVida man Frank Camorra has finally gone and colonised the whole of Hosier Lane, turning Misty cocktail bar into a mini bodega where tinned things and Rioja wines rule. Watch tourists risk death-by-garbage-truck as they take graffiti selfies while you're seated at the mosaiced bar armed with a salty seafood platter comprising oily Cuca anchovies, house-smoked salmon and trout pastrami fringed with coriander. It's a fun sport improved with a gazpacho-based bloody mary garnished with prawn that's essentially booze soup. It's an all-snack situation, but dinner can be easily achieved if you get the specials and don't mind tall bar tables. A half wheel of soft sheep's milk cheese comes studded with almonds and served bubbling with grissini-like dippers. There might be fried potatoes topped with a lacy-bottomed egg and blistered chorizo, or pan Catalan – breads rubbed in garlic and tomato – loaded with freshly filleted anchovies. Good times.

Cap off a weekend night out with one of their pork and cheese molette sandwiches, available until 3am

Open	D Tue–Sat
Price	$
Cards	AE MC V eftpos
Chef	Jackson Hunt
Features	Bar, licensed, wheelchair access
Website	bartini.com.au

Bellota

SOUTH MELBOURNE
181 Bank Street
03 9078 8381

EUROPEAN **14.5/20**

Honest, wine-friendly fare in a European-inspired setting

When Richmond's Union Dining closed in early 2017, the dining public collectively mourned the loss of chef Nicky Riemer's sweet-and-sour anchovies with charred sourdough, her pillowy gnocchi, her perfect fruit tarts. Thus the news, announced two months later, that Riemer was going to be heading up the kitchen at Bellota was met with relief. It's a good fit – Riemer's Euro-centric dishes suit both the wine list and the mahogany barred, white-floored bistro. Fans will be pleased to see the reappearance of favourites like roasted Angelica Organic Farm beetroots with crumbled goat's milk feta, walnuts and saba, and orecchiette in a light ragu made from Western Plains pork loin, finished with a smattering of salted ricotta. There's emphasis on entrees and snacks – the sausage rolls with spiced relish are a must – and sliced-to-order charcuterie and cheese are still major drawcards for those just in for a glass of wine from the short, mostly European list. Simple, fuss-free, excellent.

BYO wine from Prince Wine Store – corkage is $15

Open	L D Tue–Sat
Price	$$
Cards	AE MC V eftpos
Chef	Nicky Riemer
Features	Bar, licensed, outdoor seating, private dining, wheelchair access, BYO from Prince Wine Store only
Website	bellota.com.au

Bistro Gitan

SOUTH YARRA
52 Toorak Road West
03 9867 5853

citi

FRENCH   **14.5/20**

Homey bistro with a leafy outlook offering subtle twists on Gallic classics

You can tell a lot from the way French restaurants prepare steak tartare. Following a raft of Asian twists on classics, chef Daniel Patton has reeled things in. There are still Japanese touches, like a ponzu dressing on cured Hiramasa kingfish – but they don't crow about it. Back to the tartare, and Patton's twists are clever, not kitsch. A quail egg is cooked gently for 40 minutes to the perfect consistency for scooping up with house-made potato chips. Whole, deboned garfish is served with a salad of the tiniest squid. There's a nod to chef Jacques Reymond, whose children are the operators here, through a regular fish special from one of his old recipes. Tonight it's orange roughy, cooked gently in paper. Staff translate menu items graciously, although some wine suggestions can be a little off-piste. It's easy dining for everyone from Toorak matrons to families celebrating birthdays. A final, subtle twist on creme brulee sees the classic in a flat, round dish, leaving more surface area for crackle.

Don't have a booking? The bar area makes a comfy perch for a weeknight feed

Open	L Mon–Fri; D Mon–Sat
Price	$$
Cards	AE MC V eftpos
Chef	Daniel Patton
Features	Bar, licensed, outdoor seating
Website	bistrogitan.com.au

Bistro Guillaume

SOUTHBANK
Crown Entertainment Complex,
8 Whiteman Street
03 9292 4751

FRENCH   **14.5/20**

Classic French dining along a classic Melbourne boulevard

While the Yarra isn't exactly the Seine, you can convince yourself otherwise as you duck under the canopy of golden pendant lights and into the cosy Bistro Guillaume. The room is a rich palette of pistachio green and dark brown, the kitchen window framing focused chefs like an updated painting by Degas. The menu twirls on pitch-perfect French classics presented with thrilling simplicity – a delicate smoked salmon comes with charred brioche and a hot-air balloon of a cheese soufflé is brightened with an apple salad. A half Bannockburn chicken, leg frenched, is tender and cinnamon-scented in a tarragon jus with silken mash, while a chunky fillet of Port Phillip snapper is framed in a clean, deep shellfish bisque. Service can be distant – no greeting on arrival, offered more bread when you didn't get any in the first place – but a towering passionfruit soufflé with a plunged quenelle of matching sorbet is a powerful salve.

Look out for the new oyster bar

Open	L D Daily
Price	$$$
Cards	AE MC V eftpos
Chef	Aaron Starling
Features	Bar, licensed, outdoor seating, private dining, wheelchair access
Website	crownmelbourne.com.au/restaurants/premium/bistro-guillaume

Bistro Thierry

TOORAK
511 Malvern Road
03 9824 0888

FRENCH   **14/20**

La Belle Epoque nostalgia in Hawksburn village

It's never just about the rollcall of bistro classics at this lively two-sessions-a-night local with its appealing clutter of Gallic collectables, vintage wine posters and well-thumbed editions of *Paris Match*. Even the flirty French-accented waiters have you at bonjour. Service here has ceremony, a scene that wouldn't feel out of place in the Latin Quarter. Garlicky snails, onion soup and steak frites keep regulars vying for those paper-clad linen-laid tables but Thierry's take on the richly sauced red-wine braise of Burgundy – tender beef cheek, whole baby onions, button mushrooms and carrots on mash with a buttery puff pastry wing on the side – is a standout. Look to the chalkboard for the bouillabaisse or crisp-skinned dory on a tumble of corn and spiced sweet potato. Premier crus and varietal stemware aside, there's no shortage of fine new-world drops in the well-curated cellar. Finish with a caramel-charged tarte Tatin or creme brulee. Book ahead, though, and bring your appetite.

Opt for the fixed price two-course lunch including a glass of wine ($39.50)

Open   L D Daily
Price $$
Cards   AE MC V eftpos
Chef   Frederic Naud
Features   Licensed, outdoor seating, BYO
Website   bistrothierry.com

Bottega

MELBOURNE
74 Bourke Street
03 9654 2252

ITALIAN   **14/20**

Elegant Italian trattoria up the high-end of town

It could be a film set, a neo-baroque Fellini fantasy, with its engaging street scene backdrop and the earthy pleasures of thinly sliced beef carpaccio with truffle dressing and shaved parmesan. Classics abound here: spinning ceiling fans; peals of laughter; butcher's paper on double white linen; fine-stemmed glassware, and a simple menu that doesn't meddle with what is good and proper. Expect char-grilled squid that's suitably smoky. A caprese salad bursting with rustic flavour. A perfectly seasoned white bean puree with pan-roasted duck breast. Chocks of twice-cooked pork belly come with a house-made fennel-and-caraway-infused pork sausage that gives just the right amount of salty. And the traditional tiramisu crowned with hazelnut chocolate is sweet and creamy without being cloying. Linger on limoncello, savouring the decorum of a single sitting (no turning tables here, folks), soft lighting and muted conversation. The sweet life is alive and well at this top-end-of-town stayer.

Showtime? A two- or three-course ($55/$65) pre-theatre menu is available if you must rush

Open   L D Mon–Sat
Price $$
Cards   AE MC V eftpos
Chef   Dusty Treweek
Features   Licensed, outdoor seating, private
          dining, wheelchair access
Website   bottega.com.au

Cafe Di Stasio

ST KILDA
31 Fitzroy Street
03 9525 3999

ITALIAN   **15.5/20**

Is there a more welcoming eatery in Melbourne? We doubt it

Long, meandering lunches are a tradition in this St Kilda stalwart, where the fine Italian cooking is matched by flawless, charming, knowledgeable service. Surrounds are elegant but relaxed, full of inspiring art, unique lightwork and a crackling, anything-can-happen energy. But it's the food – classic and comfortable – that keeps this crowd of regulars coming back, some throughout its entire three-decade history. There's soup, risotto, seafood and (twice-made-daily) pasta. They're best at the basics – caprese bounces off the plate; the disarmingly simple cacio e pepe pasta melts in the mouth; insalata di rucola is just perfectly done. It takes a while to realise the completely satisfying spring lasagne has no meat – it's just tomato, mozzarella and basil, and not for the first time we find ourselves wondering how they do it. And for dessert? The booze-drenched tiramisu like every other table, of course, before heading next door to Bar Di Stasio to prolong the warm and fuzzy long lunch vibes.

Those in the know order the long-offered $39.99 two-courses-with-wine-and-coffee lunch

CAFE DI STASIO

Open	L D Daily
Price	$$$
Cards	AE DC MC V eftpos
Chef	Rinaldo Di Stasio
Features	Bar, licensed, outdoor seating, private dining, wheelchair access
Website	distasio.com.au

Carlton Wine Room

CARLTON
172–174 Faraday Street
03 9347 2626

CONTEMPORARY   **15.5/20**

Exciting new life breathed into an old Carlton classic

The name may be the same, but an expert new team, fresh fitout and made-to-share menu has turned this comfy corner classic into an upbeat local that crackles with casual cool. Nab a stool at the backlit bar or communal table and share a plate and a bottle or two for pre-or-post Cinema Nova debriefs – perhaps hunks of fluffy potato focaccia dragged through pretty zucchini flower topped-swirls of stracciatella, or grilled broccoli rescued from virtue by fat smoky lardons and creamy cured egg yolk. Up the sweeping staircase it's slightly more formal, but the laidback kitchen, cellar and service vibe continues. Let sommelier Travis Howe guide you through an ever changing 100-strong wine list spanning regions, styles and budgets. Share bigger dishes like silky whole roast baby snapper in soupy sweet tomato butter and fennel or crisp-skinned roast chicken countered by silky smooth confit potato. Don't forgo dessert – a warm, boozy rum baba with creme diplomat to leave you waltzing out the door, vowing to return.

Ask for the 'staff choice' bottle – a guaranteed good time opened every day and served by the glass

Open	L Thu–Mon; D Daily
Price	$$
Cards	AE MC V eftpos
Chef	John Paul Twomey
Features	Bar, licensed, outdoor seating, private dining, BYO
Website	thecarltonwineroom.com.au

Caterina's Cucina e Bar

MELBOURNE
Basement, 221 Queen Street
03 9670 8488

ITALIAN   **15.5/20**

Lunch-only Italian where old-school hospitality rules

The loyalty runs deep here at this the 23-year-old, lunch-only Italian run by Caterina Borsato, and it's not hard to see why. The all-woman, mostly Italian team commands the room with so much confidence it's little wonder that Melbourne's power players come here to relax. Rusted-on diners order by saying, "You know what I like". First time? Don't panic. Rattling off the daily specials at speed is this restaurant's party trick. Fresh figs, donated every season by a faithful customer, come wrapped in prosciutto, exploding with gorgonzola. Not ordering pasta is a fool's errand and both the gnocchi with rabbit ragu and olives, and squid ink linguine with tart tomatoes and tender bug do a sweet-acid dance. You pretty much can't lose, whether it's an expertly bronzed pork chop or rabbit loin rolled in hazelnut. To drink, there's mortgage-your-warehouse barolo alongside fun stuff from By Farr. Borsato herself might sneak you a nip of her mother's grappa.

Check out the keepsakes gifted by Melbourne's restaurant greats, such as the marble tables from Mietta's

Open	L Mon–Fri
Price	$$
Cards	AE DC MC V eftpos
Chef	Marcello Mariani
Features	Bar, licensed, private dining
Website	caterinas.com.au

Cecconi's Flinders Lane

MELBOURNE
61 Flinders Lane
03 8663 0500

ITALIAN   **15.5/20**

Accomplished high-end Italian from the Bortolotto clan

Down a short flight of steps, a modest entrance reveals one of Melbourne's signature dining rooms, a suave and understated blend of black and chocolate decor and well-spaced tables, presided over by an open kitchen backed by fridges crammed with hanging cuts of beast and fowl. Almost the archetypal special occasion restaurant, Cecconi's attracts deal-making business folk, celebrating families and date-night couples, all here for Maurice Esposito's sophisticated take on high-end Italian cuisine. Slow-roasted duck with betel leaf sees its oils played off against reconstituted dried figs to superb effect. Properly nutty risotto and silken pasta also appear, along with the restaurant's renowned aged beef. Really, you don't build a reputation this formidable by having gaps in your menu, and the kitchen's mastery is mirrored by the assured floor staff and fabulous wine list. Pick an occasion, put on your glad rags, and go.

Prop up the bar for a more modest menu and save some pennies

Open	B L Mon–Fri; D Mon–Sat
Price	$$$
Cards	AE MC V eftpos
Chef	Maurice Esposito
Features	Bar, licensed, private dining
Website	cecconis.com

Centonove

KEW
109 Cotham Road
03 9817 6468

ITALIAN   **15/20**

A suave eastern-suburbs Italophile with brio and braggadocio

This two-storey Art Deco stayer on a quiet corner in Kew may have antipodean heritage but its loyalty lies in the land of slow food and fast cars. All that eating around Italy and time at Cecconi's bring integrity and finesse to chef Patrick Fletcher's deft cooking. The local intel? Folks rate Centonove's quality, generosity and consistency. Expect barbecued marron – the sweet delicate meat lifted with subtle smoky char. A spin on vitello tonnato sees flash-fried saltbush sharing salty punch with capers. Next up, maybe silky house-made pappardelle tangled in hearty ragu. Crisp-skinned roast duck leg comes with a porcini torte, pearl barley and broad beans napped in glossy umami-rich sauce. Conversations compete with free-flowing Italian banter, service has swagger and though there's the odd blip in kitchen rhythm, that's part of the general pitch. Just sit back, relax in a supremely comfortable Thonet leather chair, order another Franciacorta fizz or pore over that celebrated regional wine list.

Love that lagrein from lunch? You can buy it here – the restaurateur also imports Italian wines

Open	L D Tue–Sat
Price	$$
Cards	AE MC V eftpos
Chef	Patrick Fletcher
Features	Licensed, private dining
Website	centonove.com.au

CECCONI'S FLINDERS LANE

Chin Chin

MELBOURNE
125 Flinders Lane
03 8663 2000

MODERN ASIAN   **14/20**

Party on at this high-vibe house of fun

Eight years ago Chris Lucas's
fast-paced, no-bookings humdinger
of a restaurant exploded onto
Melbourne's dining scene. It was
a bold, mod-Asian offering, not seen
in these parts before, led by exuberant
mohawked chef, Benjamin Cooper.
What's changed? Its round-the-block
queues have shortened (but only a
little), and Cooper's shifted north
(welcome, Chin Chin Sydney). The
essence of the Melbourne mothership,
however, remains true. Punters pack
the saucy charmer – in groups, solo, on
dates – for the pumping DJ-curated
playlists, fun vibes, and spicy tom yum
bloody marys made with chilli vodka.
Pair with fleshy kingfish sashimi, bright
with lime, or pulled pork roll-ups with
coleslaw and plum sauce. Most diners
have a favourite – be it the hot, green
jungle curry with scud chilli or the rich,
coconut-creamy butter chicken. Sure,
the barramundi in the crunchy green
apple and peanut salad can be a touch
overdone, but that's easily forgiven
when there's palm sugar ice-cream
and salted honeycomb for dessert.

**Waiting on a table? The basement bar,
GoGo, is perfect for a thinking drink**

Open	L D Daily
Price	$$
Cards	AE MC V eftpos
Chef	Benjamin Cooper
Features	Bar, licensed, wheelchair access
Website	chinchinrestaurant.com.au

Cicciolina

ST KILDA
130 Acland Street
03 9525 3333

🍷

EUROPEAN   **14.5/20**

Casually confident stayer serving top-shelf bistro classics

It's Campari and the crossword for
the bearded guy dining alone at a
well-worn banquette table below the
wall of nudes. In the window, suited
men sans ties confer over fat steaks
and textbook fries. Tanned tourists
strolling Acland Street take an
outdoor seat. If they're smart, they'll
start with some of the best tuna
carpaccio in town: wafer-thin petals
of high-grade yellowfin slicked with
olive oil and scattered with cress to
pile on lightly charred sourdough.
Veal saltimbocca – cut thick, medium-
rare, packing a sage-scented punch –
is meaty and satisfying with buttery
mushrooms. Serves err on the
generous side but if you last until
dessert, tangy, satiny lemon brulee
comes capped with berries, sorbet and
a single perfect tuile. Service remains
grown-up and efficient, loos remain
outside, tables are tightly packed and
the back bar is still a buzzy holding
pen. This edition marks the passing
of a quarter-century for this boho babe
who brought no-bookings dinners to
this part of town. We salute her.

**You can book at lunchtimes, with
a bonus light menu supplementing
dinner dishes and specials**

Open	L D Daily
Price	$$
Cards	AE MC V eftpos
Chef	Virginia Redmond, Michelle Elia
Features	Bar, licensed, outdoor seating, private dining
Website	cicciolina.com.au

Coda

MELBOURNE
Basement, 141 Flinders Lane
03 9650 3155

MODERN ASIAN   **15.5/20**

A spicy, sexy underground stayer

The lights are low, and the vibe is high.
Bowie's on the sound system and the
barflies by the door are nursing Aperols.
Being shown to a black-topped table in
this darkly handsome, industrial-chic
basement – maybe even a prized corner
banquette – can feel like being waved
past the velvet rope. Yet Coda is no
fly-by-night, consistently dishing up
bold flavours and beautifully contrasting
textures that bounce from south-
east Asia to Europe and back. Start
with single bites: puffy prawn fritters
wrapped in betel leaves to dip in
nuoc-cham, or signature scallops on
the shell topped with salmon roe.
Cruise on to share-friendly dishes:
maybe stir-fried lamb, bright with
lemongrass; tender duck legs in
dense, fragrant yellow curry, or a
whole baby chicken with crisp
lacquered skin and zesty house-made
plum sauce. Service can sometimes skip
a beat but the wine list is as aromatic
and excellent as the food. Rosemary
scented nectarine tarte Tatin brings
the night to a sweet conclusion.

Book well ahead of time or be ready to queue for bar seats

Congress

COLLINGWOOD
49 Peel Street
03 9068 7464

CONTEMPORARY   **14.5/20**

A Eurocentric wine bar nailing the neighbourhood algorithm

This sleek Collingwood wine bar, all
stainless steel and warm woods, serves
Eurocentric plates to Collingwood's cool
kids. Wine-friendly, Instagrammable
snacking looks like little caramelised
beer-braised sweetbreads, supple
kangaroo pastrami shrouded in fried
shallots and a kingpin pig's head sanger.
Here, white bread swaddles pork terrine
set with chicken jelly so that it causes
a fried-soup-dumpling explosion on
bite. The one-drink-one-plate dinner
might look like an Okar spritz, Jamsheed
roussanne or crunchy Pheasant's Tears
rkatsiteli and a bowl of spelt pasta
enriched with egg yolks and chives.
Or a solo serve of roast Milawa chicken
bathed in jus with a crinkled, charry
quadrant of savoy cabbage. So they've
got the goods, but it's the killer service
from co-owner Katie McCormack
(sister to front-of house royalty Astrid
McCormack of Fleet) that makes this
designer baby an absolute banger
every neighbourhood needs.

They host the Brutally Early Club – London and Berlin's power breakfast sessions

Open	L D Daily
Price	$$$
Cards	AE MC V eftpos
Chef	Adam D'Sylva, Hendri Budiman
Features	Bar, licensed
Website	codarestaurant.com.au

Open	L Fri–Sat; D Mon–Sat
Price	$$
Cards	MC V eftpos
Chef	Jack Stuart
Features	Bar, licensed, outdoor seating, private dining, wheelchair access
Website	congresswine.com.au

Copper Pot Seddon

SEDDON
105 Victoria Street
03 8590 5305

EUROPEAN   **14/20**

Cosy local for Europe-loving armchair travellers

Why aren't käsespätzle on more Melbourne menus? These adorably misshapen egg and semolina noodles, served at Copper Pot with plenty of gruyere and topped with crunchy fried shallots, are simple, comforting and the perfect antidote to a bad day. It's the way things roll here: familiar European classics (the menu is geographically annotated, in case you miss the point) cooked with care and served without flourish. Juicy, big flavoured fried Williamstown whitebait comes with a generous serve of garlicky saffron aioli. French onion soup, arriving a little colder than ideal, comes with 'tartine au fromage' (fancy cheese on toast). A superbly cooked beef short rib peels off the bone with no resistance, ready to swipe through hefty jus and celeriac mash. Service is a high point: warm, personable and perfectly pitched for a local in Seddon village, as is the well-priced wine list that mixes old world with small-producer Aussies. It's the kind of thoughtful local every neighbourhood needs.

Decision-phobic? Take the Road Trip with the well-priced wine matching

Open	L Wed–Sat; D Tue–Sat
Price	$$
Cards	AE MC V eftpos
Chef	Ashley Davis, Nick Stevens
Features	Bar, licensed, outdoor seating, wheelchair access
Website	copperpotseddon.com

Cumulus Inc.

MELBOURNE
45 Flinders Lane
03 9650 1445

CONTEMPORARY   **15/20**

Easy, breezy, all-day hangout

What a decade! Happy birthday, Cumulus Inc. Andrew McConnell's game-changer eating-house-slash-bar was borne of his frustration with the exclusivity of fine dining. He wanted somewhere accessible, where folks popped in for pre-work bircher, deals were sealed during breakfast, and lunch rolled seamlessly into dinner. So spawned Cumulus Inc., a new-breed restaurant that set Melbourne dining on a fresh course. With its marble bar, metallic fixings and sculptural lighting, it's as good as ever. Menu fixtures include Tin of Ortiz anchovies (literally, a tin of anchovies), and the now-famous lamb shoulder, cooked low and slow with smoked paprika. Salted ricotta, buried in semolina overnight, comes poached with buttery spinach, and flavour-packed Meatsmith chicken is half a bird, brined and roasted. Add crunchy roast spuds with confit garlic and sage, and it's a feast. Make sure you allow 15 minutes for the cooked-to-order madeleine, served hot from the oven. Unmissable good times, all day long.

Pick up a copy of the cookbook on your way out

Open	B L D Daily
Price	$$
Cards	AE MC V eftpos
Chefs	Andrew McConnell, Sam Cheetham
Features	Bar, licensed, outdoor seating, private dining, wheelchair access
Website	cumulusinc.com.au

Cutler and Co.

FITZROY
55–57 Gertrude Street
03 9419 4888

CONTEMPORARY   **17.5/20**

Luxurious dining where you can choose your own adventure

Oysters, vermouth, abalone katsu, hurrah! The front bar at Andrew McConnell's fine-dining flagship is a rip-roaring time, where you can spend 10 minutes with a cheeseburger, or an evening with a platter of the freshest fruits de mer. Booked for a night of relaxed luxury in the sparkling dining room? Start with a martini in the front bar first. The full carte is all about hyper-seasonal ingredients presented with sophistication. Shiso seeds and perfect leaves of basil decorate smoked curd balancing the sweetness of heritage tomatoes ("grown by our butcher," reports a floor member), while heathery lamb rack is rosy pink against juicy sweet bread crepinettes, deeply flavoured with smoked onion, garlic and sage. An early dinner is best when you can glimpse the rusted corrugated iron roofs of Fitzroy turn gold in the setting sun, matching the hue of apple confit and a buttery oat biscuit. A wine list of epic depth and intrigue completes this handsome dining package.

Sister wine bar Marion is open for kick-ons and cocktails next door

Open	L Sun; D Tue–Sun
Price	$$$
Cards	AE MC V eftpos
Chef	Chris Watson, Andrew McConnell
Features	Bar, licensed, private dining, wheelchair access
Website	cutlerandco.com.au

Da Noi

SOUTH YARRA
95 Toorak Road
03 9866 5975

ITALIAN   **15/20**

Feast with finesse, Sardinian style, on farmhouse bounty

Alongside just-baked loaves of bread and produce from the owner's farm, the early morning pasta-making ritual turns the coveted bay window table in this tiny two-storey terrace into a master class for South Yarra's passeggiata. Apart from good pasta, Da Noi's allure lies in daily changing dishes crafted from beautiful ingredients, executed with harmony and flair. There's no menu. Diners put themselves in the hands of the chefs and let Sardinian classics roll. Dishes vary from one table to another. Some take a modern spin lifted by technique but flavours rarely stray from the Italian island. Oysters and kingfish crudo here, bottarga over there. Next up, octopus on silken potato. Malloreddus in rich saffron-infused tomato sugo comes flecked with house-made pork and fennel salsiccia. Duck breast on smoked eggplant puree dressed in duck jus is a masterful combination. Changing seasons bring on hearty braises and sweet crisp-skinned slow-roasted suckling pig. Finish with a lemon meringue tart. Swift service and an all-Italian cellar add to the pleasure.

Out of staples? Take home Da Noi's bread, olive oil and house-made sugo

Open	L D Wed–Mon
Price	$$
Cards	AE DC MC V eftpos
Chefs	Pietro Porcu, Vincenzo De Candia
Features	Licensed, outdoor seating, private dining, BYO
Website	danoi.com.au

CUMULUS INC.

Dainty Sichuan

SOUTH YARRA
176 Toorak Road
03 9078 1686

SICHUAN   **14.5/20**

Superb, authentic and super spicy Sichuan

Tina Li's tiny original Collingwood digs spawned an empire that now bestrides Melbourne. But the South Yarra mothership is still the one for Sichuan aficionados and all others looking to get their chilli on. Bracingly abrupt and efficient service (a necessary style when the place fills up) ensures that the wait for dishes such as a two-chilli-rated white cut chicken served cold with equally incendiary bundles of gorgeously textured rice noodles or ridiculously addictive batons of sweet, sticky fish-flavoured eggplant, is mercifully short. Those here for one of Dainty's renowned hotpots (go the beef) should assemble a crew because portions are as generous as the chilli count. Not everything is fiery. 'Ants climbing trees', a classic dish of glass noodles and ground pork, is as much about texture as flavour while the dry stir-fried beans, also tossed with pork, are nuanced rather than numbing. The wine list is utilitarian at best but a BYO policy provides relief for the buffs.

Don't worry about over-ordering – staff are happy to supply takeaway containers

Open	L D Daily
Price	$$
Cards	MC V eftpos
Chef	Tina Li
Features	Bar, licensed, BYO

Dandelion

ELWOOD
133 Ormond Road
03 9531 4900

VIETNAMESE   **14.5/20**

An airy, sophisticated south-east Asian diner

Join the green party: it starts here at a blond-wood table beneath a vertical garden, kaffir-lime cocktail in hand, eyeing passing platters piled high with herbs and leaves. Will you start with juicy, just-cooked prawns clad in puffed green rice, or crabmeat rolled into a crisp rice paper lattice? Or jump right into larger dishes – maybe a plate-sized coconut crepe stuffed with sliced pork, prawns and crunchy bean sprouts? You'll soon be wrapping and rolling them all with lettuce, hot mint, coriander and basil, all swiped through a bright nuoc cham until your fingers are as sticky as tender braised beef short ribs with green mango salad. Vietnamese coffee creme caramel is a little grainy. Perhaps save yourself instead for another glass of something aromatic from a wine list that knows how to party with chilli. Ingredients are top-shelf, waitstaff professional and the narrow shophouse-meets-greenhouse room remains fresh and lively; co-owner Geoff Lindsay's long love affair with Indochina still has spice.

Sticky fingers? Hot towels here are lightly perfumed. If they don't come automatically, ask

Open	L Thu–Sun; D Tue–Sun
Price	$$
Cards	MC V eftpos
Chef	Sam Pinzone
Features	Licensed, wheelchair access
Website	dandelion.ws

David's

PRAHRAN
4 Cecil Place
03 9529 5199

🍷

CHINESE **14/20**

Recipes from the Shanghai countryside, served up in a Melbourne retreat

A few steps away from High Street sits a Shanghai riverhouse, cavernous and busy with the clatter of plates. It's not too rustic though – this is Prahran. There are white hanging lanterns, white painted wood, and a glassed-in display of the day's dewy seafood, resting on ice and awaiting your order. David's provides locals with a Melbourne take on Zhouzhuang comfort food. The dumplings are the biggest draw. From the soupy Shanghai steamed pork to the tender prawn with chopped chives, they're all comforting and moreish. (If there are too few of you and too many dumplings to try, the staff can sort out a sampler.) Try the Iron Buddha beef, served on crisp, dark tea leaves with a few red chillies lurking. Standards are also stand-outs here, such as Auntie's fried rice, rich with Chinese sausage, egg and vegetables, or the duck spring roll. One bit of advice: get an extra order of banana fritters for your table. They'll get eaten, trust.

Book a big crowd in for a Saturday or Sunday feast of unlimited yum cha

Open	L Wed–Sun; D Daily
Price	$$
Cards	AE MC V eftpos
Chef	Le Chen
Features	Bar, licensed, BYO
Website	davidsrestaurant.com.au

The Deck

SOUTHBANK
Upper level, Southgate, 3 Southgate Avenue
03 9699 9544

🍷

EUROPEAN **14/20**

Southbank stalwart perfect for pre-theatre dining

Theatre fans of all persuasions will find much to applaud at this Southbank stalwart. For those catching a show in the surrounding arts precinct, the riverside location and great-value pre-theatre menu round out a strong date-night plan. For improv theatre lovers without a ticket, the people-watching along the promenade – twinkling city skyline backdrop and all – is just as good. Nab a table on the eponymous deck, soak up the view and enjoy equally photogenic dishes – many prettied up with scattered petals and micro herbs. Among them, a silky rich mushroom and fontina tart, finished with a pungent slick of truffle oil. See also an at-once comforting and elegant bowl of creamy, dreamy prawn and stracciatella risotto and a cut-with-a-spoon tender beef cheek and celeriac puree. It's rich stuff, but spare a thought for dessert: a pleasingly piquant goat's cheese mousse with cinnamon crumb is a sweet way to end. And you can always undo your top button for the first act.

The pre-theatre menu (two courses for $45, three for $55 including a glass of wine or prosecco) is excellent value

Open	B Mon–Fri; L D Daily
Price	$$
Cards	AE MC V eftpos
Chef	Ron O'Bryan
Features	Bar, licensed, outdoor seating, wheelchair access
Website	thedeckrestaurant.com.au

Din Tai Fung

MELBOURNE
Level 4, Emporium Melbourne,
287 Lonsdale Street
03 9654 1876

TAIWANESE   **14/20**

A Taipei food chain industry, dominating one shopping centre at a time

Ascend an escalator to this slick dumpling house filled with Taiwanese comfort dishes. Long colonised in other world culinary hotspots, Din Tai Fung now wins over Melbourne crowds with its catchy formula: numbered tables, DIY order form, cashier at the end. In-between, enjoy the Taipei food chain's trademark xiao long bao (soup-filled dumplings that come with their own special eating instructions), or pleated shumai crowns (pork and prawn filled dumplings left open at the top), or all else from the high-stacked bamboo steaming baskets. Chopsticks clatter, pop music is up high, waistcoat-wearing waitstaff wear earpieces, spicy prawn and wonton noodles come with a nice chilli kick – it's the full Taiwanese sensory overload. Embrace the urgency. No point in idling before a crisp-fried sheet of prawn and pork potstickers. And why dwell on a bowl of sweet taro ice-cream? Sure, it's food by the numbers, made for the masses, but it's made with enough care and exactitude to have its legion of fans counting their blessings.

Prices aren't listed: as a guide, a basket of eight pork dumplings is $14.90

Open	L D Daily
Price	$
Cards	AE MC V eftpos
Chef	William Sukiri
Features	Licensed, private dining, wheelchair access, BYO
Website	dintaifung.com.au

Dinner by Heston Blumenthal

SOUTHBANK
Level 3, Crown Towers, 8 Whiteman Street
03 9292 5779

CONTEMPORARY   **16/20**

Brit-ish contemporary dining with razzle-dazzle trim at the casino

Outrageous times can be had at Heston Blumenthal's loosely history-themed restaurant at Crown casino. Behold a $1100 glass of wine on a list that rarely dips below $100 a bottle. Science meets shaker in strange but often tasty cocktails like Champagne laced with edible clay syrup, while at the table you're lashed with facts about the origin of forks and Edwardian feasts. Despite that history schtick, Dinner, with its dark walls, bare tables and big booths reflects Crown more than any royal court, and dishes are straight contemporary. Savoury porridge translates as abalone and oat flakes washed in nicely grassy parsley-garlic liquor. Salmagundi, traditionally a meaty salad, pairs chicken oysters and just-set bone marrow with heat and tang of horseradish and pickled walnut. An $84 steak is just that, though the jus is excellent and chips triple crisp. Expensive? Yes. But if you yearn to touch that Instafamous meat fruit (silky chicken parfait masquerading as a plum), and value OTT service, Dinner delivers.

The room is best at night when fire blooms outside

Open	L Sat–Sun; D Daily
Price	$$$
Cards	AE MC V eftpos
Chef	Ashley Palmer-Watts, Evan Moore
Features	Bar, licensed, wheelchair accessible
Website	dinnerbyheston.com.au

Donovans

ST KILDA
40 Jacka Boulevard
03 9534 8221

CONTEMPORARY   **15.5/20**

Sea views and stylish comfort food at this St Kilda icon

It might be a riff on a homey beach shack, but the catchcry here is luxury. An understated, sand-toned exterior gives way to a sun-dappled interior, with seagrass matting, pistachio-green tables and framed pictures of the family dogs. Service is warm and welcoming as well as efficient, while the menu is a bright and bold celebration of stellar produce. Bread doesn't just arrive with butter, but with fava bean dip and parmesan and basil-infused olive oil. The ocean snap of samphire tingles against Tasmanian scallops. Tender smoked salmon is served with fluffy blini, caviar and citrusy creme fraiche. The 'old-fashioned chicken pie' arrives in a small tureen with a billowing pastry lid, which is removed and put on your plate as a cradle for the luscious lemon and tarragon chicken filling. Sticking by the classics, beer-battered fish is accompanied by super-crisp quartered chats. With its dreamy bay view and chilled vibes, this really is something special.

Time your arrival to allow for sunset drinks on the deck

Elyros

CAMBERWELL
871 Burke Road
03 9882 8877

MODERN GREEK   **15/20**

Folksy and elegant in equal measure

A deep love of traditional Mediterranean foraging and the pastries of Crete are the key forces behind this reimagined Greek tavern. The team delivers modern elegance and home-style tradition in a well-used but still crisply appointed room. Is there a good taramasalata? You bet. But here it's built with white roe and an impressive amount of Cretan olive oil. Order the sheep and goat's cheese pastries, rich little flavour bombs that will have you thinking of one less entree and cramming more of them on your table next visit. Lamb-fat-fried potatoes laced with the perfume of well-rendered lamb are unmissable. You may find grilled quail, sticky with roasted figs on a bed of al dente barley, or fall-apart slow-cooked meats with wild herbs. Desserts could include rice pudding with sheep yoghurt, apple and caramel, where sweetness gives way to complex dairy sharpness – much like most offerings here, it's straightforward and robust with underlying finesse.

Consider the off-peak sharing menus (Tuesday to Thursday), offering up their specialties at great value

Open	L D Daily		Open	L Tue–Sun; D Tue–Sat
Price	$$$		Price	$$
Cards	AE DC MC V eftpos		Cards	AE MC V eftpos
Chef	Emma D'Alessandro		Chef	Jarrod Smith
Features	Licensed, private dining, wheelchair access		Features	Bar, licensed, private dining, wheelchair access
Website	donovans.com.au		Website	elyros.com.au

Embla

MELBOURNE
122 Russell Street
03 9654 5923

CONTEMPORARY   **15.5/20**

Flame-licked food meets low-intervention wine

There's change afoot in this boutique empire run by Melbourne's favourite New Zealand expats. The closure of The Town Mouse and the long-awaited opening of upstairs restaurant Lesa could have stolen their attention, but chef Dave Verheul and wine guy Christian McCabe are keeping things humming along happily here with a by-now-familiar roster of charred things from the wood oven and charcoal grill. Anyone wanting to humour their assertions that Embla is a wine bar can smugly point to a wine list less travelled, where low-interventionism rules, but the food says otherwise. A nakedly pink puck of finely chopped raw blue-eye mixed with a flutter of ginger and pops of finger lime gives a unique spin on the city's crudo obsessions; beef cheek with charry cabbage leaves, walnut-spiked yoghurt and caper powder mainlines comfort while the ridiculously thick, spongy bread with smoke-licked cultured cream is almost a headline act in itself. Yes, the more things change, pray Embla stays the same.

Want to get stuck into the wine list? Grab a seat at the bar and ask for some tastes

Open	L Mon–Fri, Sun; D Daily
Price	$$
Cards	AE MC V eftpos
Chef	Dave Verheul
Features	Bar, licensed, wheelchair access
Website	embla.com.au

Epocha

CARLTON
49 Rathdowne Street
03 9036 4949

EUROPEAN   **14.5/20**

Spot-on service and generous cooking in a pretty parkside dining room

With its candlesticks and cut crystal, floral crockery and Champagne coupes, elegant Epocha radiates romance. Courting couples are as much a fixture at this graceful Victorian terrace as the main dining room's marble fireplace, oversized clock and taverna-style tiled tables. But don't think for a minute it's strictly date-night territory – the charming front-of-house team handles friends-and-family tables with flair, and the refined-meets-rustic Euro-accented menu is genuinely shareable for a crew as well as for two. Beef tartare is classically hand-cut and seasoned. Creamy stracciatella might come topped with Jerusalem artichoke crisps and spicy cress. Signature roast chicken is jointed in juicy pieces for easy distribution, today with pan-seared button mushrooms. Aylesbury duck breast, with silky cauliflower puree and caramelised brussels sprouts, is reliably rosy and robustly flavoured. Wine service is a highlight – expect thoughtful advice on a glass to match with a pretty pastry from the dessert tray, or cheese from the old-school trolley.

It's tasting menus only on Friday and Saturday nights

Open	L Thu–Sun; D Mon–Sat
Price	$$
Cards	AE MC V eftpos
Chef	Gerard Curto
Features	Bar, licensed, outdoor seating, private dining
Website	epocha.com.au

Estelle Bistro

NORTHCOTE
243 High Street
03 9489 4609

CONTEMPORARY **14.5/20**

A dress-to-impress bistro pushing the neighbourhood envelope

Scott Pickett has been busy. Between closing the swish ESP next door to Estelle, running Saint Crispin in Collingwood and the deli at the Queen Victoria Market, not to mention opening newcomer Matilda in South Yarra, he's had his hands full. Yes, the Pickett empire is rapidly expanding, but Estelle shows no sign of relegation. The food bears the trademark Pickett bistronomic flourishes – light goat's cheese churros with a lick of truffled honey, parmesan-accented chickpea fries or best-in-show oysters – but the deeper reaches of the menu really showcase its sophistication, whether it's a tartare of roughly chopped wagyu hiding coyly under leaves of pickled beetroot with the added citrus tang of desert lime, or a palate-cleansing indulgence of lemon curd bedding down with mango, basil and toasty meringue. Eight years is a long time in the restaurant biz, but Estelle's doing just fine.

Check out the seasonal Sunday lunches, which are great value and child-friendly, to boot

Open	L Fri–Sun; D Daily
Price	$$
Cards	AE MC V eftpos
Chef	Scott Pickett, Justin Edwards
Features	Bar, licensed, outdoor seating, private dining, wheelchair access
Website	estellebistro.com

Etta

BRUNSWICK EAST
60 Lygon Street
03 9448 8233

CONTEMPORARY **14.5/20**

Neighbourhood wine dining

You know Etta is serious about its drinks the second you walk in and find the bar, front and centre, slinging its own house sparkling. Owner Hannah Green, former Rockpool and Attica star, bought a vat years ago and is disgorging a new batch each year. Those biscuity bubbles might kick off a snack party that starts with thick malty bread and sweet caramelised butter, some charcuterie and the fluff and crunch of an eggplant katsu sando. Confit squid strips are sharply contrasted with sparkly sheets of pickled apple and fish broth. A chickpea fritter is like a smooth savoury custard slice dressed with pickled artichoke and crisp tempura crumbs. Simpler things may appeal more, like tender, smoky lamb loin showered in shaved radishes. Let Green make you a spritz or take you on a tour of Australia, Spain and Italy's most eclectic wines then send you packing after a dense wedge of quince cake and ice cream. That's neighbourhood love.

Relinquish control to the crew on wine

Open	L Sat–Sun; D Wed–Sun
Price	$$
Cards	AE MC V eftpos
Chef	Hayden McMillan
Features	Bar, licensed, outdoor seating, wheelchair access
Website	ettadining.com.au

European

MELBOURNE
161 Spring Street
03 9654 0811

EUROPEAN   **14.5/20**

Caviar-optional continental breakfasts, power lunches and Parisian chic

Locals groan at the city's 'Paris end of town' cliche, but the European is the exception. Enter through oak double-doors and you're transported, and promptly offered an aperitif – or will that be an aperitivo? The menu straddles the Italo-French border with bistro staples and pastas, plus detours – play Russian roulette with bottarga-sprinkled padron peppers swiped through sour cream. Exclusively European wines span food-friendly by-the-glasses and big-hitting Burgundy by the bottle. Sure, there's steak, but venture to the specials board – porchetta with delicate fennel cream and a bouffant of fennel curls is a fresh take on a familiar pairing. Plump pan-fried gnocchi is served with a tumble of seasonal vegetable and mozzarella shreds. Service is similarly unstuffy – charming staff match the warm, well-worn interior, where tables are arranged Noah's ark-style or in quartets, and the solo regular and a group of theatre-going drop-ins feel equally welcome. Souffle rises over its ramekin accompanied by gelato and amaretti for an Italo-French encore.

Swing by surrounding siblings Supper Club, Siglo or City Wine Shop for a nightcap

Open	B L D Daily
Price	$$
Cards	AE DC MC V eftpos
Chef	Peter Sheldon
Features	Bar, licensed, outdoor seating, wheelchair access
Website	theeuropean.com.au

Ezard

MELBOURNE
187 Flinders Lane
03 9639 6811

CONTEMPORARY   **15/20**

Contemporary Eurasian dining at the Adelphi

There's a place for Ezard. The linen-clad fine diner at the basement of the Adelphi Hotel has been a stayer for theatre crowds and the lunch set for 19 years. There's reliability in staff who know the script and can whip tables in and out for 8pm curtains, or lay it on thick, although wine service can suffer at rush hour. Chef Jarrod Di Blasi cooks these days, adding some Japanese accents to the carte, but founder Teage Ezard's wild mix of Asian and Euro flavours lives on. It's a rollercoaster of bread with rosemary-garlic oil, but also Sichuan salt, then maybe scallop dumplings in aged mirin broth with flavour set to 11, or else risoni, peppered with broccoli and wild mushrooms redolent with truffle oil. This is pretty cooking, backed by great wines if you can grab the sommelier at peak hour. It's then that those known quantities – plush Chinese-style duck with nutty black rice and a honeycomb ice-cream tower for dessert – come to the fore.

Don't mistake the entrance for the musk-stick-scented adjoining dessert restaurant

Open	L Mon–Fri; D Mon–Sat
Price	$$$
Cards	AE MC V eftpos
Chef	Jarrod Di Blasi
Features	Bar, licensed
Website	ezard.com.au

Fancy Hank's

MELBOURNE
Level 1, 79 Bourke Street
1300 274 753

AMERICAN   **14/20**

Follow the barbecue smoke to a first-floor city hunting lodge

When Melbourne's American barbecue obsession started to rear its head, you could find these guys manning pop-ups in parks, serving smoky goodness on plastic plates. How they've grown. You'll now find their bricks and mortar operation upstairs at the top end of Bourke Street. Its ornate ceilings and expansive, curved windows are high on all old-school charisma while its walls give a wink to a kitschy hunting lodge, where mounted boar heads sit alongside framed pictures of Dolly Parton. Friendly staff welcome you into this retro-soundtracked clubhouse with its low and slow barbecue menu – smoky brisket with a molasses-sweet red-eye gravy, whole racks of lamb, tender pork shoulder sweetened with brown sugar – as well as American classics like buttermilk biscuits and mac 'n' cheese. The smoked eggplant is a textural knock-out with its juicy shiitakes and fistfuls of herbs, while a good old lemon meringue pie delivers a loud punch of citrus, soft meringue and sticky wheels of candied lemon.

Bring the fun to your backyard with Fancy Hank's mobile Roadhouse

Open	L Thu–Sun; D Daily
Price	$$
Cards	AE MC V eftpos
Chef	Daniel Inzunza
Features	Bar, licensed
Website	fancyhanks.com

Fitzroy Town Hall Hotel

FITZROY
166 Johnston Street
03 9416 5055

STEAKHOUSE   **14.5/20**

Brasserie, beer and smoke colliding just the way you need them to

There's a lot to love about this pub with a brasserie theme. Sean Donovan and staff are focused and attentive but casual. It suits the mood of the place perfectly. Sit in the atrium for a boozy lunch or the deep-blue dining room for dinner. The restaurant interior runs a take on old-world spaces with objet d'art and deep luscious colours with a timber-floored expanse. It feels playfully grand. Staff can be a little stretched across all areas, but like the menu, the focus here is professionalism and value. The steaks are outstanding, their accompanying sauces traditional and every garnish has merit. You may find a steak tartare, beautifully seasoned, textured and scattered with all the right notes sitting on deep beetroot flavours. Also braised saltbush lamb with boulangere potatoes and wild mushrooms, not to mention an incredibly chocolatey chocolate tart in a thin crisp case. This is how you want your pub food – high quality and great bang for buck.

Sit with your back to the fireplace. You want to see the wall of old-world collected chaos – there's a lot to discover

Open	L D Daily
Price	$$$
Cards	AE DC MC V eftpos
Chef	Anna Quayle
Features	Bar, licensed, private dining, wheelchair access
Website	fitzroytownhallhotel.com.au

Flower Drum

MELBOURNE
17 Market Lane
03 9662 3655

CHINESE   16.5/20

A full-service Cantonese restaurant with all the bells and whistles

It's less of a restaurant, more of a legend. A place that, since Gilbert Lau opened in 1975, has shaped the way Australians think about fine-dining Cantonese food. Where some of the waiters have been serving the Peking duck – tableside, no less – as long as the restaurant's been running. At the hands of executive chef Anthony Lui, that duck – its crisp skin deeply burnished, swaddled inside soft little pancakes with a micro spear of green onion – is served with each plate painted with a perfect hoisin bird. A tiny, but lovely touch. There's tender saltbush lamb fillet, stir-fried with ginger and leek, spooned into a sesame pancake pocket. Regulars probably have their dance card full (everyone has their favourites, whether that's the Paspaley pearl meat or thousand leaf tofu) but don't miss baby abalone – gently licked by flame, it's served in thin slices with translucent rice noodles for the most perfect, yielding, sweet sleight-of-fish.

If Jason Lui (Anthony's son) is running the floor, it pays to let him call the dance

France-Soir

SOUTH YARRA
11 Toorak Road
03 9866 8569

FRENCH   14.5/20

Buzzing French stalwart with an overload of l'esprit

To be tired of France-Soir is to be tired of life. The French bistro from central casting woos rather than wows with the practised elan of 33 years, but it woos well indeed. A favourite of the hospitality crowd and wine lovers who thrill not only to owner Jean-Paul Prunetti's magnifique French cellar but the BYO policy, France-Soir is a place beyond fashion. The narrow, mirror-lined space where linen and paper cover closely packed tables is a portal to Paris, while Gallic-accented waiters corral the crowds with varying degrees of munificence. A menu as steadfast as the laws of physics delivers the goods that give French cuisine its comfort-laden heart. Great steak frites go without saying, but also put on the radar quenelles of sea perch in a saffron-stained prawn bisque, escargot in wickedly garlicky parsley and butter sauce and oysters shucked a la minute. Really, the only variable permitted here is the age-old question: cheese or creme brulee?

That wine list can now be accessed through the online wine shop

Open	L Mon–Sat; D Daily
Price	$$
Cards	AE DC MC V eftpos
Chef	Anthony Lui
Features	Licensed, private dining
Website	flowerdrum.melbourne

Open	L D Daily
Price	$$
Cards	AE MC V eftpos
Chef	Geraud Fabre
Features	Bar, licensed, outdoor seating, BYO
Website	france-soir.com.au

THE ONLY HAT THAT COUNTS.

goodfood

AUSTRALIA'S HOME OF THE HATS

French Saloon

MELBOURNE
Level 1, 46 Hardware Lane
03 9600 2142

FRENCH   **15/20**

A clever European-style bistro that welcomes big spenders

Make your way down the laneway, through the narrow door, up the timber steps, and into a space that could be one of the latest smart casual bistros in the Marais district of Paris. Uneven timber floors, white walls, wooden tables with occasional white cloths, bentwood chairs, a lacquer-red ceiling. The mood is relaxed, the menu is small and the wine list considerable, leaning heavily to funky and upper-end French. No surprise, really, that it's in the same stable as City Wine Shop, European and Siglo – all with their fingers on Melbourne's drinks-loving pulse. Share the whipped cod's roe topped with a generous dollop of salmon roe (a small mother-of-pearl spoon for that) and plump potato blini, or a big rib of excellent beef, or roast chicken (half or whole) with cabbage and bacon. Otherwise, there's the drama of Ora king salmon and vegetables cooked en papillote, the paper parcel cut at table to release the herby aromas of a green goddess dressing.

There's a separate menu card for a range of caviars

Geralds Bar

CARLTON NORTH
386 Rathdowne Street
03 9349 4748

CONTEMPORARY   **14/20**

Rathdowne Street's most beloved local

With its atmospheric vibe and hospitable style, this local favourite is care of owner/figurehead Gerald Diffey. It's the warm hug of restaurants, welcoming diners with open arms. "The usual, thanks," is a common refrain from regulars who've been coming to this cosy, rustic haunt for over a decade. On your own? Take a padded stool at the long, curved bar while staff relay which bottles of wine are on the go (nebbiolo from the Barossa, perhaps?) Food is an equally casual affair chosen from a hand-written, oft-changing menu. There might be bresaola with a chunk of fresh mozzarella, juicy pork fillet on red cabbage alongside baked fig, or fleshy Queensland king prawns, served heads on. Years worth of mementos line the hand-built shelves – a collection of wooden deer, a photo of Johnny Cash, a lit world globe – all artfully displayed in curated vignettes. Staff flip the vinyl, a steady mix of '50s and '60s soul-jazz. Another glass? Thanks – we'll have the usual.

Drop into Gerald's other bar next time you're in San Sebastian

Open	L D Mon–Fri
Price	$$$
Cards	AE MC V eftpos
Chef	Todd Moses, Ian Curley
Features	Bar, licensed, outdoor seating, private dining
Website	frenchsaloon.com

Open	D Daily
Price	$$
Cards	MC V eftpos
Chef	Peter Savage
Features	Bar, licensed, outdoor seating
Website	geraldsbar.com.au

The Grand

RICHMOND
333 Burnley Street
03 9429 2530

ITALIAN   **14/20**

Classic comfort in a stylish gastropub

Historic pubs are a dime a dozen in this gentrified inner-city pocket, but The Grand has, for many years, been a favourite for diners wanting more than parma and chips. It's the sort of place where a younger crowd drinks craft beer in the large courtyard, while the separate dining room tucked into a front corner hosts families. There's an air of old-school formality – linen-dressed tables and plush dark carpet – playfully tempered with quirky touches such as a modern hunting scene motif on windows and walls. Expect simple Italian dishes executed well and with restraint. Rabbit's usually on the menu, perhaps shredded into a subtly orange-sweetened ragu coating house-made pappardelle, while the signature roasted half-duck, enhanced by a delicate juniper berry sauce, has been on the menu for 15 years. To finish, Italian doughnuts filled with passionfruit curd deliver an understated sweet hit. Grand, indeed.

The first weekend of the month is Italian yum cha

Greasy Zoe's

HURSTBRIDGE
Shop 3, 850 Heidelberg-Kinglake Road
03 9718 0324

CONTEMPORARY   **15/20**

Sustainable snacks, smart wines and good times at the end of the line

Forget the name. It's tricky, but you have to when chef Zoe Birch and partner Lachlan Gardner's sweet, 15-seat Hurstbridge nook is bringing fresh, spry cooking and fun wines to the fore. From a teensy corner kitchen in a room resembling a ski chalet, Birch delivers a multi-course dinner primarily in snack form. Every single thing has been made in-house or hyper-locally. Start with their funky salumi and lardo chased by nutty linseed crackers that smoosh golden Eildon trout. And then maybe a buttery, dusty tartlet of goat's cheese from Stone and Crow, perfumed with beetroot dust and amaranth. Birch loves the three-ingredient mic drop, be it her dry-aged, smoked chicken breast with golden skin and tangy mustard, a silverbeet crisp tarted up with curd and clover, or an apple-stuffed cheese-showered croissant pre-dessert. Between it all, wines trip from Kremstal to Dromana, and Nick Cave brings the tunes. All of this for $85 and a zone two Myki card.

Enjoy snacks and drinks only outside under the eucalypts

Open	L D Daily
Price	$$
Cards	AE DC MC V eftpos
Chef	Andrew Beddoes
Features	Bar, licensed, private dining, wheelchair access
Website	grandrichmond.com.au

Open	L Sat-Sun; D Thu-Sun
Price	$$
Cards	MC V eftpos
Chef	Zoe Birch
Features	Bar, licensed, outdoor seating, wheelchair access
Website	greasyzoes.com.au

Grossi Grill

MELBOURNE
80 Bourke Street
03 9662 1811

ITALIAN   **14/20**

A stylin' Tuscan grill

Want some pedigree with your Italian? This posh-but-casual Tuscan grill house has the Florentino stamp, with chefs Guy Grossi and Joel Baylon on the pans. It's a favourite of the pre-theatre city crowd who pack the close-quarters, dark-wood tables for hearty Italian dishes delivered with finesse. Wood panelling and embossed mirrors up the class factor, as does the long banquette, spotlit by hanging pendants. Two can easily share a generous slab of creamy duck parfait and sticky fig jam, which adds sweet oomph, to spread on house-made crostini. Zucchini flowers in crunchy, light batter might be stuffed with ricotta – order them if they're on. Down the back is the restaurant's engine room, an open grill firing out juicy, charred Hopkins River porterhouse steak, and the go-hard-or-go-home 'John Dee rib', a one kilogram behemoth to share between a few. The day's fish, maybe a wild barra, is also grilled. For dessert, it's gotta be Grossi's famed tiramisu, boozy with Italian liqueurs.

Ask for the corner window seat and watch the city hordes stream past

Grossi Florentino Upstairs

MELBOURNE
Level 1, 80 Bourke Street
03 9662 1811

ITALIAN   **16.5/20**

A fine-tuned fine dining institution

Memories don't come cheap at Guy Grossi's flagship, but golly this is a grand place for special occasion dinners or quiet lunches basking in natural light and seamless service. Florentine murals, chandeliers and suited floor staff indicate this is a church of classic Italian cooking and most dishes stick to the classic Italiano script. Silky egg yolk and ricotta ravioli, for example, and inked cuttlefish and cannellini blanketed by lardo and bottarga. A perfect wine match is guaranteed from a tightly curated list championing new-wave producers and classic Italian vintages. Puglian primitivo might be paired with braised suckling lamb and Dutch cream potatoes, glistening in pan juices and honed by parmigiano, or Sicilian chardonnay and wild-caught barramundi – golden skinned and holding its own buttery flavour against 'nduja and bouncy fregola. Modish desserts include a creamy puck of malted barley panna cotta, sweetened with stout gel and chewy mandarin 'leather', but a handsome cheese trolley heaving with first-rate formaggio steals the show.

Visit neighbouring sister bar Arlechin for an Americano before dinner

Open	L D Mon–Sat
Price	$$$
Cards	AE DC MC V eftpos
Chefs	Guy Grossi, Joel Baylon
Features	Bar, licensed, outdoor seating
Website	florentino.com.au/grill

Open	L Mon–Fri; D Mon–Sat
Price	$$$
Cards	AE DC MC V eftpos
Chef	Guy Grossi, Chris Rodriguez, Matteo Toffano
Features	Bar, licensed, private dining
Website	florentino.com.au/florentino

Hanabishi

MELBOURNE
187 King Street
03 9670 1167

JAPANESE   **14/20**

Nearing its 30th birthday, this CBD stayer's still got it

It's not unusual to see a lone diner seated at the front table by the window, enjoying a whole glorious large platter of sushi and sashimi for herself, or a couple indulging in the wagyu shabu shabu – a spread of raw thin sliced beef, udon noodles, and vegetables with a hotpot of steaming dashi broth for dipping. As one of the city's original sushi temples (2019 marks the restaurant's 30th anniversary), Hanabishi is no longer on the cutting edge, but the quality fish and care in presentation makes it a dependable stalwart nonetheless. That large sushi and sashimi platter comes with a roll plus 18 pieces of sashimi and 10 pieces of sushi: deep red tuna, fat slabs of salmon, buttery kingfish and more. The house-made fresh tofu, served with spring onion and ginger, may challenge your entire concept of tofu, in the best possible way. This is classic, fresh, simple, straightforward food, served in an elegant room – the basics of Japanese hospitality personified.

The daily specials menu is a goldmine – how about miso-poached foie gras?

Harley and Rose

WEST FOOTSCRAY
572 Barkly Street
03 8320 0325

PUB DINING   **14.5/20**

Imagine a hybrid of your favourite wine bar, dive bar and pizzeria

It's the all-things-to-all-people party Footscray needed. What's not to love about a wine-focused diner and bottle-o with all the cooking smarts of two ex-McConnell group chefs (Rory Cowcher and Josh Murphy), the service of wine gun Mark Williamson and a low-key, totally wipeable room pumping Aussie bangers? Everyone from wine nerds to young families is partying how they like here. In one corner, a family will be ordering char-edged margherita pizzas for their kids while next to them, winemakers nerd off about Ochota Barrels' newest release while smashing crisp-fried green tomatoes, a salad of waxy potatoes, heaped with herbs and tender octopus, and the grown-up pizza starring lemony, garlicky Goolwa pipis laced with cream. Grab a magnum straight off the shelf. Summon silky, salty cod roe dip with the crispest focaccia. Have a Sunday session armed with craft beers and lamb kofta on a fresh bed of chilled risoni and cucumber. Do it all, it's allowed.

The front terrace is built for Sunday sessions

Open	L Mon–Fri; D Mon–Sat
Price	$$
Cards	AE DC MC V eftpos
Chef	Bobby Yap
Features	Licensed
Website	hanabishi.com.au

Open	L Sat–Sun; D Tue–Sun
Price	$$
Cards	MC V eftpos
Chef	Rory Cowcher, Josh Murphy
Features	Bar, licensed, outdoor seating, wheelchair access
Website	harleyandrose.net.au

Hellenic Republic
BRUNSWICK EAST
434 Lygon Street
03 9381 1222

GREEK   **14/20**

A convivial modern Greek stayer

This boisterous Melbourne institution runs like a well-oiled machine but hasn't lost an iota of its heart and soul. Families, groups of pals and couples continue to pack the joint to feast on signature hits such as slow-cooked lamb shoulder, crisp honey glazed doughnuts and the brilliant nutty, grainy, fruity Cypriot salad bejewelled with pomegranate seeds. But there are always new Mediterranean-inspired dishes on the menu threatening to steal the show. There will be no regrets if you let charming, knowledgeable staff seduce you into ordering the likes of a fillet of pan-fried cod on smoky eggplant spiced up with a smattering of Aleppo pepper or moreish battered slices of zucchini served with dashi yoghurt. Like the food, the decor (think blue and white awnings, whitewashed brick walls, marble tabletops and cane cray pot light shades) manages to channel the Greek islands without stumbling into cliche. Order another ouzo, sit back and dream of Mykonos.

Those who are 14 and under can tuck into a kid's menu ('tapsaki') for $20

Highline at the Railway Hotel
WINDSOR
Level 1, 29 Chapel Street
03 9510 4050

citi

CONTEMPORARY   **15/20**

A serious paddock-to-plate restaurant in a knockabout pub

Many restaurants claim farm-to-plate credentials. Few deliver like Highline. Despite its urban setting – a hushed, dark room above a rollicking pub with a 24-hour bottle shop – it's the real deal. The menu is styled as a journey through the owners' working Strathbogie Ranges farm, where they farm, grow and forage much of the produce that lands in the kitchen. Simon Tarlington (ex Quay, Restaurant Gordon Ramsay, London) turns it into dishes brimming with technique. Doll-sized Vegemite scrolls and wallaby croquettes with pickled quince get the ball rolling. A paper-thin sheet of celeriac cloaks a bowl of sea treasures: dig in a spoon to dredge up clams, samphire and sea urchin custard. Rosy swatches of butter-poached lamb fillet rest on silken Jerusalem artichoke puree, under a rustling tinder pile of Jerusalem artichoke skins spangled with broccolini flowers. Chocolate marshmallows to toast over a blazing pinecone are the perfect Instagram-friendly finale.

There are a huge number of wines by the glass, plus booze-free options for designated drivers

Open	L Fri–Sun; D Daily
Price	$$
Cards	AE DC MC V eftpos
Chef	Travis McAuley, Dan Szwarc
Features	Bar, licensed, outdoor seating, private dining, wheelchair access
Website	hellenicrepublic.com.au

Open	D Tue–Sat
Price	$$
Cards	AE MC V eftpos
Chef	Simon Tarlington
Features	Bar, licensed
Website	highlinerestaurant.com.au

Host Dining

BRUNSWICK
4 Saxon Street
03 9023 5317

CONTEMPORARY   **14.5/20**

Welcoming local bistro raising the stakes in Brunswick

This stylish diner offers respite from Sydney Road's pub grub offerings. This is a mix-and-match space where you can prop the bar up, grab a date-worthy booth or do the share-plate shuffle, surrounded by house plants and ephemera. The daily menu has low food-miles and the wine list is taut and terrific. A plate of seared albacore tuna comes in a finely diced pile alongside tomato and fermented chilli, the lime sorbet melting into a zesty citrus sauce. The charred zucchini, heirloom tomatoes, feta and walnut with crisp onion will convert the most salad-shy diner and reflects the area's vego leanings. Goolwa pipis in a broth of fino sherry will set off a shell-stacking competition at your table. Saltbush lamb is partnered by a cumin-heavy green harissa – punchy and fragrant with a gentle chilli nudge. Finish with a classic battle between light and dark – a ball of orange olive oil sorbet on a rich crumble of stout cake.

Locals flock to Sunday lunch for the $45 three-course set menu

Ides

COLLINGWOOD
92 Smith Street
03 9939 9542

CONTEMPORARY   **16/20**

Delightfully fast-paced degustation dining

Chef Peter Gunn's restaurant disproves the tired trope that fine dining is dead and does it joyously, daringly, tastily. This is degustation dining but it's exciting and fun. The food is creative but confident, the service is witty and relaxed, and meals are well-paced and engaging. It's all taken in a shadowy, chic dining room that makes it easy to forget the world outside. You'll begin with a bombardment of no-cutlery snacks, perhaps baby corn and caviar, a perfect oyster, cucumber dressed with citrus. There are visual tricks – a prawn that looks whole but isn't, a mushroom that may not be – but the eating experience is paramount. That prawn, just set by heat, sits in a vegetable broth that's all sparkling, deep, honest flavour. The mushroom, when you find it, is a burst of pickled earthiness. Diners get involved with some dishes: a black box arrives for dessert, along with a gavel to smash it.

Mid-week 'sample tables' allow the adventurous to experience dishes in development at keen prices

Open	L Sun; D Wed–Sun
Price	$$
Cards	AE MC V eftpos
Chef	Roy Rosenfeld
Features	Bar, licensed, outdoor seating, private dining, wheelchair access
Website	hostdining.com.au

Open	L Sat–Sun; D Tue–Sun
Price	$$$
Cards	AE DC MC V eftpos
Chef	Peter Gunn
Features	Licensed, wheelchair access
Website	idesmelbourne.com.au

Iki Jime

MELBOURNE
430 Little Collins Street
03 9691 3838

SEAFOOD   **16/20**

A celebration of seasonal, local seafood handled with care

Shannon Bennett's latest iteration of his Normanby Chambers site (previously Vue de Monde and Bistro Vue) makes seafood the star of every savoury dish. That might mean a snapper sausage snagged with seaweed salad in the excellent bar, sweet prawns brushed with horseradish vinaigrette in the shadowy restaurant, or half a smoked trout served with blini and caviar, shimmering like a still life, retro and arch-contemporary at once. Seafood supplier Mark Eather is a crucial player: he either catches or approves the fish, which is line-caught and humanely killed with a brain spike ('iki jime') to minimise stress and keep flavours pure. Beautiful fish doesn't need fussing: it's either grilled or steamed and served with sauce on the side, perhaps burnt butter or potato dashi, there to highlight the flesh, not drown it. Desserts nod to the French bistro that preceded Iki Jime: there's always a tarte Tatin and a souffle, simple but displaying exemplary technique and indicative of the focus on diner enjoyment.

The wine list is seriously impressive, and can also be ordered in Bar Jime

Open	L D Tue–Sat
Price	$$$
Cards	AE MC V eftpos
Chef	Justin James, Sam Homan
Features	Bar, licensed, outdoor seating, private dining, wheelchair access
Website	ikijime.com.au

Il Bacaro

MELBOURNE
168–170 Little Collins Street
03 9654 6778

ITALIAN   **15/20**

An overload of Italian charm in a glowing CBD storefront

This is a place to canoodle in a corner, or to seal a business deal when you want to create a clubby sense of goodwill. There's a warmth that pervades every aspect of dining here. White tablecloths and candlelight set the scene, and waiters with heavy Italian accents address guests as Signor and Signora. For a restaurant with 23 years of history, the kitchen hits a lovely balance of classic Italian cooking and just enough modernity to keep things feeling fresh. Yes, that's blue cheese foam and horseradish powder on your beetroot and fig salad, but these touches don't distract from the tried and true combination. Wagyu beef carpaccio gets dressed up with black garlic mayo. The Moreton Bay bug spaghettini bursts with fat hunks of sweet seafood, and suckling pig finds fatty equilibrium with candied fennel and red cabbage. Regulars rave about the cheesecake with pop rocks, but don't sleep on the ricotta semifreddo that taste like sunshine on a plate.

The 400-bottle wine list has some real gems, especially for the barolo nerds out there

Open	L D Mon–Sat
Price	$$$
Cards	AE MC V eftpos
Chef	David Dellai
Features	Bar, licensed
Website	ilbacaro.com.au

IKI JIME

ISHIZUKA

Il Solito Posto

MELBOURNE
Basement, 113 Collins Street
(entry via George Parade)
03 9654 4466

ITALIAN **14/20**

Buzzy old-school Italian that delivers classics done right

From the zinc bar to the basement trattoria, Il Solito Posto is effortlessly charming and unashamedly old school. The crowd might be young city workers or couples who had a first date here two decades ago, back when graffiti-covered lanes were avoided not lauded. Staff will describe the menu with such passion you want to order it all, but try the tagliatelle con gamberi – Crystal Bay prawns, zucchini, saffron and chilli – a cooked-to-order tangle of al dente pasta that allows you to ratchet up the chilli heat if desired, or a risotto con capretto, where the rice plays second fiddle to gamey strips of goat, lifted by a quenelle of tangy curd. The specials board might have house-made linguine with spanner crab, tomato, chilli, garlic and parsley or go for the Tuscan seafood stew, where barramundi is surrounded by clams, mussels, calamari and cannellini beans in a stock with flavour deeper than the Marianas Trench. For dessert, plunge headlong into the beautifully boozy tiramisu.

Come early and soak up the atmosphere with a drink at the bar

Open	B L D Mon–Sat
Price	$$
Cards	AE MC V eftpos
Chef	Nathan Morfett
Features	Bar, licensed
Website	ilsolitoposto.com.au

Ishizuka

MELBOURNE
Basement, 139 Bourke Street
03 8594 0895

JAPANESE **16.5/20**

Traditional kaiseki dining in an underground bunker

It's no small investment. The tailored 11-course kaiseki menu costs $215 before drinks and takes place in a Bourke Street basement that's near impossible to find. But. The bangs per buck are many and varied. Beyond the unmarked entrance lies sound-sucking carpet and a rippling stone bar where you'll see chefs slicing otoro for the sushi course, easing beluga caviar onto an edamame tofu bite for a welcome snack or maybe grilling the two-bite piece of nine-score wagyu served with ice plant for the meat course. Different to a sushi omakase, this seasonal kaiseki menu features 'pretty things' (a dashi jelly pearl with uni at its heart), and soup (freshly scorched scampi washed in a delicate kombu broth) as well as nigiri. It's meditative, refined quietude here but big wines curated by ex-Rockpool sommelier David Lawler bring the drama, as does eating in soft pools of light cocooned by the gigantic linen sail.

Carve the instructions for access onto your hand or you will get lost

Open	D Wed–Sun
Price	$$$
Cards	AE MC V eftpos
Chef	Hitoshi Miyazawa
Features	Licensed, private dining, wheelchair access
Website	ishizuka.com.au

Kakizaki

SOUTH YARRA
479 Malvern Road
03 9827 9029

JAPANESE   15/20

**A serene suburban sushi bar offering
a top-notch omakase experience**

Not all of chef Yuji Matsuzaki's talents
are culinary. He created the wooden
counter, while his father made many
of the serving plates that appear
throughout the 16-course chef's menu.
Decisions are minimal and largely
reduced to wine or sake – the latter
is a little more in keeping with the
experience. Two tasting plates, including
crowd-pleasing miso-blackened cod and
tempura scallop, set the pace. Garnishes
are sparse: a disc of daikon here, a brush
of soy there. A 12-piece nigiri course
shows off chef Matsuzaki's ritual
hand-shaping of each rice ball, and
his knife skills. The seared courses are
standouts: sea perch and swordfish
among those licked by the blowtorch.
The rest are dabbed with ponzu or
garnished with just a few salt flakes.
But any sushi fan will know it's all
building to the fatty tuna belly, the oily
coating around the mouth lingering
until it's soothingly cleaned away with
silky almond tofu and peach jelly.

**Make sure to request a bar seat for
the best view of the action**

Kenzan

MELBOURNE
Collins Place, 56 Flinders Lane
03 9654 8933

JAPANESE   15/20

**Well into its fourth decade, Kenzan
continues to show 'em how it's done**

Just shy of 40, Kenzan gets a pat on
the back for longevity but a standing
ovation for consistent quality. The
dining room with its two paper-
screened tatami rooms is all neutral-
toned comfort, service is reserved and
efficient, and the wine list, particularly
when it comes to sake, agreeable. It's
all good background for a menu of
carefully prepared Japanese greatest
hits that sees Japanese pickles rubbing
shoulders with a superbly textured
chawan mushi or textbook tempura
that's all brittle shatter. There's fried
chicken, too, and dreamy ebi shumai,
but the main event is the sushi and
sashimi, either per piece at a coveted
stool at the sushi bar (one for the
culinary bucket list) or in a variety
of sizes and combinations at a table.
Quality is uniformly high, both with
the familiar tuna and wagyu and the
more unfamiliar offerings like arc shell,
making it clear how and why Kenzan
continues to pack 'em in.

**Book a seat at the sushi bar – still one
of the best in town**

Open	D Tue–Sat
Price	$$$
Cards	MC V eftpos
Chef	Yuji Matsuzaki
Features	Licensed
Website	sushibarkakizaki.com

Open	L Mon–Fri; D Mon–Sat
Price	$$$
Cards	AE DC MC V eftpos
Chef	Masay Ki Kuriki, Koichi Takeuchi
Features	Licensed, private dining, wheelchair access
Website	kenzan.com.au

Kirk's Wine Bar

MELBOURNE
46 Hardware Lane
03 9600 4550

🍷

EUROPEAN   **14/20**

Channelling Europe on Hardware Lane

Sitting streetside at Kirk's, snacking on chunky house-made duck and pork terrine and knocking back a glass of Austrian blaufrankisch, it's hard to avoid European flashbacks. Which is exactly the point. Ian Curley's menu is out and proud with its influences, listing superb oysters, natural or topped with horseradish and bottarga, perfectly grilled saganaki that hits the table warm and pliable, fettuccine tossed with a robust ragu of oxtail, peas and parmesan, fried buttermilk calamari and desserts that tick boxes from crumble to cannoli. It's a kind of armchair tour of the bars and family-run eateries of Europe, backed up by an excellent wine list that's as happy with a well-made natural local as it is with an Old World benchmark. Cheese lovers should take advantage of an all-French selection that's served at just the right age and temperature and there's top notch gelato from Gelateria Primavera for those who can't be bothered making the trek to Spring Street.

The two seats at the end of the bar are excellent for people watching

Open	B L D Daily
Price	$$
Cards	AE MC V eftpos
Chef	Ian Curley
Features	Bar, licensed, outdoor seating, private dining
Website	kirkswinebar.com

Kisume

MELBOURNE
175 Flinders Lane
03 9671 4888

🍷

JAPANESE   **14.5/20**

Bold Japanese in a luxe city setting

You'll find no hushed Japanese sushi temple here: Kisume is in thrall to the big-city sparkle of Tokyo and New York, its menu equal parts tribute to (mostly) Australian produce and a paean to the internationalisation of Japanese cuisine. It pays to request a seat at the sushi counter, where dinner and a show means watching a tight brigade of white-capped chefs powering out subtle new-style moves in the form of kingfish dabbed with minced shiso and spring onion, a just-torched sardine with garlic and sesame, or creamy scampi anointed with a trio of caviar, flying fish roe and finger lime. An a la carte menu goes gently rogue with Nippon-inflected reimaginings of steak tartare and luxe collisions of foie gras and grass-fed beef. The most ambitious of Chris Lucas' restaurant stable, Kisume offers a world of choice over its three levels.

Kuro Kisume on the top floor is now a 20-course omakase adventure

Open	L D Daily
Price	$$$
Cards	AE MC V eftpos
Chef	Joshua Bedell
Features	Bar, licensed, private dining, wheelchair access
Website	kisume.com.au

Komeyui

PORT MELBOURNE
396 Bay Street
03 9646 2296

JAPANESE   **14.5/20**

Meticulous cooking in a relaxed, low-key room

Skiing and golf, pfft. Hokkaido's great drawcard is its seafood. Not flying to Japan's northernmost island anytime soon? Uber-ing it to this discreet suburban restaurant may be your next best bet – the man behind the sushi bar, Motomu Kumano, was born into a Hokkaido fishing family. Each day he slips a freshly printed sheet listing sushi and sashimi specials inside the front cover of the menu: maybe expertly cut kingfish, supple surf clams or extravagantly marbled otoro, gently draped across rice cooked the old way, in an iron pot. Or, take a pale wooden table and ask soft-spoken waitstaff for gingery gyoza with silky skins and crisp bases, textbook tempura vegetables, or soft-as-butter Berkshire pork squares in miso-spiked broth. Wagyu sirloin comes cut into medium-rare cubes – like almost everything here, it's precisely cooked and tastes of its best possible self. Finish with deconstructed 'creme brulee' made with sake lees – or opt for another shot from the thoughtful sake list.

Sushi a la carte is always pricey but it's well worth the expense here

Lamaro's Hotel

SOUTH MELBOURNE
273 Cecil Street
03 9690 3737

CONTEMPORARY   **14/20**

Elegant and urbane neighbourhood pub

Executive chef Geoff Lindsay (Dandelion, Pearl) has breathed new life into this historic hotel in a leafy residential pocket. Sure, you can still order pub classics but there are Lindsay classics, too, such as yellowfin tuna seared on one side on a smoky Asian-style fish salad. Or a fragrant red duck curry, deconstructed and delicious. And the custom-built wood-fired grill is not just for steak lovers – a chermoula-rubbed whole baby snapper might be piled with pink grapefruit and pomegranate seeds, while seared scallops meet cubes of roasted pork belly. Co-owner Paul Dimattina has an experienced service team under his watchful gaze and is there most days welcoming regulars and amping up the convivial vibe. The stylish and comfortable separate dining room – with an open fire, padded leather chairs and red tartan carpet – might be a tad noisy on busy nights, but it's good to see a much-loved local back in vogue.

The bar area has a terrific snacks menu. Hello, Peking duck soup

Open	L D Tue–Sun
Price	$$$
Cards	AE MC V eftpos
Chef	Motomu Kumano
Features	Licensed, wheelchair access
Website	komeyui.com.au

Open	L D Daily
Price	$$
Cards	AE MC V eftpos
Chefs	Geoff Lindsay, Jay Sinclair
Features	Bar, licensed, outdoor seating, private dining, wheelchair access
Website	lamaroshotel.com.au

LAMARO'S HOTEL

Lau's Family Kitchen

ST KILDA
4 Acland Street
03 8598 9880

CHINESE   **14/20**

Cosy St Kilda mainstay has a cult following for clean Cantonese cuisine

Locals are devoted to this unassuming, ever-reliable family favourite offering fresh, traditional Cantonese with none of the weird bits. House-made classics are served at the table by experienced waitstaff who are right on the ball, dishing glossy pork and prawn sui mai, crowd-pleasing chicken dim sims or flaky spring rolls packed with slow-cooked lamb and herbs, best dunked in hoisin. Main plates are on the large side and better for groups, including tender chunks of Angus beef brisket in a dark, steaming gravy, crisp-skinned baby chicken in soy broth or comforting mapo tofu with a swift kick of chilli-spiced pork. Desserts are just like you'd make at home: banana fritters or cut strawberries with a hefty scoop of vanilla ice-cream. Devotees are willing to pay a premium for dependable fare, so always be sure to book – from a midweek winter feed to a sunny Saturday feast on the terrace, Lau's is usually jammed.

Half serves are available on request for some dishes – but you can take any leftovers home

Lee Ho Fook

MELBOURNE
11-15 Duckboard Place
03 9077 6261

CHINESE   **15/20**

Modern Chinese-Australian in an oh-so-Melbourne setting

This moody mod-Chinese restaurant embodies a lot of the components that make Melbourne a fun place to eat. Is it down an art-packed laneway? Does it have a fantastic bar scene? Does it manage to take an historic building and fit it out to feel fresh and exciting? Yup, yup, yup. Chef Victor Liong takes the legacy of deliciousness given to us by generations of Chinese Australians and takes it in highly personal and creative directions. This might mean bay scallops lightly warmed on their shell, sitting in a pool of brown butter alongside a cube of silken tofu, or spicy beef tartare with puffed rice and cucumber. Whole Murray cod comes swimming in a deeply flavourful black bean sauce, adorned by charred green garlic and a flurry of Goolwa pipis. Looking for the world's best drinking snack? The Chongqing chicken cracklings might just be that – and the neon-lit downstairs Good Luck bar is the perfect place to test this theory.

The wine list contains a treasure trove of aromatic whites – rieslings in particular

Open	L Mon–Fri, Sun; D Daily
Price	$$$
Cards	MC V eftpos
Chef	James Lew
Features	Licensed, outdoor seating
Website	lauskitchen.com.au

Open	L Mon–Fri (in the bar); D Daily
Price	$$
Cards	AE MC V eftpos
Chef	Victor Liong
Features	Bar, licensed
Website	leehofook.com.au

Lello

MELBOURNE
150 Flinders Lane
03 9654 6699

ITALIAN **14.5/20**

Handmade pasta proficiency on a buzzing city corner

Regional pasta dishes seldom seen on Australian menus have long been a strength of Leo Gelsomino's cooking, but they're squarely in the spotlight since the Flinders Lane restaurant he co-owns was given a chic refurb and renamed to reference his childhood nickname. The menu traipses across the Boot, and beautifully so. Sardinian culurgiones, intricately pleated dumplings filled with potato, lemon and mint, come with broccoli and an Amalfi-style anchovy sauce. The slippery, silken cacio e pepe is made with hand-wrapped maccheroni tubes, wonderfully nutty from burnt wheat flour imported directly from Puglia, rather than the traditional spaghetti. The rest of the menu is no slouch either, from charred calamari with green chilli, capers and vinegary zucchini to an intriguing dessert of wild fennel ice-cream. Service is smooth-sailing and the Italo-Australian wine list attractively priced – combine all this with weekday breakfasts and a bar open until late, and you'll be looked after no matter what hour you cross the threshold.

Start with a cocktail – we love the Boulevardier and white negroni

Open	B Mon–Fri; L D Mon–Sat
Price	$$
Cards	AE MC V eftpos
Chef	Leo Gelsomino, Ivan Minissale
Features	Bar, licensed
Website	lellopastabar.com.au

Lesa

MELBOURNE
Level 1, 122 Russell Street
03 9935 9838

CONTEMPORARY **15/20**

After three years, Embla's big sister has arrived

She's certainly a looker – all dark timbers, emerald-tiled kitchen and curious ephemera. The scene is ripe for renaissance nudes, but also for a wine-driven dinner. Unlike Embla downstairs, Lesa is for bottles over glasses (just a handful of the excellent, though eclectic, natural-leaning list is by glass) and groups over singles. The best tables are six-tops near the kitchen with chef Dave Verheul and wine cellar in view. It's a set menu with flexibility – four courses, three options for each, revisiting Verheul's more technique-driven days with lessons from Embla's woodfire. There's comforting hot grilled potato bread, with silky macadamia cream and ye olde 'porridge' textured with chicken, shrouded with the funk of fermented chestnut, but it's confrontingly frontier, too. See squid shaved like fat, slippery rice noodles, fresh with parsley. Miso-braised pork with extra wobble and almond-dusted flounder tartare, tasting of pure green. It's as beautiful here as it is button-pushing bold. Embrace it. Think big, drink bigger.

Word is they'll soon be open for lunch

Open	D Wed–Sat
Price	$$
Cards	AE MC V eftpos
Chef	Dave Verheul
Features	Bar, licensed, private dining
Website	lesarestaurant.com.au

L'Hotel Gitan

PRAHRAN
32 Commercial Road
03 9999 0990

citi

FRENCH   **14/20**

The Reymond family does a French gastropub. Enough said

If Bistro Gitan is the South Yarra set's sedate clubhouse, then L'Hotel Gitan is the Prahran set's raucous playground. Even on a wintry weeknight, there's an air of Celine-leather-jacket-wearing, "Ooh-look-there's-Arabella" that runs through the former Hotel Max, converted into a cosy French gastropub by the ultra-professional progeny of Jacques Reymond. The menu defies any lazy lean on French cliche. There's an excellent vol au vent: buttery pastry filled with Jerusalem artichoke and a heady garlicky note. There's leanly battered soft-shell crab tempura dabbed with avocado cream and crumbed rockling, inflected with a Mediterranean rouille. Duck magret plays it totally straight – the breast pan-seared but pink, the thigh picked, slow-cooked and set in a deeply reduced duck jus. Dessert? Mais oui. Cheesecake shouldn't need deconstructing, but Gitan's version – chevre cheesecake, with the tang of yoghurt sorbet and the textural contrast of dehydrated mandarin – is just the right mix of clever and pleasure. True to Reymond family tradition.

No tables free on the website? Try calling for a bar seat, often left free

Open	L D Daily
Price	$$
Cards	AE MC V eftpos
Chef	Rotem Papo
Features	Bar, licensed, outdoor seating, private dining, wheelchair access
Website	lhotelgitan.com.au

The Lincoln

CARLTON
91 Cardigan Street
03 9347 4666

PUB DINING   **14/20**

An education in classic pub food with flair

Remember your favourite uni professor – a little scruffy but with bags of charm and knowledge? Fittingly, Melbourne Uni's unofficial old boozer shares similar qualities. It may not be the slickest in town, but it's a real crowd-pleaser: academics and locals yabber over pints in the front bar; rowdy families and friends hook into food in slightly scuffed rooms around them. What takes the Lincoln into next-level pub territory is a classic, well-executed menu, attentive yet relaxed table service and a comprehensive wine and whisky list that spans regions, styles and price points. Share creamy cheese croquettes, fist-sized pork terrine, saved from tipping to too-rich by piquant cornichons and chutney, before tackling hearty mains. Juicy chicken schnitzel, served golden under melting garlic butter with old-school coleslaw and chips is poster-worthy pub grub, while delicate sea bream, set on a velvety potato emulsion with smoky lardons, and cooked lettuce that's anything but limp shows real cooking chops. BYO suede elbow patches.

Let the chef choose for you – either the eight-dish Full Lincoln ($75) or five-dish Half Lincoln ($55)

Open	L D Daily
Price	$$
Cards	AE MC V eftpos
Chef	Howard Stamp
Features	Bar, licensed, outdoor seating
Website	hotellincoln.com.au

Long Chim

SOUTHBANK
Crown Complex, 8 Whiteman Street
03 9292 5777

THAI   **14.5/20**

Swanky Yarra-facing Thai canteen with fiery food and icy cocktails

Renowned for his stubborn focus on authentic ingredients and finely tuned hot, sour, bitter, sweet and creamy flavours, David Thompson is Australia's king of Thai cuisine. He may not visit the Melbourne outpost of his street food empire often, but you can see where he's been. You'll spot his influence in a salad balancing soft-boiled egg, velvety, smoky eggplant flesh and crisp, fragrant sawtooth coriander with a bright but not shrill dressing. In a deeply savoury stir-fry of tender cumin-spiced beef and just-cooked onion. And especially in Chiang Mai chicken larp bundled into raw cabbage cups, a dish so fiery the charming service staff may check your spice tolerance before you order. This is a sophisticated take on a Bangkok canteen, with a fire-fighting drinks list of specialty beers, chilli-savvy wines and creative cocktails, and prices that land you firmly back in Melbourne. But in a town where bold but nuanced Thai food isn't easy to find, it exerts an undeniable pull.

On a balmy night, take a table on the riverside terrace

Open	L D Daily
Price	$$
Cards	AE DC MC V eftpos
Chef	Steven Ngo, David Thompson
Features	Bar, licensed, outdoor seating, private dining
Website	crownmelbourne.com.au/ restaurants/premium/long-chim

Longrain

MELBOURNE
40-44 Little Bourke Street
03 9653 1600

THAI   **14.5/20**

Still a swaggering giant of mod-Asian cool

It's difficult for a *Sex and the City*-era epitome of cool to maintain its status – as a viewing of *SATC 2* will quickly tell you. But a visit to Longrain, still slinging excellent Asian-inflected dishes, remains an event to anticipate. A new generation of i-banker analysts and marketing types crowd the communal tables at this ever-handsome warehouse space, here for the dim-lit buzz and big, punchy Thai flavours. Caramelised pork hock epitomises the playbook, its sweetness and richness cut through with the heat and acidity of chilli vinegar. Some dishes hit the sugary note too hard – notably the black kingfish, overwhelmed by its sweet soy yuzu dressing – but the kitchen is perfectly capable of subtlety and technique. One sip of the silky coconut broth accompanying poached chicken, julienned green papaya and Vietnamese mint is ample, perfectly balanced evidence of that. Add new rooftop bar Longsong to the mix, and Longrain looks set to maintain its reign of cool.

In a smaller group? Order half-serves of mains to maximise your menu sampling

Open	D Daily
Price	$$
Cards	AE MC V eftpos
Chef	Wee Siong Teh, Ratthawit Anankitphanit
Features	Bar, licensed, wheelchair access
Website	longrain.com

Lord Cardigan

ALBERT PARK
59 Cardigan Place
03 9645 5305

CONTEMPORARY   **14/20**

A neighbourhood bistro just off the main drag that's all calm and class

For more than a decade, this bistro has warmly wrapped locals and visitors alike in its quiet and elegant embrace. It's the sort of place where co-owner Dominique Bolger might pull up a chair to charm grey-haired regulars, while friendly staff offer savvy wine suggestions and polished service. Small bites show plenty of labour-intensive technique in the deft flavour combinations and pretty plating. Choose two or three as an entree, perhaps roasted discs of boned quail rolled in German ham, or kingfish flash-fried in a tempura-style batter. For main course, crowd-pleasers such as herb- and Dijon-crumbed veal might compete for attention with more elaborate dishes such as roast duck breast, beautifully pink and amped with shiitake mushrooms and pickled vegetables. Finish with the ever-popular mini doughnuts and head home feeling as relaxed as slipping in to your favourite chunky knit.

Lunches are a bargain: $25 for a main and glass of wine Wednesday to Saturday and $29 for Sunday roast

Open	B Sat–Sun; L Wed–Sun; D Tue–Sat (and first Sun of month)
Price	$$
Cards	AE MC V eftpos
Chef	John Singer
Features	Licensed, outdoor seating, wheelchair access, BYO
Website	lordcardigan.com.au

Lucy Liu

MELBOURNE
23 Oliver Lane
03 9639 5777

MODERN ASIAN   **14/20**

High-spirited, high-turnover, high-end laneway pan-Asian canteen

The red-neon conjures all the right desires and continues through to the finger-food fun of a fried soft-shelled crab pancake roll – north China's jianbing street eating, reworked. The menu jets from Bangkok to Shanghai, to a bang-on Korean-style crisp pork hock (served with crepes, a kimchi slaw and chilli-jazzed hoisin sauce). Brit-pack chef Michael Lambie (The Smith, Taxi, Circa) and his crew have trawled south-east and northern Asia to re-appropriate the best of its casual cuisine in this postmodern eatery that ticks all the on-trend boxes. Check that cut concrete floor, 'bamboo' lattice interior; hissing woks that perfume the room with ginger, garlic and chilli; kitsch-tacular lenticular placemats; Laminex-topped tables; chic waitstaff; deep house beats; high-ceiling and high-turnover, with fine-pinched dumplings and pork buns for days. It works. With a side of noise. As a culinary tease, from ubiquitous kingfish sashimi to one-off banana fritters (fried in rice and coconut), as a traipse through the exoticism of an imagined elsewhere.

Bewildered? Let Lucy choose with five- or seven-plate tasting menu

Open	L D Daily
Price	$$
Cards	AE MC V eftpos
Chef	Zachary Cribbes, Michael Lambie, Jenna North
Features	Bar, licensed, wheelchair access
Website	lucylius.com.au

Lume

SOUTH MELBOURNE
226 Coventry Street
03 9690 0185

CONTEMPORARY   **17/20**

Backstreet beacon of culinary excellence

Eileen Horsnell works the pass like a conductor. There's both grace and a razor-sharp intensity in the way she directs her kitchen orchestra. It was Shaun Quade in this spotlight, at this, one of Melbourne's most ambitious restaurants. But while he's concentrating on international projects, it's Horsnell's aria. The menu is as flamboyant and complex as it always has been. The opening chords of an 15-course degustation may be crab custard masquerading as a tiny cob of corn. It's cute and crazy delicious. Duck is often the menu hero, perhaps a crisp-skinned briquette of Great Ocean Road bird, basted in honey and miso, stuffed with melaleuca leaves, dry-aged, slow-roasted then smoked. It's one of the most memorable dishes in town. There is a lot of polish in both service and the room: bottles of booze sit on podiums strung from the roof, flatware is handmade, cutlery is Cutipol. After hitting some wrong notes in its early days, Lume is strongly on song.

The Lume Looking Glass is a cocktail flight of four drinks, if you're not persuaded by the full menu

Maha

MELBOURNE
21 Bond Street
03 9629 5900

MIDDLE EASTERN   **15/20**

Modern Middle Eastern fine dining in a darkly alluring room

Descend into the sleek basement room and marvel at the dimly lit, grown-up beauty of it all. This does not feel like a restaurant that's a decade old, in part because it was originally ahead of its time, and in part because it has had a slick facelift. Either way, chef Shane Delia's cooking still feels thrillingly of-the-moment. Practically every modern Middle Eastern restaurant has a slow-roasted lamb dish, but the version at Maha is a stunner. Paired with a green olive tabbouleh, the lamb is fall-apart tender, juicy and full of meaty flavour. There are other delights to be found: salmon kibbeh neya presents the buttery fish raw, with white onion and harissa jam. Charred broccoli tabbouleh gets a pop of bright fruitiness thanks to pomegranate, and the aged Persian rice is fragrant. When asked what ingredient gives that rice its distinctive perfume, the adept waitress answers, "Love. Or maybe it's passion – there's lots of that in there, too."

One of the city's best bets for a sophisticated business lunch

Open	L Sat; D Tue–Sat
Price	$$$
Cards	AE MC V eftpos
Chefs	Shaun Quade, Eileen Horsnell
Features	Bar, licensed, private dining, wheelchair access
Website	restaurantlume.com

Open	L D Daily
Price	$$$
Cards	AE DC MC V eftpos
Chef	Shane Delia, Daniel Giraldo
Features	Bar, licensed, private dining, wheelchair access
Website	maharestaurant.com.au

Marion

FITZROY
53 Gertrude Street
03 9419 6262

CONTEMPORARY   **15/20**

Razor-sharp wine bar serving up good food and good times

Think of Marion as the little black dress of wine bars, equally right for after-work drinks, a cocktail before dinner at Andrew McConnell's neighbouring flagship, Cutler and Co., or for a meal that's a textbook example of Melbourne bistronomy. You could even do the walk of shame in that LBD, returning for weekend brunch and, whatever your regrets, ordering baked eggs and braised greens with Turkish chilli won't be one of them. Flexibility is Marion's watchword. Sit at a kerbside table, on a dark leather banquette or at the kitchen bench and choose from a pithy menu that evolves daily. Confit duck salad, for example, juxtaposes rich ducky nuggets against bitter radicchio, raw onion and pickled cherries. Vitello tonnato, its blushing veal slices resting on indulgent tuna mayo, is bedazzled with capers. And a juicy crumbed pork cutlet keeps company with celeriac remoulade and a lemon cheek. Entrusting staff with wine suggestions will reward with something unusual but always delicious.

Drink something you like? You can have a mixed Deadman's Dozen ($270) delivered to your door

Open	B Sat–Sun; L Fri–Sun; D Daily
Price	$$
Cards	AE MC V eftpos
Chefs	Andrew McConnell, Natasha Burnett
Features	Bar, licensed, outdoor seating, wheelchair access
Website	marionwine.com.au

Massi

MELBOURNE
445 Little Collins Street
03 9670 5347

ITALIAN   **14/20**

A pint-size Italian restaurant dishing out maximum deliciousness

In a city block devoted to lunch on the run, Massi stands out as the place for a proper meal. In fact, its charm is that it doesn't stand out: it's a small restaurant, like little places you might find in an Italian city, devoted to the pleasures of good food and wine. The bar is an excellent spot for a pre-lunch or dinner drink and fine slices of prosciutto or salami, but the tables are where Massi shines. The precise menu covers all bases. The stuzzichini double as entrees: shared plates of tender meatballs with tomato sauce or daily-changing arancini won't stamp out the appetite for luscious ravioli filled with pumpkin and amaretto with crisp cavolo nero, or the swordfish served with caponata, Sicily's favourite sweet and warm vegetable relish. At lunch, regulars tend to the steak with thick-cut chips, the better to appreciate the impressive range of Italian reds while discussing work.

The chef's menu (two, three or four courses) includes an outstanding tiramisu among the desserts

Open	L Mon–Fri; D Tue–Sat
Price	$$
Cards	AE MC V eftpos
Chef	Joseph Vargetto
Features	Bar, licensed
Website	massi.com.au

Matilda 159 Domain

SOUTH YARRA
159 Domain Road
03 9089 6668

CONTEMPORARY   **16/20**

Flame-grilled Australian opulence beneath a boutique hotel

Bust out your YSL clutches. Scott Pickett has hit South Yarra with a 100 per cent wood-fired restaurant and some serious black Amex swagger. Beneath a barrelled ochre ceiling, hewn blackwood tables are girt by outrageously stuffed leather banquettes. Here, Melbourne's answer to the Kardashians gripe about their ungrateful teens. But you don't have to. Instead, load hot buttered charry flatbreads with spanner crab bound with creme fraiche and dressed with beach succulents. Chase with a whole liver-textured duck smoked over cherry wood served with its own confit legs sang choy bao-style. Pickled and roasted beets are perfumed with piney Geraldton wax, Blackmore wagyu bavette is nuttily seasoned with wattleseed and a spicy kangaroo tartare gets its sharp kick from muntries. The emerald-tiled, beautifully timbered toilets downstairs are worth a visit alone. But stay for the darkly caramelised apple and smoked vanilla tarte Tatin, and Australian wines straddling the interesting and investment bottle divide.

Bring a posse to delve into bigger dishes like the duck

Open	L D Daily
Price	$$$
Cards	AE MC V eftpos
Chef	Scott Pickett
Features	Bar, licensed, private dining, wheelchair access
Website	matilda159.com

Matteo's

FITZROY NORTH
533 Brunswick Street
03 9481 1177

CONTEMPORARY   **14.5/20**

A new chef breathes modern life into an old favourite

Long thriving on a rabidly devoted cadre of regulars, this wonderfully old-school dining room stands in a dignified storefront on the quiet end of Brunswick Street. The menu, which has traditionally dealt in elegant Asian fusion, isn't looking quite so Asian these days. New head chef Rhys Blackley still plays with Japanese influences – a little tempura here, a dash of ponzu there – but his main aesthetic seems to be creative, bold flavours unbound by genre. He even jumps confidently on the native ingredients train, serving tender pink wallaby tartare with daubs of slow-cooked egg yolk and riberry, and puffed beef tendon. Some dishes fall squarely in the grand tradition of Euro fine dining. Rosy fleshed duck breast is arranged on the plate next to a lovely quenelle of duck liver mousse, as well as braised witlof, glazed figs and hazelnut cream. Starched linen and deferential service complete the picture – one that's still artful, more than 20 years in.

The banquette seats that face the bar are one of the lovelier places in town to dine solo

Open	L Sun–Fri; D Daily
Price	$$$
Cards	AE MC V eftpos
Chef	Rhys Blackley
Features	Licensed, private dining, BYO
Website	matteos.com.au

The Mayfair

MELBOURNE
45 Collins Street
03 9654 8545

FRENCH **14/20**

Straight-shooting French dining in the heart of the city

There's a fine line between twee and deliciously ironic chinoiserie and this ode to the French brasserie treads it ever-so-carefully. The room, 18th-century sea captain's quarters meets Melbourne side street, is taken up by a giant brass chandelier, heavily dressed tables and bentwood chairs. The menu, Sydney's Hubert meets Paris's Le Bistrot Paul Bert, reads like a lesson in relaxed comfort. Comte custard gougeres – puff balls of cheesy pastry licked with a red wine caramel – explode on sticky-fingered impact. Crudites – heirloom carrots, radishes, cucumber, beans – are served with a mullet roe-infused aioli. The big sell here, though, isn't the Mayfair burger with its pickle-heavy special sauce, medium-rare patty, soft bun and side of herbed frites ($35 – why?). It's not the beautifully pink slices of O'Connor scotch fillet with a side of bearnaise, either. Nor is it the creme brulee, just set with a deeply caramelised sugar crust. No, it's the cocktails from bar whizz Joe Jones – drink them any way you can get them.

There's a compact menu for drinkers who'd like to dine at the bar

Open	L Tue–Fri; D Tue–Sat
Price	$$$
Cards	AE MC V eftpos
Chef	Sam Stafford
Features	Bar, licensed, wheelchair access
Website	mayfairrestaurant.com.au

Mercer's Restaurant

ELTHAM
732 Main Road
03 9431 1015

CONTEMPORARY **14/20**

French-inflected fare in a Federation cottage

Mercer's has always been a double act: chef Stephen Mercer in the kitchen and his wife Ute in the dining room. South of the Yarra and over 20 years ago, Stephen was sous chef to Jacques Reymond – his perfectly turned vegetables and delicate sauces show that that influence has remained. The tablecloths are starched and the stemware sparkling, but there's a break in formality by way of a creamy pumpkin soup amuse. A familiar pork belly and scallop entree pleases with salty crackling and an apple-mustard emulsion. The sweetly spice-glazed duck is rosy, with its accompanying Champagne-braised cabbage. A not-too-sweet bread and butter pudding arrives accompanied by a brown butter ice-cream that is practically worth the price of the degustation menu. The dining room is subdued, but features a homey array of artwork, collected from Stephen and Ute's travels, as well as pieces created by neighbours and staff. Best of all, thanks to the carpeting and the Eltham crowd, you can actually hear your tablemate.

Get someone else to drive and try one of the vineyard-focused wine dinners held throughout the year

Open	L Thu–Fri, Sun; D Wed–Sun
Price	$$$
Cards	AE MC V eftpos
Chef	Stephen Mercer
Features	Licensed, private dining, wheelchair access, BYO
Website	mercersrestaurant.com.au

THE MAYFAIR

Minamishima

RICHMOND
4 Lord Street
03 9429 5180

JAPANESE   **18/20**

Quiet perfection in the back streets of Richmond

There's an almost Pavlovian response to eating at Koichi Minamishima's hushed temple to sushi. It's the sueded, muffled sound of Koichi-san's hands clapping together as he shapes the rice for each perfect piece of nigiri, where every grain joins together yet remains separate. Crazy stuff. When it comes to the fish, things are likely to change from day to day, depending on what's available. You might be lucky enough to try King George whiting, enhanced with blood plum and black sesame. Or maybe it'll be hapuka glazed with yuzu from Beechworth and a light painting of wasabi. Hokkaido flounder comes scored and lightly torched, bringing out a toasted, buttery richness. Bluefin tuna belly is wrapped in nori like a little taco. Smoked bonito is served with a single shard of crisp garlic. It tastes like the smell of a Polish deli. Salmon roe over loose sushi rice is almost more forest than sea. This really is the epitome of quiet confidence.

This is not a restaurant for first dates, unless they're obsessed with raw fish eaten in silence

Open	D Tue–Sat
Price	$$$
Cards	AE MC V eftpos
Chef	Koichi Minamishima
Features	Licensed, wheelchair access
Website	minamishima.com.au

Mister Bianco

KEW
285 High Street
03 9853 6929

ITALIAN   **14.5/20**

Relaxed and comfortable local Italian

There's a reason Joe Vargetto has never been able to take the beef cheeks off the menu at Mister Bianco. Wine-braised and glazed until rich and sticky, then pulled back into line with a sharp kohlrabi and cauliflower puree, it's both rich and comforting. In a way, the dish epitomises how this neighbourhood restaurant manages to be both romantic and family-friendly; as suitable for business as for birthdays. Whatever the occasion, you'll want to start with the hot and salty veal-stuffed olives all'ascolana. You'll want to follow them up with the cured Hiramasa kingfish, dressed with bagna cauda and a crown of crisp potato. House-made pasta is an obvious choice, particularly the buttery garganelli with peppery duck meatballs, and you'll find plenty of options on the (almost exclusively) Australian and Italian wine list to drink alongside. If you still have room, the tiramisu is always reliable or for something different, the pumpkin creme brulee makes for an interesting finish.

Service here is friendly and attentive – let them guide you

Open	L Thu–Fri; D Mon–Sat
Price	$$
Cards	AE DC MC V eftpos
Chef	Joseph Vargetto
Features	Bar, licensed, outdoor seating, private dining, wheelchair access
Website	misterbianco.com.au

Miznon

MELBOURNE
59 Hardware Lane
03 9670 2861

MEDITERRANEAN   **15/20**

Fine dining meets street food

Chefs are often preceded by their dishes, but rarely by dishes as simple as a whole roasted cauliflower. Of course, like everything Israeli chef Eyal Shani does, the simplicity is deceptive. His food looks street, but there's some serious technique behind what goes into those pita pockets. There's one stuffed with tender lamb ribs, tahini, pickles, onion and chilli. Another has a rich ratatouille and a boiled egg. And beyond pita? There's that cauliflower, massaged in oil and roasted whole until soft. There are buttery fish wings, dressed in tahini and chilli, and a plate of lamb shawarma is rich and garlicky. Service here is fast and fun, and unsolicited shots of arak are common, especially if you choose a seat at the open kitchen on the lower level of the two-storey space. There's a couple of simple options for dessert, too, if you can fit it in, and for drinks, there's a few beers, a short, mostly local wine list, and basic spirits.

Don't forget to order the cauliflower – it's famous worldwide

Open	L D Mon–Sat
Price	$$
Cards	MC V eftpos
Chef	Eyal Shani, Afik Gal
Features	Bar, licensed, outdoor seating
Website	miznonaustralia.com

MoVida

MELBOURNE
1 Hosier Lane
03 9663 3038

SPANISH   **15/20**

A Spanish standard bearer rolls on

Sixteen years in, MoVida has retained all the electricity of a brand-new hotspot, that indefinable energy that pulses through restaurants when they're on their game. There's still a thrill in traipsing down one of Melbourne's most beautifully graffitied alleys, of stepping into the perennially packed terracotta-tiled room, and in eating flavour-packed tapas washed down with Spanish wine. Frank Camorra and team manage to balance long-time fan favourites on the menu with a dash of newness here and there to keep things interesting. Who can resist the crisp allure of the fried zucchini flowers stuffed with sweet spanner crabmeat? Mackerel with a dollop of gazpacho sorbet is intensely smoky, bolstered by the crunch of pine nuts. Ludicrously large mussels come bathed in a grassy Basque green sauce, punctuated by sweet green peas. As Camorra's empire continues to grow – he now runs a Spanish imports company, among other things – MoVida shows no signs of slowing its roll.

Those seats in the window are lovely but beware that – thanks to the graffiti outside – you'll be in the background of a lot of tourists' Instagram posts

Open	L D Daily
Price	$$
Cards	AE MC V eftpos
Chef	Frank Camorra, Ewen Crawford
Features	Bar, licensed
Website	movida.com.au

MoVida Aqui

MELBOURNE
Level 1, 500 Bourke Street
(via Little Bourke Street)
03 9663 3038

SPANISH **14/20**

MoVida's legal district sequel has the contract on city power lunches

There's hardly a deal that hasn't been sealed over lunch at this glass-and-steel stalwart overlooking the Supreme Court dome. You'll probably start with 'embutidos', cured meats sliced hard and fast with hunks of crusty bread and grassy olive oil. Then you'll order from a list of tapas dishes that are as warm and comforting as the Spanish sun. Fresh cubes of Albacore tuna on a crisp cracker lifted with pops of mullet roe is a one-bite wonder. Then there's that hulking sandwich filled with herb-flecked fingers of calamari dripping with aioli, or the Catalan potato bomb slathered with red mojo sauce: both Frank Camorra classics and hard to pass by. Larger 'raciones' are made for sharing: thin shavings of wagyu beef dabbed with black and pickled garlic, or a hefty Millbrook pork cutlet. Finish with a wobbling creme caramel served with shards of pastry, or straws of churros dunked in custardy chocolate. MoVida Aqui, it's a pleasure doing business with you.

Not talking shop? Nab a stool at the bar and watch the kitchen in full flight

Open	L Mon–Fri; D Mon–Sat
Price	$$
Cards	AE DC MC V eftpos
Chef	Frank Camorra, Kane Vokoun
Features	Bar, licensed, outdoor seating, private dining, wheelchair access
Website	movida.com.au/movida-aqui

Napier Quarter

FITZROY
359 Napier Street
03 9416 0666

EUROPEAN **14/20**

An all-day local that inspires serious postcode envy

Great local restaurants aren't just can-do places, they also understand 'can be'. Napier Quarter can be a place for croissant and, just as easily, it can be a place for a solo sandwich piled with quality charcuterie. It's great for a cosy date over pinot gris and roast chicken or a post-work wind-down with cheese and pickles. They'll sort you for a lingering after-dinner digestif, too. The watchwords are community, artisan and quality: that's expressed in connections with suppliers and neighbours, a focus on ethical, interesting produce and house-made staples (cheese, butter, preserves). It's the unbending focus on making everyday food perfect that spins a worthy philosophy into such a pleasant package. Anchovies are piled over salsa verde and crisp toast. A salad of farro, hazelnuts and the kitchen's own dazzling ricotta turns high summer zucchini into heroes. Chocolate and coconut cake supports inches of buttercream. Every dish insists quietly, deliciously, that the simple can tip into the sublime.

Ask about the daily fruit tarts, often made with produce that lobs at the back door

Open	B L D Daily
Price	$$
Cards	AE MC V eftpos
Chef	Caitlin Gray, Nikki Owen, Ximena Santurtun Balestrini
Features	Bar, licensed, outdoor seating, wheelchair access
Website	napierquarter.com.au

Neighbourhood Wine

FITZROY NORTH
1 Reid Street
03 9486 8306

🍷

EUROPEAN   **14.5/20**

The perfect neighbourhood wine bar and bistro

You'll no longer find card tables or poker chips at Neighbourhood Wine. Instead, underworld figure Alphonse Gangitano's former gentlemen's club is now a haven of a different kind. Steep steps lead to a warm, multi-roomed space, with a mismatch of tables and squishy armchairs clustered around fireplaces. The generously portioned European menu is seasonal and changes daily, although both the Cape Grim bavette steak with a serve of fat, hand-cut chips, and the pan-fried potato and ricotta gnocchi have been on for so long they're practically signatures. Start with anchovies and pickled caper berries on a potato crisp, or the house-made fresh cheese with blood plums, grilled leeks and sourdough wafers. While the food is excellent, what you're here for is the wine. Straddling the line between old world and new, the list is navigated with the help of a key noting those that are organic, biodynamic, have had extended skin-contact and more. Whether that helps you seek certain styles or avoid them, you'll find it useful.

Go early for the light in summer and to nab a spot by the fire in winter

Open	L D Daily
Price	$$
Cards	AE MC V eftpos
Chef	Almay Jordaan
Features	Bar, licensed, private dining, BYO
Website	neighbourhoodwine.com

Neptune Food and Wine

WINDSOR
212 High Street
03 9533 2827

🍷

MEDITERRANEAN   **14.5/20**

Tinder in wine bar form, with an Amalfi twist

If Chin Chin was Melbourne's first Instagram-age restaurant, then Neptune is its Tinder equivalent. Here, the gang behind the twenty-something thrills of Tokyo Tina and Hanoi Hannah sell a more thirty-something-ish mix of Mediterranean food, wine and frisson in equal and generous measures. Here for a first encounter? Tinned delicacies – say, rich tuna belly cut through with pickled onion, capers and parsley – are an easy jumping-off point for that Vilebrequin-clad, Basque coast reminiscence you wanted to share. Keep up the summer vibes with dice of gin-cured salmon, kohlrabi and cucumber, accompanied by a dramatically smoky sour cream, or hand-cut steak tartare with negroni-cured beetroot. Red-sauced pasta might seem less fashionable, but the umami-amped, spanner crab-flecked sugo through neatly folded, fresh chitarra noodles is totally worth a right swipe. Leaving aside the possibility of running into an ex – probably higher at Neptune than anywhere else in Melbourne – Neptune is date-night vibes done right.

No reservations? Kick off the night with a cocktail upstairs at Impala

Open	L Fri–Sun; D Tue–Sun
Price	$$
Cards	AE MC V eftpos
Chef	Jarad Stafford
Features	Bar, licensed, outdoor seating, private dining, wheelchair access
Website	neptune.melbourne

Noir

RICHMOND
175 Swan Street
03 9428 3585

FRENCH **15/20**

Modern French done with warmth and panache

Noir by name but not by nature, this hospitable chef-owned restaurant gives French cuisine a Melbourne rethink and serves it up in a charming timbered dining room. Sit near the pretty vestibule to feel part of the Swan Street sashay, or ensconce yourself up the back for a could-be-anywhere feast. Classic dishes are tweaked – a salade Nicoise with cured kingfish and quail eggs, say, or saltgrass lamb given the 'en croute' treatment, rolled in pastry and roasted to blushing pink. There's a jaunty playfulness to dishes like the profiteroles filled with chicken liver pâté and port jelly, and the rare venison, in a salad of broccolini, blackberries and almond cream. Creativity and technique are on show in the tortellini, filled with sweet spanner crab and elegantly dressed with caviar butter, and the signature vacherin (layered meringue) with boozy parfait and fennel cream. Wine with a story and personable service round out the picture, ensuring that diners leave planning a return.

Sunday's shared lunches are all about relaxed bonhomie

Open	L Fri, Sun; D Tue–Sun
Price	$$
Cards	AE MC V eftpos
Chef	Peter Roddy
Features	Licensed, wheelchair access, BYO
Website	noirrestaurant.com.au

O.My

BEACONSFIELD
23 Woods Street
03 9769 9000

CONTEMPORARY **16/20**

One of the most shining examples of minimal waste, farm-to-table dining in the land

A farmer stomps through the door with a box. "You want these?" he asks Matt Bertoncello, one of the three brothers who own this butcher-turned-fine diner. Matt ferries the fragrant pine mushrooms to his brother Blayne in the kitchen – they'll be straight on the menu. This is how they roll here. A deep-rooted connection to the community and the earth pulses through everything. Into the 30-seat dining room hung with a gnarled grapevine comes a riot of courses, often with one ingredient playing lead. It may be the 'zero-waste pumpkin' dish: a puree of roasted flesh, studded with pickled pellets of skin, draped with ribbons of dough made with flour from dehydrated pumpkin offcuts. It sings. As do venison fillets, brined, smoked, jewelled with preserved blueberries and crowned by kale. Vegetables star through to dessert, perhaps Jerusalem artichoke ice-cream under a soil of cacao. Oh my. Eat here and you understand the name.

Ask to see Matt's special leather-bound wine list – it's a corker

Open	L Sat–Sun; D Thu–Sat
Price	$$
Cards	AE MC V eftpos
Chef	Blayne Bertoncello
Features	Licensed, private dining, wheelchair access
Website	omyrestaurant.com.au

O'Connell's

SOUTH MELBOURNE
407 Coventry Street
03 9810 0086

BRITISH   **14/20**

Brittania rules at this South Melbourne diner

Englishman Tom Brockbank continues the epicurean pedigree of this landmark corner pub, the kitchen alma mater of Greg Malouf, Adrian Richardson, and Caths Claringbold and Kalka. It's a name-dropping end of town, where an advertising, radio and business lunch crowd loosen collars and cufflinks, talking instead about Argentinian chimichurri sauce on grilled Lakes Entrance octopus and waxy kipfler potatoes. It's a simple formula done well: choice ingredients, carefully sourced, nicely paired on a menu that doesn't disappoint. Beef carpaccio with roast beetroot cubes and shards of pecorino cheese is edible artwork. Tender-as-you-like slow-cooked lamb with French-style peas braised with butter, onion, stock, smoky bacon and a knob of creamy Yarra goat's curd makes for a slick take on comfort food. Or fall back on the classics, from beef and Guinness pie to adroitly seared scotch fillet, to a deconstructed Eton mess that turns heads and hearts. Bottoms up to a top-shelf fine dining boozer.

A few days' notice and the in-house pastry chef does birthday cakes to order

Open	L D Daily
Price	$$
Cards	AE MC V eftpos
Chef	Yall Bantawa
Features	Bar, licensed, outdoor seating, private dining, wheelchair access
Website	oconnells.com.au

Osteria Ilaria

MELBOURNE
367 Little Bourke Street
03 9642 2287

ITALIAN   **15.5/20**

No longer the new kid, Andreas Papadakis' wine bar hits its stride

At Tipo 00's bigger, easier-to-book next door sibling, the vision for modern Italian Australian is far less pasta-driven but no less convincing. The long, brick-lined wine bar with its open kitchen is as convivial as they come, and the vibe and service are a masterclass in upscale casual. The menu is intensely seasonal and changes daily, but the execution, when it comes to punchiness of flavour and cleverness, remain constant. Baby octopus are splayed across the plate enveloped in a sauce made of 'nduja and anchovy – an ingenious combination that's intensely pungent in all the right ways. Bouncy pink lamb tartare sits in a pool of pureed Jerusalem artichoke with pickled pumpkin – sweet and salty and satisfying. Main courses consist of large hunks of meat or whole fish, like a whiting split open along its back, spilling pipis and sea herbs from its perfect white flesh interior. If you're lucky enough to happen upon the wondrous pink peppercorn semifreddo, order it immediately.

Sommelier Raul Moreno Yague has a heavy tableside manner, but his guidance is en pointe

Open	L D Mon-Sat
Price	$$
Cards	AE MC V eftpos
Chef	Andreas Papadakis
Features	Bar, licensed
Website	osteriailaria.com

OSTERIA ILARIA

The Panama Dining Room and Bar

FITZROY
Level 3, 231 Smith Street
03 9417 7663

EUROPEAN   **14/20**

Inventive European cooking with sharing in mind, served in a spacious room

The label 'cavernous' is frequently misused but, applied to this third-floor bodega, it's spot on. There's space among the cascading greenery to bask in views of the eastern suburbs and city skyline. The name Panama harks from Central America but the drinks lean local – think small producers, lesser regions – and the food traverses the Mediterranean. A tricolour salad of heirloom tomatoes is dusted with goat's cheese granita – linger too long and it'll dissolve. Beef tartare is served with house-baked lavosh, strewn with sliced baby radishes and seasoned with togarashi, a Japanese spice mix that could use even more kick. Large groups can put the kitchen under pressure but the polished-yet-chummy floor staff handle the pauses with flair. The rewards include earthy chestnut gnocchi with silky fennel puree. Roasted barramundi is served with shaved kohlrabi that adds a refreshing crispness. Dessert makes the most of seasonal fruit: berries and peach, topped with a scoop of basil sorbet.

Cocktail fans can settle in with an on-trend list of smoked, fermented and salted drinks

Open	D Daily
Price	$$
Cards	AE MC V Eftpos
Chef	Ayhan Erkoc
Features	Bar, licensed, wheelchair access
Website	thepanama.com.au

Pascale Bar and Grill

MELBOURNE
QT Melbourne, Level 1, 133 Russell Street
03 8636 8808

CONTEMPORARY   **15/20**

Hotel dining that's good enough to ensnare visitors and lure locals

'Hotel restaurant' are two words that conjure a strong 'meh' feeling, unless you're here where chef Andy Harmer has aligned the food with QT's polished brand. The breakfast buffet has been replaced by a proper Melbourne brunch, room service is a drawcard and the bar menu includes a fab chicken hotdog. The flagship 80-seat restaurant is all moody gleam. An appealing menu offers multiple ways to play within a classic brasserie structure. Linguine is a luxurious twirl of house-made pasta with mushrooms and truffle. Marron is smoke-roasted over fragrant cherry wood and served with chorizo sauce in a playful nod to surf 'n' turf. Beetroot is salt-baked, pickled, candied and generally loved up in a dish that also stars macadamia and a twirling rice cracker that adds wow factor. An indigenous ingredient focus is evident in a dessert of eucalyptus-scented meringue, strawberry and coffee. Service is polished but the real impact comes from clean, balanced flavours that indicate a chef happy to let produce be the hero.

Peruse the meat display cabinet before choosing your steak

Open	B D Daily; L Mon–Fri
Price	$$$
Cards	AE DC MC V eftpos
Chef	Andy Harmer
Features	Bar, licensed, private dining, wheelchair access
Website	qthotelsandresorts.com/melbourne/eat-drink/pascale

Pastuso

MELBOURNE
19 ACDC Lane
03 9662 4556

PERUVIAN   **14.5/20**

Rambunctious, charcoal-fuelled fun

'Clink' go the pisco cocktails at this
mod-Peruvian pioneer, a rowdy ride
of ceviche and charcoal-fired meats.
This cavernous, always-busy grill-house
hums with diners at low, round tables,
propping at the bar, or sitting upfront
at the kitchen, watching the action.
There goes a plate of lush Ora salmon
from the ceviche bar, poached in a
miso-seaweed broth, topped with
crunchy green apple, daikon and
Peruvian chilli. The house sausage, a mix
of pork and annatto seeds, with a runny
egg and a dusting of spinach pollen, has
diehard fans. And then there's the meat.
The gilt-edged cabinet is stocked with
prime cuts, ethically and sustainably
sourced, and butchered in-house. The
V-shaped grill works with heat, not
flame. Witness Gippsland dry-aged
eye fillet – it comes sliced, unadorned,
and perfectly pink with a magic charry,
caramelised crust. Marinated pork
neck is smoky and tender, with a zingy
smoked salsa. It's fun trip to Peru – buy
the ticket, take the ride.

**Taste test the Patagonian pilsner or
Argentinian wines from the drinks list**

Open	L D Daily
Price	$$$
Cards	AE MC V eftpos
Chef	Alejandro Saravia
Features	Bar, licensed, private dining, wheelchair access
Website	pastuso.com.au

Philippe

MELBOURNE
Basement, 115-119 Collins Street
(enter via George Parade)
03 8394 6625

FRENCH   **14.5/20**

Old-school French luxury from a master of the form

When you're sick of share plates and
dim lights and loud music, Philippe's
old-school pomp is a welcome reminder
of the classics. Veteran chef Philippe
Mouchel's basement bistro has only
been open since 2016, but it has
the feel of an old-timer that's aged
particularly well, the brown leather
banquettes and white linen-topped
tables exuding clubby elegance. It's the
signature dishes here that deliver the
biggest thrills: the perfect bearnaise that
comes in a swoosh beside the glorious
steaks (seriously, these are some of
Melbourne's most underrated steaks).
The silken beetroot-cured salmon
gravlax. The escargot swimming in
garlic and parsley butter. And, of course,
there's the rotisserie-cooked chicken,
which earns its reputation as one of the
city's great dishes: the skin so crisp, the
flesh so juicy, thc jus a distillation of
chickeny essence. This is a restaurant
for anniversaries and birthdays, or
for that random Tuesday when
shelling out $120 for a duck for
two might cure all ills.

**Ask to sit in the front dining room:
large parties are seated in the back
and can sometimes overwhelm servers**

Open	L Mon–Fri; D Mon–Sat
Price	$$$
Cards	AE MC V eftpos
Chef	Philippe Mouchel
Features	Bar, licensed, private dining
Website	philipperestaurant.com.au

Pinotta

FITZROY NORTH
32 Best Street
03 9481 3393

EUROPEAN   **14.5/20**

A sleek-yet-friendly neighbourhood gem

Pinotta is Fitzroy North on a plate: relaxed, confident, warm. Drop in for a quick bite, or settle in for the full catastrophe (for best results, we recommend the latter). The uncomplicated wine list is a mix of local and European drops, with enough variety by the glass to allow for mixing and matching with the food. The serves are generous, as is the attentive – but never bothersome – service. Grilled, vivid green bullhorn peppers are drizzled with oily, yet delightfully sharp, goat's cheese. Raw slices of fish (whatever's been caught and hauled in that day), are amplified with the crunch of gently acidic pickled broad beans. A dark, silky tangle of squid ink tagliolini comes alive with plump pipis, teased with chilli, the shells clinking pleasingly in the bowl. Well-seasoned flat-iron steak arrives in perfect medium-rare slices: the definition of perfection in simplicity. Deconstructed panna cotta is a gorgeous mess – literally – of burnt butter crumbles, tart berries and satiny unctuousness.

There's often a special or pop-up on the go – check them out on social media

Open	L D Wed–Sun
Price	$$
Cards	MC V eftpos
Chef	Adam Racina
Features	Bar, licensed, outdoor seating, private dining, BYO
Website	pinotta.com

Piquancy

HAWTHORN
123 Auburn Road
03 9813 5160

INDIAN   **14/20**

Bollywood nights done all glam and pop-modern

Hindi music videos are projected on a wall in a loop of suggestive dance moves, bare skin and lots of razzle-dazzle. Little wonder it's a full sitting at this upstairs/downstairs Indian affair in an old Victorian shopfront. The restaurant's had a very modern Punjab makeover. With its sidekick restaurant Babu Ji in St Kilda, owner Mani Waraich knows his market. He's turned north Indian street food into street-cred fashion, from the simplicity of the tin tiffin plates to the menu of pleasing surprises. Begin with OMG, fried pani puri puff pastry shells filled with potato and chickpeas with a DIY beaker of sweet and tangy tamarind sauce. Or the sweet green mango sauce smothering squares of creamy paneer tikka. Lamb kebabs are paired with Persian feta. Much-loved old classics are given a new riff, right down to sweetly spiced cardamom kulfi ice-cream served on a stick – as sexy as any hip-jiggling in a Bollywood dance sequence.

Dig into the 'all you can eat curry and rice' night on Sundays for $29

Open	L Fri–Sat; D Wed–Mon
Price	$$
Cards	AE MC V eftpos
Chef	Ranjit Singh, Sandeep Rawat
Features	Bar, licensed, outdoor seating, private dining, BYO
Website	thepiquancy.com.au

The Press Club

MELBOURNE
72 Flinders Street
03 9677 9677

GREEK   **15/20**

Greek fine dining with an extra dose of glam

The Press Club still feels like one of Melbourne's most exclusive rooms, and stepping beyond the heavy blue curtain into its gilded intimacy is a lovely reminder of the impact of truly dramatic design. The recent move to an a la carte menu means that more of us can now experience the wonder of those vast circular leather booths, and George Calombaris' elevated ode to the food of Greece. Even with this newfound flexibility, it would be foolish to start a meal without the signature taramasalata, its creamy subtlety punctuated by the saline pop of trout roe and served with airy salt-and-vinegar loukoumades. The hearty stew, stifado, is reimagined as a restrained entree made with goat from the Barossa Valley, spooned onto a plate with goat's curd and topped with fresh herbs. Of course there is lamb, and strikingly fresh seafood, but what's more surprising is the perfect little pasta pockets of silken cauliflower, served with grapes and a sweet and sour onion broth.

The degustation menu is still available if you want to go all out

Open	L Fri–Sat; D Mon–Sat
Price	$$$
Cards	AE MC V eftpos
Chef	George Calombaris, Reuben Davis
Features	Licensed
Website	thepressclub.com.au

Project Forty Nine

COLLINGWOOD
107 Cambridge Street
03 9419 4449

ITALIAN   **14/20**

A slice of the country in inner Melbourne

'Beechworth in the city' is the maxim at Project Forty Nine; a restaurant by hospitality veterans Rocco Esposito and wife Lisa Pidutti. The Italian-leaning menu and wine list is an ode to the couple's roots, and, where possible, efforts are made to source produce from north-eastern Victoria. Not everything speaks of the region. Although both solid dishes, the salmon and prawn-filled raviolo in a heady bisque and the whipped baccala mantecato don't conjure up images of landlocked Beechworth. Still, there are echoes in a dish of stracciatella with razor-thin slices of nectarine and pink peppercorns, and the crunchy crudites that come alongside a garlicky bagna cauda sprinkled with leek ash. But mostly, the evidence is in the wine list. North-east Victorian heavyweights, including Giaconda, Castagna, Dal Zotto and Pizzini dominate, and even smaller players like Beechworth's Pennyweight, and the couple's own label Project Forty Nine get a look in. Naturally the focus is on Italian, although exceptions are made for wines produced with minimal intervention.

Rocco was once wine director at Vue de Monde – ask him for recommendations

Open	L Fri–Sun; D Mon–Sat
Price	$$
Cards	AE MC V eftpos
Chef	Tim Newitt
Features	Bar, licensed, outdoor seating, wheelchair access, BYO
Website	projectfortynine.com.au

Punch Lane

MELBOURNE
43 Little Bourke Street
03 9639 4944

EUROPEAN   **14/20**

Relaxed and intimate dining in a Melbourne backstreet

Its proximity to the city's theatres makes Punch Lane perfect for a pre- or post-show snack, but to relegate it to this one act is to do it a disservice. Dimly lit and lined with wine bottles, mirrors, and a giant chalkboard, Punch Lane is comfortable and intimate enough to while away an entire evening. If you do, the quail – its breast roasted, thighs crumbed – served with discs of rich, juicy black pudding is a good place to start. Main courses are robust. There's porterhouse steak, sliced and covered in persillade and (very) smoky mushrooms. If you want to stick to the bar menu, the silky chicken liver parfait is a must, as is a selection of local and European cheeses. And of course, the constantly changing, brilliant list of old and new world wines, poured by expert staff. At 23 years of age, this is one of Melbourne's oldest and best-known wine bars, yet somehow each visit feels like a new discovery.

The $84 five-course tasting menu represents excellent value

Pure South

SOUTHBANK
River Level, Southgate Precinct,
3 Southgate Avenue
03 9699 4600

CONTEMPORARY   **14.5/20**

A smart pub downstairs, fine dining upstairs – subtle Tasmanian fare for all

If you can't book a weekend jaunt across the Bass Strait, Pure South remains the closer option for finely-tuned Tassie and King Island delicacies. The region's sustainable farmers, growers and harvesters – namechecked throughout the menu – have been sending their products to the kitchen at this Southbank keeper since 2003. Nothing avant garde going on here, just solid cooking. Small but potent Bass Strait scallops are joined by a silky Scottsdale pork jowl and a fruity fennel confit over a light seaweed bisque. The seared King Island beef fillet, umamified with miso butter, is served with a crispy creamy stick of polenta and a dill pickle to keep you from getting too comfortable. Even after a 2016 renovation, the dining room is as Tasmanian as a corporate board room, but maybe this too ensures that the main ingredients – and the Tassie heavy winelist and city skyline view – reign supreme. Don't miss the Pyengana Dairy creme brulee, velvety with the slightest tang.

The downstairs 'feed me' menu is half the price of the degustation upstairs

Open	L Mon–Fri; D Daily
Price	$$$
Cards	AE DC MC V eftpos
Chef	Luke Fraser
Features	Bar, licensed, outdoor seating, private dining
Website	punchlane.com.au

Open	L Sun–Fri; D Daily
Price	$$
Cards	AE MC V eftpos
Chef	David Hall
Features	Bar, licensed, outdoor seating, private dining, wheelchair access
Website	puresouth.com.au

Ramblr

SOUTH YARRA
363 Chapel Street
03 9827 0949

CONTEMPORARY   **15.5/20**

Exciting Asian-skewed contemporary cooking with oodles of noodles

The experience is enveloping: there's the smell of the charcoal grill, dusky lighting and spotlit tables, curious but quenching drinks and food that's hard to pigeonhole but skews to China, Japan and Korea, augmented by European technique. If there's a theme, it's flavour. From day one, Ramblr's must-have dish has been the calamari 'noodles' with bone marrow and kimchi. It's still great, though chef Nick Stanton's obsession with handmade wheat noodles is also compelling: the spicy Chinese bolognese has South Yarra addicted. There's always raw seafood, like kingfish furled in a conversation-stopping dressing of prawn oil and burnt butter. That fragrant grill does nice things to meat – cumin-jazzed lamb skewers come with fried Chinese-style bread – but there's a focus on vegan dishes, too. Seaweed noodles are amped up with koji and topped with deeply delicious barbecued mushrooms. The pear tarte Tatin may seem an odd dessert on this ever more Asian carte but it's bolted on because it's so very, very fine.

The lunch menu focuses on Chinese pita and outstanding ramen with handmade noodles

Open	L D Tue–Sat
Price	$$
Cards	AE MC V eftpos
Chef	Nick Stanton
Features	Licensed, outdoor seating
Website	ramblr.com.au

The Recreation

FITZROY NORTH
162-170 Queens Parade
03 9042 2707

EUROPEAN   **15/20**

An old pub made modern with a great wine store and bistro

Here's a thoughtful re-creation of an old-time pub, brought brilliantly into the 21st century by hospitality good guys Joe Farrant and Mark Protheroe (ex-Grossi). It's a welcoming place for locals to eat and drink, with a bottle shop, and wide verandah to shelter outdoor diners. It's a broad offering, with house-made bread, house-churned butter, a spectacular wine list that ranges internationally and through Australia, then moving onto an open kitchen that sends out dishes small and large, perennial favourites and seasonal specials. Start with crab and sweet corn croquettes with a hint of tamarind and green chilli chutney, or char-grilled calamari with crunchy tentacles and rolls of cross-hatched body with carrot and a smooth bone marrow dressing. Proceed to pink and tender barbecued lamb rump with chestnut gnocchi and pine mushrooms, or maybe a steak with Cafe de Paris butter and fries. Locals sit back and order another glass to go with a fruit tart (fig and blood plum in season).

The wine list has takeaway and drink-in prices, and you can BYO

Open	L Wed–Sun; D Tue–Sun
Price	$$
Cards	AE MC V eftpos
Chef	Steve Nelson
Features	Bar, licensed, outdoor seating, wheelchair access, BYO
Website	the-recreation.com

Restaurant Shik

MELBOURNE
30 Niagara Lane
03 9670 5195

KOREAN   **14/20**

True mod-Korean comes to the CBD

Against a dark, clean slate, high-end soju meets natural wine and dishes that go well beyond the bibimbap. In a city overrun with roast chicken and beef tartare, here's gelatinous pig's ear terrine electrified with garlic shoots slick with chilli oil that might be the key to the fountain of youth. This is modern Korean care of Peter Jo – self-taught cook-now-sommelier. There are sticky beef intercostals for wrapping in salt-and-miso cured perilla leaves (you might also recognise the peppery green as shiso), fragrant herbs, green tomato pickles or maybe daikon tingling with raspberry wine vinegar and sancho pepper. There's the hotpot starring funky, oily bonito fillets and Korean radish. But Shik plays by its own rules, making experimental pickles of green tomatoes and beetroot for the banchan. They're serving mussels in a glossy stock pinging with pepper and ginger to start and nothing for dessert just because Jo doesn't like them. Amen.

Keep your eye out for wine parties on Sundays

Riserva

MALVERN EAST
395 Wattletree Road
03 9500 8885

EUROPEAN   **14.5/20**

A smart new food scene player with established restaurateur bloodlines

One year old and the word-of-mouth praise is true. Leisure-seekers talk schools, house prices and Tuscan holidays over oysters, muscatels, and French triple-cream brie. Lovers linger at night with rustic pork and ham hock terrine, remembering the Dordogne; or char-grilled octopus on a creamy cauliflower puree, dreaming of Positano. All congratulate themselves on being here, delighting in the assured and unheralded cookery of Andrew Marasco, in the faultless hospitality (co-owner Frank Ciorciari started way back at Cafe Di Stasio), and for ordering the stack of thickset baked polenta chips on a sticky black garlic mayonnaise that thrills in all the right places. From a seafood bisque risotto with butterflied scampi, to its staple crumbed veal rib-eye, to a textbook lemon and lime tart, all at Riserva is as it should be and is hoped for. Charcoal salt, undressed tables, fine-stemmed glassware, Parisian milk glass pendant lights, and a pleasure that comes from a success story in the making.

Ask about the Italian and French wine dinners on the ever-changing menu

Open	D Mon–Sat
Price	$$
Cards	AE MC V eftpos
Chef	Peter Jo
Features	Bar, licensed
Website	restaurantshik.com

Open	L Wed–Sun; D Daily
Price	$$
Cards	AE MC V eftpos
Chef	Andrew Marasco
Features	Bar, licensed, outdoor seating, private dining, wheelchair access
Website	riservawine.com.au

Rockpool Bar and Grill

SOUTHBANK
Crown Complex, 8 Whiteman Street
03 8648 1900

STEAKHOUSE   **15/20**

The go-to for the steak-fuelled power lunch (or dinner)

Few restaurants have such a visceral sense of occasion. The room's impressive combination of size, dramatic lighting, decor with brass and leather swagger is supercharged by the reputation of executive chef Neil Perry. The chef has built his career on meticulously sourcing the finest ingredients and that's best seen here in the quality and marquee names (Blackmore, Robbins Island) of the beef. There are an impressive 12 steak options to choose from, ranging in price from entry level to Big Win in the Mahogany Room, but the menu has plenty of space for fish and vegetable fans, too. Much of this is impressive – a thrillingly good lobster omelette, amazing Dutch cream potatoes sauteed in wagyu fat – but there are stumbles as well (citrus overpowering quality seafood, for example) that are magnified by the menu's hefty prices. The wine list continues to impress with its quality and democratic price range and is matched with some of the best wine service in town.

Don't ignore the sides – they include some of the menu's best work

Rosa's Canteen

MELBOURNE
Shop 8, Level 1, 500 Little Bourke Street
(enter via Thomson Street)
03 9602 5491

ITALIAN   **14/20**

Straightforward Sicilian from a beloved chef

Rosa's Canteen showcases the best of new Melbourne and also old Melbourne – the new being the angular room up a flight of stairs, with high tables and cantilevered windows that look out over the Supreme Court. The old being the fresh Sicilian cooking of Rosa Mitchell, and the casual smart service that assumes you know what you want and don't have time for chit chat. What do you want? Pasta, certainly. But first, lightly cured kingfish served in a pool of very good olive oil and topped with thinly sliced red onion and a sprinkle of chilli flakes. Crumbed fennel is crisp, oily goodness, like a fennel schnitzel over a schmear of parmesan custard. There's a generous shot of fennel in the house-made saffron tagliatelle, too, which brims with fat chunks of fresh fish. Dessert includes all the classics – tarts, gelato, affogato – but you're going to want the canolo. Trust us on this one.

Lunchtime can be a scrum – dinner is far more relaxed

Open	L Sun–Fri; D Daily
Price	$$$
Cards	AE DC MC V eftpos
Chef	Neil Perry, Zac Nicholson
Features	Bar, licensed, private dining, wheelchair access
Website	rockpoolbarandgrill.com.au

Open	L Mon–Fri; D Mon–Sat
Price	$$
Cards	AE MC V eftpos
Chef	Rosa Mitchell
Features	Licensed, wheelchair access
Website	rosascanteen.com.au

Rosetta Ristorante

SOUTHBANK
Crown Complex, 8 Whiteman Street
03 8648 1999

ITALIAN   **16/20**

Italian glamourpuss dates big-city corporate tycoon

Sophia Loren smoulders from behind her picture frame on the mahogany parquet wall. Flanked by fellow Italian movie stars, she invites us to time travel to the Rat Pack era, via Harry's Bar in Venice. As bottoms sink into burgundy velvet banquettes under three-tiered chandeliers and sheaths of silk curtains, white-jacketed waiters complete the jaunt as they ferry focaccia, grissini and risotto di mare. Not that the food is old fashioned – Neil Perry would never allow that. These are gently regional dishes, made from impeccably sourced ingredients, often kissed by a central wood-fired grill. While you're here for the pasta (pappardelle with fall-apart pork, spiked with oregano, say) you ought to make like a true Italian and follow this with secondi – maybe a duck breast, bronzed and lounging on sweetly yielding quince and nutty farro. Or the deep, rich osso buco made from the milkiest veal. Even Sophia would indulge in the cannoli, shatteringly crisp pastries stuffed with ricotta cream.

A private dining room with a Warhol-inspired mural of Da Vinci's _The Last Supper_ could be just the place for your next deal-closing celebration

Open	L Tue–Sun; D Daily
Price	$$$
Cards	AE DC MC V eftpos
Chef	Neil Perry, Angel Fernandez
Features	Bar, licensed, outdoor seating, private dining, wheelchair access
Website	rosettarestaurant.com.au

Rumi

BRUNSWICK EAST
116 Lygon street
03 9388 8255

MIDDLE EASTERN   **14/20**

The jewel in the crown of Melbourne's Middle Eastern corridor

Brunswick is a goldmine of Middle Eastern food, but this is one of the best bets in the neighbourhood. It's pricier, sure, but it's also slicker. There's also less cliche. No flying carpets or heavy brocade here. Instead there's Arabic script spelling out the poetry of its namesake, wooden tables and chairs, and hanging plants. There's a nice selection of food-friendly wines, but beware the overly perfumed cocktails. Start with the quail joojeh kebab, served with pickled green chilli – you may want to get a couple of orders of the juicy wee birds if you're sharing with others. Rather than settle for easy crowd-pleasers, the kitchen instead veers into creativity: wild fennel in the olives, pickled green almonds on the grilled trout. School prawns play well with tahini, as it turns out, and the marinated lamb shoulder is a must-order. This is one of the places that convinced the late, great Anthony Bourdain of Melbourne's wonder, and we can see why.

Keep an eye out for vegan feast events – a true treat for the meatfree among us

Open	D Daily
Price	$$
Cards	MC V eftpos
Chef	Joseph Abboud
Features	Bar, licensed, private dining, wheelchair access
Website	rumirestaurant.com.au

Ryne

FITZROY NORTH
203 St Georges Road
03 9482 3002

FRENCH   **15/20**

A big name brings big numbers to Fitzroy North

Donovan Cooke, still fresh after big number gigs such as the Atlantic group and the Hong Kong Jockey Club, has now pulled back and is at home in this more low-key venture. It's a moodily lit, high-ceilinged space, with a bar (complete with its own menu) and generously spaced tables. Six entrees and six mains mean enough choice for most people, and there's always the temptation of the six-course tasting menu if you can't decide. The cooking is modern, the presentation elegant, the flavours dependant on classic cuisine. A contemporary take on the French perennial coq au vin sees the chicken cooked sous-vide with wine and seasonings, presented with a wine sauce and all the traditional garnishes. An entree of miso-marinated kingfish looks (almost) too good to eat – a precise rectangle with a border of perfect curls of pickled cucumber. The pumpkin souffle with gruyere is a vegetable must – order one for the table no matter what. Go for the hazelnut semifreddo with muscovado jelly for dessert.

Sunday lunch offers four courses – hot and cold entree, main and dessert, great value for $68

Open	L Sun; D Wed–Sun
Price	$$
Cards	AE MC V eftpos
Chef	Donovan Cooke
Features	Licensed, private dining, wheelchair access
Website	ryne.com.au

Saint Crispin

COLLINGWOOD
300 Smith Street
03 9419 2202

CONTEMPORARY   **15.5/20**

Smart-casual fine diner in a former cobbler's workshop

Saint Crispin arrived with a fanfare in 2013, grabbing the Guide's Best New Restaurant title within months of opening. The win helped cement once-grungy Smith Street as an exciting eat street. Some of the gloss has come off the strip since then but Saint Crispin shines on, a gentle renovation and the addition of classically trained British chef Stuart McVeigh lending further lustre. It's a smart-casual hybrid, with the trappings of fine dining in a setting of exposed brick walls, lofty ceilings and silk curtains. The kitchen displays strong snack game, with tobiko-freckled smoked eel churros and house-made chilli sauce, and piquant kangaroo tartare with a flying buttress of potato crisp two notable examples. Mains take a more timeless path in pairings such as roast chicken funked up with mushrooms and black garlic, and pork fillet riding shotgun with black sausage and fermented turnips. Desserts such as caramelised white chocolate, fermented passionfruit sorbet and salt-baked pineapple are both creative and delicious.

There are two dining rooms upstairs for private events

Open	L Fri–Sun; D Tue–Sun
Price	$$
Cards	AE MC V eftpos
Chefs	Stuart McVeigh, Scott Pickett
Features	Licensed, outdoor seating, private dining, wheelchair access
Website	saintcrispin.com.au

San Telmo

MELBOURNE
14 Meyers Place
03 9650 5525

ARGENTINIAN　　**15/20**

An unashamedly meaty Argentinian grill

Saddles, cowhide and a glass case packed with ageing meat signal San Telmo as a chapel of char-grill. A heavily wooded dining room underscores the theme while low lights glow like the embers on the Argentinian parilla – the grill at the heart of the kitchen. The hide-bound menu treats the meat simply, leaving sides room to play and the wine list has a South American focus. Start with something you can get your teeth into. A plate of Berkshire pork jowl is crisp outside with a gelatinous centre and added crackling. The main event eye fillet is so tender, steak knives seem redundant, while fried potatoes, cornichons and aioli add crunch and cream. And everything tastes better with just one more spoonful of chimichurri (parsley, chilli, oregano, olive oil and vinegar, and the blood in any Argentinian's veins) or salsa, or both. For dessert, the glossy flan de leche is singed with toasted sugar – a final hit of San Telmo's fire.

Grab a cocktail and a lusciously lardy empanada at the bar for a quick snack

Sarti

MELBOURNE
6 Russell Place
03 9639 7822

ITALIAN　　**14/20**

A well-appointed bolthole bistro

There is something about a red neon sign, glossy door and staircase. What lies beyond? Do we dare? Up past a bouquet of chillies you'll be welcomed by gingham-clad waitstaff and politely led to the central bar for an Aperol spritz, or to a table in the distressed-brick interior with laneway views. Sarti's bistro fare begins with drinks-friendly stuzzichini – little snacks such as crunchy croquettes with unctuous centres of cheddar and mushroom – and then proceeds to a handful of pastas. These show the kitchen's proclivity for more robust fare such as cannelloni, al dente cigars of duck splashed with a mushroom consomme. Main courses – such as salty olive-dusted braised veal finished with a splash of white wine sauce, and 36-hour roast goat pepped with beetroot – ought to be finished with bread to make the most of the pan juices. Sarti's 'hot and cold' tiramisu, containing crisp chocolate and mascarpone layers, may challenge some clienti tradizionalisti. But we say embrace the nuovo.

Perfectly placed for a pre-show meal or special lunch

Open	L D Daily
Price	$$
Cards	AE MC V eftpos
Chef	Stephen Clark
Features	Bar, licensed, outdoor seating, private dining
Website	santelmo.com.au

Open	L Mon–Fri; D Mon–Sat
Price	$$
Cards	AE MC V eftpos
Chef	Paolo Masciopinto, Geoffrey Martin
Features	Bar, licensed, outdoor seating, private dining
Website	sartirestaurant.com.au

RYNE

Saxe

MELBOURNE
211 Queen Street
03 9089 6699

CONTEMPORARY   **15.5/20**

Dressed-down fine dining in a classy upstairs diner

Chef Joe Grbac (Saint Crispin, Press Club), in his first solo venture, is confidently forging his own path, combining ambitious, precise cooking with a relaxed and approachable vibe. There's some fancy footwork and clever culinary twists in the tight, French-leaning menu, but the foundation is top-notch, seasonal produce showcased creatively and with solid technique. Complimentary snacks set the scene. You might start with ginger-flecked devilled quail eggs and flavoursome roast chicken jelly fingers. Kangaroo tartare, cured in juniper and pepped with tiny cubes of heirloom beetroot, is tricked up with a velvety red wine reduction and nasturtium leaf powder. The textures and flavours are artfully balanced – ditto lemon-brined then pan-fried swordfish astride saffron-fried onion and zucchini and a silky deconstructed Brillat-Savarin cheesecake. Throw in a thoughtful, Euro-leaning wine list, sharp service and a classy fitout (full-length royal blue velvet and leather banquette, rendered white walls, pale wood floor) and Saxe is an accomplished, food-focused addition to Melbourne's legal district.

The ground-floor bar has terrific cocktails and snacks – plus the full menu if you ask

Open	L Mon–Fri; D Tue–Sat
Price	$$
Cards	AE MC V eftpos
Chef	Joe Grbac
Features	Bar, licensed, outdoor seating
Website	saxe.com.au

Scopri

CARLTON
191 Nicholson Street
03 9347 8252

ITALIAN   **15/20**

Classic neighbourhood Italian with a devoted following

Old-fashioned restaurant courtesies can be terribly underrated. Consider the pleasures of a candlelit table set with double linen, and a waiter who can recite a long list of specials without notes. Or pour peppery olive oil to accompany house-made bread, then discreetly sweep away the crumbs afterwards. Regulars don't take these touches for granted. But polished service isn't the sole reason to visit the narrow split-level room. Veteran chef Andy Logue uses vegetables from the owners' farm in dishes drawn from throughout Italy, but he's particularly adept with fish and game. Come early to order duck tortellini paddling in a butter-rich porcini sauce or risk hearing 'Tortellini finito'. Take a moment before inserting knife and fork to appreciate the skilfully deboned King George whiting, its open belly now stuffed with soft breadcrumbs, herbs, capers and raisins. And revel in wine-braised kid with carefully turned potatoes. Peas are added late so they remain green. By meal's end, everything old seems new again.

Dust off the barolo you've been saving. They'll pour it for a modest $20

Open	L Tue–Fri; D Tue–Sat
Price	$$
Cards	AE DC MC V eftpos
Chef	Andy Logue
Features	Licensed, private dining, BYO
Website	scopri.com.au

Sezar

MELBOURNE
6 Melbourne Place
03 9663 9882

Shira Nui

GLEN WAVERLEY
247 Springvale Road
03 9886 7755

ARMENIAN   **14/20**

An enticing cuisine from an ancient tradition

The Caucasus region nestles between Turkey, southern Russia and the Levant, and Armenian food is a beguiling blend of all three – meat-loving but rich in fruit, nuts, legumes, wheat and nightshades. And Sezar, in its cheery little dining room at the end of a classic Melbourne laneway, takes this bountiful and venerable heritage and adds contemporary flourishes to produce dishes that will wake up the most jaded of palates. A confit duck borek, its oils cut by the acid of miso onions and softened by braised fennel, or barbecued pork with spiced cabbage, almonds and radishes, topped with puffed pieces of pork skin. Entrees include a dense cylinder of lamb neck wrapped in shredded kataifi pastry with sesame mayo, or air-dried bastourma with a roasted corn and farro salad. The Caucasus is also the birthplace of the grape, and varietals from Armenia, Georgia and Croatia add further intrigue to a cuisine that, for the uninitiated, is well worth seeking out.

Sample the flavours of Armenia through a $40 smart lunch

JAPANESE   **14.5/20**

Long-standing and consistently good suburban star with excellent sushi counter

Since Shira Nui opened in 2002, Melbourne's Japanese dining scene has leapt ahead. So indeed has once-sleepy Glen Waverley, now a thriving multicultural mini metropolis. Shira Nui, in contrast, has very purposely stayed the same. For the diner, entering might be a little underwhelming or, conversely, a blessed relief. The small, simple shopfront is a little scuffed here and a touch tired there, though the greeting is always hearty and the diners ensconced seem happy as clams. And then the food comes – very good sushi and hot dishes, carefully prepared and served with pride. Trout belly is brushed with miso then blowtorched, salmon is draped with a shaving of kombu, beef is grilled and gently tapped with a knife before laying over perfectly seasoned rice. The best experience is at the counter, where the chefs will smilingly tell you whether soy-dipping is allowed or forbidden, though in such a cosy room there's no danger of feeling out of the action.

Choose the omakase chef's menu to outsource all decision-making

Open	L Mon–Fri; D Mon–Sat
Price	$$
Cards	AE MC V eftpos
Chefs	Garen Maskal, Nick Cornell
Features	Licensed, private dining
Website	sezar.com.au

Open	L D Tue–Sat
Price	$$
Cards	MC V eftpos
Chef	Hiro Nishikura
Features	Licensed, wheelchair access, BYO

Shukah

WINDSOR
104 Chapel Street
03 9521 3858

MIDDLE EASTERN   **14/20**

A fresh and flashy Middle Eastern party spot

The neon sign at the bar promoting 'Peace in the Middle East' hits the right cheeky/serious tone, as Shukah serves up traditional Armenian cuisine with a side of party. Service is quick and cheery, more cocktail bar than fine diner, and the wine list reps the Middle East with excursions to Greece and Australia. A small plate of kingfish sashimi with creamy avocado and finely diced cucumber is topped with salty bombs of salmon roe to offset tart black lime. Charred octopus is soft and smoky with kipfler potatoes swimming in light olive oil on an island of labne, with pistachio and green olive salsa. A large plate of barbecued spatchcock sees punchy green harissa topped with pickled onions on a plate of flatbread. The barbecue short rib with roast sweet corn and farro sighs off the bone, sweetened with pomegranate molasses. To finish, try a delicately layered poached pear with labne, and hit the town, or stay put and order a Persian Cup cocktail.

Try the Yan Yan beer, a house brew made to mimic a traditional Armenian lager

Open	L Thu–Sun; D Tue–Sun
Price	$$
Cards	AE MC V eftpos
Chef	Garen Maskal, Sean Thomas
Features	Licensed, outdoor seating, BYO
Website	shukah.com.au

Silks

SOUTHBANK
Crown Complex, 8 Whiteman Street
03 9292 5777

citi

CHINESE   **14/20**

Old-school Chinese fine dining by the Yarra

Walk through the lavishly decorated, dimly lit lobby into the honey-toned dining room complete with floor-to-ceiling views of the river and you could think you'd stumbled onto a set from *Casino Royale*. It's a spot tuxedoed high-rollers who may or may not also be debonair spies wouldn't seem out of place, but then family groups complete with laidback toddlers also look perfectly at home. Like the service, the broadly Cantonese menu is more low-key than the decor. There's exotica such as braised whole greenlip abalone to be had, but well-rendered classics are the mainstay. Expect the likes of translucent-skinned prawn dumplings, Peking duck folded into thin pancakes and ginger-spiked oysters to start. Main courses might take you from an elegant dish of cubed roasted black cod beaded with salmon roe to a moreish sweet-sour melange of silken chunks of eggplant and minced pork. Skip dessert in favour of extra side dishes such as broccoli sauteed in garlic and piled with XO crumbs, which are the big winners.

For budget-luxe dining, check out the $50 yum cha deal

Open	L D Daily
Price	$$$
Cards	AE DC MC V eftpos
Chef	Kelvyn Yeoh
Features	Licensed, private dining, wheelchair access
Website	crownmelbourne.com.au/ restaurants/premium/silks

Smith and Daughters

FITZROY
175 Brunswick Street
03 9939 3293

ITALIAN, VEGAN   **14.5/20**

Good times, booze-fuelled vegan Italian. Who knew?

Chef Shannon Martinez is Melbourne's queen of delicious lies. From this neon-filled Brunswick Street bluestone gaff she and business partner Mo Wyse have been serving a plant-based Latin American menu (including too-real blood sausage) for four years. Now, they're doing Italian and it's not just freakishly convincing but objectively delicious. Martinez' 'oxtail' ragu made with compressed mushrooms has such perfect meaty taste and fibrous texture, it's been sent back in panic. Both the polenta served with it, and an eggplant involtini, bathed in rich sugo, filled with basil not-ricotta and draped in grilled 'mozzarella' are freaks of dairy-free nature. Who knew? Martinez did. She's worked hard faking it. Now, her thick-noodle cacio e pepe with kampot pepper and vegan parmesan has real oomph. An electric-bright fennel and saffron 'squid' and rice stew is no compromise for anyone. It's witchcraft. Get your pitchfork. But stick it in the quince and pomegranate bombe alaska with fluffy torched marshmallow outer first.

Take a skeptic – preferably an Italian one – and blow their mind

Open	B L Sat–Sun; D Tue–Sun
Price	$$
Cards	MC V eftpos
Chef	Shannon Martinez
Features	Bar, licensed, outdoor seating
Website	smithanddaughters.com

The Smith

PRAHRAN
213-219 High Street
03 8563 0044

CONTEMPORARY   **14/20**

Old is new again at this (face-lifted) High Street party pub

High heels and higher hemlines endure at this ever-changing Prahran pub with the metalwork moniker. A lively crowd congratulate themselves on being here, clustered around undressed tables. Sit yourself down before two smoky, butterflied-then-barbecued king prawns, and let the sweet chilli satay tickle on your lips. The Smith is care of Michael Lambie (Taxi, Circa, Lucy Liu, etc.). A million dollar makeover and the Smith's been remade, bigger (see the adjoining glass atrium courtyard bar) and brighter (although not all are convinced by the blood-orange paint splotches). And better, with its recent Asian infusion shelved for a two-card menu of robust, fancy pub staples. Freshly shucked oysters, a creamy textured duck and pork terrine with a chicken liver parfait quenelle – the 220g pillar of perfectly tender eye fillet distracting from all else. The open kitchen. Thumping beats. Crisp service. Even the pretty-in-pink raspberry souffle with white chocolate sauce on the table next to yours. It's back, baby. Brasserie than ever.

Quiet dinnertime chat? Forget about it at weekends with the bar in full swing

Open	L D Daily
Price	$$
Cards	AE MC V eftpos
Chef	Brad Simpson
Features	Bar, licensed, outdoor seating, private dining
Website	thesmithprahran.com.au

Sosta Cucina

NORTH MELBOURNE
12 Errol Street
03 9329 2882

ITALIAN   **14/20**

Add this welcoming and warm Italian to your regular eateries list

Good Italian food is elegant, simple, classic – a sensibility applied equally to the decor, service and food found here at this North Melbourne institution where dark wood meets white napery without a hint of pretension. The service is laidback yet attentive and well-informed – especially when it comes to the enticing but gentle-on-the-wallet wine list. The menu proper is a collection of elegantly plated Italian dishes, served with generosity in mind. The subtlety of delicate scampi is dressed with a gentle, garlicky vinaigrette. Similarly, slivers of kingfish topped with discs of sweet grape and crunchy pistachios are invigorated by a little squeeze of citrus. Cappellacci – tubby, cuffed cones of satiny pasta – capture peppery sausage and broccoli chunks. Dessert brings a little more noise to the table with slices of poached peach resting on crisp layers of honeyed pastry, accompanied by a scoop of amaretto ice-cream. Elegant, simple and classic to the last.

The two-course 'business lunch' ($30 a head) focuses on a different Italian region each month

Open	L Tue–Fri, Sun; D Tue–Sun
Price	$$
Cards	AE DC MC V eftpos
Chef	Courtney Websdale
Features	Bar, licensed, outdoor seating, private dining, BYO
Website	sosta.com.au

Spice Temple

SOUTHBANK
Crown Complex, 8 Whiteman Street.
03 8679 1888

CHINESE   **15.5/20**

A brooding sexpot of a Chinese restaurant for the moneyed set

Rockpool's black-lacquered casino-dwelling ode to Chinese food may be the sexiest restaurant in the group. Cocktails riff on Chinese astrological charts, and waitresses shimmy between tables wearing black satin with blood-red brocade. The menu is far-reaching, focusing on regionally specific dishes with a little fusion. You won't generally find tartare made from large hunks of yellowfin tuna and smothered with shallots in China, but you will see it on many tables here, despite the $39 price tag. The place isn't cheap, but servings are generous, and the cooking is consistent. Ground lamb shot through with cumin comes as the filling for a flaky pancake, with a deep red chilli sauce on the side. Golf ball-sized prawn wontons come swimming in a sweet-tart black vinegar sauce. For one of the most opulent textural experiences ever, order the stir-fried quail with peanuts over egg custard, which is pure silken yolky wobble. It's as seductive as the restaurant itself, and that's saying something.

The $55 yum cha lunch special is the best way to go wild

Open	L Thu–Sun; D Daily
Price	$$$
Cards	AE DC MC V eftpos
Chef	Neil Perry, Chris Budicin
Features	Bar, licensed, private dining, wheelchair access
Website	spicetemple.com.au

Stokehouse

ST KILDA
30 Jacka Boulevard
03 9525 5555

CONTEMPORARY   **15.5/20**

Sophisticated seaside fun palace par excellence

Let's start with lunch. Social media influencers pose on sea-green banquettes, cradling rose-coloured cocktails. Rolex-wristed tourists clink glasses of Champagne over a white-draped table. Business-casual blokes glance through spreadsheets while grazing on oysters. Can anything on a plate compete with so much sensory action? Why yes it can, when it's an entree of near-translucent bug tail dotted with salmon roe and succulents, or flash-grilled calamari curls with green mango and bright romesco. Crisp flathead tails perch on planks of triple-cooked chips, sprinkled with powdered wakame. Yielding lamb shoulder couples with tender pink cutlets and a single, small smoked eggplant. Pastry princesss Lauren Eldridge kicks gimmick-free Australiana goals with zesty candied desert limes, lemon-myrtle caramel and a shower of feathery macadamia shavings. Smart, seamless service wraps up a relaxed afternoon that can easily melt into sunset drinks or – credit-card limit be damned – stay for dinner.

Arrive early for a pre-meal drink at the open-air marble bar upstairs

Open	L D Daily
Price	$$$
Cards	AE MC V eftpos
Chef	Ollie Hansford
Features	Bar, licensed, outdoor seating, private dining, wheelchair access, BYO
Website	stokehouse.com.au

Sunda

MELBOURNE
18 Punch Lane
03 9654 8190

MODERN ASIAN   **15/20**

The modern Asian restaurant on everyone's lips

Imagine a crackly pork bun filled with a riff on beef rendang accompanied by toasted-and-fermented sambal. That's the delicious reality unfolding in Punch Lane where chef Khanh Nguyen (ex-Bentley and Mr Wong) is turning edible tricks with Indonesian, Malaysian and Vietnamese flavours. The room is a brutalist dream. Behind a wide concrete bar, beneath soaring scaffolding a calm team toss smoky, sticky XO noodles with fistfuls of chicken crackling and load fresh-picked crab and finger lime onto a curried crab parfait hat-tipping Malaysia's otak otak. Native myrtles enhance a vibrant curry slicked over plump, pink lamb and a tornado of flaky, buttery roti comes with a kaffir and curry oil fragrant dip that gets its saltiness from Vegemite. It's a progressive party in a glass, too. Boatrocker sours meet Brittany ciders and Philip Lobley sauvignon blancs that drink more like chardonnays. Let manager Brad Hatch bring the fun, and order bika ambon – a caramelly yeast cake – to bring it home.

The roti is off menu and they only have about 25 serves a day. Bag it

Open	L Fri; D Tue–Sat
Price	$$
Cards	AE MC V eftpos
Chef	Khanh Nguyen
Features	Bar, licensed, private dining
Website	sunda.com.au

SUNDA

Supermaxi

FITZROY NORTH
305 St Georges Road
03 9482 2828

ITALIAN **14/20**

Upscale neighbourhood pizza favourite that thankfully never changes

Co-owner and head chef Rita Macali, who launched the legendary Ladro, is best known for her sublime pizza which is the rightful drawcard here. Irregularly shaped bases with perfect stretch and crunch are topped with simple ingredients, served good 'n' hot and cut at the table. Our favourite? The powerhouse puttanesca, scattered with salami and anchovies, olives and capers – a saucy explosion that's not too oily or heavy. Macali's partner, service wizard Giovanni Patane, might talk you into a round of oozy mozzarella sticks or piquant fried olives before moving onto gnocchi clouds in classic bolognese with extra parmesan or the 'meat of the day'. Desserts sing from the same Italian songbook, with panko-crumbed fried custard or tiramisu hitting the back of the net. The light-filled room with its terrazzo floors and bare tables is as welcoming for a family group or a solo diner at the bar. For everyone from North Fitzroy cool kids to actual kids, this is a slice of heaven.

At $11 a throw, this might be the best-value negroni in town

Supernormal

MELBOURNE
180 Flinders Lane
03 9650 8688

MODERN ASIAN **15/20**

Clanging canteen with banging mod-Asian food

Andrew McConnell's pan-Asian powerhouse is in permanent hyperdrive, delivering food that's part Korean, part Japanese, part Chinese and all A-Mac. The tonkatsu sanga has taken over where the lobster roll left off, the crumbed pork and shaved cabbage inside fluffy crustless white bread with the tangy hit of Bulldog sauce often selling out before the lunchtime peak, but there are plenty of consolations. The raw section is particularly fertile ground – a pristine selection of crudo on ice might include meaty little cockles and kingfish belly speckled with horseradish – while perfect smoky strips of the signature saltwater duck accessorise with the seasons. Excitement doesn't die down at meaty mains, either, with the flavour heft of white soy chicken, the skin golden crisp and served in an addictive slosh of miso butter. With drinks (sake, of course, and plenty more) and staff all en pointe, it argues for Supernormal's status as the Asian-accented bookend to Cumulus Inc. And that's a compliment indeed.

Pressed for time? They run a takeaway menu, too

Open	D Tue–Sun
Price	$$
Cards	AE MC V eftpos
Chef	Rita Macali
Features	Bar, licensed, wheelchair access, BYO
Website	supermaxi.com.au

Open	L D Daily
Price	$$
Cards	AE MC V eftpos
Chef	Ben Pollard, Andrew McConnell
Features	Bar, licensed, private dining, wheelchair access
Website	supernormal.net.au

Syracuse

MELBOURNE
23 Bank Place
03 9670 1777

MEDITERRANEAN   **14.5/20**

Sibley returns the glamour to this CBD grand dame

The natural order has been restored. Under the careful stewardship of Philippa Sibley, Syracuse has reclaimed its rightful position as the CBD's most civilised dining room. Soaring ceilings, elegant arches and generously spaced tables attract a well-heeled clientele, with business lunches stretching into post-work drinks and unhurried dinner dates. But it's not all style: Sibley's robust pan-Mediterranean menu brings the substance, too. Classical dishes are married with contemporary flourishes – a rump cap comes with a shiitake tart and witlof, while seared salmon channels the Middle East via eggplant caponata, tahini yoghurt and smoked almonds. But Sibley is best known for her desserts and these should not be missed under any circumstance. The 'Syramisu', which deconstructs the Italian favourite, sees coffee ice-cream, crumbs, wafered white chocolate and meringue party down. Assured staff, evening dessert-only sittings, and a wine list brimming with Australian and international varietals means Syracuse is worthy of your attention at any time of the day or night.

Try the excellent-value Express Lunch ($39/49 for two/three courses)

Open	B L Mon–Fri; D Mon–Sat
Price	$$
Cards	AE DC MC V eftpos
Chef	Philippa Sibley
Features	Bar, licensed, outdoor seating
Website	syracuserestaurant.com.au

Taxi Kitchen

MELBOURNE
Level 1, Transport Hotel, corner Swanston Street and Flinders streets
03 9654 8808

CONTEMPORARY   **14.5/20**

Casual calm in the middle of Federation Square

One floor down from the always-hopping rooftop Transit bar and just above the sometimes-deafening Transport Public Bar, chef Tony Twitchett's dining room offers a refined first-floor experience that's slightly more elegant than its neighbours but every bit as fun. Waitstaff are switched on and the Asian-influenced menu continues to evolve. Wagyu tartare miraculously balances cool meat with the heat of ginger and wasabi. Roast duck (breast and leg) is served on a slick of five-spice caramel, with a daikon citrus salad, alongside a wedge of lime to squeeze over the entire affair. One mystery: how do they make a high and foamy, picture-perfect soufflé rich with the deeply autumnal taste of pear? Even if you're not here to ponder life's bigger questions, you can take a seat at the bar and explore the expansive, Victoria-loving wine list (it comes with a map!), enjoy the 270-degree view of the sun setting over the Yarra, or just admire the 90-degree view of a very clever kitchen.

Nab the $65 pre- and post-theatre menu – two courses before curtain and then come back for dessert

Open	L D Daily
Price	$$
Cards	AE MC V eftpos
Chef	Tony Twitchett, Sam Forte
Features	Bar, licensed, private dining room, wheelchair access
Website	taxikitchen.com.au

Tempura Hajime

SOUTH MELBOURNE
60 Park Street
03 9696 0051

JAPANESE   **15/20**

Elegant omakase dining in a subdued setting

Owner/chef Shigeo Yoshihara has lovingly tended the oil-filled copper pans at one of Melbourne's best, and hardest to find, tempura counters since 2009. A nondescript entrance among office and apartment blocks leads into a waiting area, then into an austere, brightly lit, windowless room. Twelve padded, high-backed stools face the semi-hexagonal blond wood counter, with a dignified and focused Yoshihara-san in the middle. Then the performance begins: disciplined, precise and restrained. Poached sesame chicken breast and vinegar-cured snapper to start, followed by sashimi. One at a time, 10 perfect bites appear, cased in delicate gossamer-thin tempura batter with just-cooked crunch. Sweet corn, asparagus, zucchini and salmon, King Dory, mushroom with prawn mince, and more. In each case, the quality and freshness of the base ingredient shines, as it does with the small main of prawn teriyaki tempura on steamed rice. Dessert, too, is subtle, simple and light with a cleansing yoghurt jelly sweetened with Cointreau sauce. Gracious service completes an authentic and tranquil experience.

The optional sushi course is worth the small extra cost

Open	L Tue–Fri; D Tue–Sat
Price	$$
Cards	AE MC V
Chef	Shigeo Yoshihara
Features	Bar, licensed, outdoor seating, private dining, wheelchair access
Website	tempurahajime.com.au

Tipo 00

MELBOURNE
361 Little Bourke Street
03 9942 3946

ITALIAN   **15/20**

A perennially popular pasta party

It's quite an art, turning would-be diners away at the door and informing callers that no tables are free until next month. But then, the Tipo team get plenty of practice delivering the bad news gently. Since it opened in 2014, this single-room CBD pasta bar has been rammed with carb fiends fanging for bowls of midnight-black tagliolini entangled with squid, bottarga and a tickle of chilli. For precisely al dente tagliatelle with yielding chunks of braised lamb shoulder playing off bitey green olive. And for verdant pesto risotto speckled with pine nuts and daubs of smoky ricotta, so simply flavoured it works better as a shared dish. But the pithy menu isn't just carbohydrates. Across the broad white marble pass come plates of finely shaved ox tongue brightened with syrupy balsamic vinegar and pink peppercorns, and charry calamari curls with poached mussels and toasty farro grains. Postpone surrendering your seat by ordering a digestivo from the Italian-leaning drinks list.

Can't wait for a booking? Turn up at 5.30pm, put your name on the list and head next door for a drink

Open	L D Mon–Sat
Price	$$
Cards	AE MC V eftpos
Chefs	Alberto Fava, Andreas Papadakis
Features	Bar, licensed
Website	tipo00.com.au

Tokyo Tina

WINDSOR
66A Chapel Street
03 9525 2774

JAPANESE   **14/20**

All aboard the Seoul train at this pop-modern Japanese/Korean mashup

Tokyo Tina is whoever you want her to be. A cool sake bar with spinning mirror ball. Casual eating (chicken yakitori, wagyu beef tartare with taro chips) on high tables among the anything-goes spirit of Chapel Street's Windsor end. An on-trend eatery with enough wow on most plates (see sticky-sweet black sesame paste beneath roasted cauliflower florets) to please all comers. And come they do, to this shopfront temple of Japanese pop-culture, with its vintage waving cat (or maneki-neko, for the Japanophiles) slot machine in the window, Astro Boy dolls, Deborah Harry on the playlist, and a menu with just as many hits. Pork and kimchi gyoza, beautifully folded, swimming in plum and soy vinegar sauce. Bowls of miso ramen served with a holy trinity of mushrooms (shiitake, enoki, oyster). A duo of sugary home-made doughnuts, their bellies bursting with a citrusy yuzu curd. It's food to socialise over, not philosophise about. Eat in, have fun and enjoy Tina's greatest hits.

Yep, there's karaoke, with a bookable private room, and bottomless booze bingo on Sundays

Open	L D Daily
Price	$$
Cards	AE MC V eftpos
Chef	Scott Lord
Features	Bar, licensed, outdoor seating, private dining, wheelchair access
Website	tokyotina.com.au

Tonka

MELBOURNE
20 Duckboard Place
03 9650 3155

INDIAN   **15/20**

Classical Indian dishes reinvented with verve

Still hip, still madly busy – Tonka shows no signs of slowing, and why should it? Who else is offering such a captivating take on Indian cuisine, such an artful blend of subcontinental flavours so cleverly punctuated by European ingredients? Tucked amid a slew of restaurants in the Duckboard Place alley, a long bar leads to a stylish rear dining room, equally populated by old and new money, suits and ripped jeans. They're all here for elegant bites like smoked eel on fresh betel leaf with pops of pink caviar, and Kashmiri pork tikka, its richness cut by radicchio and pickles. Hungrier? Try a generous duck korma, with a creamy sauce complemented by chunks of pear and blood plum, or a Goan fish curry with padron peppers, shrimp and dill. And don't neglect the excellent breads from the tandoor. A wine list heavy on old-world varietals is another bonus of Tonka's crossover approach – and staff know their way around it, too. Bookings strongly advised.

No booking? Arrive early to snag a spot at the bar

Open	L D Daily
Price	$$
Cards	AE MC V eftpos
Chefs	Adam D'Sylva, Hendri Budiman
Features	Bar, licensed, wheelchair access
Website	tonkarestaurant.com.au

Traveller
TOURS

Bespoke itineraries created
by our travel editors and
hosted by experts in food, wine,
politics, history and the arts.

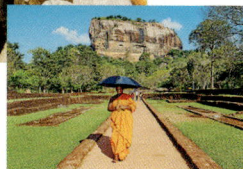

traveller.com.au

Transformer

FITZROY
99 Rose Street
03 9419 2022

VEGETARIAN   **14/20**

A slick warehouse where vegetarians plot world domination

Laki Papadopoulos and Mark Price were 30 years ahead of the curve when they opened the Vegie Bar on Brunswick Street, and going by the crowds just around the corner at their sequel Transformer, they've still got it. Three years down the track, this smartly converted warehouse proves vegetarians and their vegan cousins are after their own version of fine dining. A menu free from mock meat pushes the envelope gently with hero vegetables, umami-rich sauces and a frisson of chef-driven complexity. It's food that parties hard without missing meat. There's the straight-up delights of a black bean taco bright with guajillo salsa and winter-friendly cinnamon-roasted pumpkin in a rich slather of sherry-spiked hazelnut bread sauce. A slab of fried haloumi in a sticky honey glaze is cut with ruby grapefruit and black olive. Cumin-braised eggplant plays lead with support from smoked labne and quinoa crisps. As for drinks, you can realign your chakras with ayurvedic elixirs, or get stuck into the cocktail program.

Too full for dessert? Sibling vegan ice-cream bar Girls & Boys just around the corner might still be able to tempt you

Open	L Sat–Sun; D Daily
Price	$$
Cards	AE MC V eftpos
Chef	Bryce Edwards
Features	Bar, licensed, outdoor seating, wheelchair access
Website	transformerfitzroy.com

Trattoria Emilia

MELBOURNE
Rear, 360 Little Collins Street
(enter via Gills Alley)
03 9670 7214

ITALIAN   **15/20**

Regional Italian charmer meets Melbourne laneway

Few places sum up Melbourne's beating Italian heart quite as well. The off-Little Collins Street laneway haunt mainlines the local design passions with its lived-in mercurial quirk while shining a light on the Emilia-Romagna region thanks to proud expat chefs Francesco Rota and Luca Flammia. Their menu is an exercise in dependability, from greatest-hits antipasti boards groaning with eggplant parmigiana, vitello tonnato and oozy arancini to Italian-accented main courses such as a Tasmanian eye fillet saddling up with radicchio and olive oil mash, but it would be negligent to miss the pasta and risotto. The signature tortelloni are pure elegance, stuffed with a surprisingly delicate mortadella and prosciutto farce and finished with a lick of walnut sauce enlivened by a splash of aged balsamic, while spaghetti tricked up with with spanner crab and chilli with a salty blizzard of bottarga nails the refined-rustic brief. As for dessert, their spin on the Vienetta is an excursion into the addictive delights of primo dark chocolate.

The adjoining cafe serves some of the best baked goods in the biz

Open	B L D Mon–Sat
Price	$$
Cards	AE DC MC V eftpos
Chef	Francesco Rota, Luca Flammia
Features	Bar, licensed, wheelchair access, BYO
Website	emiliamelbourne.com.au

Tulum

BALACLAVA
217 Carlisle Street
03 9525 9127

TURKISH   **15/20**

Innovative, contemporary Turkish degustations

Searching for a fine diner in Balaclava can yield few results. But, as the rail line rattles overheard just a few metres away, you'll find a modern Turkish oasis – an intimate space with greenery and sparkling teal tones. Showcasing the seven regions of Turkey with degustations on a quarterly rotation, your soul food adventure might traverse dishes like discs of orange-infused celeriac with carrot puree, pear and labne, or a giant prawn with paprika butter and sweet, spiced borlotti beans. A thrillingly simple 'bread and dip' of warm yoghurt pide with cultured butter and Tulum cheese is served on olive wood with a carved wooden knife. Dessert might be a riff on tzatziki, with a yoghurt muhallebi with a cucumber sorbet, mint meringue and mint juice. It's exquisitely plated and as refreshing and poetic as it gets. Passionate chefs will bring dishes to your table, talking you through their incarnation and inspiration, and the atmosphere is communal and convivial. What a Turkish delight.

A three-course lunch is only $40 on Saturdays

Open	L Sat; D Tue–Sat
Price	$$
Cards	AE MC V eftpos
Chef	Coksun Uysal, Sina Sucuka
Features	Bar, licensed, outdoor seating, wheelchair access, BYO
Website	tulumrestaurant.com.au

Uncle Collins St

MELBOURNE
Level 1, 15 Collins Street
03 9654 0829

VIETNAMESE   **14/20**

Fun and fast-paced Vietnamese

A younger sister to its St Kilda sibling, this modern Vietnamese joint provides a refreshing, pop-culture counterpoint to the staid routine of the Paris end of Collins Street. Rattan, neon and glass are smooshed together to create a bamboo gazebo-feel. The service is smart and peppy, and so are the eats. Cool, salty-sweet-and-silken tofu revels under a tumble of crisp prawns. Ribbons of crisp pig's ear tossed with crunchy coleslaw are jammed into sweet little brioche buns. Shoestring fries with Sichuan-spiced salt keep the kids happy, while everyone digs chicken tenders or gelatinous short rib in soft Chinese-style steamed buns. Things get serious for a moment via a genuinely earthy and intense pho, but silken rice noodle rolls with crunchy baby zucchini bring back the brightness. Desserts are so pretty it's a shame to eat them, especially the set Vietnamese coffee topped with a net of sesame toffee, with coconut ice-cream. More fun just like this, please.

Give yourself over to the 'Uncle knows best' menu with all the 'best bits' for $65

Open	L Mon–Fri; D Mon–Sat
Price	$$
Cards	AE MC V eftpos
Chef	Dai Duong, Ankush Nagarkar
Features	Bar, licensed, wheelchair access
Website	unclerestaurants.com.au

Victoria Hotel

FOOTSCRAY
43 Victoria Street
03 8320 0315

CONTEMPORARY   **14/20**

An inviting, pokie-free pub where families can eat happily

A delight in simplicity and old-school principles filters through at this recently rejigged pub. Floral carpet is laid around the edges of the room, under high tables and generous booths – it's a noise-muffling gesture that's also amusingly retro. Beyond the front bar, there's a dining room and courtyard, both welcoming but no-frills. Chef James Cornwall is a New Zealander who was head chef at London seafood institution J Sheekey, then Hong Kong's lavish Seafood Room. The menu is a mix of pub classics like parma, fish 'n' chips and steak alongside contemporary fare. Crunchy vegetable fritters are threaded with samphire: simple, snacky, satisfying. Steak tartare is beautifully chopped, topped with an egg yolk and served with endive leaves. There's meat aplenty but also a drift to lighter, less flesh-dependent dishes. Tofu is the creamy base for a beetroot, walnut and watermelon salad. It's also the mixer for an intense berry-topped chocolate mousse.

Visit on Monday for the meat-free menu, Tuesday for curry night or Sunday for roast

Open	L D Daily
Price	$$
Cards	AE MC V eftpos
Chef	James Cornwall
Features	Bar, licensed, outdoor seating, wheelchair access
Website	victoriahotelfootscray.com

Vue de Monde

MELBOURNE
Level 55, Rialto Towers, 525 Collins Street
03 9691 3888

CONTEMPORARY   **16.5/20**

It's Vue with a view

Shannon Bennett's highline restaurant overlooking the bright lights of Melbourne city is an extremely well-oiled machine. When they say the table is to be given up at 8pm, they mean it. The bill drops on the elaborate leather-dressed table at 7.59pm. A relaxed evening it is not. But dramatic, certainly. The staff in the open kitchen led by executive chef Justin James shout a loud hail of "Yes chef!" every time a new table arrives. Which is often. Service is similarly theatrical, from the fermented mushroom tea deftly poured at the table over raw Flinders Island lamb and eggplant couscous. A cast-iron pan is brought to the table 'smoking' with a couple of plump, silky mud crab sausages along with brioche buns and kohlrabi coleslaw for DIY hotdogs. Similar showy touches like a roaring fire for toasted marshmallows (no, you're not allowed to toast them yourself) are on display but it's the straight-shooting hot suckling pig 'terrine' with salt-baked celeriac that wins the evening.

Consider stopping in at Lui bar after dinner to keep the party going

Open	L Thu–Sun; D Daily
Price	$$$
Cards	AE MC V eftpos
Chef	Shannon Bennett, Justin James
Features	Bar, licensed, private dining, wheelchair access
Website	vuedemonde.com.au

Woodland House

PRAHRAN
78 Williams Road
03 9525 2178

CONTEMPORARY   **16/20**

Contemporary French in a pretty Prahran mansion

If your tastes steer to grand mansions, iron-crisp linens, and a menu that never pulls its brakes on butter, Woodland House is a lovely time. Fires flicker, decanters sparkle and the only audio is gossip from cashmere-clad diners. Since Jacques Reymond left in 2013, chefs Thomas Woods and Hayden McFarland have made some contempo moves. Crumbed mussels capped with foie gras and Jerusalem artichokes frosted in tiny salmon roe are surprising winners setting a tasty if unrelentingly rich tone. But then come sweet roasted onions and mostly shell-less spanner crab in creamy, herbal bisque, maybe a buttery truffle-showered pasta and gently smoky abalone, drenched in Champagne sauce: proof old-school sensibility and saucework still rules this ranch. It can be heavy going, chasing supple suckling pork with spoonable beef short rib cut by tart rhubarb puree. Wine advice is less forthcoming than in the past, but the cellar remains rich in treats from the Loire, Heathcote and even the UK if you can self-navigate.

The three courses plus wine lunch special is a great deal at $55

Open	L Fri–Sun; D Daily
Price	$$$
Cards	MC V eftpos
Chef	Thomas Woods, Hayden McFarland
Features	Bar, licensed, wheelchair accessible, outdoor seating
Website	woodlandhouse.com.au

Yagiz

SOUTH YARRA
22 Toorak Road
03 9821 4758

TURKISH   **14/20**

Turkish with South Yarra glamour

This isn't your average suburban Turkish joint. It's South Yarra, so your table is precisely spotlit with flattering lighting. Couples perch at the bar with Persian fairy-floss topped cocktails. A communal table is brassy – in both senses of the word – the centrepiece of a room lined with Besser blocks and sections of salmon pink. Order pickles and keep the tart pink vegetables as a palate cleanser. Start with confit duck cigars in dinky glass jars, the bubbled pastry ends dipped in ash-like isot pepper, then make your way through share-friendly plates. Sandwich grilled ezine cheese – Turkey's answer to saganaki – between yufka pastry sheets for a savoury mille feuille of sorts. Use those same crisps to load up dukkah-tossed liver cubes and labne. More conventional: prawns in mild chilli butter, soaked up with bread that comes with whipped eggplant butter – like a whisper of baba ghanoush. Juicy char-grilled spatchock is more smoke-forward. For dessert? Classy baklava – or there's always that Turkish Delight cocktail.

Gather nine or more friends for a whole-lamb feast

Open	L Wed–Fri; D Tue–Sat
Price	$$
Cards	AE MC V eftpos
Chef	Murat Ovaz
Features	Bar, licensed, outdoor seating, private dining, wheelchair access
Website	yagiz.com.au

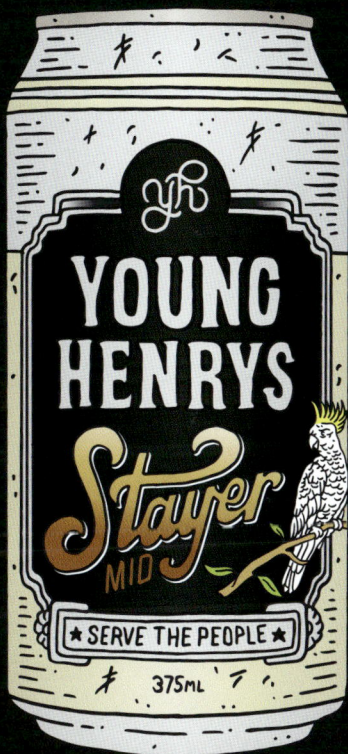

ROMEO LANE

TOP 20

MELBOURNE

BARS

By Gemima Cody
and Michael Harden

The Alps

64 Commercial Road, Prahran
03 9529 4988 • thealpsprahran.com

Wooden alcoves are stacked to the ceiling
with treats from Jura to the Savoie. It's a tight
fit up front, but there's a fire out back, 20 wines
by the glass and exactly the snacks to damp
your drinking fire in the form of meatballs,
anchovies and baked goat's cheese. Done.

Amarillo

149 Brunswick Street, Fitzroy • 03 9415 9367
amarillofitzroy.com.au

The light is gold, panels dark and vinyl correct.
The Mediterranean list is broadly Iberian,
united by universal appeal to drinkers. Drink
a cat's pyjamas (a martini rinsed with Cocchi
Americano), manzanilla sherry or something
skinsy, interesting and affordable from the
continent. Meow.

Arlechin

Mornane Place, Melbourne • 03 9662 2412
arlechin.com.au

The Grossi family's back-alley bar is as much
a draw for its proper kitchen making proper
spaghetti, toasties and ridiculous desserts
until the wee hours as for its wine list giving
access to the hefty restaurant cellar and super
fresh cocktails poured over that invisible
Navy Strength ice.

Bad Frankie's

141 Greeves Street, Fitzroy • 03 9078 3866
badfrankie.com

The all-Aussie spirits concept sounds nerdy
and the menu with seven pages of gins alone
could intimidate, but it's all easy good times.
Behold walls decoupaged with Holdens and
red roos and a well-versed crew in party
shirts. Does any bar snack trump their bangers
and mash jaffle with gravy, or supreme pizza
toastie? Doubtful.

Bar Romantica

52 Lygon Street, Brunswick East
03 9191 9410 • barromantica.com.au

Cleverly channelling the classic inner north
terrazzo-floored espresso bars from the
1960s, Romantica also keeps it modern with
an excellent selection of local craft beer on
tap, quality whisky from near and far and a
kitchen that pumps out pizza and tartare until
close, which means 4am on weekends.

Bomba Rooftop

Level 5, 103 Lonsdale Street, Melbourne
03 9650 5778 • bombabar.com.au

The freshly renovated Bomba Rooftop bar
offers a whole new space that's upgraded
everything from taplines to toilets. There's
a dedicated chef in the open kitchen
shucking oysters and pressing bikinis,
a solid range of tap beer, cocktails and
sherry made for quaffing while watching
the sun set between skyscrapers.

Cumulus Up

Level 1, 45 Flinders Lane, Melbourne
03 9650 1445 • cumulusup.com.au

Those wondering how an Andrew McConnell
cheeseburger might taste should make a
beeline for his elegant, urbane wine bar sitting
above wildly popular sibling Cumulus Inc. The
food's an obvious draw but impressive wine,
beer, cider and cocktail lists are also worth
climbing stairs for.

Dunning Kruger

436 Lygon Street, Brunswick East
dunningkrugerbar.com

Named for the syndrome where people
think they're smarter than they are, this self-
deprecating shopfront bar does what it does
very well. It knows its way around a martini for
starters. There's also a short, regularly changing
list of their own left-field concoctions. Hungry?
Choose from a small selection of house-made
American-style fruit pies.

The Elysian

113 Brunswick Street, Fitzroy • 03 9417 7441
theelysianwhiskybar.com.au

Kelvin Low and Yao Wong went as niche as
possible with their 20-seater where the focus
isn't just whiskies from countries you didn't
know made them, but one-off bottlings. Each
night they stand behind that sleek California
redwood bar, ready and waiting to pour a rare
nip of something you may never see again.

The Everleigh

Level 1, 150–156 Gertrude Street, Fitzroy
03 9416 2229 • theeverleigh.com

There's finally extra space and seats at the
glowing, tiled, golden era bar where fastidious
precise Mary Pickfords and sazeracs are
twizzled and shaken under the gaze of
a jackalope. But the rules are the same.
Relinquish control. Get the bartender's
choice. Never ask for a Midori splice.

Galah

Upstairs, 216 High Street, Windsor
03 9521 5325 • galah.melbourne

The saw-toothed warehouse space above a
bottle shop entrance (buy something on your
way in or out), hits the sweet spot between
bar and club with relaxed aplomb. The booze
is Aussie-accented, whether you're talking
the locally made spirits, minimal intervention
wine or a craft beer list of local heroes, both
packaged and on tap.

Heartbreaker

234A Russell Street, Melbourne
03 9041 0856 • heartbreakerbar.com.au

Adding New York–style pizza joint Connie's –
which slings cheesy pies and dark and stormy
slushies until 3am – turned this CBD dive bar
by the Everleigh crew into a frothing triple
threat. You're drinking bottled cocktails,
or bourbon shots with crafty Aussie and
American brews. The potential for peril is great.

Impala

1/212 High Street, Windsor • 03 9533 2827
impala.melbourne

Sibling to downstairs neighbour Neptune,
this '70s disco-chic cocktail bar knows how to
have fun but is also committed to delivering
well-constructed classic and homebrand
drinks. Want to know what a well-made mint
julep or brandy crusta should taste like? Take
a black-vinyl upholstered seat.

Lay Low

93 Buckley Street, Seddon
laylowbar.com.au

Its entrance is an unmarked door next to an
intercom inside a streetwear store. Behind the
door is a spacious, terrazzo-floored bar with
a long banquette and a burnt orange-tiled
bar where friendly bartenders pull together
flavour-forward cocktails heavy on the
quench. Who would have thought gin, carrot
juice and ginger would be such a winner?

Mr West

106 Nicholson Street, Footscray
mrwest.com.au

Footscray doesn't love new-wave interlopers,
but few have been able to argue against this
$2 shop being turned into a glorious,
wood- beamed two-level palace of craft
beers, decent wines and smart cocktails,
where it's all charcuterie and sours on
deck and takeaway treats down below.

Oscar's

Basement, 159 Domain Road, South Yarra
03 9089 6668 • matilda159.com

Scott Pickett's first southside restaurant,
leather and ochre–clad Matilda, has a similarly
stylish basement bar where the restaurant's
themes of smoke, flame and indigenous
ingredients play out in the cocktails. Sturdy,
well-priced wine and beer lists accompany
excellent snacks such as must-do salmon roe
and smoked bonito cream tartlets.

Romeo Lane

1A Crossley Street, Melbourne
03 9639 8095 • romeolane.com.au

It's the bar that looks like butter wouldn't
melt, with its perfect carved panels, flower
posies, wartime tracks and coiffed snacks,
but that tight cocktail list bringing it with a
honeyed-yet-still-sharp bees kiss, vermouth
and sherry-led lower-booze drinks and
tightrope-sharp classics can so easily
kneecap your night.

The Shady Lady

36 Johnston Street, Fitzroy
theshadylady.com.au

Sometimes only a dive bar and a gaudily
coloured frozen cocktail will do. The Shady
Lady hits all the expected marks – found,
made and salvaged decor, a neon sign and
frozen cocktail versions of pina colada,
daiquiri, mojito and margarita that are
as tasty as they are bright.

Stomping Ground

100 Gipps Street, Collingwood
03 9415 1944 • stompingground.beer

How does a cavernous former warehouse
come across as cosy? A cute fitout
helps – open fires, timber and metal detailing,
hanging plants – but it's also the reassuring
presence of the brewery, just there behind
glass. It's also there in the solidly cooked
beer-friendly food and a takeaway licence
that means the fun doesn't need to end yet.

Union Electric Gin Garden

13 Heffernan Lane, Melbourne
0450 186 466 • unionelectric.com.au

Everyone's favourite semi-open air party
bar in Chinatown is still bringing the fresh
fruit-driven drinks, craft booze, '90s hip hop
and killer attitude hard. And now there's wild
gin action upstairs, set beneath impressive
tropical plants and botanicals.

1. ORDER DOWNSTAIRS   3. TAKE A SEAT

2. WAIT FOR YOUR FOOD   4. ENJOY!!!

Evening Time:
you can also order
UPSTAIRS

FALAFEL BURGER 6   STEAK & EGG 19 LAMB KEBAB 18 PIZZA 17 WAGYU BU

RATATOUILLE 13 HOT CHICK PEAS 12 MERLAN FISH SPICY TOMATO HRAIME 16 MINUTE STEAK 22 INTIMATE WAGY

EGGS NO STEAK 14 OCEAN TROUT BELLY AND AVOCADO 6 AVOCADO GREEN DIAMONDS 13 PITA M

MIZNON

TOP 20
MELBOURNE
CHEAP EATS

By Sofia Levin and Anna Webster

Butcher's Diner

10 Bourke Street, Melbourne
03 9639 7324 • butchersdiner.com

If you find yourself hankering for a Creole
salmon cutlet at 4.30 in the morning, head
straight here. The diner, with its long orange
laminate and timber bar and floor-to-ceiling
glass meat cabinet, dishes up a consistent,
quality menu of burgers, steaks, skewers and
salads around the clock. Cash only.

Co Thu Quan

Shop 6, 234 Victoria Street, Richmond
03 8589 6339

Along with pho, noodle soups range from the
Vietnamese centre's fragrant beef and pork
bun bo hue to the south's banh canh cua crab.
But the signature is com am phu – a claypot of
fluffy rice sprinkled with candied pork mince
and served with side dishes such as crunchy
baby crabs, sticky pork belly and pickled
vegetables. You won't find it anywhere else.

Dosa Corner

587 Barkly Street, Footscray West
03 8528 5120 • Also Melbourne, Roxburgh
Park and Tarneit • thedosacorner.com.au

A plain dosa with sambar and chutneys costs
$1, but we prefer the masala version filled with
spiced potato. For a couple of dollars extra,
up-size to a dosa so big it's served folded back
on itself. The pick of the bites is biryani with
chunks of 'chicken 65', a popular street snack.

Hi Chong Qing

26 Orr Street, Carlton • 0423 262 122
hicq.business.site

Beside a Uni Lodge down a lane running
parallel to Lygon Street is one of the best
noodle soup spots in Melbourne. Hi Chong
Qing specialises in chongqing noodles from
the Chinese city of the same name.

Ippudo

Shop 18, Artemis Lane, 300 Lonsdale Street
QV Shopping Centre, Melbourne
03 9654 9057 • ippudo.com.au

The Japanese ramen chain opened its first
CBD outpost in April and crowds have flocked
for its rich, creamy signature tonkotsu ramen
with firm house-made noodles ever since.
Fortunately, with 100 seats and rapid
service, the line moves quite quickly.

Kalimera Souvlaki Art

41 Chester Street, Oakleigh • 03 9939 3912
kalimerasouvlakiart.com.au

Attica's Ben Shewry calls Kalimera's souvlaki
one of the great dishes of Melbourne. At just
$9, the char-grilled-pita-wrapped souvlaki
with juicy spit-roasted pork (or chicken),
house-made tzatziki, onion, tomato and a
couple of chips represents the best value.

Kelso's Sandwich Shoppe

271 Johnston Street, Abbotsford
03 9495 6268 • kelsossandwiches.com

Those who don't pop in for a takeaway
sandwich linger at the counter and along
walls adorned with framed magazine pages
of '50s sandwich ads. Sandwiches are steeped
in nostalgia. Tuna melts, corned beef, grilled
cheese – the latter also available in
a vegan-friendly version.

La Tortilleria

72 Stubbs Street, Kensington
1300 556 084 • latortilleria.com.au

With its brightly painted walls and food
served on plastic Corona trays, this Mexican
restaurant stands out in Kensington's
industrial backstreets. Tacos range from
al pastor (pork and pineapple) to cachete
(slow-cooked beef cheeks with green
tomatillo salsa), and there are also tostadas,
quesadillas and plates from the grill.

Little Sichuan

Box Hill Central Shopping Centre
1 Main Street, Box Hill • 03 9898 8305

Part of the Dainty Sichuan Group, this hotpot
concept involves filling a stainless steel bowl
with ingredients from shelves of trays, picking
one of five broths at the counter and paying
by weight ($3.28 for 100 grams). You'll need
both hands to count the tofu varieties.

Maker and Monger

Prahran Market, 4 Market Street
South Yarra • 0413 900 490
makerandmonger.com.au

The humble toastie is having a moment and
no one has elevated this student staple quite
like Anthony Femia, Prahran Market's resident
cheesemonger. Femia uses grated Vermont
cheddar and thick, crunchy sourdough to
make the All American Grilled Cheese. The
Fondue version is stuffed with shaved gruyere
and comte and brushed with white wine.

Mile End Bagels

14-16 Johnston Street, Fitzroy
mile-end.com.au

Owners Michael Fee and Benjamin Vaughn
are rolling some of the best bagels in town.
Their bagels are Montreal-style, which means
the dough is shaped and boiled in honeyed
water for extra sweetness before it sees the
inside of the custom-built wood oven.

Miznon

59 Hardware Lane, Melbourne
03 9670 2861 • miznonaustralia.com

A year after opening, this Hardware Lane pita
party is as popular as ever. Michelin-starred
Israeli chef Eyal Shani's food looks street, but
there's some serious technique behind those
pita pockets. Take the pita with a bone, stuffed
with tender lamb ribs, nutty tahini, pickles,
onion and chilli. Or the ratatouille, filled with a
rich vegetable stew and boiled egg.

Mocha Jo's Burger Bar

3 Glen Eira Avenue, Ripponlea
03 9086 4938 • Also rear, 87 Kingsway
Glen Waverley • 03 9545 0843
mjburgerbar.com.au

Owner Christo Christophidis slings American-
style burgers from two locations: the original
MJ's Burger Bar, attached to his flagship
Mocha Jo's restaurant in Glen Waverley,
and from the newer, pint-sized iteration
near Ripponlea station. At both, beef patties
are made from grain-fed wagyu, and served
on fluffy milk buns.

Mook Ji Bar

406 Lonsdale Street, Melbourne
03 9600 2661

What this no-frills restaurant lacks in decor it
makes up for with its menu. Complimentary
kimchi kicks things off, while entrees like
Korean pancakes and tteokbokki are
generous and filling. Mimic international
students and try fried chicken with melted
cheese. BYO wine.

Moroccan Soup Bar (Two Go)

316 St Georges Road, Fitzroy North
03 9486 3500

The verbal menu at the takeaway-only arm of
Hana Assafiri's Moroccan Soup Bar is largely
the same as at the original. Here, in lieu of the
full banquet, you can get a generous pack with
rice and couscous dishes, dhal, salad, pickles
and the famous chickpea bake for $12.50.

The Pie Shop

75 Nicholson Street, Brunswick East
0455 052 342 • thepieshop.com.au

Fans of Pope Joan will be relieved to know that
while the cafe closed, chef Matt Wilkinson's
adjoining Pie Shop is still very much in
business. Alongside the familiar chunky
beef and vegetable pies, there's the Bruce,
with a spaghetti bolognese filling, and the
cauliflower-and-cheese Shazza, which even
meat-lovers will be hard-pressed to turn down.

Ras Dashen

247 Barkly Street, Footscray • 03 9687 2748,
ras-dashen-ethiopean-restaurant.business.
site

In 2018, Ras Dashen's owners sold their
Ethiopian restaurant in Nicholson Street and
opened a bigger, brighter version in the thick
of the action on Barkly Street. It's never been
better. Order tibs (grilled) and wot (stewed),
perhaps mild and buttery beef, lamb or spiced
lentils. There's cutlery if you need, but it's
more fun to use the bread as a scoop.

ShanDong Mama

Shop 7, Mid City Arcade, 200 Bourke Street,
Melbourne • 03 9650 3818
shandongmama.com.au

A visit to Meiyan 'Mama' Wang's no-frills
Chinese restaurant isn't complete without
a serve of her boiled mackerel dumplings.
Packed with an ethereal fish mousse, ginger
and herbs, they're unlike anything else you'll
find in the city.

Soi 38

38 McIlwraith Place, Melbourne
0490 396 382 • soi38.com

Melbourne's worst-kept secret, Soi 38
specialises in Thai street-style boat noodles.
From its spot inside a city car park, it deliver
a tick-box menu of half-a-dozen types of
noodle as well as three levels of aromatic soup
(full, half or dry).

Very Good Falafel

629 Sydney Road, Brunswick
03 9383 6479 • shukiandlouisa.com

In the Melbourne falafel wars, VFG reigns
supreme. The falafels – crunchy and deeply
golden outside, chunky and green from herbs
in the middle – come from chickpeas grown
on the Allan family farm.

SMITH & DELI

SMITH & DELI

TOP 20 MELBOURNE CAFES

By Larissa Dubecki

Axil Coffee Roasters

322 Burwood Road, Hawthorn
03 9819 0091 • axilcoffee.com.au

Hawthorn remains Axil HQ – home to the roastery, training and cupping room that provides punters with a free floor show. Not to mention a menu of smart cafe fare such as turmeric and chilli scrambled eggs with pickled eggplant and smashed avo with Meredith goat's curd.

Babajan

713 Nicholson Street, Carlton North
03 9388 9814 • babajan.com.au

Simit, pastirma and tursu grace the menu here. Luckily, it's no hardship to take this primarily Turkish food trip. Even smashed avo takes a Middle Eastern spin with ezme, broad beans and goat's curd with a flutter of preserved lemon, or the Aleppo-spiced eggplant cheese toastie with sumac onions.

Brunetti

250 Flinders Lane, Melbourne
03 9347 2801;
380 Lygon Street, Carlton • brunetti.com.au

The Carlton institution that upsized into half of Lygon Court shopping centre and has now taken on the city with a Flinders Lane address almost as big as the Colosseum. There's a surfeit of Latin pride amid the slick, glamorous surroundings. Go early for colazione completa or salmone affumicato.

Burnham Beeches

1 Sherbrooke Road, Sherbrooke
03 9691 3888 • burnhambeeches.com.au

This self-sufficient cafe even boasts its own emus (for eggs, not meat thus far). The former piggery is all rugged atmosphere with food to match – this is the place you want to go the big cooked breakfast or hit the smoked chicken with slaw and pickles.

Everyday Coffee

33 Johnston Street, Collingwood
03 9973 4159;
213 Little Collins Street, Melbourne
everyday-coffee.com

We love the simplicity of a place that serves a few things to eat – sourdough toast, bagels – and very, very good coffee. They must be doing something right because they've expanded to the city and are the Svengalis behind the fabulous All Are Welcome bakery in Northcote.

Fifty Acres

65 Bridge Road, Richmond
03 9421 0296 • fiftyacres.net.au

Stripped-back red brick and covetable metallic lights provide the French provincial antidote to the Scandi design, while the menu speaks a fluent Melbourne Esperanto, flitting from citrus-cured salmon and a poached egg on dark rye to chorizo scotch eggs.

Good Times

83 Tucker Road, Bentleigh
03 9557 4868 • goodtimesmilkbar.com.au

This Bentleigh milk bar has been turned into a pastel-accented vision of Los Angeles. The speckled front counter and diner-style booths mix-and-match a bunch of nostalgic impulses, while a menu keeps the good times rolling with things like pastrami eggs benedict on golden potato hash.

Hash Specialty Coffee

113 Hardware Street, Melbourne
03 8529 0284

Sometimes all it takes to propel a cafe is for one menu item to achieve cult-like status on Instagram. Here, it's the hot chocolate: 85 per cent Mork cocoa, served in a beaker to pour over a cup topped with white fairy floss in the conical shape of Marge Simpson's hair.

Higher Ground

650 Little Bourke Street, Melbourne
03 8899 6219
highergroundmelbourne.com.au

It's not quite a cafe, not quite a restaurant. The menu does its bit for the 'breakfast is the new dinner' movement. Start the day with steamed barramundi on kohlrabi noodles and charred leek in mushroom dashi, end it with brussels sprouts, fried duck egg and XO. What a world.

Industry Beans

Warehouse 3, 62 Rose Street, Fitzroy
345 Little Collins Street, Melbourne
03 9417 1034 • industrybeans.com

Come for the award-winning fitout of a backstreet Fitzroy factory shell, stay for the addictively excellent brew made with beans roasted on-site. Just add a shamelessly populist menu where southern fried chicken burgers rub shoulders with Asian-style beef noodle broth and a next-level house-cured salmon.

Left Field

358 Koornang Road, Carnegie
03 9578 2043 • leftfieldeatery.com

This sun-filled corner shop is no stranger to the current daytime dining fads such as pork shoulder eggs benedict and cookies-and-cream doughnut sliders with smashed Oreos, as well as turmeric lattes and chia pudding taking a walk on the wild side with honeycomb and peanut butter.

Matcha Mylkbar

72A Acland Street, St Kilda • 03 9534 1111
matchamylkbar.com

Any eye-rolling about vegans taking over the world one faux poached egg at a time might just have to get in line outside this St Kilda hotspot name-checked by a glitterati of wellness bods including Chris Hemsworth. The 'eggs' get all the press but the matcha pancakes don't need to imitate anything to make an impression.

Plain Sailing

144 Ormond Road, Elwood
03 9537 7060 • plainsailingelwood.com

The fried peanut butter cookies and cream bao with banana bread, vanilla mascarpone, chocolate and popcorn crumble, banana, salted caramel and Nutella sounds more like a dare than a breakfast dish but it's the zeitgeisty excess that has cemented Plain Sailing as the Elwood cafe du jour.

Riddik

1-3 The Mall, Templestowe Lower
03 9850 2680 • riddik.com.au

Converted bank + an underserviced suburb = cafe gold. That's the equation here, where people dress for breakfast like there's a strong possibility they'll be hitting a nightclub afterwards. The French toast with strawberry cheesecake is a real diva, while the cheesy duck omelette is a more down-to-earth delight.

St Ali

12-18 Yarra Place, South Melbourne
03 9132 8960 • stali.com.au

This cafe and roastery is tucked down a pleasingly obscure South Melbourne laneway. Catnip for coffee nerds, it's easy to get lost in the siphon, espresso, pour over and filter maze, but battle through to a sprightly menu that swings from pork cotoletta to vegan pancakes.

Seven Seeds

114 Berkeley Street, Carlton
03 9347 8664 • sevenseeds.com.au

Could this be the Holy Grail of coffee in Melbourne? Mark Dundon is certainly the bean's high priest, husbanding the local coffee scene through its third-wave infancy at venues such as Ray and St Ali. It's every Melburnian's civic duty to attend one of the cupping sessions held each Wednesday.

Smith and Deli

111 Moor Street, Fitzroy • 03 9042 4117
facebook.com/SmithAndDeli

Shannon Martinez and Mo Wyse converted half of Melbourne to veganism with Smith and Daughters, then doubled down with the vegan New York-style deli we never knew we needed. But boy, how we do need the 'egg McMartinez', which gives a certain multinational behemoth an ethical run for its money.

Terror Twilight

Shop 13, 11-13 Johnston Street, Collingwood
03 9417 0129 • terrortwilight.com.au

It was an acid test for cafe culture when the team behind Wide Open Road turned their southern-fried den of iniquity into the body beautiful Terror Twilight. It's out with the pickled frankfurters, in with the build-our-own brown rice and broth bowls.

Tinker

235 High Street, Northcote • 03 9482 5264
tinkernorthcote.com.au

There's a conspiracy theory in Northcote that each new dish needs to pass a panel of Instagram influencers before being put on the menu. That could explain the excessive prettiness of plates like the mango and saffron panna cotta, or the smashed peas and haloumi with a beetroot labne popping against smoky-blue ceramics.

Wide Open Road

274 Barkly Street, Brunswick • 03 9010 9298
wideopenroad.com.au

Doing double time as a coffee roastery, the beans are good enough to feature on menus across town, while the breakfast/brunch menu is a masterclass in the way Melbourne likes to eat, from fish finger sandwiches to the thick-cut 'proper' bacon and gruyere pancake licked with chipotle mayo.

🎩 🎩 🎩

Brae

🎩 🎩

Igni
Lake House
Laura
Provenance
Wickens at Royal Mail Hotel

🎩

Captain Moonlite
Doot Doot Doot
Ezard at Levantine Hill
Ipsos
Masons of Bendigo
Midnight Starling
Montalto
Oakridge
Paringa Estate
Pt. Leo Restaurant
The Public Inn
Sardine Eatery and Bar
Source Dining
Stefano's Cantina
TarraWarra Estate
Terrace Restaurant
Tulip
Underbar

Victoria regional

A La Grecque

AIREYS INLET
60 Great Ocean Road
03 5289 6922

GREEK   **14/20**

A sunny, family-friendly corner of Greece

After 40 years in hospitality, 14 of them at this verandah-hemmed taverna on the Great Ocean Road, veteran restaurateurs Kosta and Pam Talimanidis have passed the torch to son Stratos. Little has changed in the split-level, rush-ceilinged dining room, warmed in winter by a crackling fire. But regulars may notice some differences on the menu, now pared back and more relaxed but still with a focus on clean Greek flavours and local seafood. Most tables start with house dips such as whipped feta given a good chilli nudge, and golden wedges of kefalograviera with pot-roasted quince. And baklava ice-cream is the obvious full-stop. But in-between come curls of octopus brightened with capers, green olives and cornichons, charry king prawns bedded on a rich burnt butter and almond yoghurt, and satisfying grainy salads such as mejadra. For the multi-generational family groups, the brief, wholesome kids' menu is a blessing – there's not a french fry or nugget in sight.

Over summer, they expand the opening hours for more fun in the sun

Open	L D Wed–Sun
Price	$$
Cards	MC V eftpos
Chef	Stratos Talimanidis
Features	Licensed, outdoor seating
Website	alagrecque.com.au

Bistro Elba

SORRENTO
100-102 Ocean Beach Road
03 5984 4995

EUROPEAN   **14/20**

Polished yet unpretentious bistro fare for the Sorrento set

Blame the Bard. The previous name of this bistro at the peninsula's pointy end, Cakes and Ale, was a Shakespearean reference that led the more literal-minded punters to expect a keg-filled patisserie. So owners James Langley and Mathew Guthrie recently rebranded to Bistro Elba, a name that more directly evokes the menu's coastal Mediterranean influences. Think line-caught whole baby snapper char-grilled and served with a simple dice of tomato, olive and coriander, or Roman-style baked semolina gnocchi paired with luscious confit tomato and creamy squacquerone cheese. The overall package is polished but with a welcome lack of formality that suits the beachside locale. The ambitious, globe-trotting wine list showcases several single-vineyard producers and a few wild-fermented numbers, and wine dinners are held monthly. To finish, it's hard to go past the bombe Alaska, with a tart sauce made from local strawberries to temper the sweetness of white chocolate parfait and torched marshmallow.

Order an amaro from the digestif trolley as it wheels past for the perfect finale

Open	L D Daily
Price	$$
Cards	MC V eftpos
Chef	Mathew Guthrie
Features	Bar, licensed, outdoor seating, wheelchair access
Website	bistroelba.com.au

BRAE

Bistrot Plume

BELMONT
56A Mount Pleasant Road
03 5245 8483

FRENCH   **14.5/20**

Corner store reimagined as a stylish, casual French bistro

On a broad and handsome residential street, Bistrot Plume operates quietly on the corner. Venture into the space – an intimate room of white walls, black decking, turquoise upholstery and dramatic artworks – and give in to the warmth of chef Nathan Veach's French-leaning cuisine paired with a smart wine list. Start with a twice-baked cheese soufflé, feather-light in texture but deep in three-cheese flavour, or a snappy ham-hock croquette. Swordfish comes as a chunky fillet with a bright panzanella popping with white anchovies and bell peppers, steak frites is generous with hand-cut, skin-on chips and an aromatic wedge of Cafe de Paris butter, and broccolini is charred and served with a glowing dollop of smoky paprika butter. Share dishes include a chateaubriand and a roasted duck breast with a spiced orange glaze and duck fat potatoes, while a slim chocolate mille feuille, elegantly stacked and served with coffee ice-cream and candied mandarin, is a stylish way to end the meal.

Weekday specials include $35 for an entree and main

Open	B L Daily; D Thu–Sat
Price	$$
Cards	AE MC V eftpos
Chef	Nathan Veach, Chris Dodd
Features	Licensed, wheelchair access
Website	bistrotplume.com.au

Brae

BIRREGURRA
4285 Cape Otway Road
03 5236 2226

CONTEMPORARY   **19/20**

One of the most singular dining experiences in the country, from garden to plate

It's a restaurant that lives and breathes the seasons, fed directly by what's growing in the ground out the front. Chef Dan Hunter's cooking, though, is almost otherworldly. The single mouthful combination of scallop, urchin and truffle is disconcertingly yet deliciously cooling, warm, fatty. Quite a few of Hunter's dishes have that head-versus-mouth effect, actually. The latter, however, nearly always wins. Baked beetroot, local honey and a massive spoonful of trout roe see the brine, earth and sweetness make an incredible team. Some things are just straight-up delicious. Bonito cured overnight with kelp and mountain pepper is soft and warm with just the right balance of sweetness and savour. Pork jowl and greenlip abalone is sticky and salty and gone in one bite. The smoked eel churros? Everything you've heard and more. Dining in this sprawling converted weatherboard house is all about deep, unhurried comfort from immaculate service to a pre-dessert stroll through the gardens, backlit by the setting sun.

Keep the party going by booking one of the six rooms onsite – each with its own record player and lots of vinyl

Open	L Fri–Mon; D Thu, Sat
Price	$$$
Cards	AE MC V eftpos
Chef	Dan Hunter
Features	Licensed, wheelchair access
Website	braerestaurant.com

Bunyip Hotel

CAVENDISH
17-25 Scott Street
03 5574 2205

PUB DINING   **14.5/20**

The long-haul traveller's fantasy pub

The pride of Cavendish (population 334) is a sturdy Deco-fronted pub on the banks of the Wannon River, in Victoria's sheep-dotted Western District. Under James Campbell, who returned to his hometown after a stint as co-owner and head chef of MoVida Sydney, it's become a food-lover's oasis and community hub. On the noticeboard, beside business cards for ram shearers and gardeners, is a newspaper cutting from the time *MasterChef* visited the nearby Royal Mail. Campbell's clipboard menu is a potted collection of gastropub hits, made in-house using ingredients from the district. Skinny hand-cut chips from Koroit potatoes come with runny yolked eggs and a dusting of smoked paprika. The kitchen's sparky kimchi plays off rounds of mild locally made pastrami. And a towering dome of shattery house-made puff pastry caps a bounteous fish pie. Bring an appetite sharpened by country air. The servings are large, and there's no sense leaving without a warming bellyful of golden syrup dumplings and ice-cream.

In warm weather, grab a picnic table out the back and let the kids run free in the big fenced yard

Open	L Fri–Sun; D Wed–Sat
Price	$$
Cards	AE MC V eftpos
Chef	James Campbell
Features	Bar, licensed, outdoor seating, wheelchair access
Website	bunyiphotelcavendish.com

Cape

CAPE SCHANCK
RACV Cape Schanck Resort, Trent Jones Drive (via Boneo Road)
03 5950 8038

CONTEMPORARY   **14/20**

Set the GPS for the restaurant putting the snack into Cape Schanck

Hidden from the main road, the Mornington Peninsula's newest hotel looms above the landscape like an ocean liner. It's here that young gun Josh Pelham (London's The Square) is striving to make the 160-seat restaurant a dining drawcard. Decked out in earth-toned granite, timber and leather, the dining room balances ambition and comfort, much like the menu. From the ambitious side of the ledger, there's an opulent truffled kangaroo tartare and gelled egg yolk scooped up with beef tendons puffed like prawn crackers, and a seafood raviolo shrouded in Champagne foam. In the comfort column, see crisp-skinned chicken with dabs of pureed corn and jus gras. There's also whole grilled fish with frazzled capers and a classic lemon-parsley dressing, and crimson swatches of wagyu porterhouse with a host of sauces and sides. On early visits, friendly waitstaff didn't yet match the finish of the food. But mark Cape down as a destination to watch.

The adjoining Lighthouse Lounge offers a cosy fire and all-day snacks

Open	D Daily
Price	$$-$$$
Cards	AE DC MC V eftpos
Chef	Josh Pelham
Features	Bar, licensed, private dining, wheelchair access
Website	racv.com.au/travel-leisure/racv-resorts/our-destinations/cape-schanck-resort/dining-bar/cape-restaurant.html

Captain Moonlite

ANGLESEA
100 Great Ocean Road
03 5263 2454

EUROPEAN   **15/20**

Relaxed surf club restaurant with ripper ocean views and food to match

Helping shift Anglesea to the top of any seachanger's (or sea-dreamer's) bucket list is this coastal gem, which ticks all the boxes with thick black pen. Sweeping surf coast view. Relaxed, retro room. A warming fireplace for winter and sunny balcony for summer. Easygoing hosts who won't frown at sandy feet. Tick tickety tick. How great, then, that the food smashes it, too. Unsurprisingly, seafood is the specialty. From the simple – the golden fish and chips of your final supper fantasy, a single tender charred octopus tentacle splayed across the plate with lip-tingling salt and vinegar-dusted potato cake by its side – to pillowy crab doughnuts. Or bass groper boosted by the comfort, colour and crunch of gnudi, cavolo nero and hazelnuts. Meat and sweet eaters won't go wanting, though, with share-sized wagyu rump steak (and chips, of course) juicy and generous, and a sticky warming apple tart with brown butter ice-cream to ride out a super-swell experience.

Get there before sunset to make the most of those views

DOC Pizza and Mozzarella Bar

MORNINGTON
22 Main Street
03 5977 0988

ITALIAN   **14/20**

Italian stallion of Mornington Peninsula brings the pizza goods

Mozzarella, salumi and thin-crust pizza, served with a round of "Ciao, ragazzi!" is a formula that works, and Team DOC's lively Mornington outpost is no exception. Provenance is worn with pride via the produce-annotated map of the Boot, printed on the menu along with salumi and cheese tasting notes. Start there, snacking on mortadella and bresaola with hunks of excellent ciabatta, or a lightly melted disc of smoked mozzarella paired with white anchovies and fennel. The pizza features crisp bases and chewy, lightly bubbled crusts – many come brushed with rich San Marzano tomato, but equally rewarding is the combination of creamed broccoli, mozzarella and generous nuggets of pork sausage. There's lasagne on hand, too, for pasta lovers. Booze-wise, consider skipping the Peroni to sample the several unpasteurised and unfiltered beers from Italian micro-breweries. Finish with a properly wobbly panna cotta, and be sure to swing past the terrific deli and providore to stock up on grissini and guanciale on your way out.

DOC recently added gluten-free pizza bases to their line-up

Open	B L Fri–Mon; D Thu–Sun (extended hours in summer)
Price	$$
Cards	MC V eftpos
Chef	Matt Germanchis
Features	Bar, licensed, outdoor seating
Website	captainmoonlite.com.au

Open	B L D Daily
Price	$$
Cards	AE MC V eftpos
Chef	Gianluca Clini
Features	Bar, licensed, outdoor seating, wheelchair access
Website	docgroup.net

Doot Doot Doot

MERRICKS NORTH
166 Balnarring Road
03 5931 2500

CONTEMPORARY   **15.5/20**

Degustations and sophistication in the Peninsula's swishest digs

Jumpin' Jackalope flash, what a room. A fizzing installation of golden globes bubbles across the ceiling like just-popped Champagne. Gold-flecked terrazzo tabletops twinkle against a sexy black backdrop of quilted banquettes and sheer drapes. The luxury hotel's tasting menu has been revised to a concise five courses. Service is as smooth as the futuristic frosted automated bathroom doors. Wine pairings travel wide and surprise – the sommelier's expanded descriptions peppered with anecdotes as quirky as the cocktail lounge's designer decor. Dishes and snacks are similarly personality-filled, such as spanner crab luxuriating in a buttermilk bath, balanced with finger lime and a bright, green tomato relish. Blushing duck breast, crisp persimmon discs, salt-baked beets and smoked celeriac puree as soft as a fireside cashmere throw, is pure winter on a plate. A dulcet dessert of honeyed yoghurt sorbet and softly-softly lavender custard is as comfortable as the mattress in the hotel's $675-a-night room would want to be.

For vineyard views and skillet cookies, check out the hotel's refined-casual, communal-tabled, Rare Hare

Open	L Sat–Sun; D Daily
Price	$$$
Cards	AE MC V eftpos
Chef	Guy Stanaway, Elliott Pinn
Features	Bar, licensed, private dining, wheelchair access
Website	jackalopehotels.com

Du Fermier

TRENTHAM
42 High Street
03 5424 1634

FRENCH   **14.5/20**

First-rate farm-to-table fare

In the quiet hamlet of Trentham, Annie Smithers fires up her kitchen just four times a week for lunches only, and offers just three dishes of her own choosing. And yet Du Fermier is booked out weeks in advance. Her secret? An authentic farm-to-table philosophy, with the bulk of the produce coming from her own farm, and proteins sourced where possible from local, ethical operations. These super-fresh ingredients are married with classical French technique and an utter disdain for nouvelle cuisine portions, so you might get a tart of soft egg custard concealing gooey gruyere with a huge garden salad, followed by thick slabs of stuffed roast chicken with potatoes Lyonnaise and steamed veg, then a superb lemon curd. Or perhaps Jerusalem artichoke soup, slow-cooked lamb shoulder with roasted root vegetables, then chocolate mousse. Whatever's on, it's accompanied by fine French wines and an unhurried pace, so you can relax into it all. Bring your appetite. This is abundance.

Avoid a multi-week wait by visiting on a Monday

Open	L Fri–Mon
Price	$$
Cards	AE MC V eftpos
Chef	Annie Smithers
Features	Licensed, wheelchair access
Website	dufermier.com.au

Empire Hotel

BEECHWORTH
10 Camp Street
03 5728 2743

CONTEMPORARY **14/20**

An old country pub reborn with new tricks

Welcome to the new Empire, where your steak comes with porcini butter and the menu includes a glossary explaining that cobia is the 'wagyu of the sea'. The circa 1870s pub has been given a new lease on country life by industry veterans Scott Daintry, Andrew Madden and chef Shauna Stockwell (ex-Stanley Hotel). Chesterfields, original Baltic pine floors and a crackling fireplace make the public bar a great spot for a pint, while the red brick-walled restaurant (also with fireplace) features modern cooking delivered with old-world hospitality. That cobia is cured in sake, giving an edge to the fish's smooth fat, with wakame, tobiko and pickled daikon sealing the Japanese-inspired deal. Corned and smoked ox tongue is a more European affair, sharpened by salsa verde, sliced cornichons and fennel remoulade, and later confit duck leg with golden skin is a treat, accompanied by braised lentils, parsnip cream and pistachios. Extra kudos for a wine list showcasing Beechworth vignerons. Long may this Empire reign.

There's a top-notch counter menu if you're keen for a pot pie or parmigiana at lunch

Open	L D Daily
Price	$$
Cards	AE MC V eftpos
Chef	Shauna Stockwell
Features	Bar, licensed
Website	empirehotelbeechworth.com.au

Ezard at Levantine Hill

COLDSTREAM
882 Maroondah Highway
03 5962 1333

CONTEMPORARY **15/20**

European-leaning fine dining in a flash winery restaurant

From the red chopper on the lawn to the $20,000 (yes, really) a night Homestead bed and breakfast, Levantine Hill pitches itself squarely at the cashed-up. Its signature restaurant is a calm zone at the far end of the striking Fender-Katsalidis-designed building, separated by open shelves from the hoi polloi at the wine tasting bar and all-day bistro. Settle into an upholstered armchair and a white-clothed table for a five- or-eight-course degustation menu designed by Teage Ezard, artfully presented and with clever twists. Most work well, such as rosy duck breast pepped up with pomegranate-infused yoghurt and the crunch of candied walnuts or a not-too-sweet apple sorbet dessert with shards of black sesame 'glass' and a fromage frais and yoghurt mousse. Occasional touches are trying a little too hard. A smoke-filled dome over cured kingfish doesn't really add much except a bit of theatre. Overall, though, the ambitious dishes succeed. It's a glimpse of how the well-heeled other half live – even if you have to drive home.

There are vegetarian five- and eight-course degustation menus

Open	L Wed–Mon; D Sat
Price	$$$
Cards	AE MC V Eftpos
Chef	Teage Ezard
Features	Licensed, private dining, wheelchair access
Website	levantinehill.com.au/ezard-at-levantine-hill

Giant Steps

HEALESVILLE
336 Maroondah Highway
03 5962 6111

CONTEMPORARY   **14.5/20**

Laidback luxe redefines cellar-door dining

Yarra Valley's most seductive cellar door? We think so. An intimate, relaxed yet refined refit – dark timbers, muted greens and mustards, soft leather banquettes – gives diners a chance to linger over Steve Flamsteed's stellar single vineyard drops. Beautiful produce, care in the kitchen and wine-savvy service (much like the vigilance in vineyard) elevate the experience. Snack on arancini, duck spring rolls and chicken liver parfait or paper-thin curls of jamon Iberico and wagyu bresaola. Settle in with friends for slow-cooked lamb shoulder or maple syrup-glazed duck soothed by the softly spiced dark cherry fruits of Applejack pinot noir. There's steak and wood-fired pizza. But it's sticky pork belly (master-stock braised, roasted and flash-fried) tangled in rice noodles, garlic shoots and peanuts along with a salad of spanner crab with young coconut, coriander and avocado that plays best with elegant Sexton chardonnay. Both dishes show freshness, balance and texture, and chef Jarrod Hudson's flair with modern Asian cuisine.

Nab a stool, taste and talk through award-winning wines ($10) in the towering barrel hall

Open	L Daily; D Thu–Mon
Price	$$
Cards	AE MC V eftpos
Chef	Jarrod Hudson
Features	Bar, licensed, outdoor seating, private dining, wheelchair access
Website	giantstepswine.com.au

Igni

GEELONG
Ryan Place
03 5222 2266

CONTEMPORARY   **16.5/20**

A haven for Sunday lunch where wood-fire rules

Use your nose to find this ode to smoke, ferments, pickles and things pulled straight from the dirt – the smell of the woodfire drifts down Ryan Place. Use your ears, too. The lean room is filled with the laughter of relaxed diners. But most importantly, use your mouth. The intent of chef Aaron Turner's menu is clear cut, starting with a barrage of snacks like the crunch and fun of salt- and-vinegar saltbush crisps. The chew of smoked trout. The musk and funk in a pretzel stick wrapped in lardo. The sea-meets-barnyard marriage of chicken skin crisps holding whipped bottarga. And the double act of white and breakfast radishes, lightly pickled with a splodge of green sauce. Larger dishes such as marron tail bathed in a sort of squab jus gras and finished with a tangle of kale continue the narrative helped by floor manager Joanna Smith, pouring wine and weaving stories. Use your head, and plan a return visit.

Split a wine tasting if you'd like to see some restaurant flex without the wobble home

Open	L Fri–Sun; D Thu–Sat
Price	$$$
Cards	AE MC V eftpos
Chef	Aaron Turner
Features	Licensed, wheelchair access
Website	restaurantigni.com

IGNI

The Independent

GEMBROOK
79 Main Street
03 5968 1110

🍷

ARGENTINIAN   **14.5/20**

A buzzy vegan-friendly porteno with a big heart

Swap Earl Grey tea and scones for a malbec-fuelled lunch Latin American-style. Follow the hordes from Puffing Billy to the lofty light-filled dining hall where Argentinian chef Mauro Callegari's punchy vegan dishes rival his house-made chorizo and slow-cooked lamb shoulder. The open kitchen slings plates picturing tango dancers and bulls piled high with empanadas, provoleta and grilled octopus from the all-day share menu. The joint jumps. It's perfect for families and groups. A cubby house in the beer garden caters for the kids. Will it be sticky pork belly – sweet, rich and juicy – with herb-flecked pickled green apples; subtly spiced roast pumpkin and macadamias on burnt pumpkin puree, or smoked maple carrots, carrot mayo, candied peanuts and coriander pesto? Tender beef short ribs come layered in chimichurri with crisp-skinned jacket spuds. Finish with dulce de leche-swirled ice-cream and churros. Service can slip but the Independent's a helluva ride. Just relax and top up your torrontes.

Plan ahead for Western Plains suckling pig with salsa criolla and chimichurri

Open	L Fri–Sun; D Wed–Sun
Price	$$
Cards	MC V eftpos
Chef	Mauro Callegari, Manuel Santeiro
Features	Bar, licensed, outdoor seating, private dining, wheelchair access
Website	theindependentgembrook.com.au

Innocent Bystander

HEALESVILLE
316-334 Maroondah Highway
03 5999 9222

ITALIAN   **14/20**

A sassy cellar door diner with an urban edge

Split from Giant Steps, new owners, new digs in the sweeping space once White Rabbit brewery – meet next-level Innocent Bystander. And no folks, it's not only about froth and pink bubbles. On tap alongside moscato, another eight easy-drinking drops are up for tasting. Choose your juice, pull up a high-back stool, grab a banquette, sink into a fireside sofa or take in the afternoon sun on deck and let the all-day grazing begin. Share charcuterie, go meat-free – fennel slaw, roast carrots, eggplant and tomatoes, burrata and hummus pack flavour – or do a metre-long combo board. Next up, wood-fired pizza – puffy-edged, thin based and pliable. A margherita comes topped in sweet San Marzano sugo, molten and fresh buffalo mozzarella and basil. Prefer hearty chicken and chorizo paella, perfect with, say, a 500ml lab flask of tempranillo? End sweetly with a cheesecake and blueberry-filled waffle cone. Weekends are busy but swift iPad orders beamed into the kitchen keep pace.

After lunch head to Four Pillars Distillery for a gin tasting

Open	L D Daily
Price	$$
Cards	AE MC V eftpos
Chef	Michael Themel
Features	Bar, licensed, outdoor seating, wheelchair access
Website	innocentbystander.com.au

Ipsos

LORNE
48 Mountjoy Parade
03 5289 1883

MODERN GREEK   **15/20**

A ray of Mediterranean sunshine on Victoria's Surf Coast

"Ah! Welcome back!" Charismatic host Dominic Talimanidis, son of legendary restaurateurs Pam and Kosta Talimanidis, knows most people who step into this relaxed, whitewashed taverna fronting Lorne's main strip. But even first-timers soon feel like regulars when Talimanidis stops by each table, landing plates and jokes with equal skill. It's the combination of bonhomie and clear-flavoured, contemporary Greek remixes that keep people coming back. The kitchen nudges hummus beyond humdrum with a gentle chilli warmth and a spangle of za'atar, gives crisp, flour-dusted calamari a lift with fennel seeds, dill sprigs and a schmear of taramasalata, and brightens stonkingly rich slow-cooked lamb shoulder, equal parts crusted and fall-apart, with lemon salt and almond skordalia. If you can't muster the appetite for a wedge of squishy, custardy galaktoboureko at the finish, at least try an icy ouzo sorbet scattered with mint leaves. The anise-flavoured liquor has been used as a digestive since the 14th century.

The bountiful $55 chef's selection covers all the menu's best dishes

Open	L D Thu–Mon (L D Daily in summer)
Price	$$
Cards	MC V eftpos
Chefs	Ben Macdonald, Pam Talimanidis
Features	Licensed, outdoor seating
Website	ipsosrestaurant.com.au

Jones Winery Restaurant

RUTHERGLEN
61 Jones Road
02 6032 8496

FRENCH   **14/20**

Rustic dining on local produce framed in French technique

Crunch through the gravel, past the roses and the resident bulldogs and into a rustic old shed, where an open fire, velvet armchairs, a wine bar and cosy restaurant await. Light filters in on antique dinner settings and corrugated iron walls, while clusters of cows mooch in the fields outside. The European-leaning menu is a neat showcase of hyper-local produce where possible, with a suggested Jones' wine match for each dish. A light, bright entree of blue swimmer crab is given luxurious texture thanks to silky corn puree and crisp radish, and a generous hunk of buffalo mozzarella is both sticky and sweet with baby beetroots and balsamic-drenched radicchio. Main courses are a delicious road trip, from Dijon-glazed Howlong beef to paperbark-roasted Riverina duck and slow-cooked Corowa lamb leg, grass-green in its parsley-crumb coat, a flaky, golden mini pie filled with all the offcuts. Finish with bittersweet chocolate tart on a sweetened celeriac puree with jammy blackberries.

Pre-order a picnic hamper for a delicious road trip addition

Open	L Thu–Sun
Price	$$
Cards	MC V eftpos
Chef	Briony Bradford
Features	Bar, licensed, outdoor seating, wheelchair access
Website	joneswinery.com.au

Lake House

DAYLESFORD
4 King Street
03 5348 3329

CONTEMPORARY **17/20**

Old-school charm and service teamed with new-school culinary greatness

You'd think that after 35 years in the biz, Alla Wolf-Tasker would be ready to take it easy. Apparently not: she's bought a farm. Having championed local farmers for decades, Lake House is going to grow its own produce, strengthening even further the paddock-to-plate ethos that has long kept this in the upper branches of the regional dining tree. "Mushroom season has arrived," proclaims the menu. "Many of us go out for an early morning forage in the forest's stillness." And here are the pungent pine mushrooms, sauteed and folded through pasta, topped with chestnut shavings and kale shards. A main course of pork comes as fat slices of loin grilled over coal, flanked by croquettes dripping with umeboshi puree and a soulful hotpot of baby kohlrabi, more mushrooms and buckwheat. Desserts like deep-ruby orchard quinces with local honey parfait manage to be, like this entire place, perfectly country-style yet comfortably at the culinary cutting edge.

Don't think about dining without doing an appetite-building walk around the beautiful lake first

Open	L D Daily
Price	$$$
Cards	AE DC MC V eftpos
Chef	Alla Wolf-Tasker, Brendan Walsh
Features	Bar, licensed, outdoor seating, private dining
Website	lakehouse.com.au

Laura

MERRICKS
3649 Frankston-Flinders Road
03 5989 9011

CONTEMPORARY **17/20**

Sea, sculptures and the peninsula produce story told by a gun chef

Sydney star Phil Wood has finally arrived on the Mornington Peninsula. Sure, he's been cooking at the $40 million sculpture park since November 2017, but it's in this calm terrarium of taupes and creams overlooking the Jaume Plensa statue where he's truly showing some flex. That looks like four- to-six courses celebrating the peninsula's vineyards, dairies, land beasts and fish. A fish pie is a golden pastry halo lassooing firm, crisped dogfish washed in nori-flecked almond sabayon. It's innovative cooking that doesn't shock, but soothes. Your main is a mini Sunday roast of glassy skinned, smoked duck breast, liver-enriched gravy and boudin blanc. Pavlova meets thanksgiving in a dessert of crisp meringue with gingery chopped chestnuts and spiced pumpkin creme diplomat. Add restaurant manager Ainslie Lubbock's drink matches encompassing Moriki Shuzo sake and white Burgundies for some real firepower.

Do lunch to work in a tour of the multi-million sculpture collection

Open	L Thu–Sun; D Thu–Sat
Price	$$$
Cards	AE MC V eftpos
Chef	Phil Wood
Features	Bar, licensed, private dining, wheelchair access
Website	ptleoestate.com.au/laura

Locale at De Bortoli

DIXONS CREEK
58 Pinnacle Lane
03 5965 2271

ITALIAN   **14/20**

Spacious, family-friendly trattoria for authentic Italian

It feels a bit like Sunday lunch at Nonna's – if she's an excellent cook living in an ivy-clad, redbrick villa among sloping vineyards and a colourful jumble of petunias, geraniums and roses. Septuagenarians happily mingle with toddlers at relaxed birthday celebrations, the genial hubbub kept at ear-friendly levels by partial carpeting and reasonably spaced tables. A flavoursome duck terrine is studded with plenty of pistachios, while house-made pasta is a standout. Check the pumpkin and taleggio ravioli, scattered with sage and given a spicy kick with 'nduja sausage. A generous round of rolled pork belly sits on a lentil, broad bean and pea salad. Use a piece of house-made focaccia to make the most of the leftover juices. Finish with a golden dome of glazed nougat semifreddo and dabs of rhubarb gel or pop downstairs to the tasting room for a cheese platter.

Check out the $90 wine and wildlife experience: Healesville Sanctuary, lunch at Locale and chocolate tasting

Open	L Thu–Mon; D Sat
Price	$$
Cards	AE DC MC V eftpos
Chef	Adam Mead
Features	Licensed, outdoor seating, private dining, wheelchair access
Website	debortoli.com.au/we-love-food/locale-restaurant

Macedon Wine Room

MACEDON
652 Black Forest Drive
03 5426 3030

MEDITERRANEAN   **14/20**

Fine wine and outstanding views make a jaunt very tempting

The owners who took over last November know when to leave well enough alone, and when to improve. It is essentially a showcase for the area's wines, and the range keeps growing. One benefit is that wine list prices are bottle shop prices. Enjoy a glass of local riesling, or some Champagne – the extensive wine list shows pride in its locality, but is not parochial. The menu is straightforward, with Italian influences in a selection of pizza and pasta dishes. Given the distance from the sea, it's surprising to find the fish and seafood dishes are a strength. The red pepper and white anchovy crostini topped with fried capers are hearty enough to share. Pan-cooked Cone Bay barramundi may be served on soft pillows of potato puree, freshened with salsa verde. There's a specials list, too, with some enterprising dishes such as duck breast served with plums, and a split-and-green pea puree, or a deconstructed Eton mess for dessert.

The Wine Room neighbours a resort – an overnight stopover may just be on the cards

Open	L Wed–Sun; D Wed–Sat
Price	$$
Cards	AE MC V eftpos
Chef	Daniel Kennedy
Features	Licensed, outdoor seating, wheelchair access
Website	macedonwineroom.com.au

Masons of Bendigo

BENDIGO
25 Queen Street
03 5443 3877

CONTEMPORARY   **15.5/20**

The go-to place for exploring Bendigo food and drink

Masons is deceptively casual, with paper placemats that turn over to reveal the menu of smaller and larger dishes to share. Cutlery and napkins are tucked into a cylinder embedded in the tables. Waitstaff are a class act, the cooking displays plenty of skill and imagination, and there's an incredible commitment to regional produce across the board. Smoked chicken salad with shredded kohlrabi, macadamias, fresh herbs and a hint of chilli is an exciting, flavour-packed textural construction. A special of butterflied and crumbed garfish is topped with fine-diced octopus and fried leeks, with a circle of charred cucumber sauce. Larger dishes might include buttermilk gnocchi with tiny cauliflower florets and crisp-fried kale, or lamb three-ways (shoulder, breast and loin) with black olive caramel – such a pleasure to eat that there's a dilemma. To share or not? Desserts are more limited in choice, but there is elegance in a blood orange sorbet.

Choose one of the two private dining rooms (smaller and larger) for a special occasion lunch or dinner

Open	L D Tue–Sat
Price	$$
Cards	AE MC V eftpos
Chefs	Nick and Sonia Anthony
Features	Licensed, private dining, wheelchair access
Website	masonsofbendigo.com.au

Mercato @ Daylesford

DAYLESFORD
32 Raglan Street
03 5348 4488

CONTEMPORARY   **14.5/20**

Elegant and accomplished fine dining stalwart

Mercato's classic country verandah shades a genteel, white table-clothed dining room warmed by wooden tones, cozy fires and confident and friendly staff. Lingering is the go here: let yourself be wooed by a kitchen that makes elegant use of the wonderful produce Victoria has to offer. Take your time over a dense yet juicy ballotine of quail set handsomely among a tangle of mushrooms, tempered with the sour tang of red sorrel, or an unashamedly fat chunk of pork belly, teased with star anise – crisp on top yet helplessly yielding beneath. A piece of Kyneton black Angus eye fillet resting in creamy polenta arrives perfectly medium-rare as does Tuki lamb, accompanied by a vivid green herb and parmesan puree. Both work well with bitter roasted brussels sprouts. Desserts are definitely on the agenda, especially the house-made sorbets, which may include a cucumber and sake number – as refreshing as a cool shower on a hot day.

Check out the tapas menu – Thursday to Sunday afternoons

Open	L Thu–Sun; D Thu–Tue
Price	$$$
Cards	AE MC V eftpos
Chef	Steven Orain
Features	Licensed, outdoor seating, private dining, wheelchair access
Website	mercatorestaurant.com.au

Merne at Lighthouse

DRYSDALE
650 Andersons Road
03 5251 5541

CONTEMPORARY   **14/20**

Relaxed dining overlooking the olive groves

Tucked away among the trees, fairy lights twinkling, Merne exudes warmth even on the wintriest of nights. It continues inside, with a welcome as comforting as the open fire, given a whack of wow by sweeping floor-to-ceiling views of the olive groves, the lighthouse and if you really squint, the ocean over yonder. Generosity flows from the kitchen, too. The two- or four-course sharing menu seems like at least six. Graze on olives grown within pip-spitting distance, plump dashi-grilled oysters, stracciatella swirled with smoky pepitas and burnt butter, and silky slivers of kingfish – just for starters. Then there's slippery soft sous vide trout, hunks of tender pork accompanied by bold vegetable combinations (red cabbage, pomegranate, goat's curd and puffed black rice) that reveal a strong respect for the side dish. Wines are Australian focused, but their own Oakdene label is no slouch, with their sauv blanc 'Jessie' a gem in her own right - much like the restaurant in which she's served.

Servings are generous: come hungry or wear something loose

Open	L Thu–Mon; D Fri–Sat
Price	$$
Cards	AE DC MC V eftpos
Chef	Joshua Smith
Features	Bar, licensed, outdoor seating, wheelchair access
Website	merne.com.au

Midnight Starling

KYNETON
60 Piper Street
03 5422 3884

FRENCH   **15.5/20**

A lively bistro with cave a manger spirit and fine dining flair

Word's out, there's a French revolution stirring in historic Piper Street and the locals are all over it. The owner/chef's bio reads Jacques Reymond, Pierre Gagnaire and Michel Rostang. But it's not about fuss and foams at this friendly diner with close-set tables, bentwood chairs and Hogarth's *Beer Street and Gin Lane* etched across the wall. Expect beautiful ingredients, bistro classics crafted with care and switched-on service. Nothing cliched. Utterly charming. Sweet heirloom tomatoes plucked from the kitchen garden pepped up with pickles play well with flinty petit chablis. Duck a l'orange (pink breast, tender braised leg, toffee-like skin) is napped in glossy signature sauce. Rare roast hanger steak, all charry-crusted, juicy, meaty and buttery is doused in a deep, dark red-wine reduction. The six-course degustation might roll with mackerel tartare, pickled ox tongue, garfish a la meuniere, venison in griottine jus, foot-ripe epoisses and creme caramel. Or you could just settle in for a four-course Sunday lunch. Lucky Kyneton.

Go with a gang for the tasting menu and bags the bluestone cellar

Open	L Sun; D Wed–Sat
Price	$$
Cards	MC V eftpos
Chef	Steve Rogers
Features	Bar, licensed, outdoor seating, private dining
Website	midnightstarling.com.au

VICTORIA ⟶ REGIONAL

Miss Amelie

WODONGA
Station Building, 46 Elgin Boulevard
02 6056 4170

EUROPEAN   **14/20**

**Thoroughly modern dining in
historic surrounds**

Encounter Miss Amelie lounging in an
old railway building in Wodonga. Slip
through the neon glow of the Little
Miss cocktail bar at the front and into
a slim dining room of muted greys, a
long open kitchen flanking one side.
Eurocentric food meets a super-local
wine list here, where entrees can include
clever dishes like crab with textures
of corn – sweet kernels, popped corn,
fried silk – or mushroom tortellini
in consomme, which manages to be
comforting and lavish at once. Main
course-wise, you might order seafood
linguine, duck breast with beetroot,
blueberry and boudin noir (alliterative!)
or sticky, tender lamb scotch, served
with yoghurt to cut the richness (the
accompanying ferociously salty miso
eggplant really jarrs, sadly). Similarly,
a pumpkin 'pie' (it's more tart than pie,
truthfully) with a phenomenal cheddar
custard may stumble over undercooked
pumpkin. Desserts right the ship
though, with a billowy lemon souffle
going citrus-wild with lemon curd
and lemon cheesecake ice-cream.

**Keep an eye on the socials for
twice-monthly degustations**

Open	L Fri; D Tue–Sat
Price	$$
Cards	MC V eftpos
Chef	David Kapay
Features	Bar, licensed, private dining, wheelchair access
Website	missamelie.com.au

Montalto

RED HILL SOUTH
33 Shoreham Road
03 5989 8412

MODERN AUSTRALIAN   **15/20**

**Share-friendly wood-fired cooking
in a picture-perfect setting**

It's a Peninsula postcard: children
frolicking among sculptures, parents
lolling on the wraparound deck,
vine-lined hills rolling. The winery
setting is unchanged but the glass
box of a restaurant has had a reno,
whipped off the tablecloths, and gone
back to the elements, with the kitchen
now centred on an asado grill. A
fall-apart hunk of 'overnight pumpkin'
is coaxed over the coals and further
umamified with nutty fermented
wheat and a dusting of dehydrated
nori. Saltbush scattered lamb
shoulder is practically ready-shredded,
accompanied by a pair of dense potato
pikelets. A better bet: smoke-licked
kipflers, pickled onions and gravy.
Dishes are designed to share and you'll
likely need sides, or opt for a five- or
six-course menu, which might include
battered Jerusalem artichoke that's like
an impostor fish and chips. Kitchen
garden pickings and pickles feature
through the menu to dessert – whipped
chocolate with gingerbread crumb
and ginger ice-cream brings some
old-fashioned ginger beer bite.

**Enjoy pizza under market umbrellas
in the kitchen garden piazza**

Open	L Fri–Tue; D Fri–Sat
Price	$$$
Cards	AE MC V eftpos
Chef	Gerard Phelan
Features	Licensed, outdoor seating, private dining, wheelchair access
Website	montalto.com.au

Mr + Co Wine Bar

MILDURA
138B Eighth Street
03 5021 2100

CONTEMPORARY   **14/20**

A new wine bar with a wildly international menu

Behind the huge heavy hot pink door lies Mildura's swankiest room, all kitted out in shiny black surfaces and blingy chandeliers. This wine bar takes its role as arbiter of all things cool and modern very seriously, but not so much that it doesn't also serve up a whole lot of fun. This is a wine bar first and foremost, with an impressive array of interesting local and international bottles. But it's also an A+ cocktail bar, with a tonne of small-batch spirits on hand and staff who know how to use them. The food is head-spinningly peripatetic – you can jump from China to Mexico to France in three small bites – but there's a lot of joy in this cooking. Sticky Korean chicken wings come with sliced pickle and Kewpie mayo, while a snapper fillet gets the full Vietnamese treatment, with coriander, mint, lime and basil. Or perhaps you'd just like to go for the chateaubriand for two? You won't be bored, that's for sure.

On Monday to Thursday, the kitchen offers a cracker deal: a $30 per person four-course tasting menu

Neilsons Kitchen

TRARALGON
13 Seymour Street
03 5175 0100

CONTEMPORARY   **14.5/20**

A welcome oasis from the main drag of Traralgon

This little restaurant delivers big. Executive chef Lewis Prince and maitre'd Rebecca Prince offer up an experience that is as welcoming and laid back as their raspberry gin fizz. A box of juicy, buttermilk fried chicken tenderloins (served 'OG', 'spicy', or 'Hot AF') holds its own alongside a generous house-made charcuterie board (duck liver pâté chicken and pork terrine, pickled cauliflower and tomato relish). The slow-roasted lamb shoulder is brightened with a sweet pea puree and a surprisingly unpretentious mint jelly foam. An airy, nougaty Snickers soufflé hides a dense vein of chocolate at the bottom of the ramekin and comes with a well-salted quenelle of peanut ice-cream. The modern fitout of competing tile patterns and dark wood floors and metal fireplace can get loud when the place fills up (and it does), but the local ingredients, the locavore love, and the practically telepathic staff keeps everything luscious AF.

Do a midday driveby for the two- and three-course lunch deals

Open	L Fri–Sat; D Mon–Sat
Price	$$
Cards	AE MC V eftpos
Chef	Jack Attill
Features	Bar, licensed, outdoor seating, private dining

Open	B L Tue–Sat; D Thu–Sat
Price	$$
Cards	AE MC V eftpos
Chef	Lewis Prince, Simone Gaffney
Features	Licensed, outdoor seating, private dining, wheelchair access
Website	neilsons.com.au

Oakridge

COLDSTREAM
864 Maroondah Highway
03 9738 9900

CONTEMPORARY   **15.5/20**

Innovative, delicious food in a beautiful winery setting

Chef Matt Stone's sustainability pedigree is well-known – zero waste, low food miles and organic. So it seems incongruous, at first, that he's heading up a slick winery restaurant, all gleaming glass and polished concrete, packed with snap-happy tourists and a rowdy hens' lunch. Any misgivings, however, vanish with the first bite of sourdough, made daily by Stone's partner Jo Barrett (ex Tivoli Road Bakery) from house-milled organic grain. The compact menu reflects their shared food philosophy. Expect locally farmed trout, smoked and paired with a caraway-strewn mini-croissant, and heirloom vegetables from the organic kitchen garden, such as pumpkin scattered with eucalyptus leaves, crisp and salty. Slow-cooked kangaroo shoulder is crowned with a tangy nahm jim-dressed salad and sweet plum wedges, while potato offcuts are mashed, dehydrated and shaped into sweetened wafers for a creative take on tiramisu. This is innovative, interesting food, in an innovative, interesting setting.

Between courses, stroll around the organic vegetable garden

Open	L Thu–Mon
Price	$$
Cards	AE MC V eftpos
Chefs	Matt Stone, Jo Barrett
Features	Bar, licensed, outdoor seating, private dining, wheelchair access
Website	oakridgewines.com.au

Paringa Estate

RED HILL SOUTH
44 Paringa Road
03 5989 2669

CONTEMPORARY   **15/20**

A relaxed setting of the vines that made the wine

There are larger and more glamorous vineyard restaurants, but Paringa Estate has the same charms – the view over vineyard slopes, a smart fixed-price menu (two, three, or more courses), and some excellent wines. It's cosy and welcoming, with the cellar door near the entrance, a good opportunity to taste before sitting at table. The vegetable garden is an indication of how much Adam Beckett's menu is attuned to the seasons: an early autumn dish of mushrooms with creamy goat's cheese, say, topped with fine silky slices of steamed eggplant. The pleasure of Sher wagyu is heightened further by soy and Sichuan pepper, and the crunch of grains. Elegant whiting fillets are jazzed up with capers, herbs and a garlic puree. Dishes come with recommended Paringa Estate wines, of course, but the list is broad enough that you can take your own vinous journey. The dessert selection play with flavours that go beyond the merely sweet, such as a treacle cake with figs in sour caramel served with milk ice-cream and candied lemon.

There's a five- or eight-course tasting menu in the evening

Open	L Wed–Sun; D Fri–Sat (summer L Daily; D Thu–Sat)
Price	$$
Cards	AE MC V eftpos
Chef	Adam Beckett
Features	Licensed, wheelchair access
Website	paringaestate.com.au

Petit Tracteur

MAIN RIDGE
1208 Mornington-Flinders Road
03 5989 2510

FRENCH   **14.5/20**

**Relaxed brasserie dining in a
picture-perfect pastoral setting**

It's hard to stay mad at the world as
you walk past overflowing vegetable
beds towards the weathered timber
farmhouse in the green Peninsula
hinterland. Inside, the whitewashed
weatherboard dining room and
palm-bedecked atrium are bright, airy
and relaxed. With Charles Aznavour
crooning over the speakers, textured
linen on tables and the tricolour flag
nailed to the wall, it's no surprise to
see French bistro greatest hits on the
carte, beginning with hand-cut steak
tartare and ending with tarte Tatin.
About that tarte: it's a perfect specimen,
all caramel-covered Pink Lady wedges
laid over crisp buttery pastry. And
there's plenty to enjoy in between, from
piquant white balsamic marinated
prawns to swordfish fillets three fingers
thick, zipped up with fennel shavings
and orange puree. Service is engaging
and the expansive, largely Franco-
Aussie wine list showcases several
vintages from neighbouring parent
winery Ten Minutes By Tractor. Time
seems to move more slowly here, so
loosen that belt a notch and enjoy.

**Make like a Frenchman and play
a game of petanque outside
between courses**

Open	B Sat–Sun; L Wed–Mon; D Thu–Sun
Price	$$
Cards	AE DC MC V eftpos
Chef	Charlie Yates
Features	Bar, licensed, outdoor seating, wheelchair access, BYO
Website	petittracteur.com.au

Pt. Leo Restaurant

MERRICKS
3649 Frankston-Flinders Road
03 5989 9011

CONTEMPORARY   **15/20**

**Incredible art meets casual dining with
impressive smarts**

Thank the Gandel family for snagging
ex-Rockpool chef Phil Wood for their
giant art project in Merricks. He, along
with floor boss Ainslie Lubbock and
her husband, chef Joel Alderson, are
the reason you now have the option
of a low-key Peninsula lunch that's
anything but. Here, snacking involves
tiny wallaby pies capped with bread and
butter pickles, and polenta croquettes,
totally shrouded by local caprinella
goat's cheese. An amazingly rich carrot
souffle is all butter, fluff and essence of
shellfish from luminous scampi roe. It's
tight, bright cooking gently sprinkled
with Australiana, served in a curving,
sandy-toned room with uninterrupted
eyefuls of incredible sculptures and sea.
Laura next door is the fancier sibling.
Chefs wear headsets to stay on top of
the orders of pan-roasted, buttered
flathead and nicely charred steaks with
chimichurri. Hard surfaces may make
your ears squint. But you're still eating
with Cutipol cutlery, drinking Jamsheed
roussanne or Pt. Leo's own wines from
Riedel glasses and being served by staff
who handle tourists with class.

There's a wine bar and cellar door

Open	L Daily; D Thu–Sat
Price	$$
Cards	AE MC V eftpos
Chef	Phil Wood, Joel Alderson
Features	Bar, licensed, wheelchair access
Website	ptleoestate.com.au

Port Phillip Estate

RED HILL SOUTH
263 Red Hill Road
03 5989 4444

CONTEMPORARY   **14.5/20**

Modern glamour matched with Mornington vineyard views

Beyond the imposing fortress-like approach, the interior is light, bright and spacious, with the cellar door to one side, and restaurant to the other. Big picture windows show vineyard slopes and trees in all their rural loveliness. The outdoor terrace provides an even grander perspective. Provenance is important here. Rannoch Farm quail is served on a date puree with hazelnuts and couscous, topped with shredded radicchio for colour and texture contrast. A rectangle of crisp-skinned Humpty Doo barramundi comes with a salad of grilled cos lettuce, croutons, leaves and petals, and shaved bottarga. Michel Cluizel chocolate is presented as an encased mousse with dried orange slices and an orange sorbet. The wine list features Port Phillip and Kooyong Estate in particular, and a fair number of other locals and French and Italian high-flyers. This is a popular place for groups, too, with surprisingly friendly acoustics.

Restaurant fully booked? The cellar door has its own small menu

Provenance

BEECHWORTH
86 Ford Street
03 5728 1786

CONTEMPORARY   **17/20**

Japan meets the Victorian bush in heritage surrounds

Cafe de Tokyo butter might be the best thing to happen in French-Japanese fusion since foie gras found its way onto sushi. Glistening over onglet, braised daikon and hazelnuts, it's a thundering force of shio kombu, shiitake and miso that'll have you wondering why soy sauce isn't offered with steak frites. Japanese ingredients enhance most of owner-chef Michael Ryan's dishes at this sophisticated restaurant in a cosy old bank. Kangaroo, smoked and seared, is flavoured with mullet roe and a fish sauce of wonderful clarity and depth. Duck is brined and roasted on the bone for superb texture and taste (there's no sous-vide sleight-of-hand here) and plated with a tart punch of umeboshi puree mellowed by brown rice congee. With Japanese cheesecake and yuzu mousse for dessert, Fleet Foxes on the playlist and cultivated service, Provenance is a perfect destination to recalibrate. There's even charming accommodation attached for all your bed and breakfast needs.

Whisky lovers should allow for extra time to explore the Japanese single malt collection

Open	L Wed–Sun; D Fri–Sat
Price	$$$
Cards	AE MC V eftpos
Chef	Stuart Deller
Features	Licensed, outdoor seating, wheelchair access, private dining
Website	portphillipestate.com.au

Open	L Sun; D Wed–Sat
Price	$$
Cards	AE MC V eftpos
Chef	Michael Ryan
Features	Licensed, private dining
Website	theprovenance.com.au

R.H.

RARE HARE

The Public Inn

CASTLEMAINE
26a Templeton Street
0429 820 278

CONTEMPORARY   **15/20**

Food with a feel-good flavour

Kyneton might be the current darling in these parts, but Castlemaine's Public Inn is taking the higher moral ground. New owners have converted the town's favourite fine diner into a not-for-profit outfit, with proceeds supporting community education and literacy programs. Not that you'd necessarily know it – the pale-timbered dining room with signature light fittings is unchanged and chef Ben Armstrong still offers a winning formula. Hearty servings of deceptively simple dishes make best use of superb regional produce, gussied up through subtle technique and beautiful plating. Heirloom tomatoes are heightened by basil leaves and a gentle chipotle zing, or there's highly marbled wagyu skirt steak with pickles and smoked mayo. Larger plates might include a creamy beetroot risotto or a solid wedge of pressed pork shoulder with apple, fennel and a veritable forest of multi-hued baby carrots. And a white chocolate and nutmeg mousse with vanilla custard, strawberry and ginger alone justifies a trip up the Calder.

Take a seat in the old re-PUBLIC cafe space for a more casual ambience

Open	B L Daily; D Fri–Sat
Price	$$
Cards	AE MC V eftpos
Chef	Ben Armstrong
Features	Bar, licensed, private dining, wheelchair access
Website	publicinn.org

Rare Hare

MERRICKS NORTH
166 Balnarring Road
03 5931 2501

CONTEMPORARY   **14.5/20**

The cheeky younger sibling restaurant to fine diner Doot Doot Doot

What a rollicking good time there is to be had here. With an ash-coated pizza oven a hulking presence in the dining room, you walk in expecting the margheritas to be flying. There's not one pizza in sight. Instead the open kitchen sends out vibrant sharing plates, many finished in the flames, all with a deftness that exceeds the "casual" dining tag of this second restaurant belonging to the Jackalope Hotel. Things like strips of raw kingfish curled into an edamame cream doused in tarragon oil, or a beef brisket brick, thatched with the sweetest fried carrot rounds, in a burnt onion jus. Perhaps the most magnificent thing to leave the pizza oven is a cookie, oozing with melted chocolate chips, crowned with malt ice-cream. It's a party in a cast-iron pan. Just as it is every weekend with people crammed onto the sleek communal tables, drinking wine from the vines they can see outside, served by staff who love being part of regional Australia's funkiest hotel.

Tastings of the estate's Willow Creek wines are held in the barrel room adjacent to the restaurant

Open	L Daily; D Fri–Sat
Price	$$
Cards	AE MC V eftpos
Chef	Guy Stanaway, Andrew Bryant
Features	Licensed, outdoor seating, wheelchair access
Website	rarehare.com.au

Sardine Eatery and Bar

PAYNESVILLE
Shop 3, 69A Esplanade,
03 5156 7135

SEAFOOD　　　　　　　　　　**15/20**

A fresh, fish-focused bistro with water views

Paynesville by name, but not by nature. Superyachts trawl the waters alongside super-pelicans, made enormous by the same thing that makes chef Mark Brigg's newish seafood diner so good. Most things on the plate here have best plundered from just outside – black bream, Lakes Entrance sardines, surf clams – tweaked and served in a sleek room of buffed grays, blond woods and succulents. Warm bread comes with seaweed-flecked butter studded in succulents. Dunk crisp whitebait dusted with orange salt in jalapeno aioli. A bubbly wonton crisp is loaded with a bright dice of ponzu-dressed alfonsino. From land, a juicy salt-and-pepper quail is finished with crisped up saltbush. Chasing with warm, tender octopus and salty pork belly, bright with capers, dill and gherkin, and sardines, biting their tails with a buttery, funk-neutralising herbaceous filling. Sardine brings it for all locals. Come for Gippsland charcuterie and cheese, oxtail ragu, weekend breakfast and get your water hit just from staring at the lake.

A $75 tasting menu is ludicrously large

Open	B Sun; L Tue–Sun; D Tue–Sat
Price	$$
Cards	AE MC V eftpos
Chef	Mark Briggs
Features	Bar, licensed, outdoor seating, wheelchair accessible
Website	sardineeaterybar.com

Sault

DAYLESFORD
2349 Ballan-Daylesford Road
03 5348 6555

CONTEMPORARY　　　　　　**14.5/20**

Fixed-price seasonal menus and great views to relax by in a charming stone cottage

The stone and timber building that houses the restaurant is surrounded by lavender fields and a vegetable garden, and overlooks a dam. It's such a dreamy combination that the food might be forgiven for playing second fiddle. On the contrary. The fixed price menus (three-, five- or seven-courses) are of such quality that the view takes second place. Maybe you'll order a spicy spanner crab salad to start, with avocado and mango, scattered with extra tiny crab croquettes. Or quail breast, topped with fine slices of young turnip and salted egg yolk. The menu is cleverly constructed and though plates may sound crowded, results are crowd-pleasing. Among main courses, there's a pithivier of mushrooms, artichokes and taleggio with a dark mushroom ketchup, or lamb two-ways (roast loin, slow-cooked shoulder) with asparagus, sheep's milk yoghurt and sumac. Add a great drinks list and skilled waiters, and finish with a chocolate delice with variations of raspberry (sorbet, berries, macaron).

Sault does weddings, too – propose and get married in the space of a day

Open	L Fri–Sun; D Wed–Sun
Price	$$
Cards	AE MC V eftpos
Chef	Hugh Maxwell
Features	Licensed, outdoor seating, wheelchair access
Website	sault.com.au

Source Dining

KYNETON
72 Piper Street
03 5422 2039

CONTEMPORARY **15/20**

Refined locavore-leaning diner

It's so easy to settle in here. Thoughtful widely spaced tables and modern Scandinavian furniture lifted with a high colour canvas of a party scene by artist Allan Wolf-Tasker bring pared-back luxe to the grand 19th century bluestone and brick interiors. Much of what's on the menu is orchard-fresh, home-grown, harvested from the kitchen garden or farmed locally and as carefully curated as the cellar. Your entree might be subtly smoked coffee-crusted kangaroo layered in warrigal greens, macadamia cream and plum. Roast Rockwood Cottage lamb rump – rich and hearty – rests on a pave of pulled shoulder, braised fennel and cabbage, lentils and romesco sauce. Silvanberries sharpen a pink, juicy, sticky skinned duck breast set on sauteed Asian greens with a silky onion soubise and duck jus. Olive oil sponge in a botanical flourish of figs, fennel pollen, candied rose petals, Amaro Montenegro syrup and strawberry gum ice-cream is the dessert equivalent of a fancy Sunday hat, only prettier and a little less pious.

Weekend dining? Go for the five-course degustation paired with fine regional wines

Open	L Thu–Sun; D Thu–Sat
Price	$$$
Cards	AE MC V eftpos
Chef	Tim Foster
Features	Bar, licensed, outdoor seating
Website	sourcedining.com.au

Stefano's Cantina

MILDURA
Cellars of the Grand Hotel, Langtree Avenue
03 5022 0881

ITALIAN **15.5/20**

One of regional Australia's original greats still shines

To get to Stefano's, you have to walk through two other restaurants and down an out-of-the-way flight of stairs. There's not a lot in this approach to prepare you for the legendary cosy basement room that houses Stefano's in the grand old hotel's original cellars. Brick-lined, dimly lit and fitted out in mirrors etched with scenes of Australiana, it feels like a portal to another world, one where you're whisked away by a capable staff and taken care of for a few magical hours. The nightly five-course degustation might begin with a crisp-skinned quail served simply with rocket, lemon and olive oil, its flesh perfectly rosy. A sformatino is likely to follow, a warm eggy cheesy personal souffle, spiked with stinging nettle or dandelion. Pasta and meat courses come next, and all the while the charming Italian sommelier flits over, pouring you tastes of this and that, beaming proudly when she's found just the right wine. You may never want to leave.

You won't want to go far after this feeding – luckily the hotel is quite a pleasant place to spend the night

Open	D Tue–Sat
Price	$$$
Cards	DC MC V eftpos
Chef	John Acera, Ben Trealor
Features	Licensed, private dining
Website	stefano.com.au

TarraWarra Estate

YARRA GLEN
311 Healesville–Yarra Glen Road
03 5957 3510

CONTEMPORARY **15/20**

Culture and cultivation collide

It's a bit cheeky of the Besen family. Over many years they have, by increments, created Yarra Valley World: a one-stop-shop for rolling hills, vine acreage, wine sales and, at the heart of it all, a restaurant worthy of a long drive alone. In a patina-rich room of polished concrete and rough-hewn stone, a team of affable staff glide around to the sound of porch jazz, serving up dishes that are strong parts elegance, creativity and flavour. The latter comes by dint of access to the onsite garden (not much needs doing to a salad of tomatoes with mint and macadamia pesto) driven by smarts in the kitchen. Diners are walloped by the complex aroma of tender, deeply charred octopus with yabby oil and fennel sauce. Vegetarians may love the salt-baked pumpkin disc crowned with a textural flurry of puffed grains, although one portion may not suffice. Pink slices of wagyu striploin splayed on a bed of baba ganoush is a little more generous.

At time of press, Mark Ebbels (Bacchanalia, The Fat Duck, UK) had stepped in as head chef

Terrace Restaurant

WAHGUNYAH
315 All Saints Road
02 6035 2222

CONTEMPORARY **15/20**

Laidback and lavish dining amid leafy surrounds

After you've oohed and aahed at the grand and leafy surrounds of All Saints Estate, merge into the relaxed, enclosed, marquee-style Terrace. Get snug with a window seat on eye level with the lawn, watch birds skitter through the leaves, then turn your attention to the compact, seasonal menu. Start with a glass of the phenomenal Excentrique sparkling and a hunk of warm bread with smoked butter, then on to bright, generous dishes like stracciatella with charred radicchio, sweet baby beetroot and candied walnuts. Or soft jamon with smoked ricotta and salt-baked celeriac – flavours balanced pitch-perfectly, with the hand remaining firmly on the clutch. John Dory comes with sweet little Cloudy Bay clams, Archie's Creek veal saltimbocca gets an added twang from capers and beurre noisette, while tempura brussels sprouts go Elvis under a hail of crisp bacon. A muscat-poached quince tarte Tatin arrives in a plume of steam, adding to the dream-like haze of dining here.

New on-site accommodation is now available

Open	L Tue–Sun (Daily in Jan)
Price	$$
Cards	AE MC V eftpos
Chef	Mark Ebbels
Features	Bar, licensed, private dining, wheelchair access
Website	tarrawarra.com.au

Open	L Wed–Sun; D Sat
Price	$$$
Cards	AE MC V eftpos
Chef	Simon Arkless
Features	Bar, licensed, outdoor seating, private dining, wheelchair access
Website	allsaintswine.com.au/terrace-restaurant

Tinamba Hotel

TINAMBA
4–6 Tinamba–Seaton Road
03 5145 1484

CONTEMPORARY   **14/20**

A country hotel boasting local ingredients for local (and not-so-local) fans

This cosy pub might sit quietly on the edge of a flat paddock, just across the road from the general store, but inside is the dining room that has kept this place on the culinary map for 10 years. Their recipe? The kitchen sources meat, dairy and produce from all over Gippsland. The Maffra Cheese Company (10 minutes up the road) stars here, figuring in the just-rich-enough-that-you'll-have-room-for-a-main twice-baked blue cheese soufflé, and in their pricey but luxurious take on the pub standard chicken parmigiana. The friendly staff are in on it, too, steering patrons from the distant Yarra Valley and toward the vineyards within an hour's drive. Most of the salad greens come from the garden out back – now with a full-time gardener. Some plates arrive with more strewn petals than one might expect at a pub at the intersection of two country roads, but when the 14-hour braised ox cheek comes with the onion rings everything feels just right.

Wednesday night is for locals, with a pub special that's worth the drive

Tulip

GEELONG WEST
Shop 9, 111 Pakington Street
03 5229 6953

CONTEMPORARY   **15/20**

Airy bistro dining with smarts and heart

Cooling to the eye and relaxing to the soul, this is one of those deceptively casual diners – it keeps the atmosphere warm and laidback with a snappy soundtrack, welcoming staff and an airy fitout of white and cane, then busts out knockout dishes like stracciatella with juicy shiitakes and radicchio grilled to caramel sweetness. A warm, buttery white polenta is bruleed, and served with pickled radish and hazelnut. Lamb ribs with a smoky sesame puree melt off the bone while golden roast chicken is served with Jerusalem artichokes and pickled walnuts. A festival of pumpkin (roast pumpkin, pickled, and smoked seeds) is enriched with whipped feta. Mandarin adds a bright note to a treacle-sweet, warm malva pudding, pride of South Africa. Flatware is carthy, underscoring an ethos of local, seasonal and sustainable. Oh, and house-baked bread is billed with an optional gold coin donation, which goes towards produce for meals for the underprivileged. That's food for good, right there.

Have dietaries? They are willing and able to cater

Open	L Wed–Sun; D Wed–Sat
Price	$$
Cards	AE MC V eftpos
Chef	Daniel Keck
Features	Licensed, outdoor seating, private dining, wheelchair access
Website	tinambahotel.com.au

Open	L Wed–Sat; D Tue–Sat
Price	$$
Cards	MC V eftpos
Chef	Graham Jefferies, Matt Dempsey
Features	Bar, licensed, outdoor seating, private dining, wheelchair access
Website	tuliprestaurant.com.au

Underbar

BALLARAT
3 Doveton Street North

CONTEMPORARY　　　　**15/20**

Dinner party-style fine dining in a Ballarat shopfront

Restaurant may be too strong a word since this degustation-only operation serves just 12 souls, two nights a week in a tiny Ballarat shopfront and is booked out a month in advance. But in the hands of ex-Per Se chef Derrick Boath, it's serious business. Don't be late. Dinner starts when all are sat at the long blond table where pots of sesame-fragrant prawn and daikon tartare and silky chicken parfaits await for snacking while you order hyper-local gin and tonics. Boath's toolbox is rigorous, often classic technique with an edge of play. Smoky, buttered porcini mushrooms are topped with gingery chicken stock 'tea'. He does scallops waldorf style, where walnut-oiled shellfish are dressed in celery and nasturtiums with a crisp apple juice moat. Corn is juiced, pureed, crisped and paired with as many kinds of brassica. Lamb mingles with roast peppers with black and white garlic purees. Intense flavours meet an intense dinner party scenario, but one that's worth the risk.

Put sommelier Nicolas Hinze through his paces with the $65 wine match

Wickens at Royal Mail Hotel

DUNKELD
98 Parker Street
03 5577 2241

CONTEMPORARY　　　　**16/20**

Luxurious dining room with kitchen and landscape on show behind glass

If the Royal Mail's rebooted restaurant isn't the handsomest dining room in the country, it's right up there. A stepped path through native gardens leads to a door that glides open to reveal a dramatically dark arrival lounge, where guests slough off cares and coats before taking their seats. Those Walter Knoll chairs are clad in soft black leather, with a UFO flotilla of lights gently illuminating sandstone tables. But it's the kitchen, lit like a stage set, that draws focus. Here, Robin Wickens leads a team crafting restrained dishes on exquisite ceramics. Act one, on a custom plate are cheeky canapes such as a jammie dodger of roquefort, walnuts and acorn, a tiny beetroot tart and an onion bhaji. Five or eight courses follow, drawing on the hotel's gardens for dishes such as grilled flathead in a charred broccoli thicket, or rose-pink duck, and its heart, with Chinese artichoke puree. As a curtain call, ask to see inside the kitchen.

Stay over and book a tour of the 1.2-hectare kitchen gardens or a tasting in the 28,000-bottle wine cellar

Open	D Fri–Sat
Price	$$$
Cards	AE MC V
Chef	Derek Boath
Features	Licensed, private dining
Website	underbar.com.au

Open	L Sat; D Wed–Sat
Price	$$$
Cards	AE MC V eftpos
Chef	Robin Wickens
Features	Bar, licensed, private dining, wheelchair access
Website	royalmail.com.au

The Woodhouse

BENDIGO
101 Williamson Street
03 5443 8671

STEAKHOUSE   **14.5/20**

All the wonders of the wood-fired oven, in a convivial neighbourhood setting

Woodhouse, its large space cleverly broken up into smaller areas, has been a feature of Bendigo for some years. It's best known for its steaks and its wonderful wood-fired grill. Take your pick of Sher or Cohuna wagyu, Cape Grim, or the closer-to-home Inglewood, each with three different cuts, served with hasselback potatoes. That selection would be enough in most restaurants, but Woodhouse also provides excellent pizza, and a range of other dishes cooked in the wood oven, such a corn-fed duck breast with grilled radicchio, peach, and wild fig. The sides are large enough to make good first courses – try cos salad with jamon crisps, pecorino and shavings of mullet roe for an elegant, yet full throttle play on a caesar – or keep it classic and order a charcuterie platter for the table. Everything is consistently impressive – the cooking, the drinks list that emphasises Victorian wines and beer, and waiters who are alert without being fussy.

Go for lunch: great value two- or three-course fixed price

Open	L D Tue–Sat
Price	$$
Cards	AE MC V eftpos
Chef	Paul Pitcher
Features	Licensed, outdoor seating, private dining
Website	thewoodhouse.com.au

Yering Station Wine Bar

YARRA GLEN
38 Melba Highway
03 9730 0100

CONTEMPORARY   **14/20**

A heritage vineyard grafted with modern-day dishes

The view – of river flats and Yarra Ranges – may not have changed since sod was turned here 180 years ago but Yering Station's broad atrium of a space – those spectacular windows, the resident jurassic cactus, modish padded black chairs – has a clear contemporary bent. There are around four elements on each plate, which combine wonderfully when it comes to a cloud of chilled potato with smoky octopus and the crunch of a red 'slaw. But the biscuity squid ink crumb at the base of a round glass, topped with spanner crab and braised fennel could be more at home in one of Yering's desserts. Likewise in one main course where the Jerusalem artichoke cream out-butters the fragility of a fillet of poached hapuka. Yet when equilibrium reigns, such as the duck breast, with its pink middle and crisp edges framed by a crescent of multi-hued beetroot and witlof sweetened with orange blossom, it's clear why Yering Station remains a long lunch favourite.

Diners receive a discount on wine sales at the cellar door

Open	L Daily
Price	$$$
Cards	AE MC V eftpos
Chef	Maxime Croiset
Features	Bar, licensed, private dining, wheelchair access
Website	yering.com

citi®

THERE'S A
BRAND NEW
*WORLD OF
FLAVOUR*

Find your new favourite restaurant
with the Citibank Dining Program.

citibankdining.com.au

Quay, NSW

WILDFLOWER

♔♔

Cullen Wines
Vasse Felix
Wills Domain
Yarri

Western Australia

♔

Amelia Park Restaurant
Balthazar
Billie H
Bread in Common
Garum
The Heritage Wine Bar
Il Lido
Lalla Rookh
Liberte
Long Chim
Lulu La Delizia
Millbrook Winery
Petition Kitchen
Rockpool Bar and Grill
Wildflower

Amelia Park Restaurant

WILYABRUP
3857 Caves Road
08 9755 6747

CONTEMPORARY

15/20

City looks meets country feel

Little more than a contemporary, concrete box, Amelia Park Restaurant bucks a trend or two on the outside and in. Its plush decor, including opulent chandeliers, is more metropolitan than wine paradise but the menu is refined country comfort all the way. Chef Blair Allen is no stranger to what the people of the region want – from those who call it home, to those who envy those who do. One-time chef-owner at Piari & Co, he stepped up with wife Renee to take the reins at Amelia Park and he's pulling the crowds. From the ocean he's kicking goals, with seared Abrolhos scallops against dainty confit chicken wings, and a dish of Fremantle octopus, with fresh pops of pomegranate and cucumber. Local whispers about the Amelia Park lamb shoulder are well founded – slow-roasted, it's a hefty serve even between two. A north Levantine bent is added, served with fregalone sardo, zucchini salad and wood-roasted eggplant. As luscious as it gets in wine country.

Arrive early, take time in the bar to take an aperitif or linger on a coffee after the meal

Balthazar

PERTH
6 The Esplanade
08 9421 1206

EUROPEAN

15.5/20

A stalwart fine diner has been given a new lease on life

With blinds half-drawn and a heavy wooden door to push through, Balthazar could seem like a corporate stronghold, where deals are done and fates are sealed. But under owners Daniel Morris and Emma Ferguson, this dining stalwart has renewed life. They've brought the brio of their Northbridge bar No Mafia, while maintaining Balthazar's natural old-school charm. Instructions to "smash it up" come with the lamb tartare, dabs of piquant harissa. Duck thigh bathes in a pool of buttermilk and is sliced and presented with seasonal vegetables. There's comfort in a rich marron and mussel risotto, the native shellfish tail and claw crowning the rice dish. Wine service shuns parochialism. You're as likely to be recommended a left-field Margaret River producer as a cracking Spanish albarino, or a volcanic drop from the Canary Islands.

At time of press, Luke Wakefield had stepped in as head chef

Open	L D Wed–Mon
Price	$$
Cards	AE DC MC V eftpos
Chef	Blair Allen
Features	Bar, licensed, outdoor seating, wheelchair access
Website	ameliaparkrestaurant.com.au

Open	L Mon–Fri; D Mon–Sat
Price	$$$
Cards	AE MC V eftpos
Chef	Luke Wakefield
Features	Bar, private dining, licensed, wheelchair access
Website	balthazar.com.au

Billie H

CLAREMONT
34 St Quentin Avenue
08 9384 0808

EUROPEAN   **15/20**

Good food, wine and tunes – this Claremont wine bar/restaurant hits the holy trinity

Effortlessly switching between recommendations for those who want nothing beyond easy drinking to wine geeks looking to go deep, Daniel Goodsell and his front-of-house team are reason enough to make this a regular. Throw in a stellar soundtrack and you're winning. Fremantle sardines with a whack of chilli heat are heaped on sprouted grain loaf, baked in-house. A carpaccio of hyper-seasonal Rottnest swordfish is pepped up with lemon and mustard, and doesn't disappoint. Unashamedly garlicky, half a crisp-skinned heritage chicken – local, slow – bathes in a refined stock that's as impressive as the chook, which is roasted and mounted with butter. The secret: a meeting of two birds (chicken and duck), and two garlics (black and smoked). A scattering of green beans crowns this simple, accomplished main. Billie H goes beyond a simple wine bar or neighbourhood joint. It's a dining destination.

At time of press, Skye Faithfull (Balthazar) stepped in as head chef

Open	L D Mon–Sat
Price	$$
Cards	AE MC V eftpos
Chef	Skye Faithfull
Features	Bar, licensed, outdoor seating, wheelchair access
Website	billieh.com.au

Bread in Common

FREMANTLE
43 Pakenham Street
08 9336 1032

MODERN AUSTRALIAN   **15.5/20**

Fremantle's bakery/restaurant remains head of the class with its seasonal, simple menu

Bread in Common fits effortlessly into the Freo backstreets. A heritage building, you could imagine it's been firing the ovens for decades, turning out woodfired organic bread and plates that go beyond its bakery setting. Under Scott Brannigan, one-time head chef at Balthazar, the menu isn't overly fussy, letting the ingredients shine. The carte is designed both to share and complement the excellent bread. Start with silken chicken liver parfait topped with plum jelly and a rich white bean and rosemary spread, topped with crisp saltbush. A basil and tomato salad is so fragrant you'll smell it before you see it, thanks to an onion ash salt and parmesan, lifting a much classic beyond simply great produce. Brannigan is using local and native ingredients, from Fremantle octopus, in a bold confit tomato with cumin and ginger, to kangaroo with Kakadu plum. Here, the roo is served with a bitter charred outer, and a red centre heightened by that plum. Bread in Common is anything but ordinary.

The by-the-glass wine list is great, as is Brannigan's house-made sloe gin

Open	B Sat–Sun; L D Daily
Price	$$
Cards	AE MC V eftpos
Chef	Scott Brannigan, Chris Eales
Features	Licensed, outdoor seating, private dining, wheelchair access
Website	breadincommon.com.au

Cullen Wines

WILYABRUP
4323 Caves Road
08 9755 5277

CONTEMPORARY   **16/20**

A fine dining winery restaurant with a biodynamic soul

Cullen Wines plays well on paper, from its status as biodynamic standard bearer, to the Cullens as a founding family of an extraordinary wine region. Chief winemaker Vanya Cullen's commitment to the land is well known, and in Iain Robertson they've found a chef who understands his terroir, the menu peppered with ingredients from the property or with a biodynamic focus, from honey to nettle. A warm potted rabbit with pickled grape, fresh cucumbers and sauce gribiche is enough to share with crisp salty toasts. Earthy, salt-baked celeriac has a hint of smoke, alongside a sweet caramelised nashi pear, and a light acidic note from a foam made of goat's curd and whey. It's food that nourishes, and impresses the eye. There's a moment of cringe as lamb collar with fig and smoked labne is described as 'deconstructed falafel', but if this is the result, then we'll forgive a few descriptive indulgences.

Named for the founders, a glass of Kevin John Chardonnay and the Diana Madeline Cabernet blend are a must

Garum

PERTH
Hibernian Place, 480 Hay Street
08 6559 1870

CONTEMPORARY   **15/20**

A Melbourne stalwart hits Perth, with excellent results

Guy Grossi and team have strayed from the safe clutches of Melbourne to mine the rich seam that is the Roman osteria in Perth, with the help of chef Mario Di Natale. Find Garum in Hibernian Hall, with its ecclesiastical good looks, streams of natural light and the echo of tinkling glassware and cutlery. The question of whether the west – no desert when it comes to good cucina Italiano – will embrace the Grossi ethos is answered swiftly thanks to the pasta work on show. Cacio e pepe, with hand-cut tonarelli, is on the money with its balance of pecorino and pepper, while the fettuccine carbonara – bound with egg and pecorino, with pops of salt and fat from guanciale – is worth seeking out. Billed as an homage to the quinto quarto (that's the celebration of offal for the players at home) coda alla vaccinara is a deeply flavoured oxtail stew heralding a bright future for the restaurant.

The bar menu holds its own, especially with a negroni to start

Open	L Fri–Tue
Price	$$
Cards	AE MC V eftpos
Chef	Iain Robertson
Features	Licensed, outdoor seating, wheelchair access
Website	cullenwines.com.au

Open	B L D Daily
Price	$$
Cards	AE MC V eftpos
Chef	Mario Di Natale
Features	Bar, licensed, private dining, outdoor seating, wheelchair access
Website	garum.com.au

The Heritage Wine Bar

PERTH
131 St Georges Terrace
08 9226 5596

CONTEMPORARY   **15/20**

Come for the wine, stay for the food

A small name change (once, The Heritage, now The Heritage Wine Bar) means big things for this slow burner. A corporate favourite with a reputation to match, this is the place to try any of 100 exceptional wines on rotation matched punch for punch by British head chef Matt Carulei. Old-school rules have been thrown out the window in favour of sticky lamb ribs balanced against a sharp salsa verde. Carulei's 'goose mousse', a mix of goose liver parfait, foie gras, praline paste and honey sits on a 'rich man's brioche', (that means extra butter and rendered fat in the already sweet, rich bun). Delicious, but not for the faint of heart. Fremantle swordfish is served with a slight blush in brown butter, on earthy celeriac puree – European technique meets Australian seasonality. End on a delicately presented mille feuille with rhubarb, custard and vanilla ice-cream for a real display of a kitchen that sweats every detail.

This is one of Perth's best by-the-glass lists, and perfect for solo diners

Open	L D Mon–Sat
Price	$$
Cards	AE MC V eftpos
Chef	Matt Carulei
Features	Bar, licensed, private dining, wheelchair access
Website	theheritageperth.com.au

Il Lido

COTTESLOE
88 Marine Parade
08 9286 1111

CONTEMPORARY   **15/20**

Beachside drinking and dining at its finest

There's something special about Il Lido. Is it the breezy attitude of Cottleslocals, the brio with which this place operates or the ocean views and air? Who knows, and frankly who has time to wonder as you pick your way through a wine list and menu that are equally as impressive. In recent years, this coastal wine bar and Italian restaurant opposite Cottesloe Beach has received its reputation from what's in the glass, but the food under head chef Roberto Zampogna is well worth shouting about. Veal and pork polpette, laid on charred tomato, with a generous shower of parmesan. Figs wrapped in prosciutto and loaded with gorgonzola that hit the sweet and salty spot simultaneously. House-made fettuccine, hot under the collar with 'nduja, lemon and parsley. Armed with a glass of Fiegl ribolla gialla from northern Italy, your mind may wander to the Amalfi, but this neighbourhood gem confirms just how dolce our vita is on the west coast.

Make like you live here by dropping by for coffee after your morning swim

Open	B L D Daily
Price	$$
Cards	AE MC V eftpos
Chef	Roberto Zampogna
Features	Bar, licensed, outdoor seating, wheelchair access
Website	illido.com.au

Lalla Rookh

PERTH
77 St Georges Terrace
08 9325 7077

🍷
ITALIAN

👑
15/20

LALLA ROOKH

This underground haven has nailed the art of solo wine discovery, intimate dinners and marshalling hungry groups

A small plate or two while hitting sommelier Jeremy Prus' Italian-focused list, or the old-school a la carte route both work fine, but you commit to the il Capo menu – six shared courses that dip into the regular menu, with a good few off-carte wins. Ox tongue skewers, cooked sous-vide and then grilled, are tender and a garlic, marjoram, lemon zest and juice marinade give them depth beyond a simple, smashable bar snack. House-made pasta dishes are always a hit. Dig into spaghetti tossed with cured pork jowl and mussels. There's a similar trick at play with sliced pork neck, smoked eel and savoy cabbage. It works. There's bright and bitter witlof with pickled fennel, walnuts and a good whack of a Franco-Basque hard sheep's milk cheese. Chef Alexandra Haynes' willingness to cross a few borders, be it cheese or a pinch of togarashi, only strengthens her modern take on Italian food – as versatile as it is accomplished.

For Prus' wider wine picks and a more intimate vibe, head to the adjoining Wine Store

Open	L Mon–Fri; D Mon–Sat
Price	$$
Cards	AE DC MC V eftpos
Chef	Alexandra Haynes
Features	Bar, licensed, outdoor seating, wheelchair access
Website	lallarookh.com.au

Liberte

ALBANY
160-162 Stirling Terrace
08 9847 4797

FRANCO-VIETNAMESE   **15/20**

Vive la revolution over Vietnamese pancakes and wine

Chef Amy Hamilton's restaurant might be a modern Vietnamese affair these days, but the French accent can still be discerned in the steak tartare, a profiterole dessert, and the option for baguette and butter instead of rice. The room is a homage to faded aristocratic decor with gilt floor to ceiling mirrors, red velvet drapes and a theatrical assortment of seats that span brocade armchairs and battered Chesterfields. A meal here is a casual affair but the flavours are rendered in high definition. A pillowy bao stretched around a wobbegong fritter is reminiscent of a Thai fish cake. Leafy greens are finely shredded and tamed with garlic and oyster sauce. And their famous fried noodles laced with garlic, crab, shaved parmesan and warm sunbeams of chilli will hit your umami receptors faster than mi goreng after a bender. They have a eco-friendly focus so there are no plastic straws available, but with a wine list championing local Great Southern and Denmark producers, you won't need one.

The serves are big and the menu is short so bring a group to try everything

Open	L D Mon–Sat
Price	$$
Cards	MC V eftpos
Chef	Amy Hamilton
Features	Bar, licensed
Website	libertealbany.com.au

Long Chim

PERTH
State Buildings, Corner St Georges Terrace and Barrack Street
08 6168 7775

THAI   **15/20**

Feel the heat at this spicy homage to Thai street culture

While the empire of David Thompson's stylised canteens has expanded (there are three now across Sydney, Melbourne and Perth), quality still rules and the legendary Thai chef's vision remains fully intact. A riot of street art and canteen vibes, it serves food until late, but also catches the lunch crowd. Down in the basement, time has no meaning. It's mandarin and lemongrass negroni time, anytime. A Chiang Mai-style larp of chicken – part entree, part incendiary device – still comes with warnings for newcomers. Northern Thai spices bring waves of heat. Not for the fainthearted. As with any great Thai meal, it's an exercise in contrast and balance, moving between heat, to crisp, pungent school prawns, a fresh green papaya salad, then to grilled lamb ribs, with depth of flavour from cumin and a coconut sweetness. You might consider subbing in a soothing soup to calm that spice party, before hitting the punchy Thai tea ice-cream. Or just let the good times roll.

Home base of James Connolly, Long Chim group's resident boozehound: dive into the cocktails and hit the bar menu

Open	L D Daily
Price	$$
Cards	AE MC V eftpos
Chef	Lucas Fernandes
Features	Bar, licensed, outdoor seating, private dining, wheelchair access
Website	longchimperth.com

Lulu La Delizia

SUBIACO
5/97 Rokeby Road
08 9381 2466

ITALIAN **15.5/20**

Fresh handmade pasta rules here

Chef Joel Valvasori eyes his compact, boisterous Subiaco pasta bar from the pass. It's a tight ship in this tightly packed little room with its sweet lace curtains and bentwood chairs. When it comes to handmade pasta, few come close to this pastaficio, in WA and beyond. The dedication to the mission of fresh pasta, daily, is working. Lunch service is busy, dinner busier. Starting simple, small savoury doughnuts hit the table piping hot. A plate of buttery stracciatella di burrata is dressed with lemon zest and horseradish with pickled butter beans laid on top. On this modern menu, Valvasori introduces ingredients and pasta varieties that say much about his northeast Italian heritage. Cjalson, a sweet, spicy dumpling native to Friuli, is scattered with hazelnuts. Chestnut blecs – small triangular sheets of pasta – are served with a Venetian-style sausage, made from pig's head, neck, shoulder and skin; a sharp sauerkraut accompanies, another nod to the mountains. Never short of brilliant.

Take a crew and order every pizza on the menu for WA's finest pizza party

Open	L Tue–Fri; D Tue–Sat
Price	$$
Cards	AE DC MC V eftpos
Chef	Joel Valvasori
Features	Licensed, outdoor seating, wheelchair access
Website	lululadelizia.com.au

Millbrook Winery

JARRAHDALE
Old Chestnut Lane
08 9525 5796

EUROPEAN **15.5/20**

A picturesque antidote to traditional fine dining

Deep within the estate, with an aspect to the vines and forest, Guy Jeffreys' kitchen garden makes up a good part of the culinary journey at Millbrook. The other acts are played out in the light, airy dining room. 'Kitchen's choice' is a shared three-part entree that tells you all you need to know about the ethos here: great produce cooked with bold simplicity. Salty, fresh cottage cheese, good olive oil and young fennel shoots, both raw and quickly blanched. Pink slices of grass-fed beef are sliced thinly, the flavoursome fat cut by pickled cucumber, fennel and generous dabs of mustard. Raw kingfish is served with fresh chilli paste that has wonderful depth of flavour. Larger plates impress equally. Unctuous, viognier-braised rabbit risotto an antidote to every overly-tweezered winery meal you've ever had. Jeffreys hits the comfort feels with a garden-fresh snake bean salad in a mustard dressing, minute rump steak and soft confit garlic that spreads like butter.

Take a walk down to Jeffreys' vegetable patch and take in the stunning winery location

Open	L Thu–Mon
Price	$$
Cards	AE MC V eftpos
Chef	Guy Jeffreys
Features	Licensed, outdoor seating, private dining, wheelchair access
Website	millbrook.wine

LULU LA DELIZIA

Petition Kitchen

PERTH
State Buildings, corner St Georges Terrace
and Barrack streets
08 6168 7771

CONTEMPORARY **15/20**

Perfectly honed all-day dining

With its open kitchen, bare walls and
airy interior, Petition Kitchen ticks all
the boxes, from breakfast to dinner.
Throughout the day it ebbs and flows
from early morning house-made
crumpets with labne and candied
walnuts to the more raucous evening
service where diners might get down
with cavatelli, parsnip, smoked brioche
and veal sauce. Chef Jesse Blake,
one-time sous chef at Melbourne's
Cumulus Inc., oversees not just this
venue but also the adjoining Beer
Corner and Wine Bar. Much like
the Melbourne stalwart, he pushes
a modern-facing menu that doesn't
skimp on recognisable comfort dishes.
A loosely cut beef tartare ditches
the classic egg and shallot treatment
in favour of Japanese spices and
translucent sweet potato crisps. Earthy
Jerusalem artichoke takes centre stage,
dressed with a rich anchovy cream,
while the welcome restraint of a rare
breed Manjimup pork chop served with
cider braised apple is something to
be appreciated.

**The pared-back menus of the
Wine Bar and Beer Corner are
perfect for first dates**

Open	B L D Daily
Price	$$
Cards	AE MC V eftpos
Chef	Jesse Blake
Features	Bar, licensed, outdoor seating, wheelchair access
Website	petitionperth.com

Rockpool Bar and Grill

BURSWOOD
Crown Perth, Great Eastern Highway
08 6252 1900

STEAKHOUSE **15/20**

**An old-school steakhouse, in the most
wonderful of ways**

Down the candlelit corridor, windows
onto ageing beef, there's something
almost ecclesiastical about entering
Rockpool Bar and Grill. After a session
on the casino floor or the tedium of a
corporate conference, the calm brought
by white-jacketed waiters appeases the
soul. Neil Perry's far-flung outpost is
something of a rare beast in the west:
a fine diner, offering cracking service
that doesn't demand a table-side
post-mortem of each dish. Wood-fire
grilled Fremantle octopus sits among
bitter salad leaves, dressed with pesto
and matched with steamed kipfler
potatoes. Plump sauteed marron plays
off sweet onions and earthy beetroot. It
seems almost sacrilege not to go the full
bovine route with Blackmore dry-aged,
full-blood wagyu, but an aged, grass-fed
Cape Grim rib-eye steak is spectacular,
and a fraction of the price. Hitting
the sides, load up on yet more kipflers,
sauteed in wagyu fat, and mushy
peas. The only thing that Perry's
voluminous menu doesn't cover
is a food coma disclaimer.

**Ask for a menu as you leave, if not for
posterity, but just to marvel at the scroll
and ribbon technique**

Open	L Sun–Fri; D Daily
Price	$$$
Cards	AE DC MC V eftpos
Chef	Dan Masters
Features	Bar, licensed, private dining, wheelchair access
Website	rockpoolbarandgrill.com.au

Vasse Felix

COWARAMUP
Caves Road (Corner Tom Cullity Drive)
08 9756 5000

MODERN AUSTRALIAN   **16/20**

A Margaret River founding winery, still pushing boundaries from vine to plate

When chef Brendan Pratt moved south to head up this revered kitchen, he could have trodden a worn path. Instead, it's his own vision, applied with respect to the restaurant's heritage. There's an undercurrent of Australiana here. A rummaging in the childhood larder that sees golden syrup, lavender, passionfruit and malt feature alongside emu, quandong, marron and coastal herbs. You might start with diced raw scampi, encased by slices of radish, topped with salty pops of wild scampi caviar from the northwest of WA. Bright to the eye and the palate, emu is lightly cured with sugar, salt, kombu and fennel, and sits in a baby cos leaf emulsion finished with shavings of cured, dehydrated egg yolk. Pork, eel, eggplant and miso packs some heavy artillery when it comes to umami, and delivers equal measures of satisfaction and flavour. Service leads the pack in the region, the dining room is warm and stylish, hewn from wood and stone. But the real draw here is still the meeting of culinary and wine talent.

The ground-floor wine lounge does not require a reservation. Charcuterie and cheeseboards and, of course, wine are available

Open	L Daily
Price	$$
Cards	AE DC MC V eftpos
Chef	Brendan Pratt
Features	Licensed, outdoor seating, wheelchair access
Website	vassefelix.com.au

Wildflower

State Buildings, Corner St Georges Terrace and Barrack Street
08 6168 7855

CONTEMPORARY   **15.5/20**

It's seasonal cooking, but perhaps not as you know it

This is fine dining, with a delicate edge. The concept of chef Jed Gerrard's menu is tied to the Noongar seasonal calendar. Depending when you visit, that might translate on the plate as jarrah-smoked kangaroo beneath sheets of beetroot, with dabs of duck liver mousse and dehydrated licorice bread. Abalone with squid ink, saltbush and kombu is enriched with a rich brown butter emulsion and lifted by the acidic pops of finger lime. Tender, pale White Rocks veal is served with enoki and shiitake mushrooms, black garlic and a translucent disc of pear. Gerrard hits the mark time and again, from line-caught hapuka to a botrytis semillon custard. Service is a little formal for the setting – an airy, light-filled room resting on top of the COMO hotel – but it's not a hard fix when all the other pieces fit so beautifully in place.

Time an aperitif – a Wildflower martini or rosella negroni – with the sunset

Open	L Tue–Fri; D Tue–Sat
Price	$$$
Cards	AE MC V eftpos
Chef	Jed Gerrard
Features	Bar, licensed, outdoor seating, private dining, wheelchair access
Website	wildflowerperth.com.au

VASSE FELIX

Wills Domain

YALLINGUP
Corner Abbey Farm and Brash roads
08 9755 2327

CONTEMPORARY   **16.5/20**

Margaret River experienced on a plate and by the glass

Set aside a full, lazy afternoon for the eight-course degustation, where a coastal attitude meets fine dining sensibilities. The pace ebbs and flows from a punchy snack-laden start. There's thinly sliced abalone pressed between a chicken skin crisp, a savoury potato croqueta topped with wild scampi caviar and a yabby presented on a sheet of nori with the instruction to "eat it like a taco". Beyond the opening, each course plays its part, titled as Raw (thin ribbons of apple under raw tuna, jamon, with a yuzu kosho cream), Garden (diced celeriac topped with Jerusalem artichoke crisps, finger lime), Umami (crisp shredded seaweed on a dainty pastry base, broth, marron), Ocean (bar cod, topped with finely sliced cuttlefish, and a drop of spring onion sauce held in an onion skin), Paddock (a tender beef striploin encased in crisp slices of Jerusalem artichoke) and a hit of dessert (comforting molten chocolate against a miso ice-cream). Presentation and service are lively, fun and full of warmth.

Don't have an afternoon? Hit the approachable a la carte

Yarri

DUNSBOROUGH
Cyrillian Way
08 9786 5030

CONTEMPORARY   **16/20**

Pared-back winery dining with a strong coastal vibe

You can take the chef out of fine dining, but you can't take fine dining out of the chef. Aaron Carr, the man who defined the regional West Australian dining scene (he was at the helm of Vasse Felix for 21 years) is back, this time with a pared-down offering. Perfect for the oceanside village vibe of Dunsborough, the bar/restaurant is a slower pace than the chef's previous kitchen, but no less compelling. It's smart, simple bar fare here. Banana prawns are wood-grilled and then hit with miso butter and crisp saltbush. Briny, lightly pickled sardines lie on crisp focaccia toast. Molten manchego croquettes are finger-scorchingly good. To share, there's a 550-gram dry-aged sirloin slathered in anchovy caper butter. There's daintier Carr-esque plates that hark back to Vasse Felix, too, such as lightly cured emu with muntries and macadamia. It's beautiful, but there's a lot to be said for the new direction. As second acts go, this one's a cracker.

Ask for a seat at the marble pass to watch all the action

Open	L Daily		Open	L Daily; D Mon–Sat
Price	$$$		Price	$$
Cards	AE DC MC V eftpos		Cards	AE MC V eftpos
Chef	Seth James		Chef	Aaron Carr
Features	Bar, licensed, outdoor seating, private dining, wheelchair access		Features	Bar, licensed, outdoor seating, wheelchair access
Website	willsdomain.com.au		Website	yarri.com.au

YARRI

Sails on Lavender Bay ●

The Gantry ●

Chon ● ——— ● One Ford Street

Sake Restaurant & Bar ●

Bistro Guillaume ——— Mr. Wong
Bistecca
Rosetta

Fujisaki
Flying Fish ● — 12-Micron
Bea ●
Cirrus
Banksii ●

Est. ●

The Welcome ●
Hotel Dining Room

Sushi e
O Bar & Dining
Bentley Restaurant & Bar
Bacco
Uccello
Indu

ReccoLab ●

LuMi Dining ●

Momofuku Seiobo
Sokyo

Intermezzo
The Restaurant Pendolino ●

WESTERN DISTRIBUTOR

ANZAC BRIDGE

PYRMONT

Glass Brasserie ●
PARK ST

Grounds of the City ●

The Boathouse on Blackwattle Bay ●

HARRIS ST

Tetsuya's ●
Spring Yunnan

GEORGE ST

Bodega 1904 ●

Golden Century ●

ULTIMO

SURRY HILLS

ELIZABETH ST

FOREST LODGE

A1 Canteen ●
Olio
Automata
Mekong

GREAT WESTERN HWY

LP's Quality Meats ●
Ester

THE UNIVERSITY
OF SYDNEY

Kindred ●

CLEVELAND ST

N

Bart Jr

0   500M

Ron's

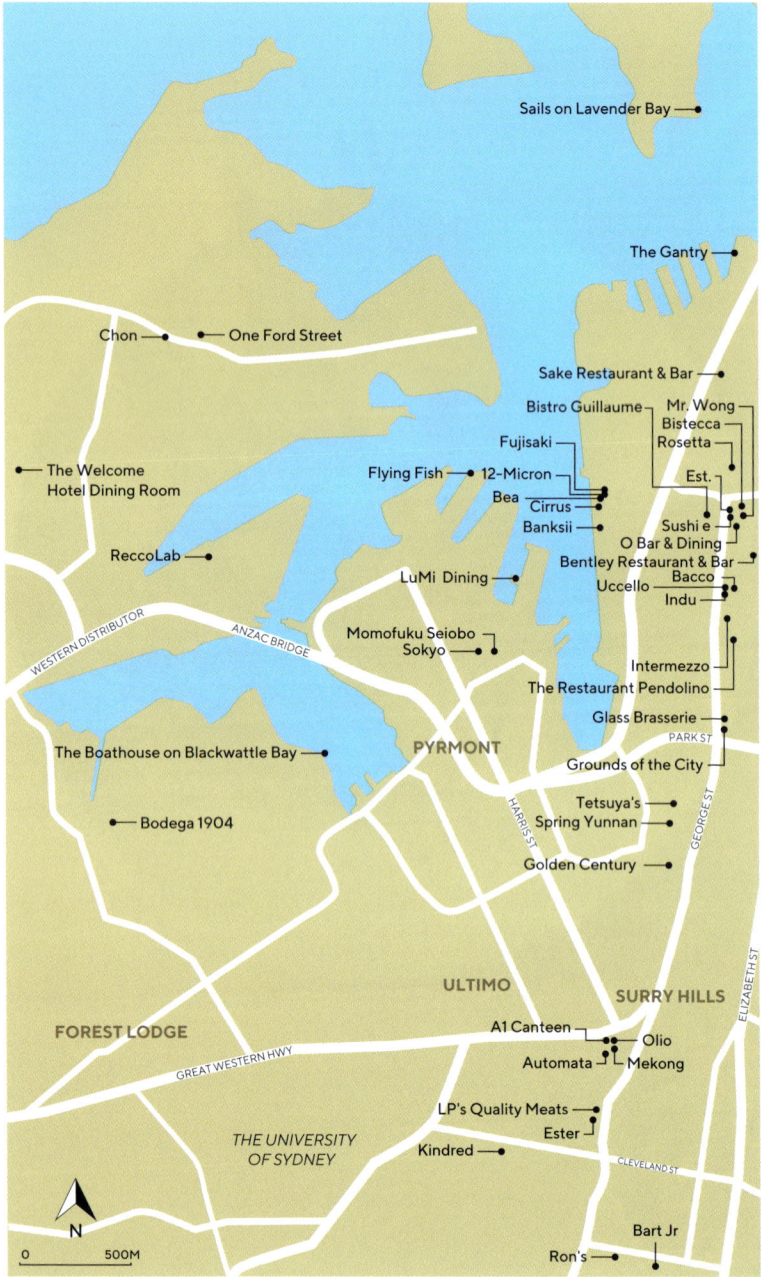

INNER SYDNEY AND CBD

KIRRIBILLI

Aqua Dining

SYDNEY HARBOUR BRIDGE

The Dining Room

Quay

Bennelong

Aria

Kid Kyoto

Chat Thai Circular Quay

Bar Patron

The Bridge Room

No. 1 Bent St

Restaurant Hubert

Spice Temple

Rockpool Bar & Grill

District Brasserie

POTTS POINT

Botanic Gardens Restaurant

Felix

Azuma

Long Chim

China Lane

Alibi

Otto

China Doll

Aki's

1821

La Rosa

The Strand

Chiswick
at the
Gallery

The Fish Shop

Billy Kwong

The Apollo

Bistro Rex

Ms. G's

Fratelli Paradiso

Yellow

Monopole

Cho Cho San

Paper Bird

Dear Sainte Eloise

SYDNEY

Bambini Trust

PARK ST

COLLEGE ST

CROWN ST

BOURKE ST

KINGS CROSS

NEW BEACH RD

Alpha

Red Lantern

Culina et Vinum

Farmhouse Kings Cross

Restaurant Moon

Chula

Acme

DARLINGHURST

Sagra

Lankan Filling Station

Sake Restaurant & Bar

NEW SOUTH HEAD RD

SURRY HILLS

Buffalo Dining Club

Bibo

Sasaki

Chin Chin

Nel.

Longrain

Chaco Bar

Big Poppa's

Buon Ricordo

Poly

Nomad

Firedoor

Bad Hombres

Bodega

Gogyo

ELIZABETH ST

Raita Noda Chef's Kitchen

Dead Ringer

Folonomo

The Unicorn

PADDINGTON

Lucio's

OCEAN ST

Chiswick

The
Bellevue
Hotel

The Dolphin Hotel

Porteno

Wyno

Nour

Mark + Vinny's

Izakaya Fujiyama

10 William St

Paddo Inn Dining Room

MOORE PARK RD

Saint Peter

Fred's

The Paddington

WOOLLAHRA

ANZAC PARADE

EASTERN DISTRIBUTOR

Bishop Sessa

St Claude's

Hotel Centennial

Bistro Moncur

N

0   500M

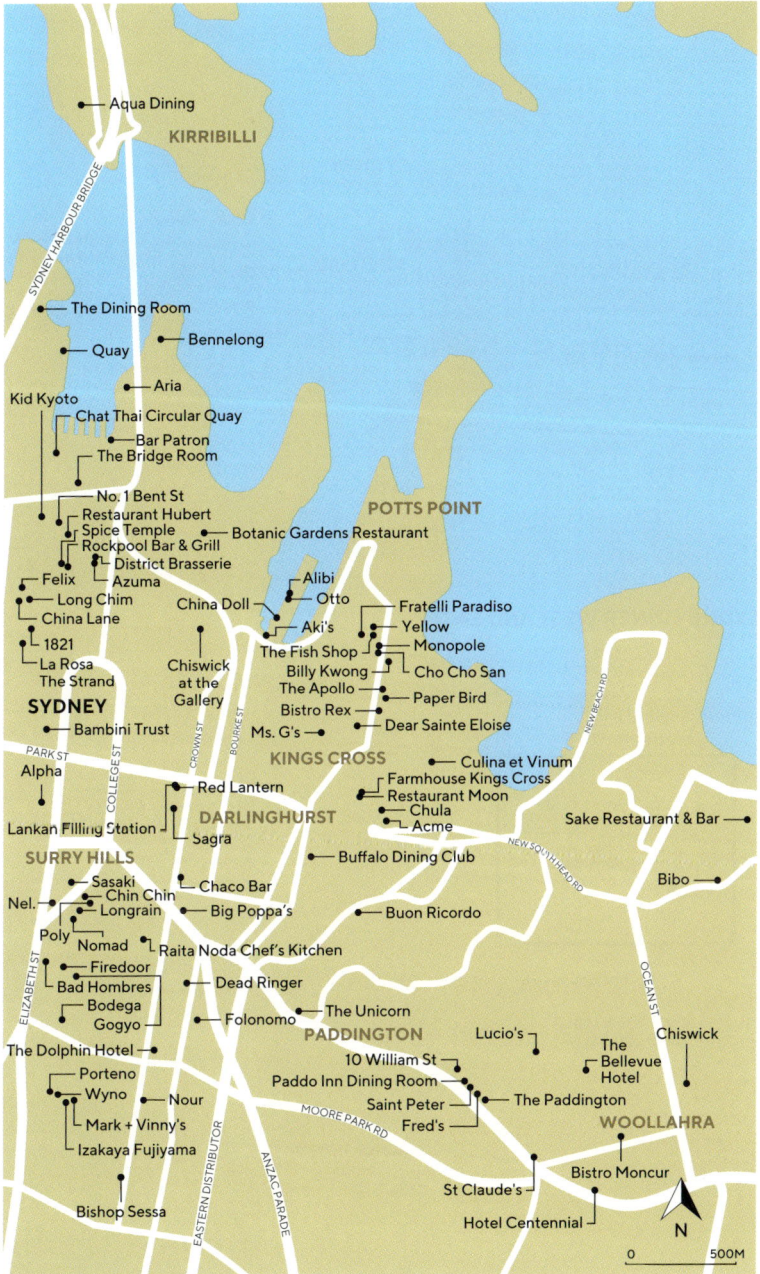

INNER SYDNEY AND CBD

CHISWICK

KIRRIBILLI

SYDNEY

DARLINGHURST

Regatta ● ● Catalina

Matteo

Rocker

OLD SOUTH HEAD RD

Capriccio

ULTIMO

GEORGES

WESTERN DISTRIBUTOR

GREAT WESTERN HWY

SURRY HILLS

One Penny Red
Continental Deli Bar Bistro
Oscillate Wildly
Sixpenny

Rising Sun Workshop

Sean's Panaroma
Da Orazio Pizza + Porchetta
Blanca
Marta
Bills Bondi
A Tavola
Bondi Trattoria
Icebergs Dining Room & Bar

BONDI

Stanbuli
Queen Chow
Osteria di Russo & Russo
Hartsyard

Kepos Street Kitchen
Luke's Kitchen
Kepos & Co.

ANZAC PARADE

TAMARAMA

Clove Lane

Pheast

Barzaari

Three Blue Ducks

Hello Auntie

Da Mario

CLOVELLY

Frenchies Bistro & Brewery

RANDWICK

Nu Bambu

EASTERN DISTRIBUTOR

Coogee Pavilion

ERSKINEVILLE

Three Blue Ducks

Yan

PRINCES HWY

Ble Restaurant
Ramsgate 8km

N

0   1KM

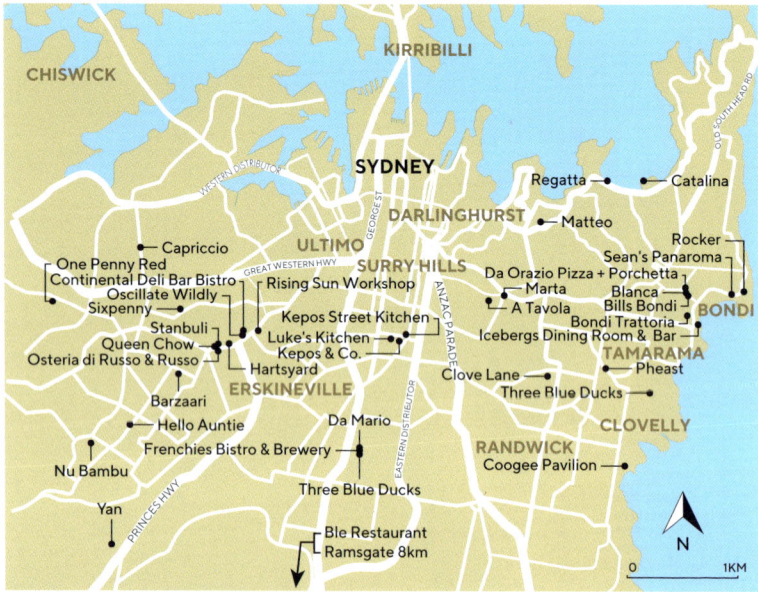

SYDNEY INNER WEST AND EAST

WOLLEMI
NATIONAL PARK

YENGO
NATIONAL PARK

N

0   10KM

HUME HWY

N

0   3KM

CENTRAL
COAST

GOSFORD

Clementine

YASS

Bombini

PACIFIC HWY

Lochiel House

Pearls on the Beach

BLUE MOUNTAINS
NATIONAL PARK

RICHMOND

Fumo

WINDSOR RD

KATOOMBA

Darley's

BLACKTOWN

CAPTAIN COOK HWY

SYDNEY

GREATER SYDNEY

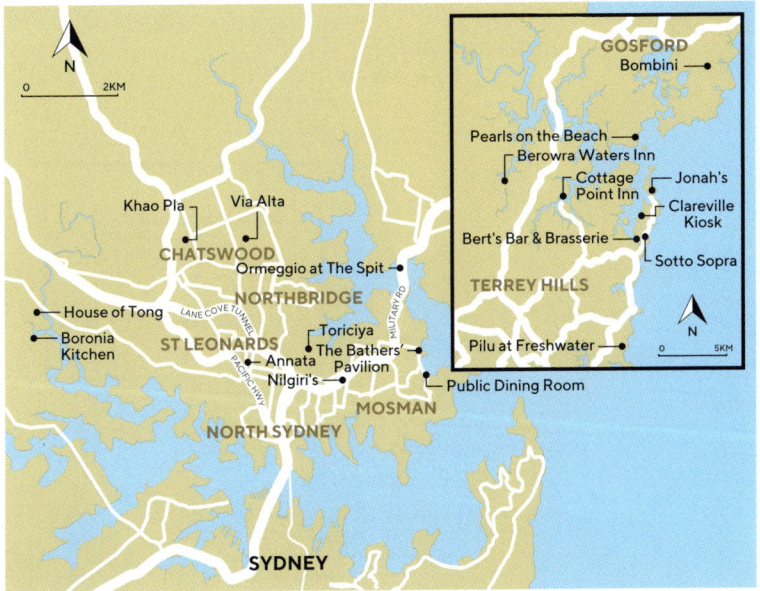

SYDNEY NORTH

Map labels:
- N — 0 2KM
- GOSFORD
- Bombini
- Pearls on the Beach
- Berowra Waters Inn
- Cottage Point Inn
- Jonah's
- Clareville Kiosk
- Khao Pla
- Via Alta
- CHATSWOOD
- Bert's Bar & Brasserie
- Sotto Sopra
- Ormeggio at The Spit
- NORTHBRIDGE
- TERREY HILLS
- House of Tong
- MILITARY RD
- LANE COVE TUNNEL
- Boronia Kitchen
- Toriciya
- ST LEONARDS
- The Bathers' Pavilion
- Annata
- Nilgiri's
- PACIFIC HWY
- Pilu at Freshwater
- Public Dining Room
- N — 0 5KM
- MOSMAN
- NORTH SYDNEY
- SYDNEY

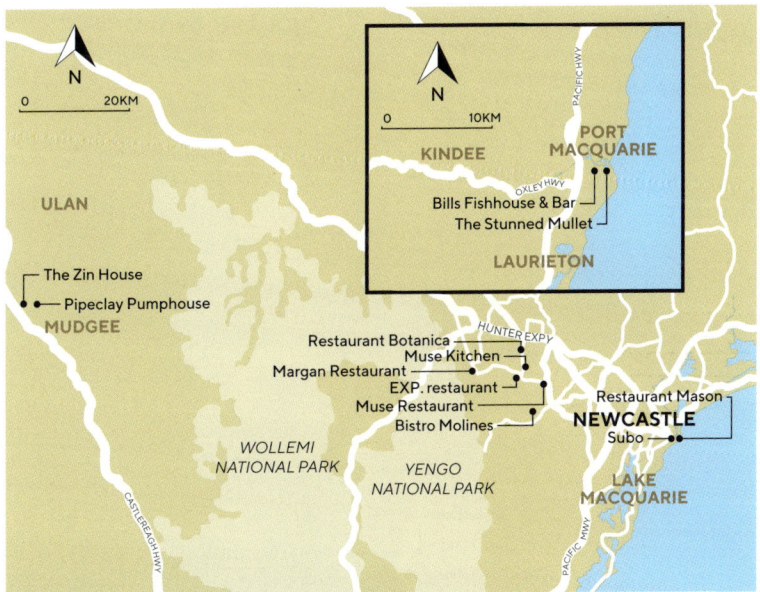

NEWCASTLE REGION AND WEST NEW SOUTH WALES

Map labels:
- N — 0 20KM
- N — 0 10KM
- KINDEE
- PORT MACQUARIE
- PACIFIC HWY
- ULAN
- OXLEY HWY
- Bills Fishhouse & Bar
- The Stunned Mullet
- LAURIETON
- The Zin House
- Pipeclay Pumphouse
- MUDGEE
- HUNTER EXPY
- Restaurant Botanica
- Muse Kitchen
- Margan Restaurant
- EXP. restaurant
- Muse Restaurant
- Restaurant Mason
- Bistro Molines
- NEWCASTLE
- Subo
- WOLLEMI NATIONAL PARK
- YENGO NATIONAL PARK
- LAKE MACQUARIE
- CASTLEREAGH HWY
- PACIFIC HWY

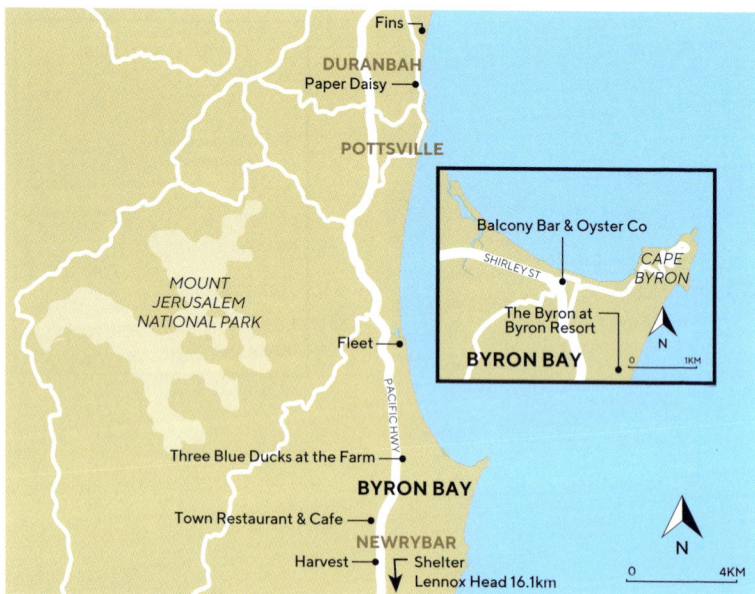

NORTH COAST NEW SOUTH WALES

Fins
DURANBAH
Paper Daisy
POTTSVILLE
Balcony Bar & Oyster Co
SHIRLEY ST
CAPE BYRON
The Byron at Byron Resort
BYRON BAY
N
0   1KM
MOUNT JERUSALEM NATIONAL PARK
Fleet
PACIFIC HWY
Three Blue Ducks at the Farm
BYRON BAY
Town Restaurant & Cafe
NEWRYBAR
Harvest
Shelter
Lennox Head 16.1km
N
0   4KM

SOUTH COAST NEW SOUTH WALES

The Argyle Inn
TARALGA
Biota Dining
WOLLONGONG
Caveau
Babyface Kitchen
BOWRAL
Bistro Officina
Ruby's Mount Kembla
ILLAWARRA HWY
BUNDANOON
KIAMA
HUME MOTORWAY
South on Albany
BUNGONIA
NOWRA
PRINCES HWY
NERRIGA
St. Isidore
MILTON
Rick Stein at Bannisters
Cupitt's Kitchen
N
0   10KM

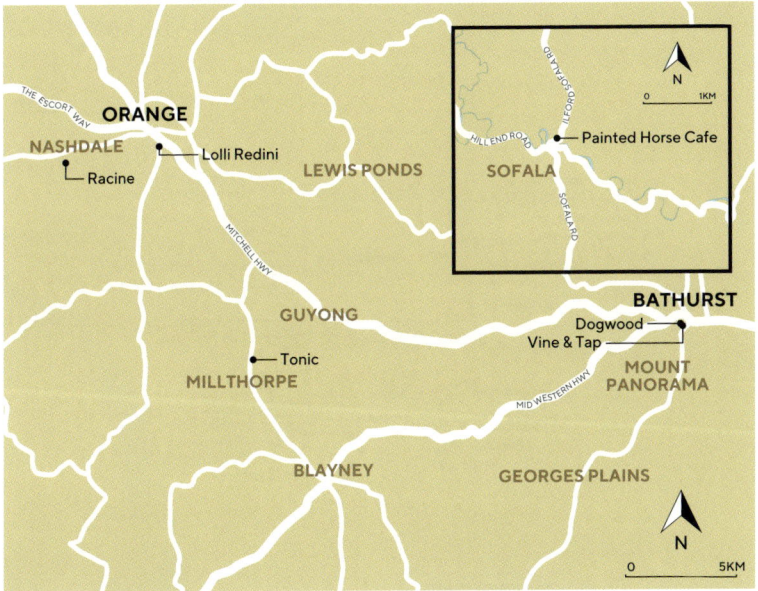

THE ESCORT WAY

ORANGE

NASHDALE

— Racine

— Lolli Redini

LEWIS PONDS

MILL END ROAD

GIBRALTAR HORSE ALLY RD

SOFALA

— Painted Horse Cafe

SOFALA RD

0   1KM

N

MITCHEL HWY

GUYONG

BATHURST

Dogwood —
Vine & Tap —

MILLTHORPE

— Tonic

MID WESTERN HWY

**MOUNT
PANORAMA**

BLAYNEY

GEORGES PLAINS

N

0   5KM

BATHURST REGION

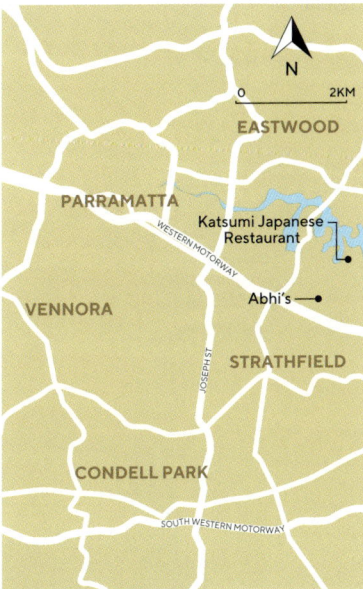

N

0   2KM

EASTWOOD

PARRAMATTA

WESTERN MOTORWAY

Katsumi Japanese
Restaurant —

VENNORA

JOSEPH ST

— Abhi's

STRATHFIELD

CONDELL PARK

SOUTH WESTERN MOTORWAY

WESTERN SYDNEY

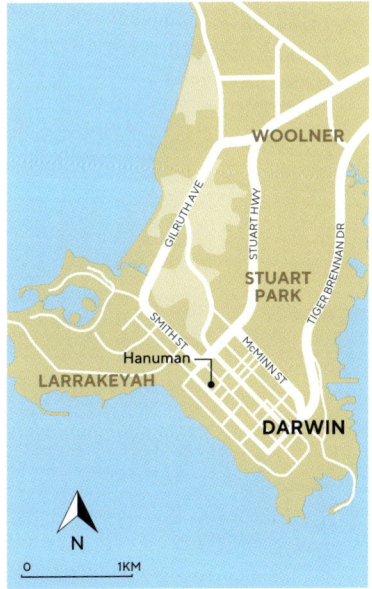

WOOLNER

GILRUTH AVE

STUART HWY

TIGER BRENNAN DR

**STUART
PARK**

SMITH ST

McMINN ST

Hanuman —

LARRAKEYAH

DARWIN

N

0   1KM

DARWIN

0   200M

VICTORIA ST

SPRING ST

European

San Telmo

Punch Lane

Bar Saracen

Longrain

Sunda

Bottega

Annam

Bar Lourinha

Uncle Collins St

Cumulus Inc.

The Mayfair

Kenzan

Cecconi's Flinders Lane

The Press Club

EXHIBITION ST

Grossi Grill

Grossi Florentino Upstairs

Flower Drum

Il Solito Posto

Fancy Hank's

Tonka

Lee Ho Fook

Pastuso

Chin Chin

Lucy Liu

Lello

Bar Tini

MoVida

Supernormal

Ezard

RUSSELL ST

Ishizuka

Lesa

Philippe

Sezar

Coda

Pascale Grill

Embla

Kisume

Il Bacaro

Sarti

Taxi Kitchen

ST KILDA RD

Din Tai Fung

MELBOURNE

The Deck

ELIZABETH ST

Tipo 00

Osteria Ilaria

Restaurant Shik

French Saloon

Kirk's Wine Bar

Miznon

Trattoria Emilia

BOURKE ST

Pure South

Maha

Caterina's

Saxe

Iki Jime

Rosa's Canteen

MoVida Aqui

Syracuse

Massi

FLINDERS ST

COLLINS ST

WILLIAM ST

Rockpool Bar & Grill

Silks

Rosetta

Spice Temple

Dinner by

Heston Blumenthal

Vue de Monde

Bistro Guillaume

LA TROBE ST

KING ST

Hanabishi

Long Chim

SPENCER ST

Harley and Rose

Victoria Hotel

Footscray 5km

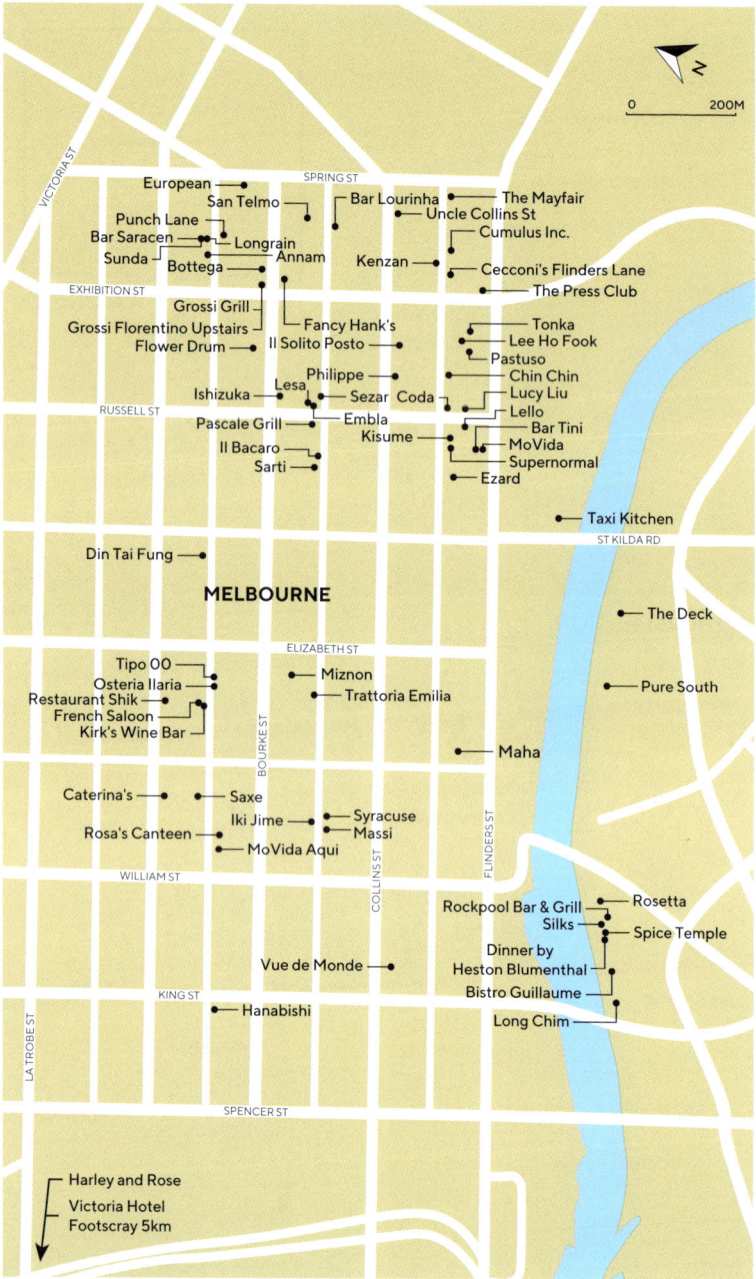

MELBOURNE CBD

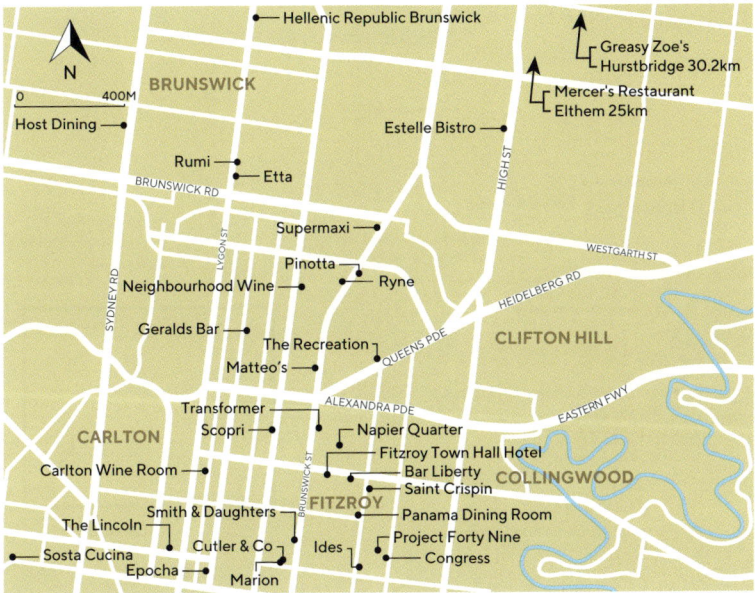

MELBOURNE NORTH

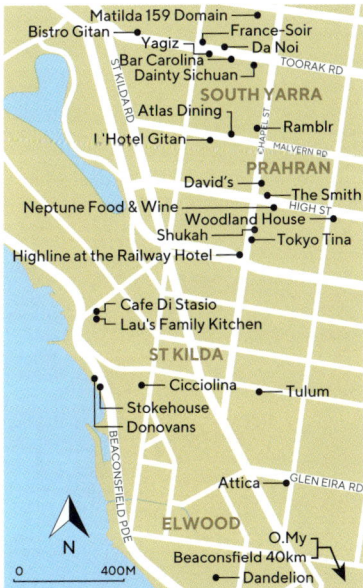

N
0 — 400M

BRUNSWICK

Hellenic Republic Brunswick

Greasy Zoe's
Hurstbridge 30.2km

Mercer's Restaurant
Eltham 25km

Host Dining

Estelle Bistro

Rumi
Etta

BRUNSWICK RD

HIGH ST

Supermaxi

WESTGARTH ST

Pinotta
Ryne

Neighbourhood Wine

HEIDELBERG RD

LYGON AV

CLIFTON HILL

Geralds Bar

SYDNEY RD

QUEENS PDE

The Recreation
Matteo's

Transformer

ALEXANDRA PDE

EASTERN FWY

Scopri

CARLTON

Napier Quarter
Fitzroy Town Hall Hotel
Bar Liberty
Saint Crispin

COLLINGWOOD

Carlton Wine Room

BRUNSWICK ST

FITZROY

Panama Dining Room

The Lincoln

Smith & Daughters

Project Forty Nine
Congress

Sosta Cucina

Cutler & Co
Ides

Epocha
Marion

MELBOURNE SOUTH

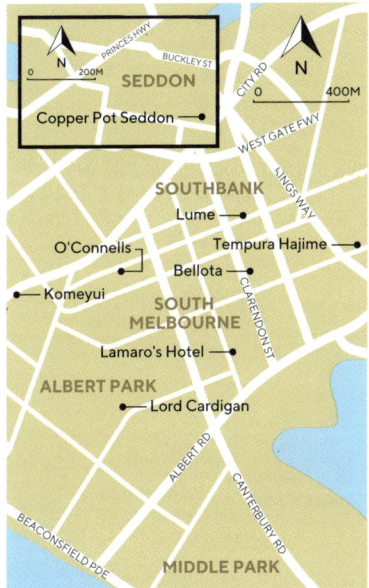

Matilda 159 Domain
Bistro Gitan
France-Soir
Yagiz
Da Noi
Bar Carolina
Dainty Sichuan

ST KILDA RD

TOORAK RD

SOUTH YARRA

Atlas Dining

CHAPEL ST

Ramblr

I.'Hotel Gitan

MALVERN RD

PRAHRAN

David's
The Smith
Neptune Food & Wine
Woodland House

HIGH ST

Shukah
Tokyo Tina
Highline at the Railway Hotel

Cafe Di Stasio
Lau's Family Kitchen

ST KILDA

Cicciolina
Tulum

BEACONSFIELD PDE

Stokehouse
Donovans

Attica
GLEN EIRA RD

N
0 — 400M

ELWOOD

O.My
Beaconsfield 40km
Dandelion

PORT MELBOURNE

N
0 — 200M

PRINCES HWY
BUCKLEY ST

SEDDON

Copper Pot Seddon

CITY RD

N
0 — 400M

WEST GATE FWY

SOUTHBANK

KINGS WAY

Lume

O'Connells
Tempura Hajime

CLARENDON ST

Bellota
Komeyui

SOUTH MELBOURNE

Lamaro's Hotel

ALBERT PARK

ALBERT RD

Lord Cardigan

CANTERBURY RD

BEACONSFIELD PDE

MIDDLE PARK

COLLINGWOOD

Mister Bianco
HIGH ST
KEW
Centonove
COTHAM RD

N
0   400M

DENMARK ST

BURKE RD

Anchovy
BRIDGE RD
Minamishima
RICHMOND

Piquancy
HAWTHORN

GLENFERRIE RD

SWAN ST
Noir
The Grand

Elyros

Bacash

France-Soir
Da Noi
Dainty Sichuan
Bar Carolina
Yagiz
TOORAK
TOORAK RD

HIGH ST RD

BLACKBURN RD

SPRINGVALE RD

Shira Nui

SOUTH YARRA
Ramblr
Kakizaki
MALVERN RD

GLEN
WAVERLEY

N
0   400M

Bistro Thierry

PRAHRAN
CHAPEL ST
Neptune Food & Wine
HIGH ST
Amaru

Riserva
Malvern 1.4km

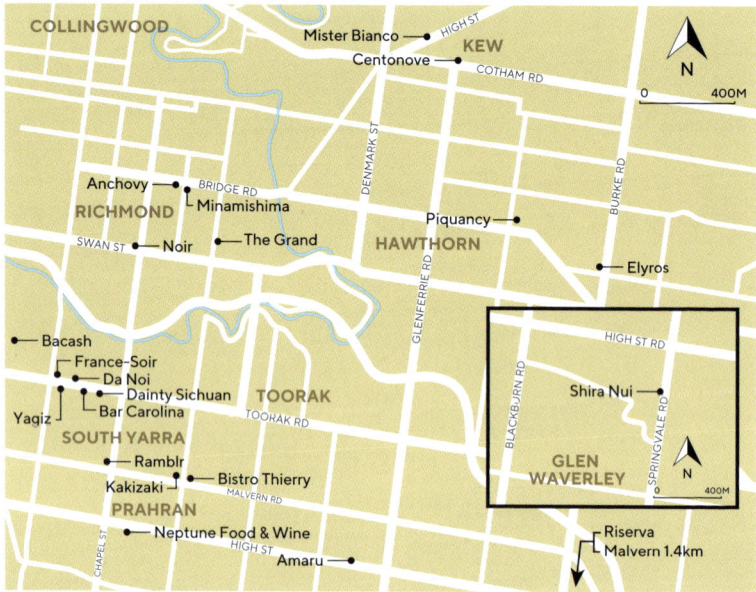

MELBOURNE EAST

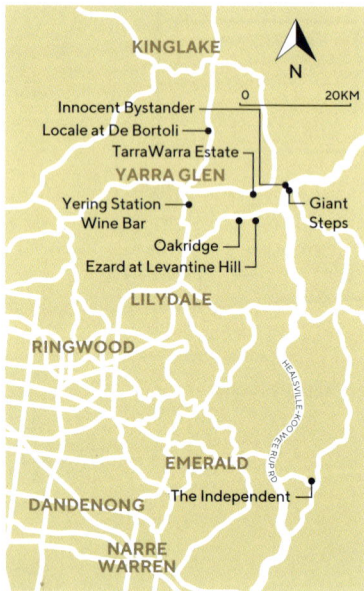

KINGLAKE

N
0   20KM

Innocent Bystander
Locale at De Bortoli
TarraWarra Estate
YARRA GLEN
Yering Station
Wine Bar
Oakridge
Ezard at Levantine Hill

Giant
Steps

LILYDALE

RINGWOOD

HEALESVILLE-KOO WEE RUP RD

EMERALD

The Independent

DANDENONG

NARRE
WARREN

YARRA VALLEY

N
0   4KM

DOC Pizza
& Mozzarella Bar

MORNINGTON

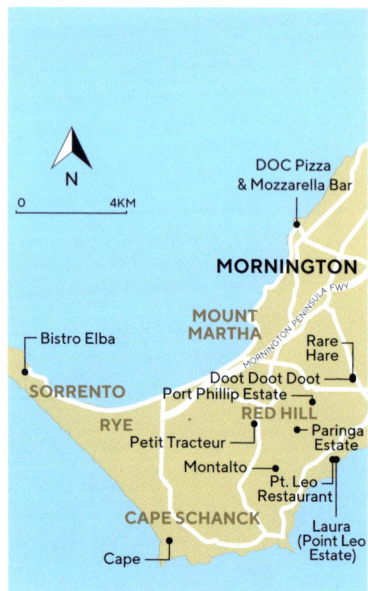

MORNINGTON PENINSULA FWY

MOUNT
MARTHA

Rare
Hare

Bistro Elba

Doot Doot Doot
Port Phillip Estate

SORRENTO

RED HILL

RYE

Paringa
Estate

Petit Tracteur

Montalto

Pt. Leo
Restaurant

CAPE SCHANCK

Laura
(Point Leo
Estate)

Cape

MORNINGTON PENINSULA

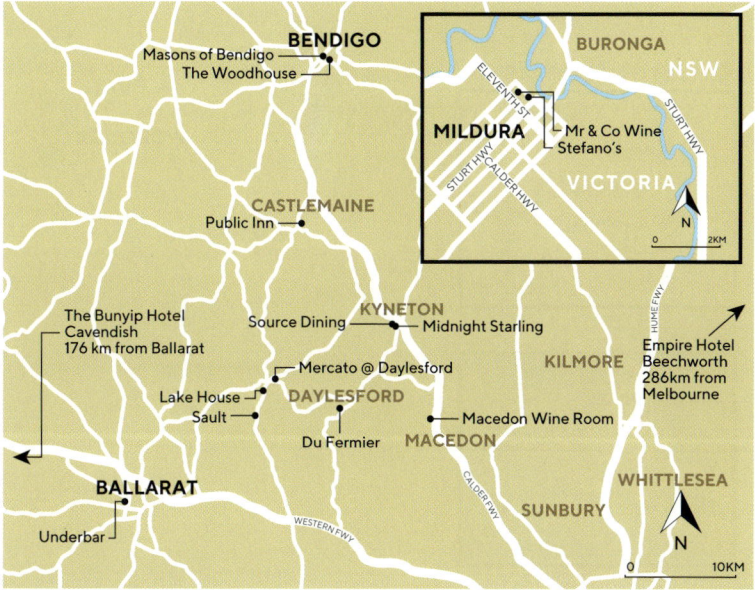

CENTRAL VICTORIA

Masons of Bendigo
The Woodhouse
BENDIGO

BURONGA

NSW

ELEVENTH ST

MILDURA — Mr & Co Wine
Stefano's

STURT HWY

CALDER HWY

STURT HWY

VICTORIA

N
0   2KM

CASTLEMAINE
Public Inn

The Bunyip Hotel
Cavendish
176 km from Ballarat

Source Dining
KYNETON — Midnight Starling

HUME FWY

Empire Hotel
Beechworth
286km from
Melbourne

KILMORE

Mercato @ Daylesford
Lake House
Sault
DAYLESFORD
Du Fermier
— Macedon Wine Room
MACEDON

WHITTLESEA

BALLARAT
Underbar

WESTERN FWY

CALDER FWY

SUNBURY

N
0   10KM

GEELONG AND BELLARINE PENINSULA

MIDLAND HWY

LARA
PRINCES FWY

POINT WILSON

Wickens
at Royal
Mail Hotel
DUNKELD

GLENELG HWY

PENSHURST-DUNKELD RD

INVERLEIGH

HAMILTON HWY

Tulip

Igni
Bistrot Plume — **GEELONG**

DRYSDALE

N
0   2KM

WAURN PONDS
PRINCES FWY

Merne at
Lighthouse

QUEENSCLIFF

BIRREGURRA
Brae

TORQUAY

Captain Moonlite

AIREYS INLET
A La Grecque

LORNE
Ipsos

N
0   5KM

NORTH EAST VICTORIA

Terrace Restaurant
YARRAWONGA
RUTHERGLEN
ALBURY
Jones Winery Restaurant
Miss Amelie
WODONGA
TINAMBA
Tinamba Hotel
HUME HWY
WINNINDOO
SALE
ROSEDALE
Neilsons Kitchen
BEECHWORTH
Provenance
TRARALGON
WANGARATTA
N
MILAWA
0   10KM

MYRTLEFORD

PAYNESVILLE
RAYMOND ISLAND
KING VALLEY
Sardine Eatery + Bar
BRIGHT
N
0   1KM

DANDONGADALE

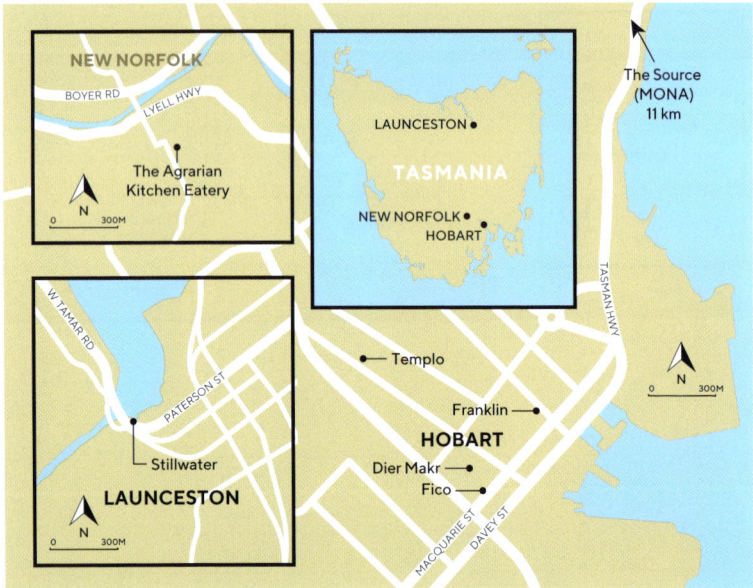

TASMANIA

NEW NORFOLK
BOYER RD
LYELL HWY
The Source (MONA) 11 km
The Agrarian Kitchen Eatery
LAUNCESTON
N
0   300M
TASMANIA
NEW NORFOLK
HOBART

W TAMAR RD
TASMAN HWY
Templo
PATERSON ST
Franklin
N
0   300M
Stillwater
HOBART
LAUNCESTON
Dier Makr
Fico
N
0   300M
MACQUARIE ST
DAVEY ST

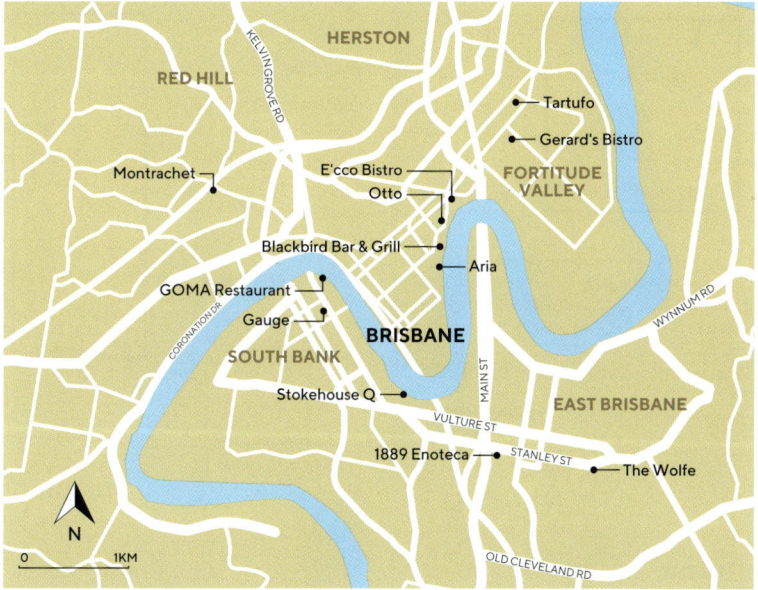

BRISBANE CBD

Map labels (Brisbane CBD):
- HERSTON
- RED HILL
- KELVIN GROVE RD
- Tartufo
- Gerard's Bistro
- Montrachet
- E'cco Bistro
- Otto
- FORTITUDE VALLEY
- Blackbird Bar & Grill
- Aria
- GOMA Restaurant
- CORONATION DR
- WYNNUM RD
- Gauge
- BRISBANE
- SOUTH BANK
- MAIN ST
- Stokehouse Q
- EAST BRISBANE
- VULTURE ST
- 1889 Enoteca
- STANLEY ST
- The Wolfe
- OLD CLEVELAND RD
- N
- 0 1KM

SOUTHERN QUEENSLAND

Map labels (Southern Queensland):
- GRANDCHESTER
- Homage
- TAROME
- QLD
- MAP INSET
- TAROME RD
- GLEN ROCK STATE FORREST
- GOOMBURRA
- MAIN RANGE NATIONAL PARK
- CUNNINGHAM HWY
- MARYVALE
- N
- 0 4KM

GOLD COAST

Map labels (Gold Coast):
- GOLD COAST
- Kiyomi
- GOODING DR
- BROADBEACH
- MERRIMAC
- BERMUDA ST
- GOLD COAST HWY
- Hellenika
- Rick Shores
- The Fish House
- PACIFIC HWY
- BURLEIGH HEADS
- N
- 0 2KM

SUNSHINE COAST

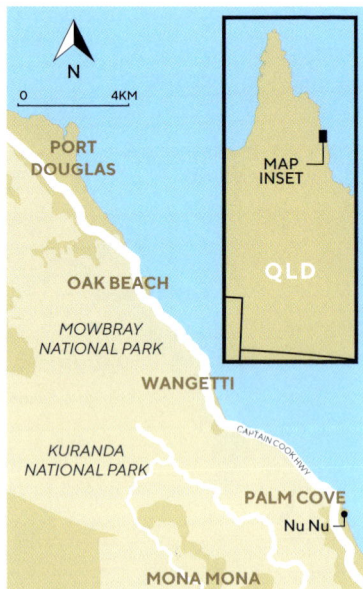

N
0   1KM

Rickys

NOOSA PDE

Wasabi

EENIE CREEK RD

NOOSA HEADS

SUNSHINE MOTORWAY

Spirit House

YANDINA

BRUCE HWY

**SUNSHINE
COAST**

MONTVILLE

The Long Apron

N

MALENY

0   5KM

SUNSHINE COAST

FAR NORTH QUEENSLAND

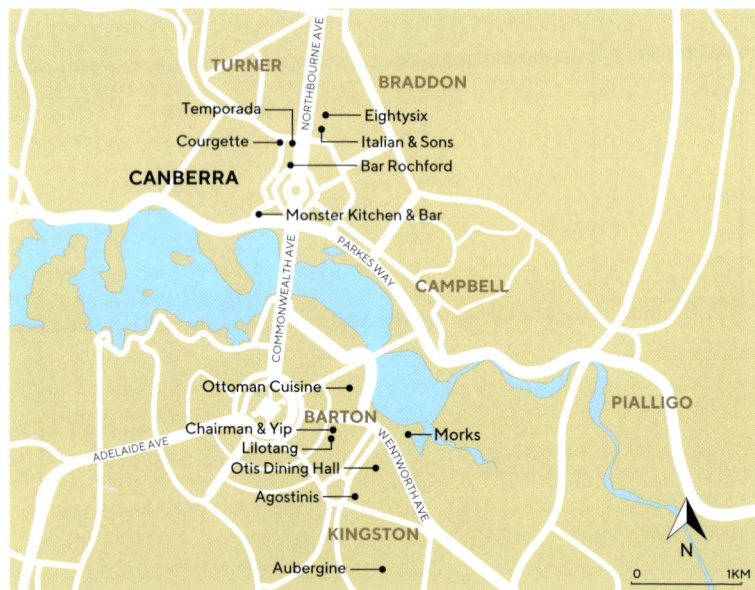

N
0   4KM

PORT
DOUGLAS

MAP
INSET

OAK BEACH

QLD

MOWBRAY
NATIONAL PARK

WANGETTI

CAPTAIN COOK HWY

KURANDA
NATIONAL PARK

PALM COVE

Nu Nu

MONA MONA

FAR NORTH QUEENSLAND

AUSTRALIAN CAPITAL TERRITORY

TURNER

NORTHBOURNE AVE

BRADDON

Temporada

Eightysix

Courgette

Italian & Sons

CANBERRA

Bar Rochford

Monster Kitchen & Bar

COMMONWEALTH AVE

PARKES WAY

CAMPBELL

Ottoman Cuisine

PIALLIGO

Chairman & Yip

BARTON

Morks

Lilotang

Otis Dining Hall

WENTWORTH AVE

Agostinis

ADELAIDE AVE

KINGSTON

N

Aubergine

0   1KM

AUSTRALIAN CAPITAL TERRITORY

WHITBY

N

0   1KM

WEMBLEY

Lulu La Delizia

The Heritage
Wine Bar   PERTH
Lalla Rookh   Wildflower
SUBIACO   Balthazar   Garum
Long Chim
Petition Kitchen

Millbrook

SERPENTINE

Rockpool Bar & Grill Perth

CLAREMONT

STIRLING HWY

SOUTH PERTH

Billie H

Il Lido

COTTESLOE

Bread In Common
Fremantle 7km

N

0   1KM

PERTH

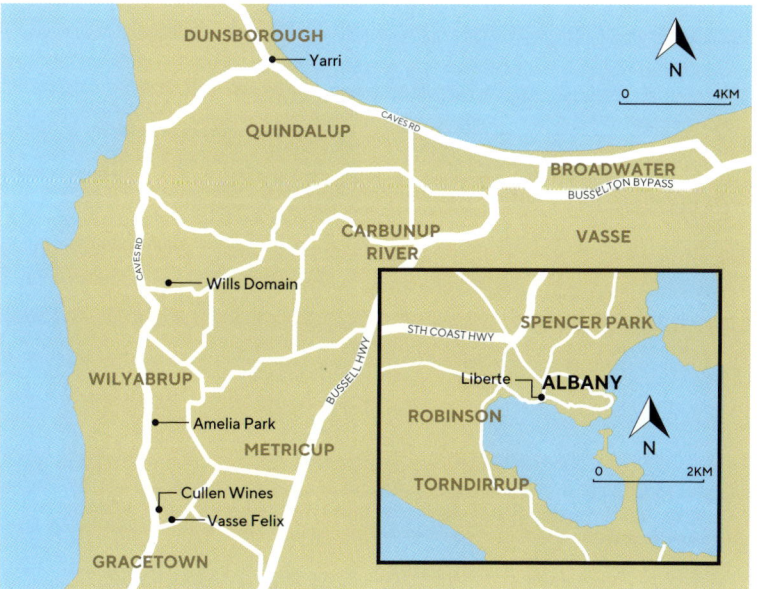

DUNSBOROUGH

Yarri

QUINDALUP

CAVES RD

BROADWATER
BUSSELTON BYPASS

CARBUNUP
RIVER   VASSE

CAVES RD

Wills Domain

SPENCER PARK

STH COAST HWY

Liberte   **ALBANY**

WILYABRUP

ROBINSON

Amelia Park

METRICUP

TORNDIRRUP

Cullen Wines

Vasse Felix

GRACETOWN

N

0   4KM

N

0   2KM

REGIONAL WESTERN AUSTRALIA

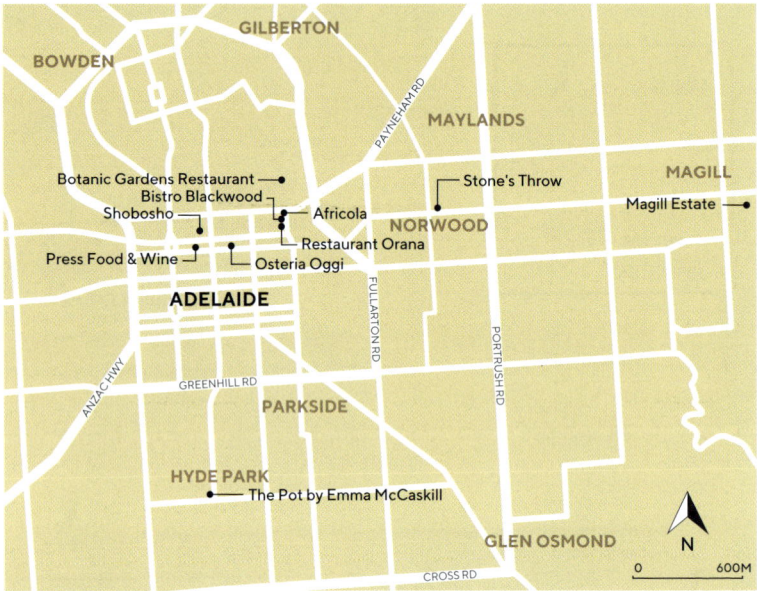

GILBERTON

BOWDEN

PAYNEHAM RD

MAYLANDS

MAGILL

Botanic Gardens Restaurant

Bistro Blackwood

Shobosho

Africola

Stone's Throw

Magill Estate

Press Food & Wine

Restaurant Orana

NORWOOD

Osteria Oggi

FULLARTON RD

PORTRUSH RD

ADELAIDE

ANZAC HWY

GREENHILL RD

PARKSIDE

HYDE PARK

The Pot by Emma McCaskill

N

GLEN OSMOND

0   600M

CROSS RD

ADELAIDE

GREENOCK

STURT HWY

MARANANGA

Appellation

Hentley Farm

SEPPELTSFIELD

TANUNDA

FermentAsian

BAROSSA VALLEY WAY

BETHANY

ROWLAND FLAT

N

LYNDOCH

0   2KM

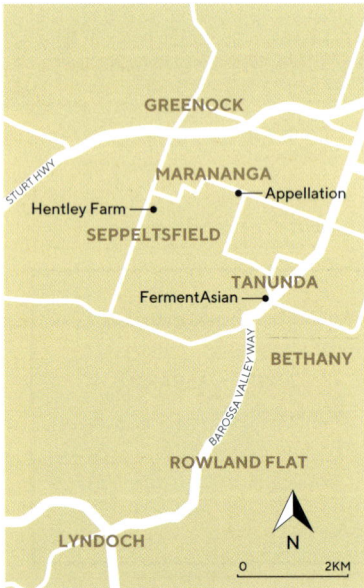

BAROSSA VALLEY REGION

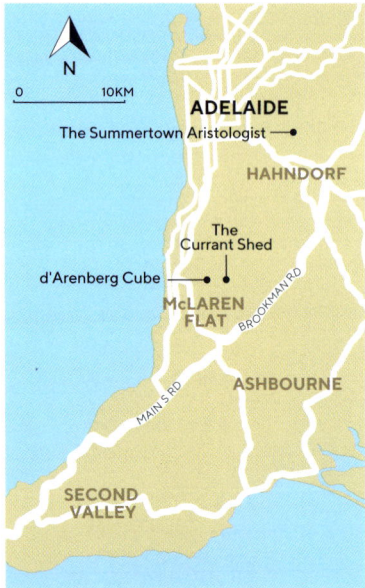

N

0   10KM

ADELAIDE

The Summertown Aristologist

HAHNDORF

The Currant Shed

d'Arenberg Cube

McLAREN FLAT

BROOKMAN RD

MAIN S RD

ASHBOURNE

SECOND VALLEY

SOUTH OF ADELAIDE

INDEX

By State

By Cuisine